GARDENING AT A GLANCE

The Organic Gardener's Handbook On Vegetables, Fruits, Nuts & Herbs

Tanya Denckla

Wooden Angel Publishing
"Towards Healthier Lifestyles"
Franklin, West Virginia

Printed On Recycled Paper

To help spread the concept of computer "shareware" to books, readers are encouraged to reproduce parts of this book for the explicit purpose of sharing information, but not for monetary gain, as noted above. If you have acquired this book or parts thereof without purchase and find the material useful we encourage you to register ownership with us. You may register for the price of this book by sending your name and address to the address below. Only registered owners will be notified of errors, updated editions, and related publications. Registration also helps defray the costs of the continued research for future offerings.

The information in this book is true and complete to the best of the author's knowledge. All recommendations are made without guarantees on the part of the author. The author and publisher disclaim all liability incurred with the use of this information.

The author gratefully acknowledges permission to reproduce the following copyrighted material:

Adapted passages from *Nut Tree Culture in North America*, edited by Richard A. Jaynes. Copyright 1979 by Northern Nut Growers Association, Inc.. Permission granted by Richard A. Jaynes.

"Pear Cold Storage Chart" and adapted passages on grape pruning from *Backyard Fruits and Berries*, by Diane E. Bilderback and Dorothy Hinshaw Patent. Copyright 1984 by Diane E. Bilderback and Dorothy Hinshaw Patent. Permission granted by Rodale Press, Inc: Emmaus, PA, 18098.

Vegetable storage conditions (temperature, humidity, and length of storage) from *Knott's Handbook for Vegetable Growers, 3rd Edition,* by James E. Knott and edited by Oscar Anthony Lorenz and Donald N. Maynard. Copyright 1988 by John Wiley & Sons, Inc. Permission granted by John Wiley & Sons, Inc.

Food storage conditions and times from *The Self-Sufficient Suburban Garden*, by Jeff Ball. Copyright 1985 by Jeff Ball. Permission granted by Jeff Ball.

Excerpts from apple and plum rootstock charts and "Intercropping For Pest Reduction: Successful Scientific Trials," from *Designing and Maintaining Your Edible Landscape Naturally*, by Robert Kourik. Copyright 1986 by Robert Kourik. Permission granted by Robert Kourik.

The USDA Plant Hardiness Zone Map, by the Agricultural Research Service, USDA, Beltsville, MD. Permission granted by the Beltsville Agricultural Research Service.

Distributed by Authors' Cooperative Publishing Services, 121 East Front Street, Suite 203-A, Traverse City, MI, 49684. For information on retail or wholesale orders write or call 1-800-345-0096.

Publisher's Cataloging in Publication   *(Prepared by Quality Books, Inc.)*
Denckla, Tanya, 1956-
   Gardening at a glance: the organic gardener's handbook on vegetables, fruits, nuts & herbs / Tanya Denckla.
   p. cm.
   Includes bibliographical references and index.
   ISBN 0-9627331-0-5
   1. Organic gardening--United States--Handbooks, manuals, etc.   2. Companion planting--United States--Handbooks, manuals, etc.   3. Pests--Control. I. Title.
SB453.5   635.0484

Cover Design: Robert Hickey
Illustrations: Melody Sarecky

Wooden Angel Publishing
Wooden Angel Farm, Building 1A
P.O. Box 869
Franklin, WV 26807

Printed in the United States of America
On Recycled Paper

10 9 8 7 6 5 4 3 2 1

CONTENTS

ACKNOWLEDGMENTS

*** *SPECIAL AWARDS* ***
For Making This Book Possible

W. Donner Denckla, for invaluable guidance on major directions, content, presentation, and concepts such as "open-field hydroponics" and "self-sustaining garden." His unflagging support and forest-from-the-trees perspective kept me going through numerous setbacks, for he deeply believed that the project was useful not only for our own purposes but also helpful to others.

Marlene Taylor, for extensive research assistance, attention to detail, proofreading, copy editing, and marketing. Her continuous technical support and enthusiasm reduced this from a herculean task to a manageable endeavor. I also am indebted to her for conceiving the final title.

*** *SPECIAL THANKS* ***
For Making This Book More Probable

The following people all generously shared their expertise and experience during their busiest of seasons. Their contributions enriched this book immeasurably and helped it grow to maturity.

Doug Britt, President of Ag Life--for reviewing both the insect and disease charts.

John Brittain, President of Nolin River--for numerous helpful suggestions on nut varieties.

Rosalind Creasy, author, edible landscaper, *L.A. Times* syndicated columnist--for a detailed review and helpful contributions to the entire manuscript, as well as for suggestions on layout and regional issues.

Dr. Galen Dively, Entomologist, University of Maryland: for a detailed review of the macro pest charts, and many valuable contributions.

Dr. Frank Gouin, Horticulturist, Chairman of the University of Maryland's Department of Horticulture--for reviewing the herb entries, and for kindly arranging review of the vegetable section too.

Patrick J. Hartmann, President of Hartmann's Plantation, Inc--for suggesting appropriate blueberry cultivars and help with *Phytophthera cinnomomi*.

Dr. Richard A. Jaynes, Geneticist, President of the Northern Nut Growers Association--for reviewing the nut entries and thoughtful suggestions on nut varieties.

Clay Stark Logan, President of Stark Bro's Nurseries and Orchards, Co., and **Dr. Joe Preczewski**, Director of Stark Bro's Field Research and Product Development--for reviewing the fruit entries and suggesting appropriate fruit varieties.

Dr. Alan MacNab, Plant Pathologist, Pennsylvania State University--for valuable contributions to vegetable disease remedies and especially for raising critical issues of presentation.

Dr. Charles McClurg, Horticulturist, University of Maryland--for reviewing the vegetable entries.

John E. Miller, President of Miller Nurseries--for reviewing the fruit entries and suggesting appropriate fruit varieties.

Tom Mills, President of Indiana Walnut Products--for suggesting nut varieties.

Dr. Carl Totemeier, Horticulturist, Retired Vice-President of the New York Botanical Gardens--for a very detailed review and contributions to the entire manuscript.

And many thanks to the following people for their kind support and assistance in various forms:

Jeff Ball, author, communicator, President of New Response, Inc.

Judy Gillan, of The Organic Foods Production Association of North America (OFPANA)

Lewis Hill, author, former owner of Hillcrest Nursery

Dr. Richard Packauskas, Entomologist, University of Connecticut

Dr. Robert D. Raabe, Plant Pathologist, University of Berkeley

Welcome

I initially started this compendium for myself and my friends. While planning to set up a large garden on our new country property, I quickly became overwhelmed. One book, I discovered, might be good on pest control but deficient on planting times. Another might be good on vegetables, but information would be scattered through various charts and sections of the book. Eventually the discouraging thought of twenty books strewn over the floor during the spring planting rush led me to create our own personal sourcebook: a centralized nuts-and-bolts reference for rapid answers, one to keep in the greenhouse or by the back door.

This book is not a primary text. A basic knowledge of gardening is assumed, but even novices will find in these pages most essentials to start a garden. For more detailed explanations or discussions, please see our Bibliography in Section 8 for a list of some excellent primary texts that cover soil preparation, clean cultivation, tilling, watering, compost and organic fertilizers, garden layout, raised beds, intensive planting, rotation, pests, and many other gardening subjects.

Please fill in the registration form at the back of this book, and let us know what you would like to see in future editions. If you wish to share successful disease and insect controls not listed in the charts, we would be pleased to hear from you, though we can't promise a personal response. Please provide your address, some information about your microclimate, and how many times or years the remedy has worked. You will be acknowledged if we decide to use your suggestion in future editions.

I am delighted to share this gardening tool with you, and hope you find it useful.

Happy Gardening!

Tanya Denckla

Garden Stewardship

An organic garden is not a machine. It is a living system of balanced forces between, for example, predator and prey, and these forces are always in flux. Soil composition, air quality, water, birds, bugs, weeds--these are just a few of the forces that determine the nature and health of your garden. Your role as garden steward is to *encourage* the balance in your favor, not to take over nature's role in the name of achieving the goal of "perfection."

Efforts to control or impose a balance for picture-perfect produce can eventually backfire. Many growers have aimed for this perfection because consumers preferred and then demanded unblemished produce. A common result is that their land may not have pests, but it also may not have earthworms in the soil, birds in the fields, or beneficial predatory insects. This may seem benign, but is not. Many practices used to obtain high yields of unblemished produce, for a variety of complex reasons, eventually promote the loss of topsoil, loss of water penetration, and loss of biologically available nutrients. Hence the soil depends more and more on human-provided nutrients.

Our desire for perfect produce, among other factors, and the associated agricultural practices of this century have led to unprecedented conditions that might be called ***open-field hydroponics***. Hydroponics is a method for growing crops in greenhouses. It mechanically delivers to plants every macro and micro nutrient. Hydroponic plants grow in various inert materials, from gravel to sand, that can structurally support plant and root growth. The term open-field hydroponics indicates a similar situation in fields where the soil is increasingly inert, where soil provides structural support but contributes little nutritionally to plant growth.

Many small and large-scale growers are alarmed by soil-depletion and related trends, for both ecological and economical reasons. Many have adopted *sustainable agriculture* as a goal. Specific definitions of sustainable agriculture may differ, but it generally refers to practices that are viable over long periods of time, both environmentally and economically. It strives for such things as soil that can produce crops reliably without nutrient depletion and with minimal human amendments. Sustainable agriculture is a philosophical shift away from control to cooperation, from master to steward.

The role of backyard steward is not hard to achieve, especially if adopted at the outset. One of its most important precepts is to *"feed the soil, not the plants."* It is perhaps most demanding during the planning phase, when you make crucial decisions about where to put your garden, what varieties to plant, when and where to plant them, how to feed the soil, where to put the compost pile (if at all), what kind of mulch to use, and--perhaps most important--how perfect you wish your produce to appear.

It is these decisions that will help you avoid the "quick" chemical fix. Some farmers actually have likened chemical sprays and fertilizers to cocaine: once started, an addictive cycle begins that is difficult to stop. The quick "fix" can take a long time to unfix. Some trials in Israel and elsewhere indicate that farms transitioning away from chemical inputs initially obtain lower yields, for a period of three to five years, following which yields increase to match and then sometimes exceed those obtained with chemicals. This is a good reminder of the long-term effects of chemical inputs and the need to maintain a long-term perspective on your garden health.

As steward, you may decide to avoid even the "organic" sprays such as copper-based fungicides because they can sometimes kill the garden's best friend: earthworms. On the other hand, your goals may dictate using some sprays for limited and highly targeted purposes. The issue is to define your own goals in advance, the reasons for them, and stick to them. In the absence of such goals, temptations to "zap" this or that pest during the growing season may become habitual.

The Self-Sustaining Garden

Perhaps another desirable goal beyond stewardship for the backyard gardener is a self-sustaining garden. A self-sustaining garden would supply all of its own essential nutrients for balanced growth, from organic matter for compost to micronutrients for healthy plants. It wouldn't require importation of beneficial insects, for example, because they would already be there. It wouldn't require the application of lime to buffer the effects of acid soil, because earthworms and compost would do the buffering for you. A self-sustaining garden is in many ways the extreme opposite of open-field hydroponics: a diametrically opposed approach with diametrically opposed results. The former has been effective without any help from humans for millions of years, and the latter has already displayed severe limitations within forty years.

As steward of a self-sustaining garden, your first job is to recognize that the forces in your garden will never be in "perfect" balance. There will always be some plant damage. The plants in your garden do not come with unconditional guarantees because they do not come out of a factory. Your second job is patience. It usually takes several years to establish an ecosystem that operates in your favor--an ecosystem with earthworms, insect-eating birds, beneficial predatory insects, soil with organic matter sufficient to both drain well and retain water to prevent runoff, and soil nutrient levels that will support healthy plant growth.

The advantage of a self-sustaining garden is that it requires the least amount of money and time in the long run. You may need to invest in a first colony of earthworms (if there are none already there), to build or buy bird houses, buy compost and organic matter (before your garden produces it for you), and perhaps even buy irrigation soaker hoses and row cover material. But these investments should pay you back many times over in several years in a healthy garden that doesn't require lots of imported materials or time-consuming pest controls.

Important Friends of the Self-Sustaining Garden

Earthworms, above all, are the gardener's best friend. Through both their tunneling and Nitrogen-rich castings (excrement) they perform all the following jobs for you--free of charge!
Earthworms will:
- Aerate the soil, improving oxygen availability to plant roots.
- Improve water retention capacity, decreasing your need to water.
- Keep the soil loose and friable, improving plant root capacity for growth.
- Raise important minerals from the subsoil to the topsoil where plants can use them.
- Counteract leaching out of nutrients by improvement of water retention.
- Break up hardpan soils, which are not hospitable to plant growth.
- Homogenize soil elements so they're more evenly available to plants.
- Create fertile channels for plant roots.
- Liberate essential nutrients into a form that is soluble and available to plants.
- Neutralize soils that are too acid or too alkaline for healthy plant growth.
- Balance out organic matter in the soil, so you needn't worry about exceeding the 5-8% optimal level.
- Generally enhance the soil's environment for growing healthy self-sustaining plants.
To protect your earthworms:

- Till minimally, because tilling can disturb and kill earthworms and other soil microorganisms through mechanical abrasion, drying out, and disruption of their environment.
- When you do till, till shallowly for reasons above. An optimal tilling depth is 3 inches. For some insect pests you may need to till more deeply to expose eggs and cocoons, but never till deeper than 6 inches.
- Avoid heavy doses of chemical fertilizers because these can harm soil microorganisms and decrease earthworm activity. Use compost instead.
- Avoid uncomposted manure of any kind because it contains disease pathogens and seeds. If you must use manure, make sure it is composted up to 160F.
- Water regularly, and avoid excesses. Flooding or overwatering, and drought or drying out of the soil, can kill earthworms as well as soil microorganisms.

Compost is another major player in the self-sustaining garden. Compost, essentially, is any organic material, including manure, that is decayed into a simpler form by the action of anaerobic or aerobic bacteria, depending on the composting method. *Humus* is any partially decomposed organic material, vegetable or animal, that is used to improve soil quality by mixing it into the soil. *Mulch* is any material used to cover the soil, whether nutrient-poor such as newspaper, nutrient-neutral such as plastic, or nutrient-rich such as compost.

Compost can be used wherever humus or mulch are recommended. The process of composting reduces the original bulk of the organic material by one-fourth to one-tenth. So where a thick mulch is desired, you may prefer uncomposted material such as straw or chopped leaves. On the other hand, if you have access to large amounts of compost, it is a highly beneficial mulch because it also feeds the soil. Compost:
- Feeds the soil and its creatures gently. By contrast chemical fertilizers can kill earthworms and other beneficial organisms.
- Lasts a long time because it releases nutrients slowly in a readily available form. By contrast chemical fertilizers usually provide a quick boost then peter out, creating a need for more.
- Improves soil drainage by adding porous organic matter (humus).
- Improves water retention, again by the addition of organic matter (humus).
- Provides food that is generally a neutral pH (unlike some chemical fertilizers), and also buffers the soil against rapid pH changes.
- Builds organic matter in the soil, which helps permit oxygen diffusion.
- Feeds the earthworms.
- Doesn't depend on chemical manufacturers and thereby doesn't contribute to any form of environmental pollution or depletion of natural resources.
- Is easy to make in any home garden or farm.

Compost is a multi-purpose tool. Some people apply large quantities to their garden, but a healthy minimum would be to spread 1 inch of compost through your garden every year in the spring before planting. It's helpful to apply another layer during the growing season. You can use compost as:
- Fertilizer, before planting, at planting, after planting, and in the fall after harvest.
- Mulch, to help retain soil moisture, to keep summer soil cool, to keep winter soil warm, to smother weeds, and in some cases to discourage pests.
- Side-dressing, during the growing season as an extra food-boost to the plant.

Compost can be bought commercially (many suppliers listed in Section 8 offer it). It is also easy to make. Compost is an ideal way to recycle many different household items such as kitchen waste, newspaper, typing paper (no gloss, no colors other than black), paper napkins, unwaxed cardboard, sawdust, or other carbon-rich materials.

There are many different ways to compost, from production of 50 pounds in the backyard to thousands of tons on a commercial scale. It can be made in dug holes or in windrows, in silos or in barrels, in layers on top of the ground or in huge concrete vats. Because there are so many different methods and possible ingredients, a full discussion of composting is beyond the scope of this book.

An understanding of the fact that bacteria are living organisms which chemically "chew up" the organic material in a compost pile will help you understand the optimal conditions for compost. Aerobic (oxygen-requiring) bacteria work faster, are usually less smelly, and generate higher temperatures in the compost pile that can help kill certain disease pathogens. To favor these bacteria, you must either turn the pile regularly, somehow introduce oxygen into the pile (such as with perforated pipes), or make the pile small enough so that oxygen can readily diffuse into the pile. In contrast, anaerobic bacteria do not require oxygen to work, take longer to accomplish the job, and do not generate high temperatures. Earthworms in an anaerobic compost pile will encourage some aerobic activity and will therefore expedite the composting process. Their castings will also make it a richer source of nutrients. Aerobic methods can produce compost in as little as 14 days, but the pile needs to be built all at once. Anaerobic methods may take up to one year to produce compost, but the pile can be built slowly over the summer.

Both aerobic and anaerobic composting methods require moisture. Dry bacteria are "dead" bacteria. Both also need a large excess of carbon compared to nitrogen, usually a ratio of 30:1. In the absence of a large excess of carbonaceous material, bacteria will digest their meal in a malodorous way, much like humans eating beans. A compost pile that smells is usually working anaerobically and either needs more carbon material, needs to be turned, or both.

Certain materials are to be avoided. Under most circumstances, extremely high sources of nitrogen--such as animal meat, and carnivorous animal manure--will not only give your pile indigestion, produce bacterial "flatulence," attract nuisance insects, but more importantly can contain disease pathogens. Diseased plant materials should also avoided. Preferably destroy diseased plant material by burial in an area away from your garden or by burning, if permitted. While some diseases can be destroyed by the high temperatures generated in aerobic composting, most backyard gardeners cannot reliably depend on this result. The hottest temperatures occur at the center of the compost pile, so unless the pile is turned adequately and evenly mixed, certain parts of the pile may never reach the temperatures needed to destroy the disease pathogens.

For a fuller discussion of composting, please consult sources in the Bibliography such as Rodale's booklet *Make Compost in 14 Days*. The following is a brief outline of basic composting principals:
  - For the most rapid composting on a small scale, aim to build a pile at least 3' x 3' x 3'.
  - Combine roughly equal parts of dry plant material and green plant material, which will achieve the desired Carbon: Nitrogen ratio of 30:1.
    Green plant material can include grass clippings, old flowers, weeds, fresh vegetable and fruit kitchen wastes. Leafy materials that were cut green and allowed to dry are still considered green.
    Dried plant material can include autumn leaves, straw, dried and cut up woody material, sawdust, and shredded white paper, newspaper, paper bags, cardboard boxes and cartons. Straw is the hollow dried stems of grain-producing plants, whereas hay ("green" material) is the entire plant (stem and leaves) and is therefore much higher in Nitrogen.
    Do not include carnivorous animal manure, wood ashes, charcoal, animal meat, soils with a basic pH (such as in California), and diseased plants.
  - Use a wide variety of materials, if possible, because this can provide a better balance of pH, nutrients and microbial organisms.
  - Do not use bug-infested or diseased plants.
  - Shred or cut material (including kitchen waste), when possible, before adding them to the pile. The smaller the particle size, the faster the pile will decompose. Some larger materials, however, can help provide better aeration.
  - Water your pile until it is evenly moist but not soggy, about a 50 percent moisture level.
  - Optional: add some commercially available composting activator, a fine powder that contains helpful bacteria to speed along decomposition. Many suppliers in Section 8 offer this product.
  - You may or may not want to turn the pile periodically. Some sources advocate turning the pile, while others point to evidence that turning may reduce the nitrogen levels in the final product.
  - For the most rapid results, do not add material to the heap once it has started composting.

Birds and Bats that eat insects are another key aspect of a self-sustaining garden. They help keep the garden clean of flying and crawling insects, and some will even eat grubs in the ground. The author and expert gardener Jeff Ball wrote that insect damage in his garden virtually disappeared after putting up bird houses that attracted insect-eaters. What more needs to be said?

Beneficial insect-eating birds include bluebirds, downy woodpeckers, barn swallows, purple martins, sparrows, blackbirds, phoebes, baltimore orioles, chickadees, juncos, purple finches, brown thrashers, warblers, chickens, ducks, and geese. Swallow family birds, such as the purple martin, are often considered the most desirable insect-eaters. Purple martin "hotel" houses are expensive but should be well worth the initial investment because these birds eat prodigious amounts of above-ground insects and, although they migrate in the fall, become a resident family that returns in the spring. Chickens, on the other hand, are always available in the fall and will eat insects in, on, and above the soil. They're one of most thorough garden cleaners to keep. If you do keep fowl, only allow them in the garden before planting, after plants have grown to maturity, and after harvest. Do not allow them in the garden when seedlings are predominant. Bats are not the blood-sucking horrors legend would make them. They have a voracious appetite for insects, eat at night, and their houses are simple structures that are becoming widely available.

Bees, Wasps and Other Beneficial Insects are vital garden friends. Bees are nature's best pollinator, making possible the fruits and vegetables we all enjoy. Wasps, like other beneficial insects, not only can prey on various destructive insects but they can also parasitize eggs, larvae, and adult insects. To attract wasps and other beneficial insects you can plant companion herbs (especially *Umbelliferae* herbs), flowers, and clovers around the edge of your garden.

Planning and Maintaining the Self-Sustaining Garden

To be self-sustaining, your garden should be able to defend itself from severe damage from most pests most of the time. Such natural defense is promoted by four major factors: sun, water, soil, and air circulation. All of these factors are interactive, so that each is necessary but, alone, not sufficient.

The place to start is with location. Choose a sunny spot that, preferably, gets a lot of morning and afternoon sun. In humid, moist, or rainy regions, where fungus can be expected, morning sun is especially important to dry the dew as quickly as possible. If possible, locate the garden where it will also get some air circulation, preferably not in a low area where it will be susceptible to pockets of fog and preferably not in a high location where it will be exposed to harsh winds.

If your soil is clay, you can mix in sand to increase the drainage, or if it is a sandy soil, mix in peat humus to increase water retention. Whatever the condition of your soil, you should consider building *raised beds*. Although they require more initial investment of time and, sometimes, money, they will pay you back in many different ways over the years. Raised beds are big step toward attaining the self-sustaining garden. Raised beds:
- Minimize soil compaction, because you never walk on the growing medium.
- Have better oxygen availability to plant roots, because there is little soil compaction.
- Drain better, because there is little soil compaction.
- Retain water better, because there is little soil compaction.
- Are easier to plant, weed, and maintain, because there is no soil compaction.
- Have greater yields, because there is better air, water, and sun penetration.
- Allow earlier and later planting as they warm up earlier in the spring and hold heat longer in fall.
- Allow greater root development, because of low soil compaction, good drainage and oxygen diffusion.
- Are space-saving. Plants can be spaced closer together because you don't need to walk around them.

There are several different types of raised beds, and different ways of preparing them, some of which do not involve double-digging. Raised beds can have rounded tops, flat tops, rounded sides, or straight sides. A good discussion of different raised beds and how to build them can be found in *High*

Yield Gardening by Marjorie Hunt and Brenda Bortz (see Bibliography). Our preferred method is to build a contained raised bed 12 to 16 inches high, which allows you to sit on the edge while weeding or planting. You can build contained raised beds with a variety of non-toxic substances, such as stone, wood (not treated with creosote as this will burn nearby plants and also leach out into the soil), concrete blocks or fiberglass. An ideal size is 4 by 12 feet, filled with a mixture of soil and organic matter.

Planning and maintenance are integrally linked with pest control. As a reminder of how important these issues are to both prevention and remedies, a detailed discussion of specific steps to be taken at the outset, *before building your garden*, is presented in Section 6.

Important Concepts Contained In The Plant Charts

You can use this handbook many different ways. For your convenience, information is organized and cross-referenced for easy retrieval. You can find overviews of each plant in the plant entry, and overviews of insects and diseases in the pest charts. Below are brief explanations of the plant entries categories, listed in order of appearance. For all major topics, especially concerning fruit and nut trees, we cover the basics, but not more. For sources with more complete discussions, please see Section 8.

VARIETIES TO TRY: We based our choice of varieties on the following criteria: (1) Disease resistance; (2) Ease of growing in organic gardens; (3) Good flavor; (4) Good storage qualities; (5) Special height, size or habit; (6) High yields; (7) Self-pollinating (fruits); (8) Open-pollinated types for seed savers (vegetables); (9) Ease of harvest, including factors such as size, bruising, or peeling; (10) Heirloom varieties grown years ago but not often found at local nurseries; (10) Unusual color or ornamental qualities; and (11) Hybrids with good yield potential. Fruit varieties are generally listed in order of ripening, not flowering. Every garden has its own microclimate, which may cause a variety to exhibit different characteristics. Consequently, the success of a particular variety in your garden cannot be predicted. In addition, varietal characteristics may differ depending on which company you order from, especially with heirloom and open-pollinated types. Obviously, the ultimate test of a variety is to actually try growing it in your garden. Because varieties are so important we intentionally allowed the remainder of the page for your personal notes.

NAMES: Genus and species are on the far left, the Family name in the center, and common name on the far right. We included the Latin names for your convenience, to help your problem solving. Because some plants may look so very different, it can be useful to know they are members of the same family for planning crop rotations and in order to be prepared for similar insect and disease problems.

GERM.TEMP: Optimum soil temperature for seed germination, in Fahrenheit. Seeds germinate at temperatures other than the optimum noted, but count on longer germination at lower temperatures and, except for extremely high temperatures, shorter times at higher temperatures.

GROW.TEMP: Optimum air temperature for plant growth, in Fahrenheit.

pH: A measure of the soil alkalinity/acidity, with 7.0 being neutral. Most plants will grow well in a range of pH from 6.0-7.0. Home test kits are widely available. See Section 8 for sources.

SPACING, Intensive: The closest spacing under optimal conditions between plants in French intensive beds, raised beds, Biodynamic gardens, and any other garden where plants are spaced very close together. NOTE: If your climate is damp and humid, you will probably want to use broader spacing to allow more air circulation and sun penetration to prevent fungal and other diseases.
Regular: Spacing between plants in conventional rows, not raised beds.
Rows: Spacing between conventional rows.

ROOT DEPTH: Wherever possible, we've given a range of average to maximum recorded root depth.

Where there isn't a range, we've just given the average. The better worked your soil, the deeper the roots will extend.

WATER: Heavy = 1 gallon per square foot, or 1.4-1.6" per week.
Medium = about 3/4 gallon per square foot, or 1-1.2" per week.
Low = about 1/2 gallon per square foot, or .8" per week.

FERTILIZER: Organic gardeners usually fertilize (often with just compost) twice in one season, once before planting and again in the middle of the growth cycle. See pages 157-158 for different types of organic fertilizers. For fruit trees, appropriate new growth is noted wherever possible because this is one of the easiest ways to determine whether the tree is obtaining proper nourishment--all other factors being equal (e.g. light, soil, moisture, temperature). If tree growth is less than the appropriate range, it may need more nitrogen, again assuming other conditions are favorable. If tree growth is greater than the appropriate range, it may be receiving too much nitrogen.

CHILLING REQUIREMENT: This is the number of hours a fruit or nut tree needs below a certain temperature, usually 45F, before it will blossom. Those with lower chilling requirements will bloom earlier and, therefore, are more susceptible to late spring frosts.

SITE: Avoid planting fruit and nut trees in low pockets or areas where fog and frost may collect. Most fruits require full sun. Morning sun is especially important for fruits to dry the dew as rapidly as possible, which helps prevent fungus problems. Some fruits that are susceptible to late frost damage are better sited on a north-sloping hill, or 12-15' away from a north wall, in order to delay budding as long as possible. To avoid nematode and verticillium wilt problems, you might choose a site where grass or cover crops were grown for the previous two years.

MULCH: Mulch is any material spread to completely cover the soil. It suppresses weed growth, keeps moisture in the soil by reducing evaporation, insulates the ground to keep it warm in winter and cool in summer, and can help prevent the emergence of certain harmful insects. Thick mulch around potatoes, for example, can help deter the Colorado potato beetle. In moister climates, some gardeners have reported using thick mulches of 4-8" or more and never having to water or fertilize again. In hot, dry climates, however, mulch should not be so thick because it absorbs rain or irrigation water, preventing water from reaching the soil. Thick mulch can also be counter-productive in areas that experience slug problems. All fruit trees should be mulched with organic matter, ideally compost. Keeping 3-12" clear around the trunk to discourage rodents and prevent rot, spread a 3-6" deep layer of mulch out to the drip line or 6', whichever is greater. In the spring lightly hoe the mulch into the ground. Avoid large amounts of hay, which releases nitrogen late in the season when tree growth slows. Examples of mulch include: compost, straw, chopped leaves, wood chips, cocoa bean shells, pebbles, plastic, landscape fabric.

SIDE-DRESS: Side-dressing is any addition to the soil, such as fertilizer, compost, or soil amendments, after the plant is already set in the soil. Create a narrow furrow 1-3" deep at the plant's drip line, or 6" from the plant base, whichever is greater. Sprinkle the amendment into the furrow and cover with soil.

ROOTSTOCKS: Most fruit and some nut trees sold today are grafted onto a rootstock. Grafting primarily aims to combine the desired fruit variety with a rootstock that controls the ultimate tree size. A more rapid form of propagation than seed-starting, grafting is also beneficial because it hastens the onset of bearing fruit and nuts. Rootstocks are numerous and not easy to sort through because most nursery catalogues and books mention certain characteristics at the expense of others, making it difficult to get an overview. Your choice of rootstock should depend on such things as ultimate size tree you desire, the natural growing height of the tree variety, your soil drainage, soil fertility, and the specific insect and disease problems in your area. When you buy a tree, be sure to find out the rootstock it is attached to, if any, and the rootstock's growing characteristics, as this can affect things such as your tree's ultimate size, how early it bears, and disease resistance. For final decisions on which rootstock is best for your garden, consult reliable nurseries, many of which are listed in Section 8.

PRUNING: Major pruning is almost always done when the tree is dormant. Do NOT prune new transplants until after the first year of growth. Old wisdom thought pruning at the time of transplanting was important to bring the tree's top growth into balance with root growth. Research has shown, however, that such pruning will stunt a tree's growth for years. Summer pruning is usually limited to balanced thinning to ensure high quality fruit.

Pruning should always remove diseased, damaged, dead, and disfigured material. It also is used to increase light penetration and air circulation for better quality fruit and better disease control. Unless diseased, pruned material can be composted. Diseased material should be destroyed.

The information we've included under pruning is intended primarily as a quick reminder for the experienced gardener. Both a science and art, pruning is above all a visual experience and, in our opinion, cannot be taught without diagrams or hands-on experience. Consult the Bibliography for books with more extensive directions on pruning, such as Lewis Hill's *Pruning Simplified*.

SEED STARTING DATES: Most catalogues and books suggest specific seed starting dates (e.g. mid-May) based on the average across the nation. Some may even break down starting dates by Zone. Such dates, however, are not necessarily the best for you and your backyard, because your micro-climate may differ significantly from these average temperatures. The equations for seed-starting dates give you the power to figure dates for your own garden, whether in Alaska or Florida, no matter how idiosyncratic your micro-climate. They also give you the flexibility to plant varieties of the same vegetable with differing maturation times. Overall, these figures should provide a higher level of confidence that each seed started will grow safely to maturity. For each part of the equation substitute your own numbers when you've done several trials.

Days Germ: The average number of days for the seed to germinate, which is when green shoots emerge through the soil.

Days Transplant: The average number of days after germination that the plant needs to grow inside until it is transplanted outside. Note: This number *includes* the 4-7 days that may be needed for hardening off.

LFD: Last Frost Date in the spring, an average date available from your local extension agent. If possible, keep your own records to figure your own average LFD.

Days Before (After) LFD: The average number of days before (or after) the Last Frost Date that the plant can tolerate living in outdoor soil. Use this number to determine the approximate dates you should transplant the seedling outside. This number will also give you a more precise measure of the plant's frost hardiness. As different sources suggest different setting out dates, we've given the widest possible range.

Maturity: The average number of days for the plant to reach horticultural maturity for harvest. For plants that are transplanted, the days to maturity are *in addition* to the germination days and days to transplant. So if you don't want to start your seeds inside and, instead, direct sow outside, figure the total days to horticultural maturity by *adding in* the "Days germ" and "Days transplant."

SDF: Short Day Factor for late summer or fall plantings. Horticultural maturity times noted in seed catalogues assume long days and warm temperatures. For late summer or fall plantings of many vegetable species you need to adjust horticultural maturity times by 2 weeks to accommodate shorter and cooler days. Some species, like the radish, require short days to form and therefore don't need such adjustments. Wherever possible, we've noted which species require this Short Day Factor adjustment.

Frost Tender: This is another 2 week adjustment needed for frost-tender vegetables, which need to mature at least two weeks before frost in order to produce a full harvest.

FFD: First Frost Date in the fall, an average date available from your local extension agent. If possible, keep your own records to figure your own average FFD.

DISEASE and ANIMAL PESTS: For more information, consult Section 6. The diseases listed by name are limited to those which are promoted by an insect vector, are highly infectious, or for which there are remedies over and above the preventive measures described at the beginning of the Section 6.

STORAGE: Parts of the storage information are reprinted from *Knott's Handbook For Vegetable Growers, 3rd Edition*, edited by Oscar Lorenz and Donald Maynard, and from Jeff Ball's *The Self-*

Sufficient Suburban Garden. Many thanks to them both. See Bibliography for complete references. The numbers in parentheses are the number of months the harvest will keep by that preservation method.

PLANTING TIME: Always plant when the fruit tree, bush, cane or vine is dormant and the ground is workable. In climates with milder winters you can plant in late fall. Where there are cold winters, plant in early spring. One evolving rule of thumb is that you can plant in the fall in zones 5 and below, and should plant in the spring in zones 4 and above. However, Windmill Point Farm & Nursery in zone 4 in Quebec, Canada still recommends fall planting. There are many advantages to fall planting, but if you're at all uncertain about your microclimate you might wait until spring.

TREE PLANTING PREPARATION: Prepare a hole that is 3-5 times larger in diameter than the root ball. The hole should be no deeper than the depth of the root system, or 10 percent shallower than the root ball. Recent studies indicate that it is more important for fruit trees to be given a wide planting hole, as opposed to older wisdom that they need the depth, because of their tendency to grow shallow roots. Add humus and compost to improve drainage. Install around the trunk a 1/4 to 1/2" hardware cloth barrier that extends 4" below ground to deter gophers and other rodents, and rises 18-24" above ground to prevent rabbit damage (especially in winter months). For trees on dwarf root stock characterized by poor anchorage, nestle in a 4-6' stake before filling the hole. Form a small trench, mounding up the sides of the trench, about 18" away from trunk. Fill the trench to the top with water. This drenching helps to eliminate soil air pockets, which are not good for roots. Wrap the bark with a spiral white plastic tree guard to protect it from mice, rodents, and other pests. If you use a wire tree guard, whitewash the trunk first while still dormant with a commercial whitewash or interior white latex (never oil-based) paint.

ALLIES: Allies are alleged to actively repel insects, or enhance growth or flavor of the target plant. Please read the introduction of Section 7 for important caveats on this subject. For all allies mentioned in the plant entries, also see Section 7 to learn the ally's reputed function and determine if that function would be useful in your garden.
　　Some evidence: These have been tested in field trials. Some sources said there was evidence for a particular claim, but failed to list the source of the evidence and where the tests were conducted. Such claims are listed as "uncertain." This is important because an ally tested in the tropics may not work in northern Maine. Further, we believe it is important to list sources because we understand certain claims were made and propagated by well-meaning but misinformed or untrained individuals.
　　Uncertain: Not scientifically tested in field trials, these are usually based on tradition, folklore and anecdotes. Presumably, for most of these, someone noticed positive correlations in order for the information to be passed down through generations. Someone's observations at an unknown place and time, however, are a long way from hard evidence. If you decide to act on this information, be aware that it falls under the rubric of experimentation.

COMPANIONS: Companions are alleged to share space and growing habits well, but do not necessarily play an active role in insect protection or growth. Again, use your own garden as a test bed. Some may work well, not at all, or may be a true ally by providing insect protection.

ENEMIES: Enemies are alleged to play an actively negative role in each other's growth by diminishing vigor or flavor, increasing the risk of insect or disease invasion, or decreasing yields. While these may not be proven any more than companions or allies, we feel it may be safer to avoid placing alleged enemies near one another.

IMPORTANT NOTE on Allies, Companions, and Enemies: For planning purposes, all allies, companions and enemies are cross-referenced. If a source says squash hinders potato growth, that does not necessarily mean potatoes hinder squash growth. Nevertheless, we decided if one plant is alleged to harm the growth of another, they should be considered enemies of each other. So squash is listed as an enemy in the potato entry, and vice-versa. The same practice applies to companions and allies.

(Genus, Species, Group)   *(Family Name)*   (Common Name)   <u>SAMPLE</u>

GROWTH CONDITIONS

Germ.Temp: Optimum soil temperature for seed germination.

Grow.Temp: Optimum air temperature for plant growth.

pH: A measure of soil acidity/alkalinity (test kits available).

Spacing:

>Intensive: The closest spacing under optimal conditions (if your climate is damp and humid, provide broader spacing for better air circulation to help prevent diseases).
>
>Reg: Spacing between plants in conventional rows.
>
>Rows: Spacing between rows.

Soil: What soil type the plant likes best (clay, clay-loam, sand, sandy loam, etc.).

Planting Depth: Best planting depth for germination, root lodging, etc.

Water: Individual watering needs. For definitions of "heavy," "medium," and "low" see page 13.

Fertilizer: Compost is almost always a good bet. See pages 157-158 for organic fertilizers.

Side-dress Times: Any addition to the soil after the plant is set in. See page 13 for more.

First and Last Seed Starting Dates: Personalize your own seed-starting dates by filling in the days that are specific to the variety you want, and dates specific to the your climate. See page 14 for definitions.

ANIMAL and DISEASE PESTS: No matter how many are listed, you probably won't see more than a few in your garden. The diseases listed are primarily for your easy to reference to textbooks; organic remedies for most diseases are simple measures described at the beginning of Section 6.

HARVEST: How and when to harvest. Special tips on how to recognize the vegetable is ready for harvest. Special preparations or directions for curing the vegetable before eating or storing.

GENERAL STORAGE REQUIREMENTS: Special tips on best ways to store the edible harvest.

Fresh: How long fresh harvest will keep, at optimum storage temperature and humidity.

Preserved: The numbers in parentheses are the number of months the harvest will keep.

OTHER GROWING NOTES: Is the plant a cool or warm season crop? How frost hardy is it? How much should you plant per person? Also look here for special tips on starting seeds, planting, spacing, and background information on the plant.

ALLIES: Plants that are alleged to actively repel insects, or enhance growth or flavor of the target plant. See the Allies Chart in Section 7 to find out what the plant is supposed to do and, if known, how and where. Please read the introductory caveat to that section!

Some evidence-- Plants for which some field trial data is available.

Uncertain-- Plants not scientifically tested. These are based on folklore and anecdotes.

COMPANIONS: Plants that are alleged to simply share space and growing habits well.

ENEMIES: Plants that are alleged to stunt the target plant's growth, diminish vigor, or increase the risk of diseases or insects.

VARIETIES

GREENHOUSE: Varieties suited for greenhouse growing and also short growing seasons.

OUTDOOR: Vegetable and herb varieties are ordered alphabetically. Fruits are ordered by fruit maturation. For vegetables, days to maturation (e.g. "51 days") can refer to either the time from seeding to harvest or the time from transplanting to harvest, depending on which catalog is used as a source. Maturation time will vary greatly by region, climate, soil conditions, annual rainfall, or a host of other reasons. So be sure to use the days to maturation only as a relative, not absolute, number with which to compare different varieties.

Vegetables

ARTICHOKE VARIETIES

GREENHOUSE
   none

OUTDOOR
   Grand Beurre-- produces early enough to bear as an annual in cold climates, not available in the United States
   Green Globe-- excellent flavor, does well in long growing seasons, mild winters and damp climates (Burpee, Fowler, Park, Seeds Blum)
   Purple Variety-- pretty violet color (write to Cook's and Shepherd's--seeds may be occasionally available, though not necessarily listed in catalogs)

NOTES

Cynara scolymus   *Compositae or Asteraceae (Sunflower)*   **ARTICHOKE**

Growth Conditions

Germ.Temp: 60-70   Height: 3-6'
Grow.Temp: 60-65   Breadth: 3-6'
pH: 6.5   Spacing, Intensive: 2-3'   Reg: 4-6'   Rows: 6-8'
Root Depth: More than 4'   Planting Depth: Set buds just above the soil surface.
Site: Sunny & sheltered
Water: Heavy
Mulch: Apply over winter, and when plants are 6-8" high.
Fertilizer: Heavy feeder. Lots of well rotted manure or compost.
Side-dress: Every 3-4 weeks.
First Seed Starting Date:
> Start 6 weeks before the LFD in 4" deep pots in an area where the temperature is about 65F. When germinated, put in full sun where the temperature is about 55F. Transplant when 4 true leaves have appeared.

Propagation Methods: Seed or suckers. To propagate by sucker, using a trowel slice 10" tall suckers off the parent plant, each with a section of root. In warm climates plant the suckers in a 4" hole. In cold climates plant the suckers in a pot to overwinter indoors.

Pests: aphid, plume moth, slug
Diseases: curly dwarf (virus), southern blight, verticillium wilt

Harvest: When heads are still closed, about the size of an orange, and while the stem 2" below the bud is still supple, cut off the head with 1-2" of stem. Heads that have already opened are tough. Always harvest the central bud first. After harvest cut the stems to the ground, or 12" above the ground to encourage side shoots. Side shoots will produce buds smaller than the first central bud.

Storage Requirements: Keep in a paper bag to increase humidity. Some say artichokes can keep for up to 1 month in the refrigerator.
Fresh: Temp: 32   Humidity: 95-100%   Storage Life: 2-3 weeks
Preserved, taste (months):   Can: hearts, good (12+)   Freeze: hearts, good (4+) Dry: N/A

Other Growing Notes: Globe Artichoke is a cool season crop, tender to frost and light freezes. Plan an average of 3 plants per person. In warm climates with mild winters artichoke is grown as a perennial, in cold climates as an annual. Before planting, add plenty of compost or rotted manure to the soil and again when 6-8" high. In cold climates plant artichokes in large containers to keep the roots alive through winter. In warm climates in the fall cut the plants to the ground. In cooler areas to prepare for winter either cut to the ground and bring containers indoors, or cut the plants to 15-20" above the ground, bend the stalks over, mulch heavily with leaves, and cover with a rain-proof tarp or basket. Some gardeners recommend removing side shoots during the growing season. This increases the size of the central head, but reduces the overall yield. One Oregon gardener harvested almost 30 heads from just the side shoots of one plant. If the bud is not harvested for your table, it will blossom into beautiful purple-blue flowers that can be cut for arrangements.

ALLIES: Some evidence-- none
         Uncertain-- none
COMPANIONS: *Brassicas*
ENEMIES: none

GREENHOUSE
none

OUTDOOR
Connover's Colossal-- open-pollinated, good for general use and raising from seeds (Bountiful Gardens)
Jersey Giant-- one of the new all-male varieties (meaning it will produce more harvest), vigorous, very high yields, resists rust, tolerates Fusarium crown and root rot, adapted to a wide variety of climates: New England across to WA and south to the Carolinas (Burpee, May, Nourse, Park)
Mary Washington-- heirloom, good flavor, rust resistant (widely available)
SYN-4-56-- hybrid, offspring of Jersey Giant, recommended until a better strain of Grenwich or Jersey Giant is released in 1990, high yields, resists rust, tolerates fusarium, there will be some female plants but most are male (Earl May, Nourse Farms)
UC 157-- a new hybrid developed by the University of California for the West coast and South, good flavor and quality (Burpee)
Waltham-- hybrid, uniform spear size, heavy producer, rust resistant (widely available)

NOTES

Asparagus officinalis   *Liliaceae (Lily)*   **ASPARAGUS**

GROWTH CONDITIONS

Germ.Temp: 60-85
Grow.Temp: 60-70
pH: 6.0-8.0
Best Planting Time: Early spring
Root Depth: More than 4'
Water: Heavy

Height: 3-8' (fern growth, depending on soil and climate)
Breadth: 2-4' (fern growth, depending on soil and climate)
Spacing: Intensive: 12"   Reg: 15-18"   Rows: 3-4'
Planting Depth: 8-10" (see Growing Notes)

Mulch: Straw or light material over winter and remove in spring. Use compost during growing season.
Fertilizer: Heavy feeder. Apply compost in autumn to first year beds, and in spring after harvest
    to established beds. Apply fish emulsion twice yearly. Beds may need P & K before
    planting, and N after planting.
Average Bearing Age: 3 years from seeds, 2 years from crowns.

PESTS: aphids, asparagus beetle (early May), cucumber beetle, garden centipede, gopher, Japanese
    beetle, mite, slug, snail, spotted asparagus beetle
DISEASES: asparagus rust, fusarium wilt

HARVEST: When spears are 3/8" thick and 6-8" high, cut spears 1/2" below soil surface to lessen
chance of disease and pest infestation. Heads should be tight and spears brittle. Stop harvesting when
stalks are less than 3/8" thick. When grown from roots do not harvest the first year. Let them go to
foliage, and when they brown in the fall cut them to ground level. The second year harvest spears for
about 4 weeks. In following years the harvest will last for 8-10 weeks.

STORAGE REQUIREMENTS: Wrap in moist towels or stand upright in glass of water, then
refrigerate in plastic bags. Blanch asparagus before you freeze it.
Fresh: Temp: 32-35   Humidity: 95-100%   Storage Life: 2-3 weeks
Preserved, taste (months): Can: good (12+)   Freeze: excellent (12)   Dry: fair (12+)

OTHER GROWING NOTES: Asparagus is a perennial early spring crop. Plan an average of 10
plants per person. Plant in a sunny spot protected from the wind and, because asparagus roots often
extend both downward and outward 5-6', plant in deeply rototilled soil that has incorporated green
manure and compost. Traditionally, roots are planted in furrows 8-10" deep and 10" wide. Spread the
roots and cover the crowns with 2-3" of sifted compost humus. Water well. As the plant grows through
the summer, add more soil but do not cover the tip. If you prefer to plant individually, dig holes 8-10"
deep and 5" in diameter, then proceed with the same method for furrow planting. Every spring,
asparagus rows should be "ridged" by drawing up to the rows several inches of topsoil or, better, newly
applied compost. This counters the crown's tendency to get too close to the surface. After harvest, sow
a cover crop of cowpeas or other legume between the asparagus rows, which will discourage weeds and
add to the organic matter when dug under. U. of Minnesota trials have shown that fall plantings of 9-11
week seedlings equal or exceed the growth of spring transplants, and also that the larger the transplant
size the better its growth after transplanting. Carl Cantaluppi of the U. of Illinois (*Organic Gardening,*
October, 1988) confirms a previous study that you can increase yields by up to 40% by planting crowns,
not at 10-12", but at a depth of 5-6". He also claims that asparagus does not need lots of fertilizer as long
as you maintain a pH between 6.0-7.0 and have good soil. Furthermore, he says it's not a heavy nitrogen
feeder and that, in fact, the ferns return most of the nitrogen to the soil. Decide for yourself.

ALLIES: Some evidence-- none
          Uncertain-- basil, goldenrod, nasturtium, parsley, pot marigolds, tomato
ENEMIES: onion family, weeds (during first 6 weeks of asparagus growth)

SHELLING or DRIED BEAN VARIETIES*

GREENHOUSE
Butterbean, short season and bush plants

OUTDOOR
Aprovecho Select Fava-- bush, large seeds, sweet flavor, good fresh or dry, hardy to below 20F, matures 2-3 weeks before pole beans, good in maritime NW and East coast (Abundant Life)
Black Coco-- bush, milder black bean, buttery flavor, good fresh or dried (Territorial)
Black Valentine-- 50 days, tall spreading plant, heirloom, meaty black bean, enjoyable flavor, bush (Abundant Life, Seeds Blum, Southern Exposure, Southwest)
Borlotto-- 68 days, beautiful bush plant with speckled rosy-red and cream pods, delicious fresh or dried, an Italian heirloom rarely seen in markets (Shepherd's)
Butterbeans or Green Vegetable Soybean (Glycine max)-- 88 days, very digestible, good fresh or frozen, stocky and highly branched plants (Garden City, Johnny's, Southern Exposure)
Buttergreen-- 45 days, bush, very short season, good dried or young as snap beans, resists bean mosaic, mellow flavor, new in 1989 (Burpee)
Chickpea or Garbanzo-- 100 days, bush, usually only one seed per pod (Burpee); **Desi**-- bush, small seeds native to India, better for home garden than large white commercial type, for interior Northwest and short-season dry areas, not good for coastal fog areas (Abundant Life); **Kabuli Black**-- 95 days, black-seeded (Ethiopian origin), small seeds, better for home garden than large white commercial type (Garden City); **Dolores de Hidalgo**-- prolific in low desert winters, produces small beans, suitable for high and low desert (Native Seed)
Cowpea (Blackeyed or Southern pea)-- **Calico Crowder**-- 79 days, very flavorful, tan with maroon splashes, good for southern and warm coastal areas (Southern Exposure); **Queen Ann**-- 68 days, compact 26" plants with no runners, no significant insects or diseases in Rodale trials [O.G., 2/89], high and reliable yields, good fresh, fried, frozen or canned (Southern Exposure); **Pima Bajo**-- excellent green or dried, suitable for low desert planting (Native Seed)
Fava (Tarahumara Habas)-- frost hardy, suitable for high and low desert (Native Seed)
French Horticultural-- 66 days, bush produces some runners, 6-8" pods, good fresh, dried, or frozen (Harris, Stokes)
Jacob's Cattle or Trout-- 85-95 days, bush 24" tall, short season baked bean type, a beautiful white with splashes of maroon, very tasty and meaty, good fresh or dry, an heirloom favorite in Vermont and Maine (Abundant Life, Garden City, Johnny's, Seeds Blum)
Pinto-- 85 days, bush 14", short half-runner plant, beans are tan with brown speckles, susceptible to mosaic damage in Rodale trials [*Organic Gardening*, 2/89], medium to high yields (Abundant Life, Burpee, Field's, Johnny's, Park); **San Juan Pinto**-- suitable for high desert planting (Native Seed)
Red Kidney-- 95 days, bush 16-22", some mosaic and Japanese beetle damage in Rodale trials [*Organic Gardening*, 2/89], bush 16", high yields (widely available)
Santa Maria Pinquito-- 120 days,
Soldier-- heirloom, kidney-shaped white bean with yellow-brown eye, very rich and meaty flavor (Blum, Territorial)

NOTES

* All varieties listed are open-pollinated.

Phaseolus vulgaris   *Leguminosae or Fabaceae (Pea)*   **Dried BEANS**

GROWTH CONDITIONS

Germ.Temp: 60-85   Height: 10-24"
Grow.Temp: 60-75   Breadth: 4-8"
pH: 6.2-7.5   Spacing: 2-6" Rows: 12-30"/ 8" on center in raised beds
Root Depth: 36-48"   Planting Depth: 1"
Water: Average and constant
Fertilizer: Light feeder. Because bean plants fix N when inoculated properly, they should require low
        N. After the plant flowers apply fertilizer low in N, medium P & K. Avoid low K at all times.
First Seed Starting Date: Transplant or direct sow when soil temperature is 60F
        Days Germ + Days Transplant - Days After LFD = Days Count BACK from LFD
        4-10   +   21-28   -   0-10   = 25-28
Last Seed Starting Date:
        Days Germ + Days Transplant + Maturity + SDF + Frost Tender = Days BACK from FFD
        4-10   +   0 (direct)   + 98-125   + 14 + 14   = 130-163

PESTS: aphid, bean leaf beetle, beet and potato leafhopper, cabbage looper, corn earworm,
        cucumber beetle, cutworm, flea beetle, garden webworm, Japanese beetle, leaf-footed bug,
        leafminer, Mexican bean beetle, mite, root knot nematode, seedcorn maggot, slug, tarnished
        plant bug, thrips, webworm, weevil, whitefly, wireworm
DISEASES: anthracnose, bacterial blight and wilt, bean mosaic, common mosaic, curly top, damping
        off, powdery mildew, rust, southern blight, white mold, yellow mosaic. Burn diseased plants
        (where allowed).

HARVEST: Wait until the plant's leaves have fallen in autumn to pick dry pods or to pull the entire
plant. Harvest before the first frost. Soybeans and limas, however, often drop beans from the shell as
they dry, so these need to be picked when any split pods are spotted. Cure for several weeks in a well-
ventilated area, piling them on screens or slatted shelves. Beans are dry and ready to thresh when your
teeth won't dent the bean. Four methods of threshing: (1) thrash the plant back and forth on the inside
of a clean trashcan; (2) place the plant in a large burlap bag with a hole in the corner and flail; (3) put
plants in a cone-shaped bag, tie the bottom, walk or jump on the bag, or hang from a tree and beat well,
then untie hole in bottom and, with the help of a good wind, the chaff will blow away and beans will fall
into container. Professional threshers are available from Peaceful Valley Farm Supply.

STORAGE REQUIREMENTS: Remove all bad beans. Place on shallow trays and heat at 170-180F
for 10-15 minutes. Cool. Store in a cool, dry area in tight jars. To avoid weevil damage see Pest Chart.

OTHER GROWING NOTES: Beans are a warm season crop, tender to light frosts and freezes. Plan
an average of 10-20 plants per person. Cold, wet weather fosters disease, so don't sow or transplant too
early, touch the plants when wet, or touch healthy plants after working with diseased ones. Most dried
beans, whether bush or semi-vining, require long growing seasons. To direct sow them try layering grass
mulch 4-6" deep on the bed in the fall. This decomposes down to about 2" by spring, will keep the soil
warm 6" deep, won't pull nitrogen out of the soil, and allows you to plant earlier in the spring. See
SNAP BEANS for comments on presoaking and inoculation. Dried beans are very high in protein. Like
other legumes, soybeans and cowpeas are excellent green manure crops that enrich soil with organic
matter and nitrogen.

ALLIES: Some evidence-- goosegrass, red sprangletop, sorghum mulch (for cowpeas)
        Uncertain-- catnip, celery, corn, goldenrod, marigold, nasturtium, oregano, potato, rosemary,
        savory
COMPANIONS: beet, cabbage, carrot, celery, corn, cucumber, eggplant, peas, potato, radish,
        strawberry
ENEMIES: fennel, garlic, gladiolus, onion family

GREENHOUSE
Fordhook 242, Henderson Bush, King of the Garden-- see below

OUTDOOR
Pole
Christmas or Speckled Calico, Giant Florida-- 85 days, rich "butter bean," nutty flavor, large beautiful red-speckled beans (Blum, Earl May, Field's, Park, Southern Exposure)
Hopi-- white, gray, yellow and red types, native to the Southwest, suitable for high and low desert (Native Seed)
Hyacinth-- new in 1989, baby white limas, some drought tolerance (Park)
King of the Garden-- 100 days, early, 5" pods, heirloom, high yields, good fresh or dried (Park, Seeds Blum, Southern Exposure)
Prizetaker-- 90 days, very large bean of good quality (Burpee)
Bush
Baby Fordhook-- 70 days, 14" bush, thick seeded, small lima, high quality (Burpee)
Fordhook 242-- 75 days, AAS winner, heat resistant, upright, early butterbean, good fresh, canned or frozen (Gurney's, Field's, Park, Seeds Blum, Stokes)
Henderson Bush-- 65 days, baby white (when dried), flat pods, withstands hot weather, good canned or frozen, good in all climates (Burpee, Earl May, Field's, Seeds Blum)

NOTES

* All varieties listed are open-pollinated.

Phaseolus limensis   Leguminosae or Fabaceae (Pea)   **Lima BEANS**

GROWTH CONDITIONS

Germ.Temp: 65-85
Grow.Temp: 60-70
pH: 6.0-7.0
Root Depth: 36-48"
Planting Depth: 1-1/2 to 2"
Water: Average and constant

Height: Pole, 8-15'   Bush, 10-18"
Breadth: Pole, 6-8"   Bush, 4-8"
Spacing: Pole, Intensive: 6"   Reg: 10-18"   Rows: 36-48"
Bush, Intensive: 4-6"   Reg: 6-8"

Fertilizer: Light feeder. Beans fix N when inoculated properly, so most need low N. Medium P & K.
Side-dress: 4 weeks after planting apply a balanced or low N fertilizer, or compost.
Support structures: Use a 6' post, A-frame, Tepee (3 poles tied at the top), or trellis for pole beans.
First Seed Starting Date:

Days Germ + Days Transplant - Days After LFD = Days Count BACK from LFD
7-18   +   21-35   -   14-28   =   14-25

Last Seed Starting Date:

Days Germ + Days Transplant + Maturity + SDF + Frost Tender = Days BACK from FFD
7-18   +   0   + 60-80   + 14 +   14   =   95-126

PESTS: aphid, bean leaf beetle, beet and potato leafhopper, cabbage looper, corn earworm, cucumber beetle, cutworm, flea beetle, garden webworm, Japanese beetle, leaf-footed bug, leafminer, Mexican bean beetle, mite, root knot nematodes, seedcorn maggot, slug, tarnished plant bug, thrips, webworm, weevil, whitefly, wireworm

DISEASES: anthracnose, bacterial blight & wilt, bean mosaic, common mosaic, curly top, damping off, powdery mildew, rust, south. blight, white mold, yellow mosaic. If legal, burn diseased plants.

HARVEST: For the best fresh flavor pick beans when young. To encourage the plant to set more beans, pick when beans are bulging through pods. For dried beans, wait until pods turn brown or leaves drop in the fall. Pick pods and cure for several weeks in a well-ventilated area, piling them on screens or slatted shelves. Beans are dry and ready to thresh when your teeth won't dent the bean. See Dried Shell Beans for threshing methods.

STORAGE REQUIREMENTS: Blanch before freezing. Store dried beans in jars in a cool, dry place.
Fresh: Temp: 37-41   Humidity: 95%   Storage Life: 5-7 days
Preserved, taste (months):   Can: fair (12+)   Freeze: excellent (12)   Dry: excellent (12+)

OTHER GROWING NOTES: Lima beans are a warm season crop, very tender to frost and light freezes. Plan an average of 10-20 plants per person. For every 2 lbs of filled pods you should get 1 lb of shelled beans. Limas are more sensitive to cold soil and calcium deficiency than snap beans. Limas don't like transplanting, so it's often recommended to sow them directly in the beds; however, seeds will not germinate if the soil isn't warm enough. See comments under Snap Beans about presoaking, inoculation, and cold, wet weather. For direct sowing, plant 5-6 seeds in a hill and thin to 3-4". Bush beans usually mature more quickly than pole beans and are determinate with one clean harvest. Pole limas generally have better flavor and are indeterminate with a continuous harvest, but they require extra effort due to their need for a trellis. Bush limas don't do well in wet weather as they'll develop an unpleasant earthy taste where pods touch the ground. A substitute support for non-rampant pole beans is to plant them between corn, if the corn isn't planted too densely, when the corn is 6-8" tall.

ALLIES: Some evidence-- goosegrass, red sprangletop
        Uncertain-- catnip, celery, corn, marigold, nasturtium, oregano, potato, savory, rosemary
COMPANIONS: Both bush & pole-- carrot, corn, cucumber, eggplant, lettuce, peas, radish
        Bush only-- beet, all *Brassicas,* strawberry
ENEMIES: Both bush & pole-- fennel, garlic, onion family
        Pole only-- beet, all *Brassicas,* kohlrabi, sunflower

GREENHOUSE
> **Tendercrop, Topcrop**-- see below

OUTDOOR
> Bush Snap
>> **Blue Lake 274**-- 55 days, 16" semi-erect plant, 6" pods, white seeds, matures all at once, long season, high yields, good fresh or frozen, resists bean mosaic (Earl May, Garden City, Gurney's, Park, William Dam)
>> **Pencil Pod Black Wax**-- 52 days, 15" plant, heirloom, stringless, tough yellow skins with black bean, fullest rich black bean flavor when mature, early and extended producer, good fresh or canned (Jung, Gurney's, Blum, Southern Exposure, William Dam)
>> **Romano or Roma II**-- 50-60 days, 2' plant, long flat stringless Italian bean, mosaic resistant, good snap or dried, canned or frozen, also available as pole (widely available)
>> **Royal Burgundy**-- 51 days, unusual purple flowers and pods, beans turn green when cooked, tolerates cold soil (widely available)
>> **Tendercrop**-- 53 days, reliable in poor weather, high yields, dark green, slender bean, thick clusters off the ground, resists mosaic, powdery mildew and pod mottle virus, good for canning (Gurney's, Field's, Nichols, Park)
>> **Topcrop**-- 49 days, AAS winner, stringless, slender, meaty bean, mosaic resistant, hardy (Burpee, Gurney's, Field's, William Dam)
>
> Pole Snap
>> **Blue Lake**-- 62 days, 8', 6" pods, stringless, excellent flavor, white seeds also good as shell beans, very sweet and tender (widely available)
>> **Kentucky Wonder**-- 65 days, 9" stringless pod, heirloom, very popular, good flavor, resists rust, also available as bush (widely available)
>> **Wren's Egg**-- 65 days, pretty streaked pods, large shelling beans (Blum)
>
> Pole Runner (perennial in warm climates; dig up bulbous root and replant in spring)
>> **Scarlet Runner (*P. coccinus*)**-- 70 days for fresh, 115 days for shell beans, vine to 10', pretty ornamental red flowers are edible, 8" pods, good soup bean, tolerates cool weather, pods won't set in hot weather (widely available)
>> **Scarlet Runner (*Tarahumare Tecomari*)**-- red flowering variety that produces purple, lavender, black and mottled beans, suitable for high desert (over 4,000 ft) (Native Seed)
>
> Filet (pencil-thin)
>> **Aramis**-- 65 days, bush, best taste raw and cooked in Rodale trials [*Organic Gardening*, 4/88], disease resistant, very uniform high yields, stringless (Garden City, William Dam)
>> **Camile**-- most productive in Rodale trials [*Organic Gardening*, 4/88], disease resistant, good sweet flavor, best lightly steamed (Cook's, Horticultural Products)
>> **Finaud**-- a true filet that doesn't need to be picked every day, new in 1988 (Cook's)
>> **Fin de Bagnols**-- very slender pods, early, uniform, tender, sweet, delicate flavor, grow like bush beans (Cook's)
>
> Flageolet (rich, meaty shelling beans often eaten fresh like limas)
>> **Chevrier**-- a delicacy when eaten fresh, flageolet are also grown as shell beans for drying, pick when seeds are 1/2" in the shell (Cook's)

NOTES

* All varieties listed are open-pollinated.

Phaseolus vulgaris   *Leguminosae or Fabaceae (Pea)*   **Snap BEANS**

GROWTH CONDITIONS

Germ.Temp: 60-85   Height: Pole: 8-15'   Bush: 10-24"
Grow.Temp: 60-70   Breadth: Pole: 6-8"   Bush: 4-8"
pH: 6.2-7.5   Spacing: Pole: Intensive: 6"   Reg: 12"   Row: 18-36"
Soil: Loam   Bush: 2-4"   4-6"   "   "
Root Depth: 36-48"   Planting Depth: 1" spring, 2" fall
Water: Low until the plant flowers, then average.
Fertilizer: Because bean plants fix N when inoculated properly, they should require low N. After it
        flowers you might apply light N. Avoid low K.
Support structures: Use a 6' posts, A-frame, Tepee, or trellis to support pole beans.
First Seed Starting:

        Days Germ. + Days Transplant - Days After LFD = Days Count BACK from LFD
        4-10   +   21-28   -   7-14   = 25-28
Last Seed Starting:

        Days Germ + Days Transplant + Maturity + SDF + Frost Tender = Days BACK from FFD
        4-10   +   0 (direct)   +   48-95   + 14   +   14   = 80-134

PESTS: same as LIMA BEANS.   Also European corn borer.
DISEASES: anthracnose, bacterial blight & wilt, bean & common mosaic, curly top, damping off,
        powdery mildew, rust, south. blight, white mold, yellow mosaic. If legal, burn diseased plants.

HARVEST: For best flavor pick early in the morning, after leaves are dry. Harvest before seeds bulge, when beans snap off the plant and snap in half cleanly. Continual harvest is essential for prolonged bean production. **Bush, snap:** pick when 1/4 - 3/8" diameter. **Filet:** pick daily and, for peak flavor, when no larger than 1/8" diameter, regardless of length.

STORAGE REQUIREMENTS: Blanch before freezing.
Fresh: Temp: 40-45   Humidity: 95%   Storage Life: 7-10 days
Preserved, taste (months): Can: fair (12+)   Freeze: excellent (12)   Dry: excellent (24)

OTHER GROWING NOTES: Beans are a warm season crop, tender to light frosts and freezes. Plan an average of 10-20 plants per person. Bush beans are usually determinate with one clean harvest, so plant every 10 days for continuous harvest. Pole beans are usually indeterminate with a continuous harvest for 6-8 weeks--if kept picked--so only one planting is necessary. Bean roots don't tolerate disturbance so handle seedlings minimally. Plant outside at the same depth they grew in the pot. For pole beans, pinch off growing tips when plants reach the top of their support system. While some gardeners recommend presoaking the seeds, recent research indicates that presoaked seeds absorb water too quickly, split their outer coats and spill out essential nutrients, which encourages damping-off seed rot. Yields can increase 50-100 percent by inoculating with Rhizobia bacteria. To inoculate simply roll seeds in the powder. Cold, wet weather fosters disease, so don't sow or transplant too early, touch plants when wet, or touch healthy plants after working with diseased ones. For a substitute support, plant non-rampant pole beans between corn that isn't too densely planted, when the corn is 6-8" tall.

ALLIES: Some evidence-- goosegrass, red sprangletop
        Unproven-- catnip, celery, corn, marigold, nasturtium, oregano, potato, rosemary, savory
COMPANIONS: Both pole & bush-- carrot, corn, cucumber, eggplant, peas, radish, strawberry
        Just bush-- beet, all *Brassicas*
ENEMIES: Both pole & bush-- basil, fennel, garlic, gladiolus, onion family
        Pole only-- beet, all *Brassicas*, sunflower

GREENHOUSE: Greenhouse beets are usually grown for their greens.
  Detroit Dark Red, Green Top Bunching, Lutz Green Leaf-- see below

OUTDOOR
  Albino White-- 50 days, unusual white beet won't "bleed," mild, sweet (Blum, Cook's, Field's, Stokes)
  Burpee's Golden or Golden-- 50-55 days, unusual yellow beet that won't bleed into other foods, both root and greens are tasty, this is a poor germinator so sow more thickly (widely available)
  Chioggia-- 50 days, open-pollinated, gourmet red and white striped beet, try the Improved variety (Cook's, Johnny's, Seeds Blum, Shepherd's)
  Crosby's Egyptian-- 60 days, open-pollinated, heirloom, flattened shape, sweet and rich, 1 of the best in Harrowsmith 1988 trials [*Harrowsmith,* 1/89] (Southern Exposure, Seeds Blum)
  Cylindra-- 60 days, up to 8" (like carrot), needs deep soil (widely available)
  Detroit Dark Red-- 60 days, most widely sold beet, reliable, high-quality (widely available)
  Green Top Bunching-- 65 days, roots and greens retain color in cooler weather (Stokes)
  Kleine Bol-- 50 days, a true baby beet which grows fast (Shepherds)
  Lutz Green Leaf-- 70 days, open-pollinated, good yields, improves in storage & stays tender, high in Vitamins A & C, one of best in Harrowsmith 1988 trials [*Harrowsmith,* 1/89] (Abundant Life, Burpee, Cook's, Southern Exposure, Park)
  Red Ace-- 52 days, hybrid, midseason, milder than "Detroit Dark Red", sweet and rich, stays tender when older, one of best in Harrowsmith 1988 trials [*Harrowsmith,* 1/89] (widely available)

Swiss Chard (*B. vulgaris* var. *cicla*)-- closely related to the beet, chard is grown for its greens which taste like spinach. Rich with Vitamin C, calcium and iron, its leaves can be used fresh in salads, or cooked in stir-fry dishes, in quiches, or even in stuffing. Its stalks can be cooked with the leaves, or separately like asparagus. It can be grown year-round in zones 9-10, and as an annual elsewhere. Harvest outer leaves, or cut to a few inches above the ground following which new leaves will grow. It can withstand fall frosts to 15-20F.
  Fordhook Giant-- 60 days, easy to grow, large dark green, crinkled leaves, yields well even in hot weather (Burpee, Harris, Johnny's, Stokes, Territorial)
  Large White Ribbed-- 60 days, smoother and more tender leaves with white ribs (Blum, Harris)
  Lucillus-- 60 days, extremely heat tolerant and non-bolting (Field's, Gurney's, Jung, Park, Southern Exposure)
  Ruby or Rhubarb-- 60 days, a beautiful red-stalked plant, pretty in the garden among flowers or vegetables, some of the color bleeds in cooking, excellent flavor (widely available)

NOTES

GROWTH CONDITIONS

Germ.Temp: 50-85   Height: 12"
Grow.Temp: 60-65   Breadth: 4-8"
pH: 5.8-7.0 (5.3 for scab)   Spacing: Intensive: 3-4"   Reg: 6"   Rows: 18-24"
Root Depth: 24" -10'   Planting Depth: 1/4"
Water: Average and evenly moist
Fertilizer: Heavy feeder. Needs high P. Avoid high N. Good tops may mean the roots are poorly developed and the plant is getting too much N.
Side-dress: Every 2 weeks provide a light and balanced feeding. When tops are 4-5" use low N.
First Seed Starting Date:

> Days Germ + Days Transplant + Days Before LFD = Days Count BACK from LFD
> 5-10   + 0 (direct)   + 9-18   = 14-28 days

Last Seed Starting Date:

> Days Germ + Days Transplant + Maturity + SDF + Frost Tender = Days BACK from FFD
> 5-10   + 0 (sow direct)   + 55-80   + 14 + 0   = 74-84

PESTS: mostly pest free; occasional beet leafhopper, carrot weevil, earwig (seedlings), garden webworm, leafminer, mite, spinach flea beetle, whitefly, wireworm
DISEASES: the eating beet is mostly disease free; occasional cercospora, downy mildew, leaf spot, rust, scab

HARVEST: Pull or dig when beets are 1-2" across. They become tough and woody-flavored when allowed to grow larger.

STORAGE REQUIREMENTS: Remove all top greens, leaving about 1" of stem with the beet. Do not wash. Pack beets in straw or moist sand. Beets can also be left in ground and dug up from under the snow.
Fresh: Temp: 32   Humidity: 98-100%   Storage Life: 4-7 mos. topped; 10-14 days bunched
Preserved, taste (months):   Can: good (12+)   Freezing: fair (8)   Drying: fair (12+)

OTHER GROWING NOTES: Beets are an annual cool season crop, half-hardy to frost and light freezes. Plan an average of 10-20 plants per person. Most beet cultivars are open-pollinated and multigerm, where one seed yields a clump of 4-5 plants which need to be thinned. These multigerm seeds, also known as "seed balls," germinate better if soaked an hour before planting. There are three main types of eating beets: Long (Cylindra), Medium (Semiglobe), and Short (Globe). Cylindra types mature slowly and, because they grows as long as 8", require deep soil. They can also be a good organic matter crop. For all types, look for cultivars resistant to bolting as well as to downy mildew. Yellow and white beets are sweeter than red varieties. Newer hybrids are usually sweeter than older varieties and offer more green leaves. Most beets contain about 5-8% sugar while the newer hybrids such as BIG RED run about 12-14%. Hybrids tend to mature 7-14 days earlier, are more upright, and tend to have higher yields. Like kale and some other vegetables, most beets in hot weather get tough, woody, and develop an "off" flavor. An exception, according to some, is "Detroit Crimson Globe." If your summers are hot generally choose a variety that matures in 45-60 days. In greenhouses beets are often grown for just their greens.

ALLIES: Some evidence-- none
          Uncertain-- garlic, onion family
COMPANIONS: all *Brassicas,* bush beans, head lettuce
ENEMIES: field mustard, all pole beans

BROCCOLI VARIETIES

GREENHOUSE
DeCicco, Green Comet, Italian Green Sprouting, Spartan Early-- see below

OUTDOOR
DeCicco-- 65 days, open-pollinated, old Italian variety, small heads, long harvest with side-shoots (Garden City, Hi Altitude, Johnny's, Southern Exposure, William Dam)
Green Comet-- 55 days, hybrid, extra large and tight heads, heat and disease resistant (Burpee, Gurney's, Park, William Dam)
Green Goliath-- 55 days, open-pollinated, high yields, early and extended harvest, many side shoots, good for freezing (Burpee, Jung, William Dam)
Green Valiant-- 66 days, hybrid, large heads, good for intensive planting, good for fall planting, frost resistant, dense heads and heavy stalks, develops side shoots (Johnny's, Territorial)
Italian Green Sprouting (aka: Calabrese)-- 65-80 days, open-pollinated, forms many sideshoots after central harvest, prolific (Abundant Life, Cook's, Nichols, Seeds Blum, Stokes)
Mercedes-- 58 days, hybrid, new in 1990, reliable for fall planting and harvest before winter, matures in 2 months from seed (Shepherd's)
Premium Crop-- 60-80 days, hybrid, large heads, good for summer and fall crops, uniform, compact, holds firmness well (widely available)
Purple Sprouting-- 220 days (from seed), open-pollinated, one of oldest heirlooms (pre-1835), profusion of tender, very sweet shoots, hardy to -10F, in some areas must overwinter before it flowers in the spring (Abundant Life, Bountiful Gardens, Cook's, Territorial)
Rapini or Broccoli Raab or Ruvo Kale (*B. rapa ruvo*)-- 60 days, not a true broccoli, Italian specialty item, doesn't develop real heads, grown for leaves, ribs and flower buds. Sow very early spring with radishes, or in fall. Saute with garlic and olive oil, or use like kale. (Nichols)
Romanesco-- unusual yellow color, open-pollinated, spiralling large head, needs a long season so start seeds early, also needs extra feeding, there are apparently many different strains with different maturation times for short or long seasons, before ordering check to make sure their strain will do well in your area (Bountiful Gardens-says good for Northern climates, Burpee-75 days, Gurney's-105 days, Johnny's-75 days for cultivar "Minaret", Shepherd's-100 days)
Silvia-- new in 1989, more resistant to powdery mildew than most (Earl May, Letherman's)
Spartan Early-- 47-76 days, open-pollinated, extra early, good sized solid center heads, doesn't go to seed, good flavor (Earl May, Field's, Seeds Blum, Southern Exposure, Stokes)
Waltham 29-- 74 days, open-pollinated, for early fall planting, will mature in cold weather, long harvest, good for freezing (Abundant Life, Earl May, Seeds Blum, Southern Exposure)

NOTES

Brassica oleracea, Botrytis Gr.   **Brassicaceae (Mustard)**   **BROCCOLI**

GROWTH CONDITIONS

Germ.Temp: 50-85

Grow.Temp: 60-65

pH: 6.0-7.5 (7.2 deters clubroot)

Root Depth: 18-36"

Water: Medium and evenly moist

Height: 18" - 4'

Breadth: 15-24'

Spacing: Intensive: 15" Reg: 18-24" Rows: 24-36"

Planting Depth: 1/4"

Fertilizer: Heavy feeder. Before planting add compost to the soil. If clubroot is a problem, raise the pH
by adding lime or taking other measures (see page 159).

Side-dress: When buds begin to form side-dress the plant with compost.

First Seed Starting Date:

Days Germ + Days Transplant + Days Before LFD = Days Count BACK from LFD

3-10   +   42   +   14   = 59-66

Last Seed Starting Date:

Days Germ + Days Transplant + Maturity + SDF + Frost Tender = Days BACK from FFD

3-10   +   21   + 55-74   + 14 +   0   = 93-119

PESTS: aphid, cabbage butterfly, cabbage looper. cabbage maggot, cutworm, diamondback moth,
flea beetle, harlequin bug, imported cabbage worm, mite, root fly, slug, weevil, whitefly

DISEASES: alternaria leaf spot, black leg, black rot, club root, damping off, downy mildew, leaf
spot, rhizoctonia, yellows

HARVEST: Broccoli is ready to harvest when the heads are dark green. Purple varieties should be a
dusky violet. If heads turn yellow you've waited too long. For the best flavor heads should be no more
than about 4" across. The exception is "Romanesco," whose natural color is chartreuse and head can
grow up to 1' in breadth. For most varieties, smaller compact heads are best. Harvest the central head
first. Some varieties will produce side shoots that develop small head clusters; these plants will produce
for 1 to 2 months, or until frost. Cut the stalk so that several inches remain on the plant.

STORAGE REQUIREMENTS: Fall crops are better than summer crops for freezing.

Fresh: Temp: 32   Humidity: 95-100%   Storage Life: 10-14 days

Temp: 32-40   Humidity: 80%   Storage Life: 1 month

Preserved, taste (months):   Can: fair (12+)   Freeze: good (12)   Dry: fair (12+)

OTHER GROWING NOTES: Broccoli is an annual cool season crop, hardy to frost and light freezes.
Plan an average of 5-10 plants per person. Transplant seedlings when they're 6" high, and place in the
ground 1" deeper than they were grown in the pots. Broccoli is usually sensitive to heat. If the weather
is too hot, it will flower quickly and won't produce an edible head. Cover with fabric immediately after
planting. This not only protects broccoli from pests but also helps trap heat for early plantings. To
prevent spreading clubroot and other soil borne diseases, don't compost *Brassica* roots. Some gardeners
won't compost any part of a plant in the *Brassica* family. Pull and destroy infected plants. Also, rotate
the placement of *Brassica* plants in your garden so they aren't in the same 10' radius for at least 3 years.
Some experts recommend a rotation of 7 years.

ALLIES: Some evidence-- candytuft, shepherds purse, wormseed mustard
Uncertain-- catnip, celery, chamomile, dill, garlic, mint, nasturtium, onion family, radish,
rosemary, sage, savory, tansy, tomato, thyme, wormwood

COMPANIONS: artichoke, beet, bush beans, cucumber, lettuce, peas, potato, spinach

ENEMIES: pole lima and snap beans, strawberry, tomato (Note: also might by an ally.)

BRUSSELS SPROUTS VARIETIES

GREENHOUSE
Early Dwarf Danish, Jade Cross, Long Island Improved-- see below

OUTDOOR
Early Dwarf Danish-- 95 days, early, open-pollinated, well suited for short seasons, dwarf habit aids mulching, large sprouts (Abundant Life, Garden City)

Jade Cross-- 80 days, dwarf hybrid, good for short season, sweet and mild (but can be bitter), heat tolerant (widely available)

Long Island Improved (Catskill)-- 80 days, excellent standard variety, open-pollinated, tall variety, small globe-shaped heads, tender, delicate flavor, good frozen (Earl May, Nichols, Stokes)

Oliver-- hybrid, earliest variety, easy to grow (Burpee, Harris, Johnny's)

Ormavon-- 117 days, hybrid, grows sprouts up the stem and "cabbage" greens on top, harvest tender greens after sprouts, interesting dual-purpose item (Thompson & Morgan)

Peer Gynt-- 140 days, dwarf, long maturation and high quality sprouts (Thompson & Morgan)

Prince Marvel-- 90 days, tall plant, firm and excellent quality sprouts, tolerates bottom rot, reduced cracking (widely available)

Rubine Red-- 80 days, open-pollinated, beautiful red, late variety (Cook's, Gurney's, Harris, Nichols, Seeds Blum, William Dam)

Silverstar-- hybrid, good flavor, early sprouts, very hardy variety, can overwinter in mild areas or where good snow cover (Cook's)

Valiant-- 110 days, hybrid, 2' plant, cylindrical sprouts, tender and sweet, not bitter, resists rot and cracking, reliable heavy producer (Shepherd's)

NOTES

B.oleracae, Gemmifera Gr. Brassicaceae (Mustard)   **Brussels SPROUTS**

GROWTH CONDITIONS

Germ.Temp: 50-80   Height: 24-48"
Grow.Temp: 60-65   Breadth: 24"
pH: 6.0-7.5   Spacing: Intensive: 16-18"   Reg: 18-24"   Rows: 24-40"
Root Depth: 18-36"   Planting Depth: 1/4"
Water: Medium and evenly moist
Fertilizer: Heavy feeder. Use compost, or 2-3 bushels of manure per 100 sq.ft.
Side-dress: Apply 2 weeks after transplanting, then twice more at monthly intervals.
First Seed Starting Date:
        Days Germ + Days Transplant + Days Before LFD = Days Count BACK from LFD
        3-10   +   28-49   +   14-21   = 45-153
Last Seed Starting Date:
        Days Germ + Days Transplant + Maturity + SDF + Frost Tender = Days BACK from FFD
        3-10   +   21   + 80-100 + 14 +   0   = 115-142

PESTS: aphid, cabbage butterfly, cabbage looper, cabbage maggot, cutworm, flea beetle, harlequin
        bug, mite, root fly, slug, thrips, weevil, whitefly
DISEASES: black leg, black rot, club root, damping off, leaf spot, rhizoctonia, yellows

HARVEST: For the best sprout growth, when a sprout node begins to bulge remove the leaf below it. Harvest from the bottom of the stalk up. When sprouts are firm and no more than about 1" across, use a sharp knife to cut off the sprouts and remove lower leaves. Leave enough trunk so that new sprouts can grow. As the harvest slows pinch out the top of the plant to direct nutrients to the sprouts. For maximum Vitamin C, harvest when the temperature is around freezing. Some say to never harvest unless you've had at least two frosts, as frost improves the flavor. It has also been reported that sprouts can be harvested throughout the summer (and still be tender) if they're continuously picked when they reach the size of marbles. If you want to harvest all at once instead of continuously, cut or pinch off the stalk top about 4-8 weeks before your intended time of harvest. When done harvesting, remove the entire plant from the ground to minimize the chance of disease next season.

STORAGE REQUIREMENTS: Store entire plant "logs" in a cool root cellar. Otherwise leave the stalk in the ground and pick sprouts when ready to eat. Some report harvesting through the snow.
Fresh: Temp 32   Humidity: 95-100%   Storage Life: 3-5 weeks
Preserved, taste (months):   Can: fair (12+)   Freeze: good (12)   Dry: poor

OTHER GROWING NOTES: Brussels sprouts are an annual cool season crop, hardy to frost and light freezes. Plan an average of 2-8 plants per person. There are two basic types of Brussels sprouts varieties: (1) the dwarf (e.g. "Jade Cross") which matures early and is winter hardy but more difficult to harvest, and (2) the taller (e.g. "Long Island Improved") which is less hardy but easier to harvest. Brussels sprouts have shallow roots, so as they become top heavy you may need to stake them, particularly if exposed to strong winds. As with other *Brassicas*, Brussels Sprouts are susceptible to pests and diseases which early in the season must be kept under control. Row covers are one of the easiest pest controls, provided no pest eggs are already present under the covers. This vegetable is high in calcium and iron, as well as a good source of Vitamins A and C. To prevent spreading soil borne diseases, don't compost *Brassica* roots. Rotate at least on a 3-year basis, or optimally on a 7-year basis.

ALLIES: Some evidence-- candytuft, clover (white), cover grass, french beans, shepherd's purse,
        weedy ground cover, wormseed mustard
           Uncertain-- celery, chamomile, dill, garlic, mint, onion family, radish, rosemary, sage,
        savory, tansy, tomato, thyme, wormwood
COMPANIONS: artichoke, beet, peas, potato, spinach
ENEMIES: kohlrabi, all pole beans, strawberry, tomato (Note: might also be an ally.)

CABBAGE VARIETIES

GREENHOUSE
    All **Chinese cabbages, Market Prize**-- see below

OUTDOOR
    Red
        Pierette-- hybrid, midseason, large, round heads, tolerates splitting (Stokes)
        Red Danish-- open-pollinated, resists thrips, cabbage looper and moths (Stokes)
        Ruby Ball-- hybrid, early, red leaves retain color in cooking (Earl May, Harris, Territorial)
    White
        Danish Ballhead-- 100 days, open-pollinated, late keeper, good for kraut, resists thrips, sweet flavor, resists cracking, keeps through winter (widely available)
        Early Jersey Wakefield-- 63 days, open-pollinated, heirloom, space saving pointed heads, good flavor, reliable, well-adapted to different soils, resists yellows (widely available)
        Grenadier-- 65 days, 2 lb heads, hybrid, excellent fresh eating, tender, juicy, resists cracking and long holding qualities, prefers cool weather, doesn't tolerate yellows (Shepherd's, Stokes)
        Lariat-- 125 days (from seed), 5-8 lb heads, open-pollinated, very late season, best long-term keeper, still high quality after several months storage (Johnny's)
        Market Prize-- 76 days, hybrid, blue-green, good yields under a wide variety of conditions, good holding quality, resists yellows and splitting (Harris)
        Perfect Ball-- 87 days, hybrid, midseason, sweetest & smallest core of midseasons, resists yellows, good holding quality in field, large wrapping leaves (Johnny's)
        Prime Time-- 76 days, hybrid, midseason, especially good for salads if picked early as a loose, round head (Stokes)
        Multikeeper-- 86 days, hybrid, late season, tolerates yellows, black rot (Stokes)
        Savoy Ace-- 85 days, AAS winner, resists heat and frost, holds well for long harvest, resists yellows and insects (widely available)
        Savoy King-- 90 days, very dark green crinkled (savoyed) leaves, high in Vitamin A, semi-flat heads resists yellows and insects (widely available)
        Stonehead-- 67 days, AAS winner, hybrid, early, popular for firm, solid interior, resists cracking, resists yellows, good for small areas (widely available)
    Chinese (good in soups, stir-fried, or in salads)
        Jade Pagoda (Michihi type)-- 68 days, hybrid, tall cylinder shape, thick, leafy and savoyed, mild, sweet, vigorous, high yields, easy to grow, resists bolting (Harris, Park, Stokes)
        Nagoda-- 50 days, tolerates heat and cold, standard in stores (Johnny's)
        Joi Choi-- 45 days, hybrid between Pak Choi and Lei Choi, slow bolting stands warm weather, excellent flavor (Harris, Park, Stokes,

NOTES

B.oleracea, Capitata Gr.   *Brassicaceae (Mustard)*   **CABBAGE**

GROWTH CONDITIONS

Germ.Temp: 45-95   Height: 12-15"
Grow.Temp: 60-65   Breadth: 24-40"
pH: 6.0-7.5 (7.2 deters clubroot)   Spacing: Intensive: 15"   Reg: 18"   Rows: 24-30"
Root Depth: 12" - 5'   Planting Depth: 1/4 - 1/2"
Water: Heavy early and medium late in the season.
Fertilizer: Heavy feeder. High N & K. You may need to add lime to raise the pH to deter clubroot.
Side-dress: Every 2 weeks.
First Seed Starting Date:

Days Germ	+	Days Transplant	+	Days Before LFD	=	Days Count BACK from LFD
7-12	+	42	+	14-21	=	63-75

Last Seed Starting Date:

Days Germ	+	Days Transplant	+	Maturity	+	SDF	+	Frost Tender	=	Days BACK from FFD
4	+	21	+	65-95	+	14	+	0	=	104-120

PESTS: aphids, cabbage butterfly, cabbage looper, cabbage maggot, cabbageworm, cutworm, diamond-back moth, flea beetle, green worm, harlequin bug, leafminer, mite, mole, seedcorn maggot, root fly, slug, stink bug, weevil
DISEASES: black leg, black rot, club root, damping off, fusarium wilt, leaf spot, pink rot, rhizoctonia, yellows

HARVEST: For eating fresh, as soon as the head feels solid cut it at ground level. Smaller heads may grow from the remaining leaves and stems. For the best storage heads, pick when still firm and solid and before the top leaves lose green color. Pull the entire plant and roots from the ground. If left too long in the ground the cabbage core becomes fibrous and tough, and the head may split.

STORAGE REQUIREMENTS: Some recommend curing heads in the sun for a few days before storing for long periods. Such curing requires covering at night. Because of the strong odors emitted, store in either a well-ventilated place or a separate room reserved for *Brassicas*. To store, trim off all loose outer leaves. Hang by its roots, or wrap individually in paper, or layer in straw in an airy bin, or place several inches apart on shelves.
Fresh: Temp: 32-40   Humidity: 80-90%   Storage Life: about 4 months
Preserved, taste (months):   Can: poor   Freeze: good (8)   Dry: fair (12+)

OTHER GROWING NOTES: Cabbage is an annual cool season crop, hardy to frost and light freezes. Plan an average of 3-5 plants per person. Young plants may bolt if grown at 50F for a long time; mature plants of late varieties improve flavor in cold weather. A smaller cabbage head has better flavor and can stay in the field longer without splitting. To keep them small, plant close together or, when the head is almost full, give the plant a sharp twist to sever feeder roots. After harvest continued growth causes cabbage to need additional food reserves. Rapid growers, then, keep poorly as they use up their food reserves faster. Early varieties are generally the smallest, juiciest, and most tender, but they store poorly and split easily. Midseason varieties keep better in the field. Late varieties, best for sauerkraut, provide the largest and longest keeping heads. Yellow varieties tend to be hotter than white. To prevent spreading soil borne diseases, don't compost any *Brassica* roots and pull and destroy infected plants. Also, rotate these plants on at least a 3-year basis, or optimally on a 7-year basis.

ALLIES: Some evidence-- candytuft, clover (red & white, shepherd's purse, wormseed mustard
        Uncertain-- celery, chamomile, dill, garlic, hyssop, mint, nasturtium, onion family, radish,
        rosemary, sage, savory, tomato, tansy, thyme, southernwood, wormwood
COMPANIONS: artichoke, beet, bush beans, cucumber, lettuce, peas, potato, spinach
ENEMIES: all pole beans, basil, strawberry, tomato (Note: might also be an ally)

CARROT VARIETIES

GREENHOUSE
Early Scarlet Horn, Planet, Caramba, or other shorter carrots-- see below

OUTDOOR
A-Plus-- 71 days, hybrid, rich in vitamin A, nantes-type (widely available)

Caramba-- 75 days, Dutch, open-pollinated, grow for "mini" or regular size, crispy, makes sweet juice (Shepherd's, Territorial)

Chrisna-- 68 days, hybrid, nantes type, high flavor & texture rating by Rodale (Earl May)

Danvers Half Long-- 75 days, open-pollinated, good keeper in underground storage, adapted to many soil types (Burpee, Garden City, Fields, Gurney's, Southern Exposure, William Dam)

Early Scarlet Horn-- open-pollinated, heirloom "baby" carrot, good for greenhouse forcing and early outdoor planting (Abundant Life)

Ingot-- 68 days, hybrid, nantes type, high flavor & texture rating by Rodale (Johnny's, Stokes)

Lindoro-- 63 days, hybrid, nantes type, high flavor & texture rating by Rodale (Park)

Mokum-- hybrid, good for early spring crop under row covers (Cook's)

Nantes Half Long (aka: Coreless and Scarlet Nantes)-- 70 days, open-pollinated, sweet and tender eating carrot, coreless, standard home gardener variety (widely available)

Nantes Tip Top-- 73 days, Dutch, excellent eating quality, for wide range of soils (Shepherd's)

Napoli-- 58 days, hybrid, new in 1989, tender, sweet, early, blight-tolerant (Johnny's)

Planet-- 68 days, French, open-pollinated, a small round "baby" carrot of deep orange/red color, doesn't need deep soil (Shepherd's, Stokes)

Royal Chantenay-- 70 days, excellent for heavy, clay or shallow soils, popular (widely available)

Touchon-- 75 days, French, open-pollinated, nantes type, fine texture, sweet, flavor suffers in hot summers, good for juicing (Abundant Life, Blum, Cook's, Nichols, Stokes)

White Belgium-- 75 days, unusual white all the way through, taste may get too strong in hot summers (Nichols)

NOTES

Daucus carota v. *sativum*   *Umbelliferae or Apiaceae (Parsley)*   **CARROT**

GROWTH CONDITIONS

Germ.Temp: 45-85   Height: 12"
Grow.Temp: 60-65   Breadth: 12-24"
pH: 5.5-6.5   Spacing: Intensive: 2-3"   Reg: 6"   Rows: 16-30"
Root Depth: 24" - 7'   Planting Depth: 1/4 - 1/2"
Water: Medium
Fertilizer: Light feeder. Too much top growth may mean too much N.
Side-dress: Apply 3 weeks after germination, then again when 6-8" high.
First Seed Starting Date:

> Days Germ + Days Transplant + Days Before LFD = Days Count BACK from LFD
> 6-14   +   0   +   8-14   =   14-28

Last Seed Starting Date:

> Days Germ + Days Transplant + Maturity + SDF + Frost Tender = Days BACK from FFD
> 6-14   +   0   + 65-70   + 14 +   0   =   85-98

PESTS: carrot rust fly, carrot weevil, cutworm, flea beetle, leafhopper, nematode, snail, slug, parsleyworm, weevil, wireworm
DISEASES: alternaria leaf spot, cercospora, damping off, leaf blight, soft rot, yellows

HARVEST: Gently pull the roots out by their green tops. For most newer varieties don't let carrots grow fatter than 1-1/2" across or they'll become woody. Some older varieties can still be succulent and delicious when large.

STORAGE REQUIREMENTS: Remove the green tops, but do not wash the carrot before storing. Store in sawdust or sand in containers.
Fresh: Temp: 32   Humidity: 90-95% / 95-100%   Storage Life: 4-5 mos. / 7-9 mos.
Preserved, taste (months): Can: fair (12+)   Freeze: good (8)   Dry: fair (12+)

OTHER GROWING NOTES: Carrots are an annual cool season crop, half-hardy to frost and light freezes. Plan an average of 10-40 plants per person. One way to break the soil crust for carrot seeds is to plant a few fast-germinating radish seeds in the carrot bed. Carrots produce best in friable soil, so dig well before planting or grow smaller carrots that don't need deep soil. Sow seeds evenly in a very shallow furrow, about 1/4" deep, and keep seeds moist so they will germinate. When the first leaves emerge, thin to 1" apart; when true leaves emerge, thin to 3" apart. If you delay the final thinning a bit, you can use the removed roots as baby carrots. The darkest and greenest tops indicate the largest carrots. To prevent greening at the shoulders hill dirt up around the greens. The sweetest and best textured carrots are the Nantes-types, cylindrical and blunt-tipped. The long and tapered characteristics are typical of Imperator varieties. Nantes-types absorb more water and therefore have less dry matter, making them more succulent and crisp. They are also lower than other types in terpenoids, which cause a soapy turpentine-like taste; the amount of terpenoids depends entirely on variety, not on the soil. Terpenoids break down in cooking so that carrots taste sweeter when cooked. "Nantes" now describes any carrot with the above traits, not true lineage to the French region where the type originated.

ALLIES: Some evidence-- onion family
>   Uncertain-- black salsify, chives, corinader, flax, lettuce, onion family, pea, pennyroyal, radish, rosemary, sage, wormwood
COMPANIONS: all beans, leek, pepper, tomato
ENEMIES: celery, dill (retards growth)

CAULIFLOWER VARIETIES

GREENHOUSE
Extra Early Snowball, Purple Head, Snow Crown, Snow King-- see below

OUTDOOR
Early Purple Sicilian-- open-pollinated, purple heads, like purple broccoli (Abundant Life)
Extra Early Snowball-- 50 days, open-pollinated, early variety, pest resistant, yellows resistant (Seeds Blum, Southern Exposure, Stokes)
Purple Head-- 80-85 days, open-pollinated, easier to grow than white types, turns green when cooked (Burpee, William Dam)
Snow Crown-- 50-53 days, hybrid, AAS winner, early and reliable producer, vigorous, tolerates adverse weather (Burpee, Harris, Jung, Stokes, Territorial, William Dam)
Snow King Hybrid-- 50 days, AAS winner, very early, excellent flavor (Gurney's, Field's, Park, Thompson & Morgan, William Dam)
White Sails-- 68 days, hybrid, good for fall planting, leaves self wrap to protect inner curds, deep large heads (Southern Exposure, Stokes)
Violet Queen-- 54 days, hybrid, earliest purple, considered by some as best purple variety, easy to grow, uniform (Cook's, Harris, Johnny's)

NOTES

B.oleracae, Botrytis Gr.   *Brassicaceae (Mustard)*   CAULIFLOWER

GROWTH CONDITIONS

Germ.Temp: 45-85
Grow.Temp: 60-70 day, 50-60 night
pH: 6.0-7.5
Root Depth: 18" - 4'

Height: 18-24"
Breadth: 2 to 2-1/2'
Spacing: Intensive: 12-15"   Reg: 18"   Rows: 24-46"
Planting Depth: 1/4 - 1/2"

Water: Medium (critical early in season and during warm weather).
Fertilizer: Heavy feeder. Needs high N & K.
Side-dress: Every 3-4 weeks.
First Seed Starting Date: If covered, transplants can be set out almost 4 weeks earlier (see below).

Days Germ	+	Days Transplant	-	Days After LFD	=	Days Count BACK from LFD
4-10	+	35-49	-	14 (no cover)	=	25-45 (uncovered at transplanting)
			+	14 (covered)	=	53-73 (covered once transplanted)

Last Seed Starting Date:

Days Germ	+	Days Transplant	+	Maturity	+	SDF	+	Frost Tender	=	Days BACK from FFD
4-10	+	21	+	50-95	+	14	+	N/A	=	89-140

PESTS: aphid, cabbage butterfly, looper and maggot, cutworm, diamondback moth, harlequin bug, mite, root fly, root maggot, slug, snail, striped flea beetle, weevil
DISEASES: black leg, black rot, clubroot, damping off, downy mildew, leaf spot, rhizoctonia, seed rot, yellows

HARVEST: When heads are 8-10" in diameter, harvest by pulling the entire plant from the soil. Cauliflower heads deteriorate quickly, so check periodically and harvest when ready.

STORAGE REQUIREMENTS: Wrap individual plants, head and roots, in plastic. Store in a root cellar or cool place.
Fresh: Temp: 32   Humidity: 95-98%   Storage Life: 3-4 weeks
Preserved, taste (months):   Freeze: good (12)   Pickled: good (12)

OTHER GROWING NOTES: Cauliflower is an annual cool season crop, half-hardy to frost and light freezes. Plan an average of 3-5 plants per person. Cauliflower can be difficult to grow as it bolts in heat and is also the most sensitive of all *Brassicas* to frost. Note on the seed starting dates that cauliflower shouldn't be transplanted outdoors until all danger of frost is past, unless covered. It also needs to mature before hot summer arrives. A compromise might be to choose an intermediate starting date and cover the plants when set out to protect from cold. Purple cauliflower is an easier crop because it's more pest resistant and hardier than white varieties. Early in the season it looks and tastes more like broccoli, but after a cold snap its flavor will be more like cauliflower. Depending on your area, cauliflower might be better grown as a fall weather crop to reduce the threat of insect damage and bolting. Plant transplants 1" deeper than they were grown in your starting pots, and cover with netting to protect from pests. Spacing between plants determines head size, the closer together the smaller the head. When heads start forming, tie the leaves over them to prevent yellowing. To prevent spreading clubroot and other soil borne diseases, don't compost any *Brassica* roots. Pull and destroy all infected plants. Also, rotate *Brassica* plants on at least a 3-years basis, or optimally on a 7-year basis.

ALLIES: Some evidence-- candytuft, corn spurry (spergula arvensis), lamb's quarters, shepherd's purse, tomato, white or red clover, wormseed mustard
Uncertain-- chamomile, celery, dill, mint, nasturtium, onion, rosemary, sage, savory, thyme, wormwood
COMPANIONS: artichoke, aromatic plants, beet, bush beans, garlic, lettuce, peas, potato, spinach
ENEMIES: pole bean, strawberry, tomato (Note: also might be an ally)

CELERIAC VARIETIES

GREENHOUSE
celeriac, as a root vegetable, won't grow well in the greenhouse

OUTDOOR
Alabaster-- 120 days, open-pollinated, large thick roots (Burpee)
Large Smooth Prague-- 110 days, open-pollinated (Jung, Seeds Blum, Stokes, William Dam)
Jose-- 110 days, open-pollinated, resists pithiness and hollow heart, relatively smooth, good taste (Cook's, Johnny's)

NOTES

Apium graveolens v. *rapaceum*   *Umbelliferae (Parsley)*   **CELERIAC**

GROWTH CONDITIONS

Germ.Temp: 70   Height: 12"
Grow.Temp: 60-65   Breadth: 12"
pH: 6.0-6.5   Spacing: Intensive: 4-7"   Reg: 12"   Rows: 15-26"
Root Depth: 18-24"   Planting Depth: 1/8"
Water: Heavy, infrequently. But keep evenly moist especially during hot spells.
Fertilizer: Heavy feeder.
First Seed Starting Date: Usually 8-12 weeks before last frost.

Days Germ + Days Transplant - Days After LFD = Days Count BACK from LFD
10-21   +   46-60   -   0-14   = 56-67

Last Seed Starting Date:

Days Germ + Days Transplant + Maturity + SDF + Frost Tender = Days BACK from FFD
10-21   +   50   + 110-120 + 14 +   N/A   = 184-205

PESTS: aphid, celeryworm, slug, weevil, wireworm
DISEASES: septoria leaf spot

HARVEST: After the first fall frost, and when the bulbs are 2-4", carefully dig or pull out the roots. The larger the root (more than 4") the more it will be contaminated by involutions of the skin.

STORAGE REQUIREMENTS: Do not wash the root before storing. Rub off side shoots. Store in boxes of moist peat. When covered with a thick mulch, the roots will keep in the ground for about one month beyond the first frost.
Fresh: Temp: 32   Humidity: 97-99%   Storage Life: 6-8 months
Preserved, taste (months): Can: unknown   Freeze: unknown   Dry: unknown

OTHER GROWING NOTES: Celeriac is a cool season root crop, half-hardy to frost and light freezes. Plan an average of 1-5 plants per person. It is a pest, disease and problem-free biennial vegetable that is usually grown as an annual. In zones 5 and northward, this root can be overwintered in the ground if mulched heavily with straw to prevent frost penetration. Sow seeds thickly in pots indoors. Thin seedlings to 1 per pot. Set out when 2 to 2-1/2" tall. Remove side-shoots from the base of the plant. When transplanting, keep as much as possible of the original potting soil around the root. After setting in the roots, reach under and gently squeeze the soil around the roots to eliminate air gaps. Too much oxygen exposure during transplanting will cause them to dry out and die. Root quality drops when they're watered regularly, so water deeply and less frequently. To achieve the deep fertile soil needed for celeriac, try adding 1 bushel of well-rotted manure for 20' of row, and spading it in 8-10" deep. Celeriac has been enjoyed in Europe for ages and only recently has begun to make a showing in the United States. It is an unsightly root that tends to develop involutions filled with dirt, which causes wastage in food preparation. With it's delicious delicate flavor similar to celery heart, however, it is worth the preparation effort of cutting off all skin and involutions with dirt. It can be boiled and added to potatoes, or eaten raw as an addition to salads. We cut it into thin strips, blanch and tenderize it for 30 minutes by adding lemon juice and a little salt, then toss and serve it with a remoulade sauce.

ALLIES: Some evidence-- none
          Uncertain-- none
COMPANIONS: squash, tomato
ENEMIES: none

CELERY VARIETIES*

GREENHOUSE
> try the self-blanching varieties

OUTDOOR
> Blanching
>> **Fordhook**-- stocky, early, 15-18", good keeper, silvery white after blanching (Seeds Blum)
>> **Red**-- unusual red-bronze stalks, stay red when cooked, hardier than green varieties (Blum)
>> **Summit**-- 100 days, very dark green, tolerates fusarium wilt, compact, 10" (Stokes)
>> **Tall Utah 52-70R Improved**-- 98 days, long, dark green, thick stalks, high yields, resists boron deficiency, high quality (Abundant Life, Burpee, Garden City, Jung, Park, Stokes)
>> **Tendercrisp**-- 105 days, early, high yields, more upright than most, Pascal type, ribless, pale green stalks (Field's, Stokes)
>> **Ventura**-- 100 days, tall Utah type, some tolerance of fusarium wilt (Johnny's, Stokes)
> Self-Blanching
>> **Golden Self-Blanching**-- 115 days, early, crispy, delicate flavor, dwarf (widely available)
> Seasoning or Cutting Celery
>> This has the same general culture as celery, but is generally grown only for its leaves. It is easier to grow than other celery due to fewer pest and disease problems, and less requirements for water and feeding. Cutting celery also can be harvested over a longer period of time.
>> **Leaf Celery**-- pungent seasoning, excellent as dried flavoring (Seeds Blum)
>> **Amsterdam Fine Seasoning Celery**-- 12-18" tall, leaves are like a shiny flat-leafed parsley, easy to dry and retains its flavor (Shepherd's)

NOTES

* All varieties listed are open-pollinated.

Apium graveolens v. *dulce*   *Umbelliferae or Apiaceae (Parsley)*   **CELERY**

GROWTH CONDITIONS

Germ.Temp: 60-70

Grow.Temp: 60-65, nights higher than 40

pH: 6.0-7.0

Root Depth: Shallow, upper 6-12"

Water: Heavy

Height: 15-18"

Breadth: 8-12"

Spacing: Intensive: 6-8" Reg: 8-12" Rows: 18-36"

Planting Depth: 1/4 - 1/2"

Fertilizer: Heavy feeder. 2-3 weeks before planting, apply compost worked 12" into soil.

Side-dress Times: Apply every 2 weeks, especially 3 weeks after transplanting and then 6 weeks later.

First Seed Starting Date:

Days Germ	+	Days Transplant	-	Days After LFD	=	Days Count BACK from LFD
5-7	+	70-84	-	14-21	=	89-112

Last Seed Starting Date:

Days Germ	+	Days Transplant	+	Maturity	+	SDF	+	Frost Tender	=	Days BACK from FFD
6	+	30	+	90-135	+	14	+	0	=	130-185

PESTS: aphid, cabbage looper, carrot rust fly, carrot weevil, celery leaftier, flea beetle, earwig, leafhopper, mite, nematode, parsleyworm, slug, tarnished plant bug, weevil, wireworm

DISEASES: black heart, celery mosaic, damping off, early and late blight, fusarium, pink rot, yellows

HARVEST: Harvest self-blanching celery before the first frost. Harvest blanched varieties after the first frost. Dig out each plant whenever needed.

STORAGE REQUIREMENTS: Celery is best stored at cold temperatures in a perforated plastic bag. To refresh wilted stalks simply place them in a tall glass of cold water.

Fresh: Temp: 32   Humidity: 98-100%   Storage Life: 2-3 months

Temp: 32   Humidity: 80-90%   Storage Life: 4-5 weeks

Preserved, taste (months):   Can: fair (12+)   Freeze: good (5)   Dry: good (12+)

OTHER GROWING NOTES: Celery is a cool season crop, half-hardy to frost and light freezes. Plan an average of 3-8 plants per person. Soak seeds overnight to help germination. The seedlings will need to be transplanted at least once before setting outside. Transplant outside when seedlings are 4-6" tall and night temperatures don't fall below 40F. Water plants before they are transplanted. There are two basic types of celery: the blanching and self-blanching. Self-blanching varieties are much easier to grow, as they can be grown in flat soil without trenches. Their harvest, however, is earlier and more limited. For celery that needs blanching, (1) plant in the center of 18" wide trenches, (2) remove suckers in midseason and wrap stalk bunches with something like brown paper, newspaper or cardboard to prevent soil from getting between the stalks, (3) 2 months before harvest fill the trench with soil up to the bottom of the leaves, and (4) keep mounding soil around the base of the plant every three weeks. Make sure the mound is sloped to help drainage.

ALLIES: Some evidence-- none

Uncertain-- black salsify, cabbage, chive, coriander, garlic, nasturtium, pennyroyal

COMPANIONS: all beans, all *Brassicas,* celery, spinach, squash, tomato

OTHER: cucumbers provide shade and moisture to other plants such as celery

ENEMIES: carrot, parsnip

CORN VARIETIES

KEY: OP = Open-pollinated   HL = Heirloom

OUTDOOR

Flour Varieties: These have soft starch, are easiest to grind, and make flour not meal.

Hopi Blue-- OP, HL, drought tolerant, vigorous, colors vary from black to purple, makes pretty blue flour (Abundant Life, Native Seed--their strain good for high and low desert) Note: most other sources of "Hopi Blue" are flint varieties

White Posole-- OP, makes white flour (Plants of the Southwest)

Dent or Field Varieties: These have hard starch on the side and soft starch on the top of the kernel, are easier to grind than flint types, and are good for fresh eating, roasting, and grinding. Versatile.

Beasley's Red Dent-- 105 days, 9', OP, HL, high blight and drought resistance, red kernels (Southern Exposure)

Bloody Butcher-- 110-120 days, 10-12', OP, pretty red kernels sometimes interspersed with other colors (Seeds Blum, Southern Exposure)

Mayo Batchi-- 90 days, OP, HL, short flat ears, staple of region, for low desert (Native Seed)

Northstine Dent-- 105 days, 7', OP, HL, excellent for cornmeal and cereal, yellow, good for short seasons, high quality (Johnny's)

Reids Yellow Dent-- 85-110 days, 7', OP, HL, very hardy, good in Southern heat, high yields, good for tortillas, meal, hominy (Field's, Southern Exposure)

Flint Varieties: These have very hard starch and make cornmeal. Generally good insect resistance and storage.

Hispanic Pueblo Red-- OP, HL, orange, red & maroon kernels, long ears, for high & low desert (Native Seed)

Longfellow-- 117 days, OP, orange kernels, makes a sweet cornbread, good in Northern gardens (Johnny's)

Sweet Varieties: **Supersweet** corn has the Shrunken-2 (sh$_2$) gene which causes shriveled seeds with weak seed coats, resulting in poor germination. Supersweets are often twice as sweet as "eh" types. They develop a watery texture when frozen. **Sugar Enhanced** corn has the "se" gene which causes higher sugar levels than "eh" types and also longer retention of sugar and tenderness, for up to 10-14 days. **Everlasting Heritage** corn has the "eh" gene designed for sweetness and texture.

Country Gentleman or Shoepeg-- 96 days, OP, HL, white, tender, resists drought and wilt, kernels are not in rows (widely available)

Florida Staysweet-- 87 days, supersweet, yellow, great flavor and yields, tight husks (Johnny's)

Hopi Early-- cold tolerant, short season crop, plant in early spring, small ears, for high and low desert (Native Seeds)

Honey and Cream-- 78 days, "eh," white & yellow, tight husks (Burpee, Gurney's, Shepherd's)

Illini Gold-- 80 days, supersweet, yellow, excellent in trials (Jung, Park)

Improved Golden Bantam-- 82 days, OP, yellow, midseason, flavorful, performed well in Harrowsmith 1988 trials (Abundant Life, Nichols)

Iochief-- 86 days, AAS winner, 7-1/2', hybrid, yellow, top rated by *Organic Gardening* readers for reliability, productivity, drought tolerance and taste (Earl May, Gurney's, Field's)

Kandy Korn-- 84 days, "eh," yellow, good flavor, doesn't require isolation, stays sweet several days after harvest, pretty purplish stalks and husks (widely available)

Polar Vee-- 53 days, yellow, produces well in cool regions (Field's, Gurney's, Stokes)

Silver Queen-- 92 days, standard hybrid, white, late season, top rated for flavor, productivity, drought tolerance & disease resistance, tolerates Stewart's wilt and leaf blight (widely available)

Popcorn: These have the hardest starch of all corns.

Strawberry-- 105 days, 4', HL, OP, stalks bear several ears, red kernels (widely available)

Tom Thumb-- 85 days, dwarf 3-1/2', yellow, can grow closely spaced (Johnny's)

White Cloud-- 95 days, hybrid, not heavy producer but one of best for popping (Stokes)

NOTES

Zea Mays v. *rugosa*　　　*Graminae or Poaceae (Grass)*　　　Sweet **CORN**

GROWTH CONDITIONS

Germ.Temp: 60-95　　　　　Height: 7-8', but some flour & field corns grow much higher
Grow.Temp: 60-75　　　　　Breadth: 18" - 4'
pH: 5.5-7.0　　　　　　　　Spacing: Intensive: 8-12"　Reg: 18"　Rows: 30-42"
Root Depth: 18" - 6'　　　　Planting Depth: 1-2"　sh_2 types, 1/2"
Water: Medium. Provide more when the stalks flowers.
Fertilizer: Heavy feeder. Apply manure in the fall, or compost a few weeks before planting.
Side-dress: Apply every 2 weeks, and additionally when stalks are 8-10" and knee high.
First Seed Starting Date: Sow every 10-14 days for continuous harvest.

　　　　Days Germ + Days Transplant - Days After LFD = Days Count BACK from LFD
　　　　4-21　　　 + 　0 (direct)　 - 　0-10　　　　 = 4-11
Last Seed Starting Date:

　　　　Days Germ + Days Transplant + Maturity + SDF + Frost Tender = Days BACK from FFD
　　　　4　　　 + 　0　　　　 + 65-95　+ 14　+ 14　　　　　 = 97-127

PESTS: aphid, birds, corn borer, earworm, maggot and rootworm, cucumber beetle, cutworm, earwig, flea beetle, garden webworm, Japanese beetle, June beetle, leafhopper, sap beetle, seedcorn maggot, thrips, webworm, white grub, wireworm
DISEASES: bacterial wilt, mosaic viruses, rust, smut, southern corn leaf blight, Stewart's wilt

HARVEST Sweet Corn: About 18 days after silks appear, when they're dark and dry, make a small slit in the husk (don't pull the silks down), and pierce the kernel with a fingernail. If the liquid is (1) clear, wait a few days, (2) milky, pick and eat, (3) pasty, the ear is past its prime and is best for canning. **Popcorn (v. *praecox*):** Pick when the husks are brown and partly dried. Finish drying corn on the husks. A solar drier is the most rapid method , drying the corn in about 5 days. When the kernels fall off easily by rubbing a thumb over them or twisting them off, they're ready for storage. Before using, store in bags or jars to even up the moisture content. The ultimate test, of course, is to pop them.

STORAGE REQUIREMENTS: Corn is best eaten immediately. Some gardeners won't even go out to pick ears until the cooking water is already boiling.
Fresh: Temp: 40-45　　Humidity: 80-95%　　Storage Life: 4-10 days
Preserved, taste (months): Can: excellent (12+) Freeze: good (8) Dry: good (12+)

OTHER GROWING NOTES: Corn is a warm season crop, tender to frost and light freezes. Plan an average of 12-40 plants per person, depending on your needs. For good pollination and therefore full ears, plant in blocks of at least 4-6 rows and about 15" on center. If birds are a problem in your garden, stealing seeds or eating seedlings, cover your corn patch with a floating row cover immediately after planting seeds. Corn easily cross-pollinates, so isolate popcorn and field corn from sweet corn by at least 50-100'. Or plant varieties that have different pollination times, which is when tassels appear. For seed saving, isolate corns by 1000' for absolute purity. Once pollinated, corn matures rapidly, usually in 15-20 days after the first silks appear. Corn has shallow roots, so mulch heavily and avoid cultivating deeper than 1-1/2". In small patches don't remove suckers; they may bear corn if well side-dressed. Once harvested, cut stalks and till under or compost immediately. White and yellow corn vary in nutrition; white corn contains twice as much potassium, and yellow corn contains about 60 percent more sodium.

ALLIES: Some evidence-- all beans, chickweed, clover, giant ragweed, peanut, pigweed, shepherd's purse, soybean, sweet potato
　　　　Uncertain-- alfalfa, goldenrod, odorless marigold, white geranium, peas, potato
COMPANIONS: cucumber, melon, parsley, pole beans (corn can be a support for pole beans)
ENEMIES: tomato (attacked by some similar insects)

CUCUMBER VARIETIES

KEY: Resistance to CMV = Cucumber Mosaic Virus, DM = Downy Mildew, PM = Powdery Mildew

GREENHOUSE
Bush Champion, Gourmet #2, Pot Luck, Salad Bush, Salty, Spacemaster, Sweet Success-- see below. See Stokes and Thompson & Morgan for other varieties specifically for the greenhouse.

OUTDOOR
Salad
Bush Champion-- 55 days, short compact vines, 9-11" fruit, long season producer in all weather conditions, good for containers and greenhouse (Burpee, Thompson & Morgan)

County Fair 87-- 48 days, hybrid, parthenocarpic, seedless,, 7 disease resistances, bitterfree, isolate from others with cheesecloth to assure 100% seedless fruits (Park, Stokes)

Gourmet #2-- 60 days, gynoecious greenhouse type, 14-16" long, crisp, sweet, tolerates scab and leaf spot (Nichols)

Marketmore 80-- 68 days, bred for resistance to CMV, DM, PM and scab, straight slicer, bitterfree (widely available)

Pot Luck-- 45 days, hybrid, developed for small spaces, 18" long vine, 6-8" fruit, space these 8-12" in rows (Earl May, Jung)

Salad Bush-- 57 days, AAS winner, resists PM, DM, CMV, leaf spot and scab, small 24" vines, 8" fruit, monoecious (widely available)

Surecrop-- 60 days, hybrid, AAS winner, early, 8"long, weather resistant, high yields, good taste (Gurney's, Field's, Jung)

Sweet Success-- 58 days, hybrid, AAS winner, early, 12-14", burpless, CMV, resists scab and leafspot, parthenocarpic, provides seedless fruit (widely available)

Spacemaster-- 60 days, open-pollinated, best dwarf, CMV, resists scab, 7-1/2", white spine, plant early (widely available)

Picklers
Edmonson-- open-pollinated, heat and disease resistant (Seeds Blum)

Green Knight Hybrid-- 60 days, burpless, heat-resistant, vigorous, thin-skinned (Burpee)

Pickalot-- 54 days, hybrid, new in '89, bush, PM, gynoecious, continuous bearer (Burpee)

Salty-- 53 days, hybrid, tolerates CMV, PM, DM, crispy, a white spine gynoecious (Stokes)

Novelties
Armenian Long (aka: Yard Long)-- 65 days, open-pollinated, long, good slicer, mild, sweet, bitterfree (Abundant Life, Burpee, Nichols, Seeds Blum, Shepherd's)

China-- 75 days, open-pollinated, oriental type, 12"-15", tolerates CMV, crisp, firm, mild, weather tolerant (Stokes)

Crystal Apple-- 65 days, open-pollinated, non-bitter skins, good slicing & pickling, 2-3" globes, creamy white skin and spine (Bountiful Gardens, Thompson & Morgan)

Lemon-- 60 days, open-pollinated, sweet, size and color of lemon (widely available)

White Wonder-- 58 days, open-pollinated, early bearing, all white, heirloom, high yields, crisp, resist Fusarium Wilt (Garden City, Seeds Blum)

NOTES

Cucumis sativus   *Cucurbitaceae (Gourd)*   **CUCUMBER**

GROWTH CONDITIONS

Germ.Temp: 60-95   Height: 6'
Grow.Temp: 65-75   Breadth: 12-15", trellis or 12-20 sq.ft. on ground
pH: 5.5-7.0   Spacing: Intensive: 12"   Reg: 24-48" Rows: 4'
Root Depth: 12", tap root to 2-3'   Planting Depth: 1/2 - 1"
Water: Heavy during fruiting. All other times average and evenly moist. Deep watering.
Fertilizer: Heavy feeder. Before planting apply compost.
Side-dress: Every 2-3 weeks.
Support structures: Use a 6' post, A-frame, Tepee (3 poles tied together at the top), or a trellis.
First Seed Starting Date:

       Days Germ + Days Transplant - Days After LFD = Days Count BACK from LFD
       6-10   +   28   - 14-21   = 17-21

Last Seed Starting Date:

       Days Germ + Days Transplant + Maturity + SDF + Frost Tender = Days BACK from FFD
       6-10   +   28   + 22-52 + 14 + 14   = 84-118

PESTS: aphid, cucumber beetle, cutworm (seedlings), flea beetle, garden centipede, mite, slug, snail, squash bug, squash vine borer

DISEASES: alternaria leaf spot, anthracnose, bacterial wilt, belly rot, cottony leak, cucumber wilt, downy mildew, leaf spot, mosaic, pickleworm, powdery mildew, root-knot, scab

HARVEST: When the fruit is slightly immature, before seed coats become hard, pick with 1" of stem to minimize water loss. In warm weather, all cucumber plant types should be picked daily. Always pick open-pollinated varieties underripe. Harvest pickling cucumbers at 2-6", and slicing cucumbers at 6-10".

STORAGE REQUIREMENTS: Keep the short piece of stem on each fruit during storage.
Temp: 45-55   Humidity: 85-95%   Storage Life: 10-14 days
Preserved, taste (months): Can: good (as pickles) (12+)   Freeze: poor   Dry: poor

OTHER GROWING NOTES: Cucumbers are a warm season crop, very tender to frost and light freezing. Plan an average of 3-5 plants per person, depending on your pickling needs. In warm climates, some recommend planting cucumbers in hills spaced 3-5' apart, with 6-8 seeds per hill. In cooler climates, transplant seedlings on a cloudy day or in the afternoon to minimize transplanting shock. Allow the main stem to grow as high as possible by pinching back some of the lateral shoots and letting others grow into branches. By picking the fruit early you won't have to support heavy fruit or risk arresting plant production. Variety information: Most cucumbers are Monoecious, which produce both male and female (fruit-bearing) flowers. Gynoecious types bear only female flowers, therefore a few male-flowering pollinators are included in the seed packets. Both require pollination by bees. Parthenocarpic types produce few if any seeds and require no pollination, so they can be grown to maturity under row covers. Bitterfree are resistant to damage from cucumber beetles. Dwarfs are good candidates for intercropping with tomatoes and peppers, but they must have a constant water supply. All types must also be picked daily in warm weather.

ALLIES: Some evidence-- broccoli, corn
        Uncertain-- catnip, goldenrod, marigold, nasturtium, onion, oregano, radish, rue, tansy
COMPANIONS: all beans, cabbage, eggplant, kale, melon, peas, sunflower
OTHER: radish can be used as a trap plant; celery is companion plant under the "cuke's" A-frame
ENEMIES: anise, basil, marjoram, potato, quack grass, rosemary, sage, summer savory, strong herbs

EGGPLANT VARIETIES

GREENHOUSE
  Black Beauty, Ichiban, Jersey King-- see below

OUTDOOR
  Agora-- 68 days, improved variation of "Dusky" (see below) (Shepherd's)
  Black Beauty-- 73-80 days, open-pollinated, almost round fruit, heavy yields, reliable, a common standard-size fruit (widely available)
  Burpee Hybrid-- 70 days, drought resistant, tall, semi-spreading, vigorous (Burpee)
  Dusky-- 60 days, popular early variety, pear-shaped, glossy, tolerates tobacco mosaic virus, good for northern gardens (widely available)
  Early Long Purple-- open-pollinated, very early, a smaller variety for smaller growing areas, heirloom, slender 12" fruit (Seeds Blum)
  Florida Market-- 85 days, open-pollinated, resists phomopsis, good for southern growing (Blum)
  Ghostbuster-- 80 days, open-pollinated, new in 1989, sweet, excellent for cooking (Harris)
  Ichiban-- 61 days, open-pollinated, slender 12" fruit, 36" plants (Gurney's, Park) An improved variation on this is "Tycoon" (Nichols)
  Jersey King-- 73 days, hybrid, dark purple, very long 10" fruit (Stokes)
  Little Fingers-- 68 days, long and very slim oriental-type fruit, easier to pick because spineless (Harris, Shepherd's)
  Orient Express-- 58 days, hybrid, slender 8-10" fruit, excellent early yields, sets fruit in cool weather, also tolerates heat (Johnny's)
  Rosa Bianca-- open-pollinated, unusual beautiful bright lavender color, high yields, vigorous, mild flavor (Seeds Blum, Shepherd's)
  Violette di Firenze-- open-pollinated, oblong-round fruit are rich lavender, beautiful (Cook's)
  White Egg-- unusual shiny white-skinned fruit, top quality (Seeds Blum)

NOTES

Solanum melongena v. *esculentum*   *Solanaceae (Nightshade)*   EGGPLANT

GROWTH CONDITIONS

Germ.Temp: 75-90
Grow.Temp: 70-85
pH: 5.5-6.5
Root Depth: 4-7'
Water: Heavy

Height: 24-30"
Breadth: 3-4'
Spacing: Intensive: 18"   Reg: 18-30"   Rows: 24-48"
Planting Depth: 1/4"

Fertilizer: Heavy feeder. Apply manure water or tea every two weeks.
Side-dress: Apply after the first fruit appears.
First Seed Starting Date:

Days Germ	+ Days Transplant	- Days After LFD	= Days Count BACK from LFD
5-13	+ 42-56	- 38-45	= 14-21

Last Seed Starting Date:

Days Germ	+ Days Transplant	+ Maturity	+ SDF	+ Frost Tender	= Days BACK from FFD
5-13	+ 42-56	+ 50-80	+ 14	+ 14	= 125-177

PESTS: aphid, Colorado potato beetle, cucumber beetle, cutworm, flea beetle, harlequin bug, lace bug, leafhopper, mite, nematode, tomato hornworm, whitefly
DISEASES: anthracnose, bacterial wilt, botrytis fruit rot, phomopsis blight, tobacco mosaic, verticillium wilt

HARVEST: Pick when the fruit is no more than 3-5" long or 4" in diameter, and before the skin loses its lustre. Cut the fruit with small amount of stem. Fruit seeds should be light-colored. Brown seeds indicate the fruit has ripened too long. Eggplant vines are spiny, so be careful to avoid pricking yourself.

STORAGE REQUIREMENTS: Keep a small piece of stem on the eggplant during storage, so the skin isn't pierced. Eggplant is best used fresh.
Fresh: Temp: 46-54   Humidity: 90-95 %   Storage Life: 1 week
              Temp: 32-40   Humidity: 80-90 %   Storage Life: 6 months
Preserved, taste (months):   Can: fair (12+)   Freeze: fair (8)   Dry: fair (12+)

OTHER GROWING NOTES: Eggplant is a warm season crop, tender to frost and light freezes. Plan an average of 2 plants per three people. All parts of the plant except the fruit are poisonous. For indoor seed starting in flats, once the seedlings are well-established block out the plants; run a knife through the soil midway between the plants, cutting the roots, and leaving each plant with its own soil block. If you start seeds in individual pots this procedure is unnecessary. Make sure outdoor soil temperature is at least 55-60 before transplanting; otherwise they become stunted, turn yellow, and are slow to bear. As frost approaches pinch back new blossoms so that plant nutrients are channeled into the remaining fruits. Eggplant is a versatile fruit often used in Italian dishes such as ratatouille, caponata, and lasagna. It's virtue is that it easily absorbs the flavors of whatever sauce it is cooked in, from herbal tomato sauces to chinese szechuan.

ALLIES: Some evidence-- none
                  Uncertain-- coriander, goldenrod, green beans, marigold, potato
COMPANIONS: all beans, pepper
OTHER: potato can also be used as a trap plant for pests
ENEMIES: none

KALE VARIETIES

GREENHOUSE
All varieties. You can also try bringing plants inside after the first light frost.

OUTDOOR
Dwarf Blue Curled Vates (a.k.a. Vates Dwarf Blue Curled Scotch)-- 55 days, open-pollinated, very hardy, compact, lasts nearly all winter (widely available)
Ornamentals-- frost is needed to bring out the spectacular colors of ornamentals (widely available)
Ragged Jack-- unusual beautiful red oak-type leaves, open-pollinated, heirloom, maintains quality in heat, also good as baby kale (Blum)
Red Russian-- 65 days, American heirloom, beautiful red 2-3' leaves in cold weather (leaves are blue-green in warm weather), sweet even in warm weather (Nichols, Shepherd's)
Verdura-- 60 days, Dutch, very sweet, compact, extended harvest in cold weather (Shepherd's)

NOTES

Brassica oleracea v. *acephela*   *Brassicaceae (Mustard)*   **KALE**

GROWTH CONDITIONS

Germ.Temp: 45-95   Height: 12-18"
Grow.Temp: 60-65   Breadth: 8-12"
pH: 6.0-7.0   Spacing: Intensive: 15-18"   Reg: 18-24"   Rows: 24-46"
Root Depth: 6-12"   Planting Depth: 1/2"
Water: Heavy
Fertilizer: Heavy feeder. Use compost.
Side-dress: Apply when plants are about one-third grown.
First Seed Starting Date:

Days Germ	+	Days Transplant	+	Days Before LFD	=	Days Count BACK from LFD
3-10	+	35-70	+	14-28	=	52-108

Last Seed Starting Date:

Days Germ	+	Days Transplant	+	Maturity	+	SDF	+	Frost Tender	=	Days BACK from FFD
3-10	+	21	+	56-63	+	14	+	N/A	=	94-108

PESTS: aphid, cabbage maggot, cabbage looper, celery leaftier, club root, diamondback moth, flea beetle, harlequin bug, imported cabbage worm, Mexican bean beetle, mites, thrips, weevil
DISEASES: alternaria leaf spot, black leg

HARVEST: Harvest younger leaves from the middle and work your way up the stalk as it grows. Keep some of the leaves on the bottom to feed growth at the top. You can also harvest the plant all at once by cutting its stem near the bottom.

STORAGE REQUIREMENTS: For fresh storage don't wash the leaves. For drying, cut the leaves into strips and steam for 2-5 minutes. Spread on trays no more than 1/2" thick, and dry. If using an oven set the temperature below 145; check and turn every hour.
Fresh: Temp: 32   Humidity: 95-100%   Storage Life: 2-3 weeks
         Temp: 32-40   Humidity: 80-90%   Storage Life: 10 months (only fair taste)
Preserved, taste (months): Freeze: good (12)   Dry: fair (12+)   Can: good (12+)

OTHER GROWING NOTES: Kale is a cool season crop, hardy to frost and light freezes. Plan an average of 4 plants per person. Kale's flavor is reputed to improve and sweeten with frost. An easy vegetable to grow, it is generally more disease and pest resistant than other *Brassicas,* although it can occasionally experience similar problems. Kale is also the best of the *Brassicas* in terms of using the least space. Use it as a spinach substitute in a wide variety of dishes. Kale maintains body and crunch much better than spinach and so can be used in dishes where spinach might not be suitable; it's especially delicious in stir-fry dishes. Author and edible landscaper Rosalind Creasy recommends cooking kale over high heat to bring out the best flavor and prevent bitterness. Creasy also noted that "many specialty growers are planting kale in wide beds only 1/2" to 12" apart and harvesting kale small as salad greens." In England close plantings of kale have been shown to prevent aphid infestations through visual masking. Although kale is usually disease and pest free, some gardeners won't compost any *Brassica* roots, to prevent spreading clubroot and other soil borne diseases. Pull and destroy plants. Kale is not as likely as other *Brassicas* to suffer from clubroot, but if you experience problems be sure to rotate plantings so they're not in the same 10' radius for at least 3 years, optimally 7 years.

ALLIES: Some evidence-- none
         Uncertain-- chamomile, dill, garlic, mint, nasturtiums, rosemary, sage, tansy, tomato
COMPANIONS: artichoke, beet, bush bean, celery, cucumber, lettuce, onion, peas, potato, spinach
ENEMIES: pole beans, strawberry, tomato (Note: might also be an ally. See Ally Chart.)

LETTUCE VARIETIES*

GREENHOUSE

Arctic King, Bibb, North Pole, Parris Cos, Tom Thumb-- see below. Also see Cook's and Johnny's for special greenhouse varieties.

OUTDOOR

Head lettuce (Butterhead and Iceberg types) Note: Butterheads are more resistant to leaf aphids, according to Dutch scientists.

Arctic King-- 80 days, for fall and winter only, butterhead, "cut and come again" lettuce, tasty crinkled leaves (Cook's, Thompson & Morgan)

Au-Isbell-- developed at Auburn University, apparently not bothered by insects or rabbits, a spring crop reseeds itself for fall crop, a fall crop reseeds for spring crop, non bitter, heirloom. Look for it in future years.

Bibb or Limestone-- 55 days, early spring, favored for its delicacy (Cook's, Nichols, Park)

Buttercrunch-- 50 days, matures mid-summer, bibb, favorite with home gardeners, slow-bolting, tolerates heat, very tender (widely available)

Continuity-- 70 days, summer bibb, similar to "Four Seasons" but stands longer in dry summer weather (Cook's, Territorial)

Four Seasons (Merveille des Quatre Saisons)-- 60 days, spring bibb, also for late summer and fall, beautiful red outer leaves, pink and cream interior (Blum, Cook's, Shepherd's)

Ithaca-- 72 days, spring iceberg, popular, reliable, only iceberg good in Northeast, also good in warm climates, resists tip burn in hot weather, flood to avoid "slime" (Cook's, Dam, Field's, Garden City, Harris)

North Pole-- 50 days, for fall and winter, butterhead, high cold resistance (Cook's, Nichols)

Red Riding Hood-- summer, pretty red butterhead, tolerates heat, resists bolting (Cook's)

Sangria-- new in 1990, beautiful butterhead, resists bolting, superior flavor (Johnny's)

Tom Thumb-- 65 days, spring, tiny solid butterhead, good for containers (widely available)

Valprize-- new in 1989, butterhead, non-bitter, resists bolting and downy mildew (Jung)

Non-heading, Loose Leaf, or Cutting Lettuce (Romaine, Cos and other types)

Green Ice-- 45 days, spring, very sweet, very crinkled leaves, slow to bolt (Burpee, Park)

Little Gem or Sugar Cos-- 60 days for baby heads, 80 days to maturity, summer, 5-6", troublefree (Burpee, Cook's, Shepherd's, Territorial, Thompson & Morgan)

Lolla Rossa-- 56 days, spring, beautiful crinkly leaves with red margins, mild, keep cut to avoid bolting and bitterness (widely available)

Parris Island Cos-- 68-76 days, all seasons, romaine, mild sweet flavor, slow bolting, 8-10" heads, resists tip burn and mosaic, vigorous (Burpee, Garden City, Harris, Johnny's, Stokes)

Red Sails-- 45-50 days, spring, AAS winner, dark red leaf lettuce, resists bolting, little bitterness, fast growing, easy to grow (widely available)

Victoria-- 52 days, best for summer but also good for spring and fall, new in 1989, very crisp, sweet and juicy, heat tolerant, resists bolting and bottom rot, sweet (Johnny's)

Winter Density-- 60 days, winter or year-round in mild climates, like a tall buttercrunch (Cook's, Johnny's, Seeds Blum)

NOTES

* All varieties listed are open-pollinated.

Lactuca sativa   *Compositae or Astraceae (Sunflower)*   LETTUCE

GROWTH CONDITIONS

Germ.Temp: 40-80   Height: 6-12"
Grow.Temp: 60-65   Breadth: 6-12"
pH: 6.0-7.5   Spacing: Head, Intensive: 10-12"   Reg: 12-14"   Rows: 14"
                                  Leaf,   6-8"
                                  Romaine,   10"
Root Depth: 18-36", with a taproot to 5'.
Planting Depth: 1/4- 1/2"
Water: Low to medium. Heavy in arid climates. Water early in the morning to minimize diseases.
Fertilizer: Heavy feeder.
Side-dress: Every two weeks apply balanced fertilizer or foliar spray.
First Seed Starting Date:

Days Germ + Days Transplant + Days Before LFD = Days Count BACK from LFD
4-10   + 14 (leaf & head) + 7-28   = 25-46

Last Seed Starting Date:

Days Germ + Days Transplant + Maturity   + SDF + Frost Tender = Days BACK fr. FFD
4   + 14   + 60-95, head + 14 +   0   = 92-127, head
                             45-65, leaf   77-97, leaf
                             55-80, romaine   87-112, romaine

PESTS: aphid, beet leafhopper, cabbage looper, cutworm, earwig, flea beetle, garden centipede, leafminer, millipede, slug, snail

DISEASES: bacterial soft rot, botrytis rot, damping off, downy mildew, fusarium wilt, lettuce drop, mosaic, pink rot, powdery mildew, tipburn

HARVEST: For leaf lettuce, start picking the leaves when there are at least 5-6 mature leaves of usable size. Usable size means about 2" long for baby lettuce and 5-6" long for more mature lettuce. Keep picking until a seed stalk appears or the leaves become bitter. For head lettuce, when the head feels firm and mature simply cut it off at the soil surface. Harvest all lettuce in early morning for the maximum carotene and best taste. Refrigerate immediately.

STORAGE REQUIREMENTS: Lettuce doesn't store well for long periods, and is best eaten fresh.
Fresh: Temp: 32-40   Humidity: 80-90%   Storage Life: 1 month
       Temp: 32   Humidity: 98-100%   Storage Life: 2-3 weeks

OTHER GROWING NOTES: Lettuce is a cool season crop, half-hardy to frost and light freezes. Plan an average of 10-12 plants per person. Closer spacing results in smaller heads, which may be preferable for small families. Specialty growers are spacing lettuce very close for selling baby lettuces, a rapidly growing produce market. There are two basic categories of lettuce, heading and non-heading. Head lettuces include crisphead (e.g. iceberg) and butterhead (e.g. bibb & Boston). Non-head lettuces include leaf and romaine. For head lettuce, one source suggests that you strip transplants of outer leaves to help the inner leaves "head up" better. This is not tested, so treat it as experimental. Head lettuces tend to be milder in flavor but are harder to grow. Lettuce doesn't do well in very acid soils, and some say the pH shouldn't be lower than 6.5. During hot weather sow lettuce in partial shade, as it doesn't do well in the heat, and use heat resistant varieties.

ALLIES: Some evidence-- none
         Uncertain-- chive, garlic, radish
COMPANIONS: beet (to head lettuce), all *Brassicas* (except broccoli: see "Enemies" below), carrot, cucumber, onion family, pole lima beans, strawberry
ENEMIES: none. Some studies have shown lettuce sensitive to plant residues of broccoli, broad beans, vetch, wheat, rye and barley.

MELON VARIETIES

GREENHOUSE   KEY: OP = Open-pollinated   HL = Heirloom
    Minnesota Midget-- see below

OUTDOOR
    Muskmelon and "Cantaloupe"
        Ambrosia Hybrid-- very popular, juicy, sweet, firm salmon flesh, some resistance to downy and powdery mildews (Burpee, Earl May, Park, Stokes)
        Canada Gem Hybrid-- new in 1989, tolerates downy and powdery mildews and fusarium wilt, good flavor, deep orange flesh (Stokes)
        Chaca Hybrid-- 68 days, gourmet French Charantais type, salmon flesh, resists powdery mildew and fusarium wilt, high yields (Nichols)
        Edisto 47-- 88 days, OP, excellent disease resistance, said to exceed disease resistance of many hybrids, resists or tolerates alternaria leaf spot, powdery mildew and downy mildew (Southern Exposure)
        Golden Golpher-- OP, resists fusarium wilt, orange flesh (Seeds Blum)
        Goldstar Hybrid-- 87 days, early and long bearing, deep orange flesh, high yields, excellent quality, a standard for Mid-Atlantic states (Harris)
        Green Nutmeg (or Extra Early Nutmeg)-- 84 days, OP, HL, green flesh with salmon center, small fruits, unusual (Abundant Life, Seeds Blum, Southern Exposure)
        Honeyloupe-- 75 days, unusual cross of honeydew and cantaloupe, skin is smooth and creamy white, interior is salmon, resists verticillium wilt (Stokes)
        Jenny Lind-- OP, HL, green flesh, excellent flavor, rediscovered and offered in 1987 (Abundant Life, Burpee, Seeds Blum, Thompson & Morgan)
        Minnesota Midget-- OP, uses only 3' of space, earliest maturing melon, 4" fruit, orange flesh, sweet, spicy (Earl May, Garden City, Gurney's, Seeds Blum, Thompson & Morgan)
        Old Time Tennessee-- 100 days, OP, HL, elliptical fruit 12-16" long, flavor is outstanding if picked at peak, salmon flesh (Southern Exposure)
    Honeydew (*C. melo, Inodorous Group*)
        Hybrid Milky Way-- 80 days, early enough for the North, pale green, resists wilt (Gurney's)
        Kazakh-- OP, early, bright yellow when ripe, white flesh, not good keeper (Abundant Life)
        Limelight Hybrid-- 96 days, big melons, juicy, green flesh, fairly early (Burpee)
        San Juan-- compact vines, desert hardy, delicious, prolific, for low & high desert (Native Seeds)
        Venus Hybrid-- 88 days, green flesh, medium fruit, very juicy, sweet, aromatic (Burpee)
    Crenshaw
        Crenshaw-- OP, very sweet, perishable, needs a long season (Seeds Blum)
        Early Crenshaw Hybrid-- 90 days, early enough to be grown in the North, very sweet, yellow-green flesh, each up to 12-14 lbs. (Burpee, Earl May)
    Watermelon (*Citrullus lanatus*): These require more space, usually 8' x 8' minimum. They should be harvested when tendrils shrivel and brown, the bottom turns green, and the skin becomes hard.
        Charleston Gray-- 85 days, OP, resists fusarium wilt, anthracnose and sunburn, red and crisp flesh, 24" long, 28-35 lbs, good in the North or South (Blum, Burpee, Gurney's)
        Sugar Baby-- 75 days, OP, very popular, one of easiest watermelons to grow, small and sweet, 8" diameter, thin and hard rinds, 8-12 lbs (widely available)
        Sugar Baby Bush-- 80-85 days, space-saver, bush-type vines grow to 3-1/2', bears 2 oval-round fruits, 8-10", 8-12 lbs (Burpee, Gurney's) Also see Park's disease-resistant **Bush Baby II**
        Yellow Doll or Yellow Baby Hybrid-- 65-70 days, AAS winner, one of earliest watermelons, juicy yellow flesh, sweet, 7" diameter, to 10 lbs (Burpee, Fields, Harris, Jung, Shepherd's)

NOTES

Cucumus melo, Reticulatus Gr. Cucurbitaceae (Gourd) **MUSKMELON**

GROWTH CONDITIONS

Germ.Temp: 75-95   Height: 24"
Grow.Temp: 65-75   Breadth: Bush, 36-48"   Vine, 30-40 sq.ft. on ground
pH: 6.0-6.5   Spacing: Intensive: 2' Reg: 4-8' Rows: 5-7'
Root Depth: Shallow, some to 4'   Planting Depth: 1/2"
Water: Medium. Apply in deep watering. Withhold water when fruits begins to ripen.
Fertilizer: Heavy feeder. Before planting work in compost or rotted manure.
Side-dress: Apply balanced fertilizer or compost when vines are 12-18" long and again when fruits form.
Support structures: Use an A-frame or trellis to grow vines vertically.
First Seed Starting Date:

Days Germ + Days Transplant - Days After LFD = Days Count BACK from LFD
4-10   +   21-28   -   14-21   = 18

Last Seed Starting Date:

Days Germ + Days Transplant + Maturity + SDF + Frost Tender = Days BACK from FFD
4   +   21   + 59-91 + 14 + 14   = 112-151

PESTS: aphid, cucumber beetle, cutworm, flea beetle, mite, pickleworm, slug, snail, squash bug and vine borer, whitefly

DISEASES: alternaria leaf spot, anthracnose, bacterial wilt, cucumber wilt, curly top, downy mildew, fusarium wilt, mosaic, powdery mildew, scab

HARVEST: Harvest melon as soon as the ends are soft when pressed, at "full slip" when it separates easily from the stem, when there's a crack all around the stem, and when it smells "musky." The skin netting should be cord-like, grayish, and prominent. Winter melons don't "slip" but should be soft.

STORAGE REQUIREMENTS: Store fruits in a cool area.

Fresh: Temp: 45-55   Humidity: 80-90%   Storage Life: about 1 month
Preserved, taste (months): Can: poor   Freeze: good (3)   Dry: poor   Other: pickling

OTHER GROWING NOTES: Melons are a warm season crop, very tender to frost and light freezes. Plan an average of 2-6 plants per person. Muskmelons (Reticulatus Group) are often called cantaloupes, but they're not the same botanical variety. True cantaloupes are rarely grown in North America. Winter melons (Inodorus Group) include honeydew and casaba. Like all *Cucurbits*, bees are needed for pollination. Melons can be sown directly outside, but several gardeners report better germination with pre-sprouting the seeds. If you start indoors, do so in individual cells or peat pots, not flats, as the roots are too succulent to divide. When you direct sow, plant 4-5 seeds in a hill and then thin to appropriate spacing, depending on whether you train them on a trellis or let them spread on the ground. For either direct sowing or transplants, cover seedlings with cloches or a hot cap to protect them from frost, speed their growth, and keep out pests. To encourage side shoots, when the seedling has three leaves pinch out the growing end. When new side shoots have three leaves pinch out the central growing area again. When fruits begin to form, pinch back the vine to two leaves beyond the fruit. Make sure fruits on a trellis are supported by netting or pantyhose, and fruits on ground vines are lifted off the ground by something like steel (food) cans to prevent disease and encourage ripening. When watering, avoid wetting the leaves or fruits to help prevent diseases. Troughs near the plants can be flooded for effective watering. Melon rinds are good for compost; they decompose rapidly and are high in P and K.

ALLIES: Some evidence-- none
Uncertain-- corn, goldenrod, nasturtium, onion
COMPANIONS: radish
OTHER: morning glories, radish & zucchini are succession trap plants for cucumber beetles
ENEMIES: none

GREENHOUSE
   Any variety

OUTDOOR
   Long Day (need 15+ daylight hours): plant in early spring in Virginia and northward to obtain large bulbs; can plant later in regions south of Virginia.
      Early Yellow Globe-- 102 days, early, high yields, keeps 6-12 months, moderately strong (Abundant Life, Burpee, Dam, Garden City, Johnny's, Southern Exposure)
      Red Giant-- open-pollinated, mild, semi-flat, keeps 6-12 months (Seeds Blum)
      Sweet Spanish-- 110 days, some are hybrid and some open-pollinated, large globe-shaped yellow bulbs, sometimes known as "hamburger onion," mild, sweet (widely available)
      Walla Walla Sweet-- 125 days spring-seeded, 300 days late-summer seeded and overwintered, open-pollinated, large flattened bulbs, mild, plant in August-September for next summer harvest and sweetest onions, short keeper (widely available)
   Intermediate Day (needs 12-14 daylight hours): best for intermediate latitudes.
      Fiesta Hybrid-- 110 days, firm, yellow, Spanish-type, tangy flesh, high yields, keeps 4-6 months (Park, Shepherd's)
      Red Hamburger or Red Mac-- large, semi-flat bulb, red skin, red and white flesh, best in salads, doesn't store for long periods (Burpee, Earl May, Gurney's, Park)
      Ringmaker Hybrid-- 108 days, early, large yellow spanish type, mild, keeps 4-6 months (Johnny's, Stokes)
      Ruby-- open-pollinated, red, strong flavor, keeps 6-8 months (Cook's, Seeds Blum)
   Short Day (12 daylight hours): best type for fall planting South of Virginia, and spring or fall planting in Mid-Atlantic; not good in North where long days force them to bulb too fast.
      Granex Hybrid or Vidalia-- 170 days, large flat yellow bulbs, very mild flesh, especially good for Mid-Atlantic and South, good for overwintering in the South (Burpee, Field's, Park, Southern Exposure)
   Pearl Onions
      Barletta-- 70 days, cocktail onions, mild flavor, good in soups, stews, good for continuous harvest throughout summer (Shepherd's, Stokes)
   Multiplier (perennial): includes potato onions, Welsh onions and shallots
      He-shi-ko-- 70-80 days, Welsh scallion, resists bulbing, good in North and South (Field's, Gurney's, Nichols)
      Tohono O'odham (Papago) I'itoi's-- good for winter growing in low desert areas and summer growing in cooler regions, multiplier type, has a shallot-like flavor (Native Seeds)
      Yellow Potato Onion-- open-pollinated, very popular, good drought resistance, resists pink root, good keeping quality, heirloom, flavorful but not too strong (Southern Exposure)
      Shallots-- open-pollinated, French, red-pink bulbs known for culinary uses, tops can be used for scallions (Gurney's, Johnny's, Southern Exposure, William Dam)
   Bunching
      Beltsville Bunching-- 65 days, stands dry summer heat, best for August harvest crisp and mild (Seeds Blum, Stokes)
      Evergreen Hardy White-- 60 days for scallions, open-pollinated, little or no bulbing, hardiest bunching type can be perennial, protect in severe winters (widely available)
      Red Beard-- 60 days, unusual red stems develop color in cool weather, harvest late summer and early fall (Burpee, Shepherd's)

NOTES

Allium cepa   *Liliaceae (Lily)*   **ONION**

GROWTH CONDITIONS

Germ.Temp: 50-95   Height: 15-36"
Grow.Temp: 55-75   Breadth: 6-18"
pH: 6.0-7.5 (Multiplier types: 6.5-7.0.) Spacing: To grow scallions, 1" To grow bulbs, 3"
Root Depth: 18" - 3'   Planting Depth: Seeds, 1/2" Sets, 1"
Water: Medium. Dry soil will cause the onion to form two bulbs instead of one. Don't water one week
     before harvest.
Fertilizer: Light feeder. Use compost.
First Seed Starting Date: The average time to maturity is 100-160 days.

     Days Germ + Days Transplant + Days Before LFD = Days Count BACK from LFD
     4-10   +   28-42   +   14-40   =   46-92

PESTS: Japanese beetle, onion eelworm, onion maggot, slug, thrips, vole (storage), white grub,
     wireworm. Try radish as trap crop for onion root maggot; when infested, pull & destroy.
DISEASES: botrytis, damping off, downy mildew, pink root, smut, storage rot, sunscald, white rot

HARVEST: Wait until tops fall over; pushing tops over can shorten the onion's storage life. When
bulbs pull out very easily, rest them on the ground to dry and cure. Treat them gently as they bruise
easily. Turn the onions once or twice in the next few days; cover if it rains. When completely brown,
they're ready for further curing. For regular onions, clip tops 1" from the bulb. Do not clip tops of
multipliers or separate their bulbs. Spread onions no more than 3" deep on wire screens in a shady,
warm, dry, well-ventilated area. Cure this way for up to 2 months before storing for the winter. The
flavor and quality of multipliers keeps improving. After 2 months, check for spoilage and remove all bad
or marginal onions. Only now separate multiplier bulbs, clean and cut off dried tops about 1" above the
bulbs. Keep the smallest bulbs for spring planting.

STORAGE REQUIREMENTS: Onions will sprout in the presence of ethylene gas, so never store
them with apple, apricot, avocado, banana, fig, kiwi, melons, peach, pear, plum, or tomato. Eat the
largest onions first as they're the most likely to sprout.
Fresh: Temp: 36-40   Humidity: 65-70%   Storage Life: 1-8 months (dry)
Preserved, taste (months):   Can: good (12+)   Freeze: fair (3)   Dry: good (12)

OTHER GROWING NOTES: Onions are a cool season crop, hardy to frost and light freezes,
although certain varieties are exceptions. Plan an average of 40 plants per person. The common or
regular onion reproduces by seed and is usually started by seed. Multiplier onions (*A. aggregatum*) such
as shallots and perennial potato onions, reproduce vegetatively and are usually started by sets. Bunching
onions (*A. fistulosum*), such as scallions, Welsh, and Japanese, don't form full bulbs and are usually
started by sets. Onions started from seeds are larger and store longer, while sets are easier and faster
to grow. Sweet onions are best started from seed. To start from sets, choose small bulbs, 3/8 -7/8".
Storage quality is directly related to the length of daylight growing hours, so match onion varieties with
your day length. Also, sweet onions store poorly, while pungent varieties store well because of a high
content of aromatics which act as preservatives. For a perennial patch, grow potato onions. Almost a
lost variety, they're stronger flavored than shallots and can substitute for regular onions. Buy them once
and plant in the fall or spring, and grow them for decades. Fall planting yields twice as many. For
details, see *Fine Gardening,* Dec88.

ALLIES: Some evidence-- carrot
          Uncertain-- beet, caraway, chamomile, flax, summer savory
COMPANIONS: lettuce, pepper, spinach, strawberry, tomato
ENEMIES: all beans, asparagus, peas, sage

PEA VARIETIES*

GREENHOUSE

Alaska, Burpee Sweetpod, Dwarf Grey Sugar, Frosty, Green Arrow, Little Marvel, Sugar Rae-- see below

OUTDOOR

Bush Green Peas

Alaska-- 55 days, 18-36" tall, plump, good dried as split peas (Abundant Life, Earl May, Gurney's, Field's, Seeds Blum)

Corvallis-- 65 days, 2-3' semi-bush, good for cool, damp areas, especially in Northwest, like Little Marvel, resists mosaic and enation mosaic (Nichols)

Frosty-- 65 days, sturdy 18-24", excellent for freezing, high yields (Earl May, Harris)

Green Arrow-- 70 days, 28", resists downy mildew, fusarium wilt, excellent freezing quality, high yields, long pods (widely available)

Laxton's Progress No.9-- 62 days, 14-20", resists fusarium wilt, good flavor and quality (Blum, Earl May, Gurney's, Field's, Jung, William Dam)

Little Marvel-- 63 days, 18", very early, summer, good fresh or frozen (widely available)

Novella-- 65 days, 18-24" bush, fewer leaves provides better air circulation and lower disease and insect damage, resists powdery mildew (widely available)

Waverex-- 65 days, 15" bush needs staking, true French petit pois, good in any cool climate, good frozen (Bountiful, Thompson & Morgan)

Vine Green Peas

Alderman or Tall Telephone-- 68 days, 5-6' tall, extra sweet, high yields and quality, sow in early warm weather, late maturing (Blum, Bountiful, Harris, Gurney's, Stokes, Territorial)

Tarahumara-- peas are good fresh or dried, not heat adapted, plant in spring in cool climates, for high desert planting (Native Seed)

Wando-- 68 days, 30" tall, tolerates heat and drought, good yields, best pea variety for late sowing, good for southern areas (widely available)

Edible Pod Peas (Snow peas)

Burpee Sweetpod (Mammoth Melting Sugar)-- 68 days, 4' vines, resists wilt, can be trellised inside greenhouse (Burpee)

Dwarf Grey Sugar-- 65 days, 18" bush, no staking needed, high yields (widely available)

Norli-- 58 days, 4-5' vine, very early, sweet, good producer (Shepherd's, William Dam)

Oregon Sugar Pod II-- 64 days, 28"-6' vines, good fresh or frozen (widely available)

Snap Peas -- introduced in the 1980s, edible pods, sweet, excellent raw, cooked, or frozen)

Sugar Bon-- 56 days, 18-24" vines, matures 2-3 weeks earlier than Sugar Snap, compact 18" plant, resists powdery mildew and pea leafroll, high yields (Burpee, Field's, Park)

Sugar Mel-- 68 days, 30" vines, very heat and powdery mildew resistant (Cook's, Park, Southern Exposure)

Sugar Rae-- 67 days, dwarf 30" vines, its powdery mildew resistance makes ideal for greenhouse (Bountiful Gardens, Southern Exposure)

Sugar Snap-- 70 days, AAS winner, sweet, good raw any size, resists wilt (widely available)

NOTES

* All varieties listed are open-pollinated.

Pisum sativum   *Leguminosae or Fabaceae (Pea)*   **PEA**

GROWTH CONDITIONS

Germ.Temp: 40-70   Height: Garden peas, 21" - 4'   Snap peas, 4-6'
Grow.Temp: 60-65   Breadth: 6-10"
pH: 6.0-7.5   Spacing: Intensive: 2-4"   Reg: 1-3"   Rows: 18"-48"
Root Depth: Shallow to 3'   Planting Depth: 1" Or 1/2 - 3/4"
Water: Low initially. Heavy after bloom. Shallow watering is said to increase germination.
Fertilizer: Light feeder. When inoculated, peas are N-fixing and need low N. Apply liquid seaweed 2-3
        times per season.
Side-dress: When vines are about 6" tall apply compost or an amendment high in P & K, and light in N.
Support structures: Use a 6' post, A-frame or trellis.
First Seed Starting Date: Plant every 10 days in case of poor germination.
        Days Germ + Days Transplant + Days Before LFD = Days Count BACK from LFD
        7-14   + 0 (direct)   + 28-42   = 35-56
Last Seed Starting Date:
        Days Germ + Days Transplant + Maturity + SDF + Frost Tender = Days BACK from FFD
        6   + 0 (direct)   + 50-80   + 14 +   0   = 70-100

PESTS: most problems affect seedlings: aphid, cabbage looper, cabbage maggot, corn earworm, corn
        maggot, cucumber beetle, cutworm, garden webworm, pale-striped flea beetle, seed
        corn maggot, slug, snail, thrips, webworm, weevil, wireworm
DISEASES: bacterial blight, downy mildew, enation mosaic, fusarium wilt, leaf curl, powdery
        mildew, root rot, seed rot

HARVEST: When pea pods are plump, crisp, and before they begin to harden or fade in color, harvest
them with one clean cut. Sugar snaps are best picked when plump and filled out. Harvest snow peas
when the pods are young and peas undeveloped. Pick peas every day for continuous production. Pea
shoots, the last 4-6" of the vine, can also be harvested for stir-fry dishes and salads.

STORAGE REQUIREMENTS: Blanch before freezing.
Fresh: Temp: 32   Humidity: 95-98%   Storage Life: 1-2 weeks
Preserved, taste (months):   Can: good (12+)   Freeze: excellent (12+)   Dry: good (12+)

OTHER GROWING NOTES: Peas are a cool season crop, hardy to frost and light freezes. Plan an
average of 25-60 plants per person, depending on how much you want to freeze, dry, or can for the
winter. Add organic matter to the beds in the fall; in the spring when the soil is thawing, gently rake the
soil surface. Gardeners with mild winters can plant peas in both spring and fall. Peas have fragile roots
and don't transplant well. While some gardeners recommend presoaking seeds, recent research indicates
that presoaked legume seeds absorb water too quickly, split their outer coatings and spill out essential
nutrients, which encourages damping off seed rot. Yields can increase 50-100 percent by inoculating with
Rhizobia bacteria. Peas can cross-pollinate, so for seed-saving space different varieties at least 150 feet
apart. Dwarf varieties don't need a trellis if you plant them close together. Pole and climbing peas
produce up to five times more than dwarf bush varieties and over a longer period. If a plant only has
a few peas on it, pinch back the growing tip to encourage further fruiting. After the harvest turn under
the plant residues, which improve the soil.

ALLIES: Some evidence-- tomato
        Uncertain-- *Brassicas,* caraway, carrot, chive, goldenrod, mint, turnip
COMPANIONS: all beans, coriander, cucumber, radish, spinach
ENEMIES: garlic, onion, potato

PEANUT VARIETIES

GREENHOUSE
   The smaller dwarf bushes ("Spanish") might be grown in a greenhouse.

OUTDOOR: Peanuts are good container plants.
   Mammoth Jumbo-- 120 days, early ripening, can grow as far north as Wisconsin (Earl May)
   Spanish or Early Spanish-- 100-120 days, dwarf bushes, rich flavor, small kernels, can be grown as far north as Canada, provide light, sandy soil and southern exposure (Burpee, Field's, Gurney's, Jung, Park, Stokes)
   Valencia Tennessee Red-- 120 days, large and sweet kernels, southern warm-season type, can be grown as far north as New York (Park)
   Virginia or Jumbo Virginia-- 120 days, 3-1/2' spreading vines, large kernels, grows in the north and corn belt, too, good rich flavor fresh or in peanut butter (Burpee, Field's, Gurney's, Park)

NOTES

Arachis hypogaea   *Leguminosae or Fabaceae (Pea)*   **PEANUT**

GROWTH CONDITIONS

Germ.Temp: 60-80   Height: 12-18"
Grow.Temp: 70-85   Breadth: 15-20"
pH: 5.0-6.0   Spacing: 3-6" (in 4" high ridge), thin to 12"   Rows: 30-36"
Root Depth: Shallow   Planting Depth: 1 to 1-1/2"

Water: Average. When the plant begins to blossom, stop all watering.
Fertilizer: Add rotted manure in the fall so its decomposition won't affect peanut seeds. At blossom
        time, add calcium (Calcium Sulfate or limestone). Additional Potassium may also be required.
First Seed Starting Date: Try presprouting extra-large peanuts, which germinate poorly in wet, cool soil.
        Days Germ + Days Transplant + Days Before LFD = Days Count BACK from LFD
        7-14   +   0   +   15-28   = 22-42
Last Seed Starting Date:
        Days Germ + Days Transplant + Maturity + SDF + Frost Tender = Days BACK from FFD
        7-14   +   0 (direct) + 110-120 + 14 + 14   = 145-162

PESTS: weeds. Otherwise backyard gardeners should experience no significant pests except occasional
        corn earworm, cutworm, pale-striped flea beetle, potato leafhopper, spider mite, thrips
        and different caterpillars
DISEASES: no significant diseases, except occasional leaf spot and Southern blight

HARVEST: As the first frost approaches, when the leaves turn yellow-white, kernels drop, and pod
veins darken, dig up the entire plant. In short-season areas, you may want to wait to harvest after the
first few light frosts; although the top growth may be killed, the pods will continue to mature. Shake off
all loose dirt. Dry roots in the sun for a few days to facilitate separation of the pods, or hang roots in
a dry, airy place. Make sure they're out of reach of small animals.

STORAGE REQUIREMENTS: Spread peanuts on shallow trays or hang the entire plant from rafters
in a garage or attic. Cure this way in a warm, dry place for a minimum of 3 weeks and up to 2-3
months. Peanuts are best stored shelled, in airtight containers in the refrigerator for short periods, or
in the freezer for long periods--because they are very susceptible to a fungus that produces a highly toxic
substance called aflatoxin. To be safe, don't eat any moldy peanuts. Roast nuts at 300F for 20 minutes
before eating.
Fresh: Temp: 32   Humidity: low   Storage Life: 12

OTHER GROWING NOTES: Also known as goober peas and groundnuts, peanuts are a warm season
crop, very tender to frost and light freezes. Plan an average of 10-20 plants per person. Peanuts require
full sun and can be grown wherever melon grows, as far north as Canada, although commercial
production is generally limited to the South. In short-season areas, you may want to start seeds, which
are the nuts, inside. Transplant seedlings outside into soil warmed with plastic, choosing a sheltered
south-facing site. For higher yields, inoculate with special peanut inoculant available from nurseries.
Plant nuts that are not split and still have their papery skin; they sprout more easily without their shell
but filled shells can be planted. They need loose, enriched, sandy soil. For succession planting, peanuts
are good planted after early crops of lettuce or spinach. The plant produces peanuts after the stem
blossoms; its lower leaves drop and in their place peduncles grow. The peduncles eventually bend over
and root in the nearby soil, where clusters of peanuts then grow. When the plants reach 6" begin to
cultivate the rows to control weeds and keep the soil aerated. When about 1' high, hill the plants in the
same manner as potatoes, mounding soil high around each plant. Hilling is important to help the
peduncle root quickly. Mulch between rows with 8" of grass clippings or straw. Peanut hulls are good
for mulching and composting as they're rich in nitrogen. For rotation planning, follow peanuts with
nitrogen-loving plants.

ALLIES: Some evidence-- corn
ENEMIES: none

PEPPER VARIETIES

GREENHOUSE
Ace, Anaheim, E. Jalapeno, Hungarian Y.W., Staddon's, S. Cayenne, Thai -- see below

OUTDOOR
Sweet

Ace Hybrid-- 50 days, green stuffing pepper, medium thick flesh, short sturdy plants reliable even in adverse conditions, ripens to red (Burpee, Johnny's)

California Wonder-- 75 days, open-pollinated, very mild flavor, good stuffing pepper, blocky deep green fruit (widely available)

Golden Bell or Golden Summer Hybrid-- 70 days, unusual bright yellow when ripe, excellent flavor, open growing habit, good yields (widely available)

Gypsy Hybrid-- 62 days, AAS winner, early, prolific, thin, yellow-red, mild flavor, good for salads and frying, 3-4" fruits, resists tobacco mosaic virus (widely available)

Large Sweet Cherry-- 70 days, open-pollinated, red, small fruit 1-1/2" across, excellent in salads (Nichols, Seeds Blum, Southern Exposure)

Pepperoncini (Italian)-- 65 days, open-pollinated, shrubby 3' plant, red pencil-thin fruit, prolific good fresh or pickled for antipasto (Blum, Nichols, Shepherd's, Stokes)

Staddon's Select-- 72 days, open-pollinated, early, meaty, prolific even under adverse conditions, resists mosaic, popular in the North (Garden City, Seeds Blum, Stokes)

Sweet Banana or Sweet Hungarian-- 75 days, open-pollinated, pretty light yellow, slender 6-8" fruit, thin flesh, good for pickling or salads, high yields, sturdy plants (widely available)

Sweet Pimento-- 65 days, open-pollinated, heart-shaped peppers, bright red, eat fresh in salads or out of hand, roasted, peeled, canned (widely available)

Yolo Wonder-- 76 days, open-pollinated, thick flesh, bell pepper, ripens green to red, resists mosaic, thick foliage protects against sunscald (Bountiful Gardens, Jung, Stokes))

Hot

Anaheim-- 74 days, open-pollinated, chili type, relatively mild, 7-8", thick flesh, good fresh in salsa and chili rellenos, canned, frozen or dried, may resist tobacco mosaic virus (Cook's, Garden City, Harris, Nichols, Park, Seeds Blum)

Early Jalapeno-- 70 days, open-pollinated, very hot Mexican type, compact plant, thick flesh, good fresh, in jelly and as pickles (Earl May, Garden City, Johnny's, Jung, Shepherd's)

Hot Shot-- 54 days, open-pollinated, larger jalapeno type, medium hot, earlier than jalapeno and larger 4" fruit, high yields and good quality under both heat and cold stress (Johnny's)

Hungarian Yellow Wax-- 70 days, open-pollinated, pretty yellow, red when ripe, 6-7", strong upright plants, medium hot, considered best hot pepper for cool climates (widely available)

Large Red Cherry-- 80 days, open-pollinated, red 1-1/4" hot fruit (Blum, Harris, Nichols)

Sandia-- 6-9", good for rellenos, enchilada sauce, stews, for low & high desert (Native Seeds)

Serrano-- 75 days, popular in Southwest, extremely hot (Burpee, Fields, Gurney's, Shepherd's)

Super Cayenne-- 72 days, 1990 AAS winner, 20" plants, more compact and manageable than other cayennes, hot and spicy pepper (Burpee, Park)

Thai Hot-- extremely hot, pretty 8" plant, small 1-1/2" fruit, good for containers (Park)

Novelty

Ariane-- 70 days, unusual orange, first sweet orange bell, beautiful, good flavor when green or orange, early, high yields, resists tobacco mosaic virus (Nichols, Shepherd's)

Paprika-- 80 days, open-pollinated, mildly hot and sweet, thick peppers, open-pollinated, excellent dried and ground (Abundant Life, Nichols, Seeds Blum, Southern Exposure)

Szentese-- 60 days, open-pollinated, unusual lime yellow ripens to orange, semi-hot, an unusual hot Hungarian type, good for greenhouse production too (Stokes)

NOTES

Capsicum annuum   *Solanaceae (Nightshade)*   **PEPPER**

GROWTH CONDITIONS

Germ.Temp: 65-95   Height: 2 -3'
Grow.Temp: 70-85   Breadth: 24"
pH: 5.5-7.0   Spacing: Intensive: 12"   Reg: 12-24"   Rows: 18-36"
Root Depth: 8", some to 4'   Planting Depth: 1/4"
Water: Medium-heavy
Fertilizer: Medium-heavy feeder. High N. Rotted manure or compost. Some soils may need calcium.
Side-dress: Apply at blossom-time and 3 weeks later. Apply liquid seaweed 2-3 times per season.
First Seed Starting Date:

> Days Germ + Days Transplant - Days After LFD = Days Count BACK from LFD
> 10-12   +   32-44   -   14-21   = 28-35

Last Seed Starting Date:

> Days Germ + Days Transplant + Maturity + SDF + Frost Tender = Days BACK from FFD
> 6-9   +   21   + 60-90   + 14 +   14   = 115-148

PESTS: aphid, Colorado potato beetle, corn borer, corn earworm, cutworm, flea beetle, leafminer, mite, snail, slug, tomato hornworm, weevil

DISEASES: anthracnose, bacterial spot, cercospora, mosaic, soft rot, southern blight, tobacco mosaic. Environmental disorders: blossom end rot, sunscald.

HARVEST: For sweet peppers, pick the first fruit as soon as they're usable in order to hasten growth of others. For storage peppers, cut the fruit with 1" or more of stem. For maximum Vitamin C content wait until peppers have matured to red or yellow colors.

STORAGE REQUIREMENTS: Hot varieties are best stored dried or pickled. Pull the entire plant from the ground and hang it upside down until dried. Alternately, harvest the peppers and string them on a line to dry. For sweet peppers, refrigeration is too cold and encourages decay.
Fresh: Temp: 45-55   Humidity: 90-95 %   Storage Life: 2-3 weeks
Preserved, taste (months): Can: good (12) Freeze: fair (3) Dry: excellent (12) Pickled: excellent (12+)

OTHER GROWING NOTES: Peppers are a warm season crop, very tender to frost and light freezes. Plan an average of 5-6 plants per person. All parts of the plant except for the fruit are poisonous. To start indoors use pots at least 1-1/2" wide to minimize transplant shock, to make a stockier plant, and to encourage earlier production. Growers report the following cold treatment of seedlings significantly improves yields and fosters earlier production: (1) when the first leaves appear, lower the soil temperature to 70 and ensure 16 hours of light with grow lamps; (2) when the first true leaf appears, thin seedlings to 2-3" apart or transplant into 4" pots; (3) when the third true leaf appears, move the plants to a location where night temperatures drop to 53-55 and keep there for four full weeks; (4) move the seedlings back to a location where temperature averages 70; (5) finally, transplant the peppers into the garden 2-3 weeks after all danger of frost has passed. Soil temperature should be at least 55-60 for transplanting, otherwise the plants turn yellow, become stunted, and are slow to bear. Some recommend feeding pepper seedlings weekly with half-strength liquid fertilizer until transplanted. Peppers do better planted close together. Except in the West where peppers may be mostly pest free, use row covers immediately because pepper pests will be out. If the temperature rises over 95, you might sprinkle plants with water in the afternoon to try to prevent blossom drop. At blossom time try spraying leaves with a weak epsom salt mixture (1 tsp. per quart) to promote fruiting.

ALLIES: Some evidence-- none
          Uncertain-- caraway, catnip, nasturtium, tansy
COMPANIONS: basil, carrot, eggplant, onion, parsley, tomato
ENEMIES: fennel, kohlrabi

POTATO VARIETIES

GREENHOUSE
none, potatoes won't grow well in the greenhouse

OUTDOOR
White: good for a variety of purposes

Kennebec-- late, white, delicious big tubers, thin skin, resists mosaic & blight, reliable high yields, good storage (Burpee, Earl May, Gurney's, Field's, Jung)

Elba-- 1987 Cornell release, late, white, resists early & late blight, verticillium wilt and golden nematode, high yields, good boiled or baked (Gurney's)

Russet (brownish skin, white flesh): best baking potatoes

Butte-- baking potato, higher in protein and Vitamin C than most (Gurney's, Field's)

Burbank-- the famous "Idaho potato", late maturing (Territorial)

White Cobbler-- early season, the standard popular white potato, smooth skin, best baked, dependable yields under wide growing conditions, not good for storing (Field's)

Red (red skin and white flesh): good for boiling

Red Norland-- very early potato, very large tubers, resists scab, one of best flavors, smooth skin (Abundant Life, Earl May, Gurney's, Field's)

Red Pontiac-- early to midseason, tolerates heat for Southern growers, excellent for boiling, stays firm for potato salads (Field's, Gurney's)

Yellow Flesh

Lady Finger-- small 1" wide and 4-5" long fruits, brown skin and yellow flesh, good for baking, excellent boiled or fried (Gurney)

Ruby Crescent-- late season, similar to "Lady Finger" but higher yields, rosy skin with yellow flesh, delicious in potato salads or fried with onions, prized by chefs (Seeds Blum, Shepherd's)

Yukon Gold-- round, yellow flesh, all purpose, good flavor, excellent storage (Abundant Life, Burpee, Garden City, Nichols, Seeds Blum)

Yellow Fingerling-- salad potato, yellow flesh, long and slender crescent-shaped tubers (Jung, Seeds Blum)

Yellow Finn-- bakes and boils nicely, prized in Europe, natural butter flavor (Shepherd's, Territorial)

Novelty

All-Blue--good yields, unusual blue flesh all the way through, good baked, boiled, roasted, makes beautiful violet vichyssoise (Field's, Seeds Blum)

Blossom-- pretty pink skin and pink flesh, oblong, somewhat flat with tapered ends, plant is also pretty with pink flowers (Seeds Blum)

NOTES

Buy only certified disease-free potatoes.

Solanum tuberosum   *Solanaceae (Nightshade)*   **POTATO**

GROWTH CONDITIONS

Germ.Temp: 65-70   Height: 23-30"
Grow.Temp: 60-65   Breadth: 24"
pH: 5.0-6.0   Spacing: Intensive: 9-12" (seed potatoes) Reg: 10-12" Rows: 24"
Root Depth: 18-24"   Planting Depth: 3-4"

Water: Medium, except heavy watering when potatoes are forming, from blossom time to harvest.
Fertilizer: Light feeder. Apply compost at planting.
Side-dress: 2-3 weeks after 1st hilling apply fertilizer 6" away from plant, and hill again.
First Seed Potato Planting Date: 2-4 or 6-8 weeks before LFD. In the South and West potatoes are
      usually started in February or March and harvested in June and July.
Last Seed Potato Planting Date: 90-120 days (average days to maturity) before FFD.

PESTS: aphid, cabbage looper, Colorado potato beetle, corn borer, corn earworm, cucumber beetle,
      cutworm, earwig, flea beetle, Japanese beetle, June beetle, lace bug, leaf-footed bug, leafhopper,
      leafminer, nematode, slug, snail, tomato hornworm, white grub, wireworm
DISEASES: black leg, early blight, fusarium wilt, late blight, mosaic, powdery mildew, psyllid yellows,
      rhizoctonia, ring rot, scab, scurf, verticillium wilt. Environmental disorders: black heart

HARVEST: For small "new" potatoes harvest during blossoming or, for varieties that don't blossom,
about 10 weeks after planting. Harvest regular potatoes when the vines have died back half-way, about
17 weeks after planting. Gently pull or dig out tubers with a garden fork. If not large enough, pack the
soil back and try again at 2-3 week intervals. If you have many plants, remove the entire plant when
harvesting to make room for another crop. For storage potatoes dig near the first frost, when plant tops
have died back. To minimize tuber injury, always dig when the soil is dry.

STORAGE REQUIREMENTS: Spring or summer-harvested potatoes aren't usually stored, but can
keep for 4-5 months if cured first at 60-70F for at least 4 days and stored at 40F. Dry fall-harvested
potatoes for 1-2 days on the ground, then cure at 50-60F and a high relative humidity for 10-14 days.
Don't cure potatoes in the sun, which causes them to turn green. Once cured, store them in total
darkness in a single layer. Never layer or pile potatoes more than 6-8" deep.
Fresh: Temp: 55-60   Humidity: 90-95%   Storage Life: 5-10 months
Preserved, taste (months):   Can: fair (12+)   Freeze: good (8)   Dry: good (12+)

OTHER GROWING NOTES: Potatoes are a warm season crop in the North, tender to frost and light
freezes, and a cool season crop in the South and West. Plan an average of 10-30 plants per person. All
plant parts except the tubers are poisonous. They require full sun. Most potatoes are started from small
potato pieces called seed potatoes. Each piece should contain 1-3 "eyes," small indentations which will
sprout foliage. If desired, you can presprout the eyes by keeping the seed potato at 40-50F for two
weeks before planting to break dormancy. Two methods of preparing seed potatoes for planting: (1) cut
the potato into 2" pieces about 2 days before planting, and cure indoors at about 70F in high humidity.
This helps them retain moisture and resist rot better; (2) plant small whole potatoes, which are less apt
to rot, have more eyes, and don't need curing prior to planting. Potatoes are very disease-prone, so it's
important to use buy certified disease-free seed potatoes. Place potatoes in trenches 6" deep by 6" wide.
Space them 10-12" apart and cover with 3-4" of soil. About 1 week after shoots emerge start mounding
soil around their base, leaving a few inches exposed. "Hilling" keeps tubers covered with soil to prevent
greening. Side-dress and "hill" again 2-3 weeks later. Cover plants if a hard frost is expected.

ALLIES: Some evidence-- none
          Uncertain-- all beans, catnip, coriander, "dead" nettle, eggplant, flax, goldenrod,
          horseradish, onion, nasturtium, tansy
COMPANIONS: all *Brassicas,* corn, marigold, pigweed
ENEMIES: cucumber, peas, pumpkin, squash, spinach, sunflower, tomato, raspberry

GREENHOUSE
America, Bloomsdale, Melody-- see below

OUTDOOR (Note: Savoyed = crinkled leaves)
America-- 43 days, open-pollinated, AAS winner, milder taste when fresh, excellent taste stir-fried, holds quality long, good for canning, spring or fall crop, dark green crinkled leaves, slow bolting, 40-50 days (Earl May, Southern Exposure, Stokes)
Bloomsdale Long Standing-- 48 days, open-pollinated, late spring-early summer crop, best flavor for salads, heavy yields, glossy crinkled leaves, bolt resistant, long harvest, can be overwintered (widely available)
Hybrid No.7-- 42 days, for early spring plantings, and fall or winter crop, upright, semi-savoy type, resists downy mildew and mosaic, dark green, large crinkled leaves (Nichols, William Dam)
Melody-- 42 days, hybrid, spring or fall crop, quick growing, 40-50 days, resists downy mildew and mosaic, bred for the home garden, upright, easy harvest of dirt-free leaves, good fresh, frozen or canned (widely available)
Savoy, Cold-resistant-- 45 days, open-pollinated, late summer or fall crop, good for overwintering for early spring crop, tolerates heat, cold and blight, good fresh flavor, well-savoyed (Seeds Blum, Southern Exposure, Stokes)
Tyee-- 42 days, hybrid, excellent savoy type, upright habit makes easier harvest, tolerates downy mildew, good for spring, summer and fall crops, very slow to bolt, stands longer than "Melody" (Johnny's, Southern Exposure)
Wolter-- 45 days, Dutch hybrid, rapid growing, high yields, high resistance to downy mildew, very fine flavor (Shepherd's)

HOT WEATHER SPINACH SUBSTITUTES
Basella Malabar Red Stem Summer Spinach-- open-pollinated, a new vegetable introduced in 1987 from the Orient, harvest all summer, mild but not as flavorful as spinach, tolerates heat, vigorous, can grow up to 6', easily trained on a trellis, ornamental red stems are also good in salads, not recommended in northern areas (Bountiful Gardens, Park, Seeds Blum)
New Zealand Everlasting Spinach (Tetragonia expansa)-- open-pollinated, perennial, tastes like spinach, tolerates heat and drought, crisp green leaves, continuous harvest (widely available)
Red Orach-- open-pollinated, also called "Mountain Spinach", not really like any other listed above, but flavor is mild and sweet, use in salads and sandwiches like lettuce, can grow to 9' tall if allowed to go to seed, often grown as potherb in France and Asia, goes to seed quickly in warm weather but can be kept productive if you pinch out seed heads, pretty red seedheads are beautiful in arrangements, leaves are pretty red in salads (Seeds Blum)

NOTES

Spinacia oleracea **Chenopodiaceae (Goosefoot)** **SPINACH**

GROWTH CONDITIONS

Germ.Temp: 45-75
Grow.Temp: 60-65
pH: 6.0-7.5
Root Depth: 1', tap root to 5'
Water: Light but evenly moist

Height: 4-6"
Breadth: 6-8"
Spacing: 2", thin to 6-12" as leaves touch   Rows: 12-14"
Planting Depth: 1/2"

Fertilizer: Heavy feeder. Before planting apply compost.
Side-dress: Apply 4 weeks after planting, and thereafter every 2 weeks.
First Seed Starting Date: Sow directly every 10 days, starting 4-6 weeks before last frost.

Days Germ	+	Days Transplant	+	Days Before LFD	=	Days Count BACK from LFD
7-14	+	28	+	21	=	56-64

Last Seed Starting Date: Sow later crops directly, as transplanting encourages bolting.

Days Germ	+	Days Transplant	+	Maturity	+	SDF	+	Frost Tender	=	Days BACK from FFD
5	+	0	+	40-50	+	14	+	N/A	=	59-69

PESTS: aphid, beet leafhopper, cabbage looper, cabbageworm, flea beetle, leafminer, slug, snail
DISEASES: curly top (spread by beet leafhopper), damping off, downy mildew, fusarium wilt, leaf spot, spinach blight (caused by cucumber mosaic virus spread by aphids, see Mosaic)

HARVEST: Cut individual leaves when they're large enough to eat. Continual harvest prevents bolting. When the weather warms, cut the plant to ground level. Its leaves will grow back. For the best nutrition, harvest leaves in the morning.

STORAGE REQUIREMENTS: For freezing and drying, cut the leaves into thick strips. Blanch for 5 minutes before drying, or 2 minutes before freezing. It's best to use only the smallest and most tender leaves for freezing.
Fresh: Temp: 32   Humidity: 95-100%   Storage Life: 10-14 days
Preserved, taste (months):   Can: good (12+)   Freeze: good (12)   Dry: unknown

OTHER GROWING NOTES: Spinach is a cool season crop, hardy to light frosts and freezes. Plan an average of 10-20 plants per person. Spinach can be grown as soon as the soil is workable. After thinning to 4-6", cover the plants with row covers to keep pests away. Fall crops usually taste better and suffer no leafminers or bolting. Also, if you plant a late fall crop and mulch it, a very early crop will come up in the spring. Spinach will bolt when there's 14-16 hours of light, regardless of the temperature, although warmer temperatures will cause it to bolt faster. The exceptions are New Zealand and Basella Malabar "spinach," which thrive in warm weather. They aren't true spinach, but when cooked they taste like the real thing. Malabar is also a pretty ornamental vine which is easily grown on arbors where it provides summer shade and a constant supply of summer greens.

ALLIES: Some evidence-- none
          Uncertain-- strawberry
COMPANIONS: all beans, all *Brassicas,* celery, onion, peas
ENEMIES: potato

SQUASH VARIETIES

GREENHOUSE

Aristocrat, Greyzini, Gld. Nugget, Grm. Globe, Ptty. Pan, Scallopini, Table King-- see below.

OUTDOOR

Pepo: Almost all bush varieties are Pepo, including the most commonly grown such as summer squash, acorn, spaghetti, and pumpkin.

Summer

Aristocrat-- 53 days, hybrid zucchini, AAS winner, upright bush, early, high yields, excellent quality, dark green, smooth, long harvest (Earl May, Jung, Nichols, T & M)

Cocozelle or Italian Vegetable Marrow-- 50 days, OP, slim zucchini, striped, very flavorful raw or cooked (Garden City, Johnny's, Nichols, Stokes)

Golden Bush Scallop-- OP, HL, long season, space-saving bush (Blum, Southern Exposure)

Gourmet Globe-- 50 days, hybrid zucchini or "apple squash," compact bush, very early, small round flavorful fruits (Earl May, Park, Shepherd's, Thompson & Morgan)

Greyzini-- OP, zucchini, high eating quality, long harvest (Stokes)

Patty Pan-- OP, flat with scalloped edges, excellent flavor, picky when very young, survives well even in English climate (Blum, Bountiful)

Scallopini Hybrid-- new summer squash, All American Bronze winner, best when 3" or less, good raw, boiled or fried (Jung, Stokes, Territorial)

Winter

Delicata or Peanut or Sweet Potato-- 100 days, OP, acorn type, oblong 8" fruits with dark green stripes, superb keeper, good taste, compact vines (widely available)

Gold Nugget-- 85 days, OP, runnerless bush plants, each bears about 4 slightly flattened orange fruits, 5" across, stores well (Blum, Johnny's)

Jersey Golden Acorn-- 80 days, OP, AAS winner, smaller, good for small gardens, when picked 1-3 days after flowering tastes like corn with sweet nutty flavor, also good when matured for winter storage (widely available)

Spaghetti Squash-- 100 days, OP, use pulp like spaghetti (widely available)

Table King-- OP, winter acorn, AAS winner, compact bush, dark green with small seed cavity, improves with storage (Earl May, Garden City, Stokes, Territorial)

Winter Luxury Pumpkin-- OP, best for smooth tasty pie fillings, ripens early, excellent keeper, high yields, about 10" fruit (Jung)

Maxima: These are excellent keepers, tolerant of borers, and include the largest fruit such as buttercup and banana.

Buttercup (Burgess strain)-- 105 days, OP, turban-shaped with light stripes, deep orange, rich, sweet and very dry flesh, tastes like sweet potato, excellent keeper (widely available)

Blue Banana-- OP, best and sweetest banana, makes good pies, heirloom (Blum)

Mayo Blusher- large fruit turns pink when ripe, keeps well, good for low desert (Native Seed)

Red Kuri-- 92 days, beautiful red-orange, teardrop-shaped, good for pies & purees (Johnny's)

Moschata: The sweetest squashes, such as butternut, cushaws and cheese, are all Moschata. They have high pest resistance and also have the highest vitamin content.

Early Butternut-- 92 days, hybrid, AAS winner, compact vines, high quality fruit, stores 2-3 months (widely available)

Magdalena Big Cheese-- large, ribbed, flat pumpkin shape, good for low desert (Native Seeds)

Mixta: This is a Southern growing group like Moschata.

Cushaw-- 115 days, OP, green-striped, resists squash vine borer, light yellow flesh, good for pies, excellent canned (Blum, Gurney's, Field's, Southern Exposure)

Hopi "Vanta"-- striped or solid green, thick hard shells (sometimes used for music instruments), for high and low desert (Native Seeds)

NOTES

GROWTH CONDITIONS

Germ.Temp: 70-95   Height: winter, 12-15"   summer, 30-40"
Grow.Temp: 65-75   Breadth: bush, to 4 sq.ft.   vining, to 12-16 sq.ft.
pH: 6.0-7.5   Spacing: Intensive: 12-18" Reg: 24-28"   Rows: bush, 36-60"
Root Depth: 18" - 6'   Planting Depth: 1/2 - 1" in hills   vine, 72-96"
Water: Heavy
Fertilizer: Heavy feeder. Apply lots of compost. High N requirements.
Side-dress: Apply compost midseason. In boron deficient soils, apply 1 tsp borax per plant.
Support structures: Use an A-frame or trellis to grow vines upright.
First Seed Starting Date:

> Days Germ + Days Transplant - Days After LFD = Days Count BACK from LFD
> 7-10   +   28-42   -   21-28   =   14-24

Last Seed Starting Date: (summer/winter varieties)

> Days Germ + Days Transplant + Maturity + SDF + Frost Tender = Days BACK from FFD
> 3   +   0 (direct)   + 40-50   + 14   + 14   = 71-81 (summer)
>   80-110   111-141 (winter)

PESTS: aphid, beet leafhopper, corn earworm, cucumber beetle, Mexican bean beetle, pickleworm, slug, snail, squash bug, squash vine borer, thrips, whitefly
DISEASES: alternaria leaf spot, anthracnose, bacterial wilt, belly rot, cottony leak, cucumber wilt, downy mildew, mosaic, powdery mildew, scab

HARVEST: Cut all fruit except hubbard-types with a 1" stem. Don't ever lift squash by the stem. Treat even those with hard skins gently to avoid bruising. **Summer**-- Cut before 8" long, when skin is still soft, and before seeds ripen. **Patty Pans**-- Cut when 1-4" in diameter and the skin is soft enough to break with a finger. **Winter**-- Cut when the skin is hard, not easily punctured, and mature.

STORAGE REQUIREMENTS: Cure winter squash after picking by placing in a well-ventilated, warm or sunny place for 2 weeks. If you cure fruit in the field, raise them off the ground and protect from rain. Alternately, dip fruit in a weak chlorine bleach solution (9 parts water:1 part chlorine), air dry, and store. Store only best fruit. Don't allow fruit to touch. Wipe moldy fruit with a vegetable-oiled-cloth.
Fresh: Temp: 50-60   Humidity: 60-70%   Storage Life: 4-6 months
Preserved, taste (months): Can: good (12+)   Freeze: good (8)   Dry: good (12+)

OTHER GROWING NOTES: Squash is a warm season crop, very tender to frost and light freezes. Plan an average of 2 winter squash plants per person, and 2 summer squash plants per 4-6 people. Fabric row covers boost and prolong squash yields. In cooler climates, you can keep row covers on all season; when the female (fruit) blossoms open, just lift the cover for 2 hours in early morning twice a week to ensure pollination. Bee pollination is essential. To keep vines short for row covers, pinch back the end of the vine, choose the best blossoms, and permit only 4 fruits per vine. Winter squash doesn't transplant well but can be sown inside if you use individual pots that won't disturb the roots. Squash is usually planted in small hills. To prepare these dig 18"-deep holes, fill them partly with compost, and complete filling the hole with a mixture of soil and compost. Traditionally, 6-8 seeds are placed 1" deep in each; when seedlings reach 3", thin to 2 seedlings. Others say to plant only 1 or 2 seeds due to squash's high germination rate. Raise fruits off the ground to prevent rot.

ALLIES: Some evidence-- corn
>   Uncertain-- borage, catnip, goldenrod, marigold, mint, onion, nasturtium, oregano, radish, tansy
COMPANIONS: celeriac, celery, corn, melon
ENEMIES: potato, pumpkin (pumpkin cross-pollinates with other *pepo* plants, which is only important to prevent if you are saving seeds; keep distant or plant 3 weeks later)

SWEET POTATO VARIETIES

GREENHOUSE
> **Bunch Port Rico, Vardaman**-- see below

OUTDOOR
> White -- White sweet potatoes, not very well known, have less beta-carotene but still more Vitamin C than tomatoes. They are a good substitute for white potatoes.
>> **Sumor**-- very white sweet potato, an excellent & more nutritious substitute for Irish white potato, some disease and insect resistance, stores well, must boil before removing skin (South Carolina Foundation Seeds)
>> **White Delight**-- heavy yields, unusual white flesh, texture and sweetness resembles orange-flesh varieties (South Carolina Foundation)
>
> Yellow-orange
>> **Allgold**-- moist flesh, resists viral disease, internal cork and stem rot, grows well in the Midwest, good keeper (Fred's)
>> **Bunch Port Rico**-- compact vines to 18", good for containers and greenhouses (Fred's)
>> **Centennial**-- 100 days, very popular, bright copper skins, high yields, keeps well, good for Northern climates, tolerates clay soils, resists wilt (Burpee, Earl May, Jung, Park, South Carolina Foundation)
>> **Excel**-- excellent flavor, earlier and higher yields, good shapes, good resistance to wilt, rootknot nematodes and soil insects (South Carolina Foundation)
>> **Jewel**-- 100 days, leading commercial variety, excellent keeper (up to 50 weeks), bright copper skin, highest yields of all, disease resistant, prefers sandy soil (Earl May, Field's, Fred's, Jung, Park, South Carolina Foundation)
>> **Southern Delight**-- dark orange flesh, high pest resistance, especially rootknot nematodes, resists diseases, excellent baking quality, new in 1988 (South Carolina Foundation)
>> **Vardaman**-- 110 days, a "bush" with short vines of only 4-5', resists fusarium wilt better than longer vined types, worth trying in the greenhouse (Field's, Jung, Park)

NOTES

Ipomoea batatas   *Convolvulaceae (Morning Glory)*   SWEET POTATO

GROWTH CONDITIONS

Germ.Temp: 60-85   Height: 12-15"
Grow.Temp: 70-85   Breadth: 4 - 8 sq.ft.
pH: 5.0-6.0   Spacing: Intensive: 10-12"   Reg: 12-16"   Rows: 36-40"
Root Depth: Length of the potato   Planting Depth: 4 - 6"
Water: Dry to medium. Water well the first few days until anchored, then ease back on water.
Fertilizer: Light feeder. Low N. Before planting place 1-2" of compost in furrows.
Side-dress: Once anchored apply high P fertilizer like bone meal, about 1 Cup per 10 row-ft.
First Slip Starting Date:

Days Germ	+	Days Transplant	- Days After LFD	= Days Count BACK from LFD
8-12	+	42-56	- 7-21	= 43-57 (6 to 8 weeks)

Last Slip Starting Date:

Days Germ	+	Days Transplant	+ Maturity	+ SDF	+ Frost Tender	= Days BACK from FFD
8-12	+	42-56	+ 100-125	+ 14	+ 14	= 178-221

PESTS: flea beetle, nematode, weevil, wireworm. Problems vary by region, so check with your extension agent.

DISEASES: black rot (fungal), fusarium surface rot (storage), rhizoctonia, soil rot or scurf

HARVEST: Some say to harvest after the vines are killed by frost, but most warn that frost damages the root. Always harvest on a dry day. Start digging a few feet away to avoid damaging sweet potatoes with the fork. Bruises or cuts as small as that left by a broken hair root will shorten the shelf life by serving as an entry point for fusarium surface rot. Dry for 1-3 hours on the ground. Do not wash them unless absolutely necessary. Never scrub them.

STORAGE REQUIREMENTS: Cure sweet potatoes before dry storage to help seal off wounds and minimize decay. Place them in a warm, dark, well-ventilated area at 85-90 degrees and high humidity for 4-10 days. Store in a cool place, making sure they don't touch each other. Temperatures below 55 cause chill injury. Do not touch potatoes in storage until ready to use.
Fresh: Temp: 55-60   Humidity: 85-90%   Storage Life: 4-7 months
Preserved, taste (months):   Can: good (12+)   Freeze: excellent (6-8)   Dry: good (12+)

OTHER GROWING NOTES: The sweet potato is a warm season crop, very tender to frost and light freezes. Plan an average of 5 plants per person. Other than extreme sensitivity to frost, sweet potatoes are easy to grow, mostly pest free, and, once the transplants are anchored, drought-hardy. Start slips with a sweet potato cut in half length-wise. Lay the cut-side down in a shallow pan of wetted peat moss or sand. Cover tightly with plastic wrap until sprouts appear, then unwrap. The slip is ready when it has 4-5 leaves, is 4-8" tall, and has roots. A second method is to place a whole potato in a jar, cover the bottom inch with water, and keep warm. When leaves form above the roots, twist sprouts off and plant in a deep flat or, if warm enough, outdoors. A third method is to take 6" cuttings from vine tips in the fall just before frost. Place cuttings in water and, when rooted, plant in 6" pots set in a south window for the duration of winter. By late winter you can take more cuttings from these. To prepare the ground in April, fill furrows with 1-2" of compost. Mound soil over compost to form at least 10" high ridges. This creates a kind of mini-"raised bed" to optimize both tuber size and quality, because tuber growth is easily hindered by obstructions in the soil. After all danger of frost is past transplant slips into these ridges. Unlike potatoes, sweets are not true tubers and keep expanding as the vine grows.

ALLIES: Some evidence-- none
        Uncertain-- radish, summer savory, tansy
COMPANIONS: none
ENEMIES: none

GREENHOUSE
Coldset, Patio Prize, Small Fry, Sub-Arctic Plenty, Tiny Tim-- see below

OUTDOOR: IND= Indeterminate, DET=Determinate   OP=Open-pollinated H=Hybrid
Resistance To V=Verticillium, F=Fusarium, N=Nematodes, T=Tobacco Mosaic, L=leafspot
  Standard
        Ace 55 VF-- 70 days, H, DET, suited well for hot, dry areas in West (Burpee, Tomato)
        Beefmaster VFN-- 80 days, H, IND, tomatoes up to 2 lbs, need staking (Park, Tomato)
        Better Boy VFN-- 72 days, H, IND, midseason, popular, sturdy plant, large, meaty, resists sunscald, ranked well in '87 by Auburn Ag. station (Gurney's, Jung, Nichols, Tomato)
        Bonny Best-- 76 days, OP, IND, early season, heirloom, meaty and good flavor, best grown in a wire cage (Nichols, Seeds Blum, Tomato Growers)
        Brandywine-- 95 days, OP, IND, late, large rich fruit, heirloom (Seeds Blum, Tomato)
        Coldset-- OP, DET, medium fruit, withstands soil temperature of 50F, can sow directly, doesn't tolerate wet, humid conditions well (Gurney's, Southern Exposure, Stokes)
        Delicious VFN-- 77 days, OP, IND, midseason, very large fruit, good for slicing, little cracking (Burpee, Gurney's, Field's, Seeds Blum, Tomato Growers)
        Early Girl VFF-- 54 days, H, IND, earliest slicing/canning, sweet-tart, improved variety has more disease resistance (Burpee, Gurney's, Jung, Nichols, Tomato Growers)
        Floramerica VFFA-- 70 days, H, DET, AAS winner, developed in the South to resist 15 diseases, resists cold, heat and humidity, good fresh or canned (Dam, Field's, Jung, Tomato)
        Lemon Boy VFN-- 72 days, H, IND, lovely yellow, mild, adaptable (widely available)
        Patio Prize VFNT-- 68 days, H, DET, bush, no staking, medium-sized fruit (4oz), excellent disease resistance (Earl May, Park, Stokes, Tomato Growers)
        Pink Ponderosa-- 80 days, OP, IND, late, very large, meaty and solid beefsteak fruit, low acid (Nichols, Seeds Blum, Stokes, Tomato Growers, William Dam)
        Quick Pick VFFNT-- 68 days, H, IND, excellent flavor and texture, high yields (Tomato)
        Rutgers VF-- 76 days, OP, DET, high disease resistance (widely available)
        Sub-Arctic Maxi-- 62 days, OP, DET, early, sparse foliage for quick ripening, vigorous, no staking (Gurney's, Field's, Johnny's, Tomato Growers, Southern Exposure)
        Yellow Oxheart F-- OP, stores 3-6 mos., excellent flavor (Southern Exposure)
  Cherry -- Most are determinate. Indeterminate are better flavored but need more space.
        Chiapas-- sprawling, survived curly top in low desert, prolific, for low desert (Native Seeds)
        Pixie II VFT-- 52 days, H, DET, very early, compact, sturdy plant, meaty, fruit 1-3/4", ideal for pots, small gardens or greenhouse (Burpee, Tomato Growers, William Dam)
        Small Fry VFN-- 65 days, H, DET, AAS winner, very early and prolonged yields, compact bush, excellent taste, good for salads and canning (Earl May, Jung, Tomato Growers)
        Sweet 100-- 65 days, H, IND, excellent sweet flavor, midseason, plants are tall and need staking, high yields over prolonged period, disease resistant, high Vitamin C (widely available)
        Tiny Tim-- 60 days, OP, DET, early, plants 15", good for containers, fruit 3/4", not as sweet as large cherry types (Blum, Burpee, Southern Exposure, Stokes, William Dam)
        Yellow Pear-- 75 days, OP, IND, pretty yellow, resists heat (Southern Exposure)
  Sauce and Paste -- Most are determinate but can be staked.
        Del Oro VFNA-- 72 days, H, DET, best disease resistance of paste types (Harris, Tomato)
        Roma II VF-- 80 days, OP, DET, late season, compact plants, heavy bearer, very solid and meaty with few seeds, good canned whole and good for paste (readily available)
        San Marzano-- 80 days, OP, IND, popular, rectangular pear-shaped fruit, meaty excellent paste tomato (widely available)
        Super Italian-- OP, IND, midseason, excellent meaty tomatoes for paste (Seeds Blum)

NOTES

Lycopersicon escutentum   *Solanaceae (Nightshade)*   **TOMATO**

GROWTH CONDITIONS

Germ.Temp: 60-85   Height: determinate, 3 - 4' indeterminate, 7 - 15'
Grow.Temp: 70-75   Breadth: 24 - 36"
pH: 5.8-7.0   Spacing: Intensive: 18"   Reg: 24-36"   Rows: 3-6'
Root Depth: 8", some to 6'   Planting Depth: 1/2"
Water: Medium and deep watering until harvest. Even moisture helps prevents blossom end rot.
Fertilizer: Heavy feeder. Fertilize 1 week before and the day of planting. Avoid high N
       & K at blossom time. Too much leaf growth may indicate too much N or too much water.
Side-dress: Every 2-3 weeks apply light supplements of weak fish emulsion or manure tea.
Support structures: Use a wire cage, stake or trellis. Most gardeners prefer cages.
First Seed Starting Date: Set out 2 to 4 weeks after the last frost. In FL, TX, and southern CA, you can
       transplant tomatoes in late winter and remove them in summer when they stop bearing.
       Days Germ + Days Transplant - Days After LFD = Days Count BACK from LFD
       7-14   +   42-70   -   14-28   = 28-56 (average 6 weeks/42 days)
Last Seed Starting Date: In FL, TX, and southern CA, gardeners often plant fall crops.
       Days Germ + Days Transplant + Maturity + SDF + Frost Tender = Days BACK from FFD
       7-14   +   42-70   + 55-90 + 14 + 14   = 132-202

PESTS: aphid, beet leafhopper, cabbage looper, Colorado potato beetle, corn borer, corn earworm,
       cucumber beetle, cutworm, flea beetle, fruit worm, garden centipede, gopher, Japanese
       beetle, lace bug, leaf-footed bug, mite, nematode, slug, snail, stinkbug, thrips, tomato
       hornworm, tobacco budworm, whitefly
DISEASES: alternaria, anthracnose, bacterial canker, bacterial spot, bacterial wilt, botrytis fruit rot,
       curly top, damping off, early blight, fusarium wilt, late blight, nematode, psyllid yellows,
       septoria leaf spot, soft rot, southern blight, spotted wilt, sunscald, tobacco mosaic,
       verticillium wilt. Environmental disorders: blossom end rot, sunscald.

HARVEST: Pick when fruit is evenly red but still firm. If warmer than 90F harvest fruit earlier.

STORAGE REQUIREMENTS: Wash and dry before storing. Pack no more than two deep.
Fresh: Temp: 45-50 - ripe/55-70 - green   Humidity: 90-95%   Storage Life: 4-7 days/1-3 weeks
Preserved, taste (months): Can: excellent (12+)   Freeze: good (8)   Dry: good (12+)

OTHER GROWING NOTES: Tomatoes are a warm season crop, very tender to frost and light
freezes. Plan an average of 2-5 plants per person. All parts of the plant except the fruit are poisonous.
Never plant near the walnut family trees (see Walnut entry). To start in flats sow seeds at least 1/2"
apart. Seedlings will be spindly with less than 12-14 hours of light per day. When seedlings have four
leaves transfer to a deeper pot and again when 8-10" tall. Each time place the uppermost leaves just
above the soil line and remove all lower leaves. Transplant into the garden when the stem above the
soil has again reached 8-10" tall. Allow up to 10 days to harden off. Soil temperature should be at least
55-60 to transplant, otherwise plants turn yellow, become stunted and are slow to bear. To transplant,
pinch off the lower leaves again, lay the plant on its side in a furrow about 2-1/2" below the soil surface.
This shallow planting helps it grow faster due to being in warmer soil. Put in stakes on the downwind
side of the plants. Some sources suggest that indeterminate and larger semi-determinate varieties be
pruned of all suckers (tiny leaves and stems in the crotches of larger stems) because they may steal
nourishment from the fruits. However, the Erie City Extension Service has shown that removing leaves
decreases photosynthetic production. Hand pollinate in greenhouses.

ALLIES: Some evidence-- cabbage
       Uncertain-- asparagus, basil, bee balm, borage, coriander, dill, goldenrod, mint,
       parsley, marigold, sage
COMPANIONS: *Brassicas*, carrot, celery, chive, melon, marigold, nasturtium, onion, pea, pepper
ENEMIES: cabbage (Note: might also be a companion), corn, dill, fennel, kohlrabi, potato, walnut

Training an Espallier

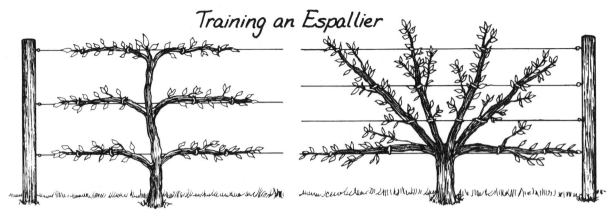

Six-arm Cordon

Fan

Grape Vines

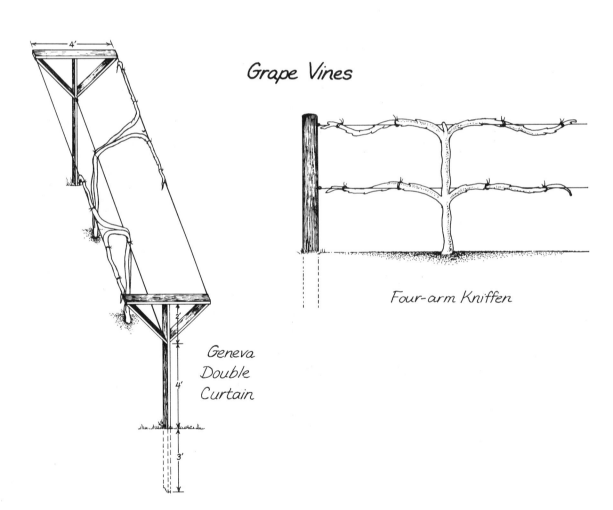

Geneva
Double
Curtain

Four-arm Kniffen

Fruits & Nuts

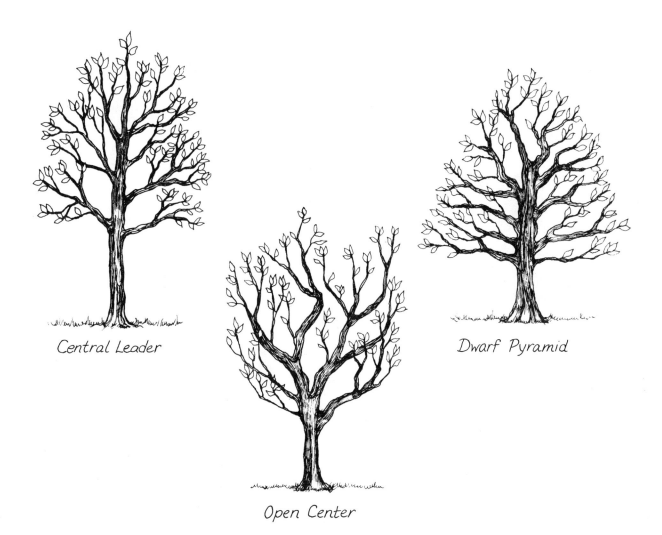

Central Leader

Open Center

Dwarf Pyramid

ALMOND VARIETIES

Nonpareil-- good pollinator, the best almond, large thin shell, can be shelled by hand, regular bearer, one of the most widely grown in the U.S., ripens early, hardiness similar to peach (Fowler, Van Well)

All-in-one Almond-- semidwarf, self-pollinating, soft-shelled, very good to excellent quality, pollinates Nonpareil, zones 6-9, (Fowler, Stark)

Garden Prince-- genetic dwarf, 10-12', self-fertile, low chill requirement, sweet and tasty kernels, bears young and heavily in climates without heavy February rains, zone 9 (Sonoma Apple, Stark)

Hall's Hardy-- up to 20', beautiful ornamental, good pollinator of others, late-blooming, good for the Northwest, most hardy almond. Bitter flavor can be leached out by boiling but we wouldn't recommend eating the nuts because they were suspected in one case of causing cyanic poisoning (however, we don't know how much he ate). This is self-pollinating, though has better yields when planted near a peach or other almond. Hardy through zone 6 (Burpee, Gurney's, Henry Field's, Northwoods, Raintree)

NOTES

Root Stocks: Almond seedlings grow slower than those grafted onto peach rootstock, but mature to a large height and produce well. They resist drought but are susceptible to crown rot, crown gall, and nematodes. Peach rootstocks produce rapidly growing trees that have a better survival rate than almond seedlings. Some are nematode resistant. All will need irrigation. Marianna 2624 is a good semidwarfing rootstock (see Plum Rootstock Chart). The Almond X Peach Hybrid is a good rootstock for poor soils as it's vigorous with deep roots.

Prunus dulcis   *Rosaceae (Rose)*   **ALMOND**

GROWTH CONDITIONS
Height: dwarf, 8-10'   semidwarf, 10-20'   standard, 20-30'
Spacing: dwarf, 8' semidwarf, 8-20'   standard, 24-30'
Pollination: Most need cross-pollination. The pollinate cultivar can be grafted to main cultivar.
Chilling Requirement: 300-500 hours below 45.
Bearing Age: 3-4 years
Root Depth: Very deep
pH: 6.0-6.5
Site: Full sun. South or south-east exposure. Can withstand poor soil.
Water: Medium. Water deeply and let roots dry out between applications. Watering in fall and
          winter is very important. Mature trees are drought resistant and prefer dry summers.
Fertilizer: Heavy feeder. Low N for trees under 2 years. Appropriate new growth is 6-10".
Side-dress: Apply compost in late autumn.
Training: Free-standing tree-- open center, vase   Espalier-- N/A
Pruning: Prune young trees minimally with little or no heading back, which delays bearing
          stimulates extra leaf growth. When more mature, thin out crowded or competing branches, as
          well as the short, stubby spurs which bear nuts.

PESTS: boxelder bug, brown almond mite, codling moth, filbertworm, leaf-footed bug, mite, navel
          orangeworm, nematode, peach twig borer
DISEASES: bacterial canker, brown rot, crown gall, crown rot, leaf blight, leaf scab, peach leaf curl

HARVEST: Unlike walnuts, as almonds mature the outer hull splits to expose the inner nut. As the
nuts dry they fall out of the split outer hull to the ground. Alternatively nuts can be knocked down onto
canvas sheets. Don't harvest until the hulls on the inner part of the tree split open, which will be last.
Spread nuts in a thin layer before hulling those that haven't fallen out of the hull. Unless wet, hull
immediately.

STORAGE REQUIREMENTS: Place hulled nuts in water. Remove rotten or diseased nuts that float.
Dry immediately at 110F. They're ready for storage when the kernels rattle in the shell, or, when
unshelled, the nutmeat snaps when bent. Avoid big piles of nuts which encourage rot.
Fresh or frozen, shelled or unshelled: Temp: below 40   Humidity: low Storage Life: 12+ mos.

OTHER GROWING NOTES: All almond trees, even the *dulcis* which are grown for nuts, are pretty
ornamentals. Their culture is very similar to the peach. Almonds bloom extremely early in the spring
with white or pink blossoms, and are even more susceptible than peaches to bud damage from spring
frosts. As a result, cold northern areas require hardy, late-blooming varieties. Before you plant, cultivate
the soil as deeply as possible for the almond's deep roots. Rain and high humidity during the bloom
season can interfere with pollination, reduce yields, and promote fungal and bacterial diseases. Also, in
humid summers the hulls may not split. If your area is noted for this type of spring or summer, almonds
may not be for you. Almonds thrive in long, dry summers supplemented by irrigation and can produce
nuts for up to 50 years.

ALLIES: Some evidence-- none
          Uncertain-- caraway, coriander, dill, wildflowers
ENEMIES: none

APPLE VARIETIES

EARLY (SUMMER APPLES)

Williams Pride (Co-op 23)-- very early, large red fruit, 1988 Purdue release, best flavor of disease resistant apples, immune to scab, resists mildew, cedar rust and fire blight, stores 1 month refrigerated, naturally moderate-sized tree, tested in zones 5-6 (Raintree, Rocky Meadow, Stark)

Jerseymac-- red fruit, one of the best early apples but bruises easily, susceptible to scab and blight, productive, naturally large tree (Hilltop, NYFT, Van Well, Windmill)

Redfree-- large bright red fruit, immune to scab and cedar rust, moderate resistance to mildew and blight, excellent flavor, naturally small tree (Adams, Raintree, Stark)

MIDSEASON

Royal Gala™, Imperial Gala™, and Scarlet Gala™-- yellow background with red-orange blush, excellent quality, considered one of the best early apples, firm, sweet, juicy, compact tree, prolific, heavy spur-bearing, hardy, excellent keeper, best on rootstocks and with cultural practices that maximize fruit size, susceptible to fire blight, zones 5-8 (Hilltop, Rocky Meadow, Stark, Van Well)

Gravenstein-- yellow with red stripes, old favorite, great flavor, vigorous, bears biennially, ideal for sauce & cider, infertile pollen, requires pollinizer, loved on the West Coast (widely available)

Jonafree-- red, good for fresh eating, immune to scab, resists fire blight and cedar apple rust, good keeper, high yields, vigorous and spreading tree, zones 5-8 (Adams, Hilltop, Stark)

Liberty-- red with yellow, McIntosh-type, resists scab, mildew, rust, fire blight, good dessert apple, naturally large tree, zones 4-8 (widely available)

Cox's Orange Pippin-- historical apple, good fresh, baked or as sauce, excellent for espalier, needs 600 hours or less chill, naturally medium-sized tree, hardy through zone 3 (Miller, NYFT, Northwoods, Raintree, Sonoma Apple, Windmill)

Freedom-- red with yellow, very resistant to scab, resists mildew, rust and fire blight, stores until January, one of the best for no-spray organic orchards, excellent pie apple, naturally large tree, zones 3-8 (Adams, Kelly, Miller, NYFT, Northwoods, Raintree, Windmill)

LATE ("Braeburn" and later bearers need about 150 frost-free days for fruit to mature)

Ashmead's Kernel-- historical yellow apple with orange-brown blush, russet, natively large tree, excellent flavor fresh or juiced, excellent keeper, resists mildew, tart when tree ripe, mellows with storage, naturally moderate-sized tree, hardy through zone 3 (Northwoods, Raintree, Rocky Meadow, Sonoma Apple, Southmeadow, Windmill)

Jonagold-- large yellow and red fruit, newer apple, cross between Jonathan and Golden Delicious, good taste fresh and in pies, stores until spring if kept at 31F, heavy yields, naturally large tree, zones 4-8 (widely available)

Golden Delicious-- universal pollinator, vigorous spreading tree, precocious, heavy crops, resists scab, crops well, susceptible to cedar apple rust, discovered in West Virginia (widely available)

Tydeman's Late Orange-- excellent storage apple, reaches full flavor around Christmas, some say has better flavor than Ashmead's Kernel, naturally moderate-sized tree (Southmeadow)

Braeburn-- yellowish with red blush, new from New Zealand, crisp, juicy, stores 6-12 months, bears young, manageable by homeowner because only moderately vigorous, susceptible to powdery mildew, doesn't appear susceptible to fire blight (Adams, Northwoods, Rocky Meadow, Stark)

Brown Russet-- very late, russet with patches of green and red, good fresh, stored or as sweet cider apple, resists scab and mildew, naturally moderate-sized tree (Raintree)

CRAB

Dolgo-- early, best all purpose crab, excellent pollinator for all apples, excellent ornamental, excellent jelly, high disease resistance, needs chill 400 hours or less, naturally small to moderate-sized tree, hardy through zone 1 (Hilltop, Northwoods, NYFT, Raintree, Southmeadow, Windmill)

NOTES

Rootstocks: see pages 76-77.

Malus pumila   *Rosaceae (Rose)*   **APPLE**

GROWTH CONDITIONS
Height: dwarf, 6-12'   semidwarf, 12-18'   standard, 20-40'
Spacing: dwarf, 8-20'   semidwarf, 15-18'   standard, 30-40'
Pollination: Most require cross-pollination.
Chilling Requirement: 900-1000 hours below 45, though some require less.
Bearing Age: dwarf & semidwarf, 2-3 years   standard, 4-8
Root Depth: 10' or more, with a spread 50% beyond drip line
pH: 6.5-7.0 (6.0-6.5 for bitter pit)
Site: South-east exposure.   Clay loam.   To espalier, some experts suggest in very hot
          summer climates siting apples on an eastern wall or slope to avoid sunburn.
Support Structures: Branches may need support when fruiting. Branch separators can increase yields.
Water: Medium
Fertilizer: Low N for young trees. Appropriate new growth is 6-14".
Side-dress: Apply compost in late autumn and work into soil.
Training: Free-standing-- central leader Wire-trained-- all cordons, espalier, fans, stepovers, palmettes
Pruning: Spur-types require little annual pruning since spurs bear for about 8 years, but each spring
          remove 1 out of 10 spurs and thin fruit by 10%. Tip-bearers fruit on 1-year old wood. For
          these, prune back some of the long shoots and some of the spurs. For bitter pit, a sign of
          unbalanced growth, at the end of the summer remove the most vigorous shoots.

PESTS: aphid, apple maggot, cankerworm, codling moth, European apple sawfly, European red mite,
          flea beetle, fruit worm, gypsy moth, leafhopper, leafroller, mice, oriental fruit moth,
          pearslug, plum curculio, potato leafhopper, scale, tent caterpillar, weevil, whitefly,
          white grub, woolly apple aphid
DISEASES: apple scab, baldwin spot, canker dieback, cedar apple rust, crown gall, crown rot, cytospora
          canker, fire blight, powdery mildew, sunscald

HARVEST: For summer apples pick fruit just before fully ripe, otherwise the apples become mealy.
In the fall, pick fruit only when fully ripe. Make sure you pick with the stems, or a break in the skin will
occur that will permit bacteria to enter and foster rot.

STORAGE REQUIREMENTS: Wrapping in oiled paper or shredded paper helps prevent scald. Some
apples stored over the winter develop a rich flavor that is excellent for pies. Israeli research shows that
summer apples keep better if held at high temperatures several days before storage.
Fresh: Temp: 32-40   Humidity: 80-90%   Storage life: 4-8 months
Preserved, taste (months): Can: good   Freeze: unknown   Dry: good (12+)

OTHER GROWING NOTES: Thousands of apple varieties have been grown since ancient times.
Many are lost to posterity, but more varieties of apple still exist today than of any other fruit. Breeding
for disease resistance has focussed on the apple more than other fruits, so organic orchardists may have
the greatest chance of success with this fruit. Crab apples are any apple smaller than 2" in diameter.
After the June drop and when the fruit is no more than 1" in diameter, thin to 8" apart, or remove about
10% of the total fruit. Also thin all clusters to just one fruit. The inclination of the apple branch is
thought to determine its fruitfulness: the more horizontal, the more fruit. U.S. researchers have shown
that shining red lights on apple trees for 15 minutes each night, beginning 2 weeks before harvest, delays
fruit drop for two weeks. Other researchers are experimenting with inoculating bare roots with hairy
root organism, previously thought to be a problem disease but now shown to promote early root growth
and fruiting. Watch for this to become available in future years.

ALLIES: Some evidence-- buckwheat, *phacelia* genus of herbs (e.g. California bluebells), *eryngium*
          genus of herbs (e.g. button snakeroot and sea holly), weedy ground cover
                    Uncertain-- dill, caraway, coriander, garlic, nasturtium, tansy, wildflowers, wormwood, vetch
ENEMIES: mature walnut trees, potato

APPLE ROOTSTOCKS *

Most growers now choose dwarf apples; standard trees grow very large, don't bear for years, and are difficult to harvest because of their height. To choose a rootstock you must know your soil type, drainage, and depth. Then consider the specific variety's natural growing habit and size, which affects how dwarfing a rootstock you need. In rich, fertile soil all rootstocks grow more vigorously than predicted and need extra spacing. Buy smaller trees when possible because they suffer less transplanting shock, and are more productive and vigorous.

Most nurseries don't offer a choice of rootstocks for a particular variety, but choice can be found between nurseries. The purpose of these charts is not to help you make an independent decision; it is to help you conduct an informed discussion with the nursery. We urge you to seek and follow the nursery growers' advice.

Names	Malling 27 EMLA 27/ M27	Poland 22 P22	Malling 9 EMLA 9/ M9	Malling 26 EMLA 26/ M26	MARK Mac-9	M9/111
Size (% of Standard)	mini-dwarf 15-30%	mini-dwarf 15-30%	dwarf 20-40%	dwarf 30-50%	dwarf 30-45%	dwarf 25-50%
Height	4-8'	5-6'	8-10'	8-14'	8-14'	10-15'
Width	2-8'	2-8'	8-10'	10-14'	8-12'	10-15'
Best Soil	clay loam	--	sandy & gr.loam	sandy & gr.loams	clay	--
Anchorage	poor/ stake	poor/ stake	poor/ stake	fair/might stake	good/no stake	good/no stake
Crown Rot	VR	--	VR	S	R	R
Wlly.Aphid	LR	--	S	S	S to LR	R
Nematodes	--	--	S	--	--	--
Fire Blight	R	--	VS	S	S	S (in early yrs)
Pdwr.Mildew	MR	--	MR	MR	--	--
Hardiness	L	VH	--	VH	VH	--
Drought	--	--	--	--	--	Tolerant
Precocious	P	--	VP	VP	P	--
Other	Remove fruit first 2 yrs. Stops growing when bears fruit. Good for espalier when grafted to vigorous varieties.	Roots are brittle. Union with some types is brittle when young.	Mice love this root stock, so use tree guard. Produces large fruit. Defruit or thin fruit in 1st 2 years to prevent loss of leader.	Can form root galls at graft union. Defruit or thin 1st 2 years to prevent loss of leader. Doesn't sucker much. Produces large fruit.	Open structure & roots well in stoolbeds. Hardy to zone 4 but not as hardy as M26.	Combines benefits of 111 and 9. Bury rootstock so MM111 part is underground and M9 part is exposed.

* We gratefully thank Robert Kourik for permission to reprint information on rootstocks from his book *Designing and Maintaining Your Edible Landscape Naturally* (see Bibliography).

APPLE ROOTSTOCKS, continued

R = Resistant   MR = Moderately Resistant
S = Susceptible   MS = Moderately Susceptible
L = Low Hardiness H = Hardy   VH = Very Hardy
P = Precocious (early bearing)   VP = Very Precocious

Names	M7a Malling VII EMLA 7	MM106 Merton- Malling 106	MM111 Merton- Malling 111	Other Notes
Size (% of Standard)	dwarf 40-60%	dwarf 55-85%	dwarf 65-85%	
Height	11-20'	14-21'	15-24'	
Width	12-16'	14-18'	15-20'	
Best Soil	most soils; avoid heavy clay	sandy loam; avoid poor drainage	all soils; can also tolerate wet soils	
Anchorage	good/no stake	fair to good	very good/no stake	
Crown Rot	L-MR	R	R	
Wlly.Aphid	LR	HR		
Nematodes	--	--		
Fire Blight	R	VR		
Pwdr.Mildew	--	S		
Hardiness	VH	LH	VH	
Drought	Tolerant	Tolerant	Tolerant	
Precocious	P	P	No	
Other	Susceptible to burr knot. Better than M26 on wet soils. Remove suckers each year.	Susceptible to burr knot. Good stock for spurs. Fumigate site for nematodes which spread union necros. & ringspot. Stake in hardpan soil.	Smaller harvest than a stock like M106, but still productive. Ideal for an interstem or under low vigor varieties.	Stark Bro's Nurseries cautions that the extremely dwarfing rootstocks (M27 & P22) won't do well in for most gardeners. Unless you're very experienced, use one of the other rootstocks. Miller Nurseries also notes that Malling 9 is very difficult for homeowners; its roots are shallow and brittle. It must be securely staked or the tree will blow over. The British Inst. of Hort. Research showed that wrapping M9 stems in July with black poly. film to 6" above ground will increase root production.

APRICOT VARIETIES

Harcot-- early ripening, freestone, firm and sweet, cold hardy, late blooming, vigorous, good resistance to perennial canker, bacterial spot and brown rot, self-fertile, Zones 5-8 (Kelly, Hilltop, NYFT, Northwoods, Windmill)

Sungold & Moongold-- early midseason, very cold hardy for the North, developed by the U. of Minnesota, recommended to pollinate each other, good fresh, canned or as jam, zones 3-8 (Gurney's, Miller)

Lisa Sweet-Kernel or Sweet Pit-- midseason, fruit and nut tree, edible kernel is sweet, easy to extract, stores well and tastes similar to an almond, juicy, tree is compact, hardy, vigorous, self-pollinating, zones 5-8 (Gurney's, Miller, Raintree)

Precious-- midseason, very hardy variety, original tree estimated over 100 years old, bears large crops even with cold winters, late frosts and spring temperature fluctuations, sweet and juicy fruit, kernel usually has sweet almond flavor, disease resistant, self-fertile (Windmill)

Manchurian Bush-- midseason, bush type, good for small areas, grows about 12', juicy, sweet, a good choice if you don't know rootstocks, very hardy, tolerates both heat and cold, good fresh, dried or as jam (Gurney's, St. Lawrence)

Aprium™-- late season, apricot-plum hybrid, self-fertile, medium-large apricot-sized fruit, clear yellow skin, tree can be maintained at 10', zones 6-9 (Northwoods, Raintree, Sonoma Apple, Stark)

Royal Blenheim-- late season, grown in California, needs warm, dry weather during bloom, medium to large fruit, good fresh, canned or dried, high yields, fruit is subject to pitburn in warmest springs, good pollinizer (Fowler, Sonoma Apple, Van Well)

Stark GoldenGlo-- late season, genetic dwarf, 4-6', productive, good dried or fresh (Stark)

NOTES

Rootstocks: Generally don't use peach rootstocks, because they're susceptible to peach tree borer, root knot and lesion nematodes, root winter injury, and uneven growth which weakens the graft. Try not to use plum rootstocks, those dwarfed on nanking cherry (P. Tomentosa), or sand cherry (P. Besseyi). While more tolerant of wet soil, these sucker continuously and cause a different fruit flavor. Apricot rootstock offers the best chance for tree survival, is resistant to nematodes, and has some resistance to peach tree borers.

Prunus armeniaca   *Rosaceae (Rose)*   **APRICOT**

GROWTH CONDITIONS
Height: dwarf, 6-7'   semidwarf, 12-15'   standard, 20-30'
Spacing: dwarf, 8-12'   semidwarf, 12-18'   standard, 25-30'
Pollination: Most are self-pollinating, but yields are higher with more than one variety.
Chilling Requirement: Very low, 350-900 hours, which results in early blooming.
Bearing Age: 3-9 years
Root Depth: 50-100% farther than drip line
pH: 6.0-6.5
Site: Not too rich or sandy. In the North plant 12-15' from the northern side of a building. This
       delays buds and minimizes late frost injury but ensures full summer sun. Avoid windy
       locations. Also see PEACH about hydrogen cyanide.
Water: Medium.
Fertilizer: Appropriate new growth on a young tree is 13-30", a bearing tree 10-18". Since the tree
       is naturally vigorous, go easy on N.
Side-dress: Apply compost or well-rotted manure mixed with wood ashes annually in the spring,
       before leaves appear.
Training: Free-standing-- open center, dwarf pyramid. In colder areas use central leader.
       Wire-trained-- fan
Pruning: If the tree bears fruit only in alternate years, prune heavily when over half of the flowers
       are blooming. Pruning aims to encourage new spurs, each of which bears fruit for about 3
       years. Prune yearly to encourage fruiting spurs. Remove wood 6 or more years old.

PESTS: aphid, cankerworm, cherry fruit sawfly, codling moth, gopher, gypsy moth caterpillar, mite,
       peach tree borer, plum curculio, white fly
DISEASES: bacterial canker, bacterial spot, black knot, brown rot, crown gall, cytospora canker, scab,
       verticillium wilt

HARVEST: When all green color is gone and the fruit is slightly soft, twist and gently pull upward. If
possible, harvest apricots when fully ripe. If plagued with animal problems, you may want to pick them
slightly green and ripen them at 40-50F.

STORAGE REQUIREMENTS: For canning, use only unblemished fruits or all fruits in the container
will turn to mush. For drying, split the apricot first and remove pit. If after drying the fruit is still softer
than leather, store in the freezer.
Fresh: Temp: 60-65 / 40-50   Humidity: Storage Life: a few days / 3 weeks
Preserved, taste (months):   Can: good (12+)   Freeze: after partially drying, excellent (12+)
                              Dry: good (12)   Jam: good (12+)

OTHER GROWING NOTES: Apricots are good additions to the orchard. They're pretty with glossy
green leaves, easily managed, and one of the most drought resistant fruit trees. They are, however,
vulnerable to winter damage and their buds are very susceptible to late frost damage (see Siting).
Apricots grow vigorously and require annual pruning and thinning. After the natural fruit drop in late
spring and when the fruit is about 1" in diameter, thin fruit to 3-4" apart. Summer temperatures over
95F will cause pit burn, a browning around the pit. Apricots enjoy long lives of about 75 years.

ALLIES: Some evidence-- alder, brambles, buckwheat, rye mulch, sorghum mulch, wheat mulch
       Uncertain-- caraway, coriander, dill, garlic, nasturtium, tansy, wildflowers, wormwood, vetch
ENEMIES: Persian melon, plum. Also don't plant where any of the following have grown in the
       previous 3 years: eggplant, pepper, potato, raspberry, strawberry, tomato

BLACKBERRY VARIETIES

TRAILING *(Rubus procerus)*

Dirksen-- early, thornless, trailing, very sweet, hardy, vigorous, resists leaf spot, mildew and anthracnose, zones 6-10 (Fowler, Henry Field's)

Hull-- midseason, thornless, trailing, very sweet, good fresh or in pies, hardy, zones 5-8 (Burpee, Nourse, Rayner)

Chester Thornless-- late season, trailing, large berry, productive, good fresh, frozen, canned, or as juice, firm, good keeping qualities, zones 5-8 (Burpee, Nourse, Raintree, Stark, Windmill)

UPRIGHT *(Rubus macropetalus)*

Darrow-- early crop with smaller fall crop, upright, bred in the North, one of the top crops in the Northeast, large berries, low acid fruit good for jelly, very cold hardy, zones 4-8 (Gurney's, Henry Field's, Kelly, Miller, Rayner, Stark)

Ebony King-- early, upright, large purplish berry, sweet, withstands temperatures to -20F, resists orange rust, zones 5-8 (Gurney's, Windmill)

Thornfree-- midseason, semi-upright, from the USDA, hardy, plants don't sucker, tart flavor good for jam, some disease resistance, zones 6-8 (Kelly, Miller, Stark, Van Well)

NOTES

Propagation: Erect blackberry-- by suckers. When dormant, dig up root suckers no closer than 6" to mother plant. Thornless and trailing-- tip layering. Late in the season (August-September) bend and bury the primocane tips 4" deep in loose soil. In the spring cut off the cane 8" from the ground and dig up the new plants.

Rubus (2 species)   *Rosaceae (Rose)*   **BLACKBERRY**

GROWTH CONDITIONS
Height: 4-10' when pruned
Spacing: Erect and Semierect Blackberry-- 2-3' in a row (suckers/new canes fill out row)
    Trailing Blackberry-- 6-12' in a row (no suckers, but canes grow very long)
Pollination: Self-pollinating.
Chilling Requirement: Hours needed depend on the variety.
Bearing Age: 2 years
Root Depth: More than 12"
pH: 5.0-6.0
Site: Full sun. Rich loam. Due to verticillium wilt, avoid planting where nightshade family plants
    were grown in the last 3 years. Plant at least 300 ft away from wild brambles which harbor
    pests and diseases, and from raspberries to prevent cross-pollination.
Water: Medium. Drip irrigation is essential to avoid water on the berries, which is absorbed and
    dilutes their flavor. Water regularly because of vulnerability to water stress.
Mulch: In summer apply 4-8" of organic mulch. In winter apply 4-6" of compost.
Fertilizer: In spring apply well-rotted manure or compost before canes break dormancy.
Training: A trellis is very important for disease and pest reduction, quality fruit, and easy harvest.
    For erect blackberries use a 4' top wire, and for trailing blackberries a 5' top wire. Fan out
    canes and tie with cloth strips.
Pruning: After harvest or in spring, cut out old canes done bearing. Erect blackberries-- thin to 5-
    6 canes per row-ft. To encourage branching, when primocanes are 33-40" cut off the top 3-4"
    and, late next winter, cut the lateral branches back to 8-12" long. Trailing blackberries-- thin
    to 10-14 canes per hill. Don't prune in the first year. In late winter cut canes back to 10'.

PESTS: caneborer, mite, raspberry root borer, strawberry weevil, whitefly, white grub
DISEASES: anthracnose, botrytis fruit rot, cane blight, crown gall, powdery mildew, rust, septoria
    leaf spot, verticillium wilt

HARVEST: When berries slide easily off without pressure, harvest into very small containers so berries
on the bottom won't be crushed. After harvest, cut back floricanes to the ground. Burn or dispose of
all cut canes for disease control.

STORAGE REQUIREMENTS: Freeze within 2 days by spreading out berries on cookie sheets and
freezing. When rock hard store in heavy freezer bags. When refrigerated they keep 4-7 days.
Fresh, taste (months): Can: excellent as jams (12+)   Freeze: excellent (6) Dry: unknown

OTHER GROWING NOTES: Bramble fruits are very easy to grow. The key to good yields is
adequate spacing, light, and, because of shallow roots, good weed control and thick mulch. Rather than
several short close rows which will limit berry development to only the upper cane parts, plant one long
narrow row which will produce berries to the bottom of the canes. Blackberries are biennial. First year
green stems, primocanes, bear only leaves. Two-year old brown stems, floricanes, produce fruit. Upright
or erect canes are shorter while trailing varieties, also known as dewberries in the South, grow flexible
canes as long as 10'. Blackberries are usually hardy to Zones 5-8; upright varieties are the hardiest.

ALLIES: Some evidence-- grape
    Uncertain-- none
COMPANIONS: If berries are planted down the center of a 3' bed, plant beans or peas in the first
    summer to keep the bed in production, and also to add organic matter and N to soil.
ENEMIES: black walnut, and all members of nightshade family due to transmittal of verticillium wilt.

BLUEBERRY VARIETIES

NORTHERN AND ORNAMENTALS
Highbush *(Vaccinium acorymbosum)*
Bluetta-- very early, small-medium berry, 10-20 lbs/plant, compact, spreading, 3-5', good ornamental due to low stature, zones 5-7 (Hartmann's)

Blueray-- early midseason, large berry, 10-20 lbs/plant, very sweet, leading U-pick, upright, 4-6', excellent ornamental, zones 4-7 (Fowler, Hartmann's, Miller, NYFT)

Bluecrop-- midseason, large berry, 10-20 lbs/plant, upright, 4-6', very hardy, drought resistant, leading highbush, excellent ornamental, zones 4-7 (widely available)

Elliot-- late, small-medium berry, 10-20 lbs/plant, one of highest yielding blueberries, very tart until 60% of fruit are ripe, upright, 5-7', good ornamental, zones 4-7 (Hartmann's, Raintree)

Patriot-- early, large berry, 10-20 lbs/plant, upright, 4-6', resists Phytophthera cinnomomi, good ornamental, very cold hardy, zones 3-7 (Fowler, Hartmann's, Henry Field's, Miller)

Northblue-- midseason, large berry, 3-7 lbs/plant, 20-30", best with snow protection, good ornamental, very cold hardy, zones 3-7 (Hartmann's, Miller, Northwoods, NYFT, Raintree)

Lowbush *(Vaccinium angustifolium)*
Vaccinium Angustifolium-- Maine wild blueberry, ornamental and commercial uses, 6-18", spreads rapidly once established, excellent plant, zones 3-7 (Hartmann's)

Tophat-- very beautiful and one of the best ornamentals, 20" high and 24" breadth, medium berry, profuse blooms, cold hardy, bonsai type, zones 4-7 (Hartmann's)

Wells Delight-- late, creeping, 5-8", evergreen similar to holly, excellent low maintenance ground cover, zones 5-7 (Hartmann's, Raintree)

SOUTHERN AND ORNAMENTALS
Highbush: All Southern highbush are self-pollinating and ripen 20-30 days earlier than Rabbiteye. Low chill varieties can be grown farthest South.

Sharpblue-- early, large berry, 8-16 lbs/plant with irrigation, vigorous, 5-6', needs little chill, very good ornamental, zones 7-10 (Hartmann's)

Challenger-- early midseason, medium berry, good quality and attractive fruit, slender and upright, 6', needs little chill, good ornamental, zones 6-10 (Hartmann's)

Sunshine-- late, medium berry, 5-10 lbs/plant, very hardy but needs little if any chill, excellent patio or pot culture, excellent southern ornamental, zones 6-10 (Hartmann's)

Rabbiteye *(Vaccinium ashei)*: Pollinate with another in same maturation group.
Climax-- early midseason, large berry, 8-22 lbs/plant, very good quality, tall and spreading, 6-10', leading pollinator, good ornamental, zones 7-9 (Hartmann's)

Bonitablue-- early midseason, large berry, 8-22 lbs/plant with irrigation, excellent quality, stores well, very sweet, upright, 6-10', very good ornamental, zones 8-9 (Hartmann's)

Woodard-- midseason, very large berry, 8-16 lbs/plant, good in the northern South, good fresh or processed, not good commercial, good ornamental, zones 7-9 (Hartmann's, Stark)

Choice-- late, small berry, 8-12 lbs/plant when irrigated, good quality, used in process market, upright, some spreading, 8-12', best Rabbiteye ornamental, zones 7-9 (Hartmann's)

Powderblue-- late, large berries, 8-14 lbs/plant when irrigated, very good quality and flavor, upright, vigorous, 8-12', very good ornamental, zones 7-9 (Hartmann's)

Tifblue-- late, large berry, 8-25 lbs/plant, vigorous, 8-14', excellent in Georgia and Texas, good ornamental, zones 7-9 (Hartmann's, Stark)

NOTES

Propagation: layering-- bend and bury the tip of a lower branch and cover with soil. Rooting hormone helps. Next spring cut off the cane 8" from the ground and dig up the new plant.

Vaccinium (3 species)   *Ericaceae (Heath)*   **BLUEBERRY**

GROWTH CONDITIONS
Height: Lowbush, 2-4'   Highbush, 5-6'
Spacing: Lowbush, 3-4'   Highbush, 7-8'   Rows: 10'
Pollination: All varieties require cross-pollination.
Chilling Requirement: 650-800 hours below 45 for Low and Highbush, 200 hours for Rabbiteye
Bearing Age: 3-8 years
Root Depth: Very shallow, top 14" of soil
pH: 4.0-5.6
Site: Full sun. Choose a site where plants won't be disturbed, away from paths, roads, driveways.
Water: Heavy and evenly moist
Mulch: 3-6" acid mulches such as pine needles, peat moss, shredded oak leaves, or rotted sawdust.
Fertilizer: Apply 1" of compost under mulch. Avoid high N. Avoid aluminum sulphate or urea. If you
        must, apply ammonium sulphate, 1/2 oz in year 1, and 1 oz for every additional year thereafter.
Pruning: Don't prune until the third year after planting because blueberries fruit near the tips of 2-year
        and older branches. To prune, cut out diseased tips and, for larger fruit, cut branches back to
        where buds are widely spaced. Also cut out weak and diseased branches, or canes as they're
        called by commercial growers. Every 2 or 3 years you may need to cut out the 5-year or older
        canes back to the main stem. Don't leave any stubs as suckers will be weaker than new canes
        growing from the roots. A good rule of thumb is to allow one branch per year of age plus one
        or two vigorous new branches. If new branch growth on an old bush (15-years) is thinner than
        1/4", cut out half of the new canes.

PESTS: apple maggot, birds, cherry fruitworm, fruit fly, mite, plum curculio, weevil
DISEASES: bacterial canker, cane gall, crown gall, mummy berry, *Phytophthera cinnomomi*, powdery
        mildew. Many problems are due to not enough acidity.

HARVEST: Leave berries on the bush 5-10 days after they turn blue. They're fully ripe when slightly
soft, come easily off the bush, and are sweet. Pick directly into the storage bowl or container so that as
little as possible of their protective wax is removed.

STORAGE REQUIREMENTS: Don't wash the fruit if you're going to freeze them.
Fresh: Temp: 35-40 (refrigerated)   Humidity: 80-90%   Storage Life: 7 days
Preserved, taste (months): Can: fair   Freeze: good (6) Preserves: good (12+)

OTHER GROWING NOTES: Blueberries lack abundant root hairs and have shallow, underdeveloped
roots concentrated in the top 14" of soil. As a result, regular watering and thick mulch are critical to
keep the weeds down. A very acid pH is necessary to enable the plant to extract iron and nitrogen from
the soil. Most blueberry problems are caused by stress relating to pH, under or over fertilization, and
under or over watering. Plant 2-year old bushes. When your plants arrive, do not put them in water.
Follow directions and "heel in" until ready to plant. Try inoculating the roots with the beneficial
mycorrhizal fungi, which increases yields significantly. Lowbush varieties are grown primarily in New
England, highbush throughout the nation, and rabbiteye only in the South and West. Lowbush and
rabbiteye require another variety for cross-pollination; highbush types don't, but yields increase with
cross-pollination. To encourage root growth, remove all blossoms for a full 2-3 years. The delayed
harvest will pay you back in higher yields and healthier plants. Blueberries mature about 50-60 days
from pollination. For areas prone to late spring frosts, blueberries are a good choice because of good
frost resistance. Consider adding blueberries to your landscape for they can be beautiful ornamentals.

ALLIES: Some evidence-- none
        Uncertain-- none
COMPANIONS and ENEMIES: none

Montmorency-- early, the standard of sour cherries, very large, bright red fruit, resists cracking, tart, semi-dwarfish tree, hardy to zone 2-3 depending on rootstock (widely available)

North Star-- midseason, genetic dwarf only 6-7', small red fruit, more concentrated flavor than Montmorency, good for pies and jam, self-fertile, hardy, high yields, resistant to brown rot, great for the home garden due to size, zones 3-8 (widely available)

Meteor-- late, natural semidwarf, 10-14', considered superior to Montmorency, very hardy, large fruit, good fresh, canned, frozen, baked or juiced, hardy to zone 2 (Gurney's, Hilltop, Northwoods, NYFT, Rocky Meadow, Windmill)

NOTES

If possible buy certified virus-free trees.

Root Stocks: Mahaleb (Prunus mahaleb) rootstock is good for sour cherries. It produces trees 60-75% of standard size that are susceptible to root rot and gophers, less long-lived than Mazzard, but more resistant than Mazzard to crown gall, drought, and cold injury. Colt rootstock produces semidwarfs, about 80% of full size, that may be more resistant to bacterial diseases and crown rot. North Star rootstock also produces semidwarfs that are hardy and resistant to wet soil. For other sour cherry rootstocks, especially GH 61-1, see SWEET CHERRY.

Prunus cerasus   *Rosaceae (Rose)*   **Sour CHERRY**

GROWTH CONDITIONS
Height: dwarf, 6-10'   semidwarf, 12-18'   standard, 15-20'
Spacing: dwarf, 8-10'   semidwarf, 18-20'   standard, 20'
Pollination: All sour types are self-pollinating.
Chilling Requirement: 800-1200 hours below 45.
Bearing Age: 2-7 years
Root Depth: 50% beyond dripline
pH: 6.0-6.5
Site: Full sun to partial shade. A Southern exposure or 12' from north-facing walls to delay blooming.
    Well drained soil and good air circulation. Likes 4' of top soil. Don't plant on former
    apricot, cherry or peach sites; when waterlogged, their roots release hydrogen cyanide
    which may linger and hinder growth. Also don't plant between other fruit trees,
    because cherries bear at a time others may need to be sprayed.
Water: Heavy and even supply. Cherries are especially sensitive to water stress.
Fertilizer: Low N until 2 years old. Appropriate new growth is 12-24" when young, and 6-12" bearing.
Training: Free-standing-- central leader or open center. Wire-trained-- fan-trained against a south
    or north-facing wall, using the same method as for peaches. All sizes of sour cherries are
    suitable for training because they're not vigorous growers.
Pruning: The lowest branch should be about 2' off the ground and limbs about 8' apart. Both sour
    and sweet cherries bear on spurs as well as 1-year old wood. Sour cherries, however, produce
    on the 1-year wood several adjacent fruit blossoms, which causes future bare spaces on the
    wood without foliage. If there are too many of these lateral flower buds, trim 1-2" off the
    branch ends in June to stimulate leaf buds. Sour cherry spurs bear 2-5 years.

PESTS: apple maggot, blackberry fruit fly, birds, cherry fruit fly, cherry fruit sawfly, codling moth, peach
    leaf curl, peach tree borer, plum curculio
DISEASES: bacterial gummosis, black knot, black rot, brown rot, cherry leaf spot, crown rot, peach leaf
    curl, mildew, peach leaf curl, verticillium wilt

HARVEST: Wait to pick until the fruit is fully ripe, which is when the flesh slides off the stem leaving
the pit behind.

STORAGE REQUIREMENTS: Use immediately if possible. Freeze sour cherries immediately.
Fresh: Temp: 34-40   Humidity: high   Storage Life: soft flesh, 7 days   firm flesh, 2-3 weeks
Preserved: Can: both sweet & sour   Freeze: sour only

OTHER GROWING NOTES: Sour cherries are the easiest cherries to grow because they're more
tolerant than sweet cherries of cold winters and hot humid summers. They also are less vigorous and
therefore require less pruning. Cherries live about 30-35 years. For insect egg control apply dormant
oil spray every spring before the leaf buds open, covering all areas of the trunk and branches.

ALLIES: Some evidence-- alder, brambles, buckwheat rye mulch, sorghum mulch, wheat mulch
    Uncertain-- caraway, coriander, dill, garlic, nasturtium, tansy, wildflowers, wormwood, vetch
COMPANIONS: alfalfa, bromegrass, clover
ENEMIES: none

SWEET CHERRY VARIETIES

RED

Starkrimson-- early, genetic dwarf, 12-14', self-pollinating, large fruit, very sweet, high yields, zones 5-8 (Stark)

Compact Van-- early, fruit similar to Bing, highly crack resistant, very hardy, large crops, excellent crops, zones 5-7 (Windmill)

Compact Stella-- midseason, genetic dwarf, 8-14', self-pollinating, dark red fruit, zones 6-7 (Henry Field's, Miller, Stark, Windmill)

Lambert-- midseason, flavor and looks of the Bing cherry, later season so more resistant to cracking, excellent fresh or canned, hardy, high chill requirement, pollinated by Rainier (Hilltop, Northwoods, Sonoma Apple, Van Well)

Compact Lambert-- midseason, same as Lambert, but only 7-10', suited for pot culture or in the ground, thrives in Northwest (Northwoods, Raintree)

Parkhill-- midseason, purplish soft flesh, excellent flavor, recommended by Southmeadow for the amateur home gardener, believed a seedling of Lambert (Southmeadow)

Lapins Sweet Cherry-- late midseason, self-pollinating, Bing-type fruit, crack resistant, firm, meaty texture, from British Colombia, one of best of the Bing-type for home orchards (Stark)

Spate Braun (Late Brown)-- late, very large, very sweet, crack resistant, considered the best garden cherry for its size and texture, high yields (Southmeadow)

YELLOW

Rainier-- early, large fruit with red blush, like Royal Ann, firm yellow-white flesh, resists splitting, productive, spreading tree (Hilltop, Northwoods, NYFT, Rocky Meadow, Sonoma)

Stark Gold-- late, unusual yellow fruit with unique, tangy flavor, survived -30F, attracts very few birds, crack resistant, pollinate with any other sweet cherry, zones 5-7 (Stark)

Compact Royal Ann-- genetic dwarf, large, light yellow cherry with red blush, firm, good flavor, can maintain under 10' (Raintree)

DUKE CHERRIES

The Duke cherry, not widely grown since the beginning of the 20th century, is still available. They're hardier than sweet cherries and excellent substitutes. Their fruit is yellow-red, soft and juicy. Pollination is less difficult than with sweet cherries. If you can't grow sweet cherries because the climate is too cold, you might try these. (Windmill)

NOTES

If possible select certified virus-free trees.

Root Stocks: Mazzard (Prunus avium) rootstock is good for sweet cherries. It is a vigorous grower, producing large trees, is slow to bear, and tolerant of wet soil. Mazzard is particularly good in the West, Northwest, and areas of the East where moisture is sufficient and winter hardiness is not a problem. GM 61 is a new rootstock from Belgium and is considered by some to be the best overall dwarfing stock for cherry. Its trees are 50-60% of standard size, can be maintained below 15', are hardy to at least -20F, spreading, precocious, do well in heavier soils, and are good for both sweet and sour. Trees propagated on GM61 are available from Northwoods, Raintree, Rocky Meadow, and Stark Nurseries. For more on other rootstocks, see SOUR CHERRY.

Prunus avium   *Rosaceae (Rose)*   **Sweet CHERRY**

GROWTH CONDITIONS
Height: dwarf, 6-12'   semidwarf, 10-15'   standard, 25-40'
Spacing: dwarf, 8-10'   semidwarf, 15-18'   standard, 25-30'
Pollination: All sweet, except "Stella", must be cross-pollinated, although not all are compatible because of different bloom times. Further pollination difficulties arise because early spring flowers are receptive for only about 1 week. Also, a late frost and/or a wet spring can interfere with bee activity.
Chilling Requirement: 800-1200 hours below 45
Bearing Age: 2-7 years
Root Depth: 50% beyond dripline
pH: 6.0-6.5
Site: Full sun. Needs light, well-drained soil for successful survival. See other notes for Sour Cherry.
Water: Heavy and even supply. Cherries are particularly susceptible to water stress.
Fertilizer: Low N until 2 years old. Appropriate new growth is 22-36" when young, and 8-12" bearing.
Training: Free-standing-- central leader. Wire-trained-- fan-trained against a south wall where the summer sun is not blistering hot, or 12-15' away from a north wall. Only dwarf sweet cherries are suitable for training.
Pruning: The lowest branch should be about 2' off the ground and limbs about 8' apart. Sweet cherries bear on spurs as well as 1-year old wood. Sweet cherry spurs produce for 10-12 years, so exercise extreme caution to not damage these when harvesting or pruning.

PESTS: See SOUR CHERRY
DISEASES: See SOUR CHERRY

HARVEST: Wait until the fruit is fully ripe. Gently pull on the stem and twist upward. Be extremely careful to not damage or rip off spurs, as these bear for 10 or more years.

STORAGE REQUIREMENTS: Use immediately if possible. If not possible, place in an airtight container like a crisper, and refrigerate. There is a controversy over whether or not sweet cherries store best with or without their stems; decide for yourself.
Fresh: Temp: 34-40   Humidity: high   Storage Life: soft flesh, 7 days   firm flesh, 2-3 weeks
Preserved: Can: good   Freeze: not good

OTHER GROWING NOTES: Standard sweet cherries grow very large and require consistent pruning in order to be managed properly. Cherries live about 30-35 years. For insect egg control apply dormant oil spray every spring before the leaf buds open, ensuring that all areas of the trunk and branches are coated.

ALLIES: See SOUR CHERRY
COMPANIONS: See SOUR CHERRY
ENEMIES: none

CHESTNUT VARIETIES

CHINESE and CHINESE HYBRIDS: Suited for East of the Rocky Mts., where blight is widespread.

Au-leader-- grafted Chinese variety, large nut, good flavor, hardy, disease-resistant, grows only 25-35', zones 4-9 (Stark)

Crane-- 32 nuts/lb, flavor and keeping quality is excellent when cured, good annual bearer, good anywhere from north FL to the Great Lakes region, hardy to -20, (Nolin River)

Douglass-- Chinese-American hybrid, well-filled nuts, good flavor, available as graft or seedling from different nurseries, zones 5-7 (Grimo, Windmill)

Eaton-- ornamental and high quality nut tree, 30-40 nuts/lb, good texture, flavor and sweetness. You will need 2-3 trees for a good crop. Originally from CT. Good from northern FL to MI and WI, zones 5-6 (Nolin River)

Layeroka-- Chinese-European hybrid, combines blight resistance of Chinese with timber and nut quality of European, very hardy, good for commercial orchards, early ripening, available as graft or seedling from different nurseries, not a very big nut, zones 6-7 (Grimo, Northwoods, Raintree, Saginaw, Windmill)

Manchurian-- Chinese-American hybrid, flavor and size nut of American, vigorous grower, hardy to -28F (Miller)

Sleeping Giant-- good quality nut, also good for timber, spreading crown, originally from CT, not prone to frost problems (Nolin River)

AMERICAN (*C. dentata*): suited only for the Northwest where blight is not a problem

American seedlings-- excellent, huge timber tree (Grimo, Northwoods, Raintree, St.Lawrence)

EUROPEAN (*C. sativa*): suited only for areas west of the Rocky Mountains

European seedlings-- planted widely on West coast (Northwoods)

NOTES

Most seedlings do better than grafted trees in the northern zones (5-6).

Castanea mollisima   Fagaceae (Beech)   # Chinese CHESTNUT

GROWTH CONDITIONS
Height: 30-40'   Breadth: 20'
Spacing: 8' if thinned out in 5 years; 20' if thinned out to 40' in 20 years; 40' if not thinned
Pollination: All require cross-pollination. Plant two of the same or different variety.
Chilling Requirement: Low number of hours are required for nut blossoms development.
Bearing Age: 3-4 years
Root Depth: Deep
pH: 5.0-6.0
Site: Full sun. Preferred soil is light and sandy but it can be rocky or silty as long as it isn't alkaline
        or very dry. Soil must be very well-drained. Avoid frost pockets, areas that are subject to soil
        compaction, and sites with potential disruption of the root system.
Water: Medium. However, established trees are fairly drought resistant.
Fertilizer: Medium feeder. Low N for trees under 2 years; you don't want rapid growth when the
        tree is young. Unlike some nuts, throughout its life the chestnut likes to be fed and produces
        better quality nuts with regular feeding. If you want to add lime in order to add calcium, make
        sure the pH is 5.0-5.5 initially, as chestnut thrives in acid soil.
Side-dress: Apply compost in late autumn, or rotted manure and leaf mold in the early spring.
Training: Free-standing-- central leader.   Wire-trained-- N/A.
Pruning: Prune young trees minimally, only that which is needed to train the tree to a single trunk
        and basic scaffold. Too much pruning stimulates extra vegetative growth and delays bearing.

PESTS: chestnut weevil, gall wasp (in GA), mite, nut curculio, squirrel
DISEASES: chestnut blight, blossom end rot, oak wilt

HARVEST: Use thick gloves to protect your hands from the spines of the outer chestnut hull. To minimize daily gathering, when the burs begin to crack open in late summer pick or knock down small bunches of burs onto a harvest sheet. For final ripening store them at 55-65F for about 1 week or until the burs split open. If unable to pick them in bulk, you must gather fallen nuts each day, for chestnuts are particularly susceptible to rapid degradation on the ground by fungi and bacteria.

STORAGE REQUIREMENTS: The chestnut can be eaten raw if cured first to maximize the nut's free sugar. To cure, dry de-burred nuts in a shady, warm, dry place for 1 to 3 days until the nut texture is spongy. To roast, cut an X in the shell and cook at 400F for 15 minutes. If not eaten immediately, store uncured nuts in a cold place that is either dry or has high humidity but no free moisture. A good method is to mix freshly harvested and dehulled nuts with dry peat moss, pack in plastic bags, seal, and refrigerate. You can also dry and grind nuts into a baking flour.
Fresh, uncured: Temp: 32   Humidity: high but no free moisture   Storage Life: 6-12 months

OTHER GROWING NOTES: The Chinese chestnut is an attractive, globe-shaped landscape shade tree. It also offers rot-resistant timber and regular annual crops of one of the sweetest nuts. In early summer the tree is decked with pretty (but odiferous) yellow catkins, and its glossy, dark green serrated leaves cling late into the fall. Chestnut fungal blight swept through North America in the early 1900's, destroying nearly all American (*C. dentata*) and European (*C. sativa*) chestnuts, both of which are now planted on the West coast where blight is less a problem. The Chinese chestnut, introduced in 1853, resists blight and grows well in zones 5-8 in a wide variety of soil and climatic conditions, although it's grown primarily in the East and Northwest. Like the peach it is hardy to about -20F, but unlike the peach late blooming permits it to escape spring frosts. For rot-resistant poles, chestnuts can be coppiced: cut down the tree to cause suckers to grow, let suckers grow to desired pole thickness, and cut again. Chestnuts can live 50 or more years.

ALLIES, COMPANIONS, and ENEMIES: none

FILBERT VARIETIES

EUROPEAN species *(C. avellana)*: commonly known as filberts. These are a major commercial crop in the Northwest, grow best in maritime climates, and are the kind of nut usually found in supermarkets. They have been occasionally grown in the East, but generally are poorly suited there due to its great susceptibility to Eastern filbert blight.

Butler-- good pollinizer for **Ennis**, medium-large nut, good flavor, smooth kernel, moderate bud mite resistance, very hardy (Northwoods)

Ennis-- European, replaces the prime commercial **Barcelona** cultivar, more productive, very few blanks, larger nut, smooth kernel, moderate hardiness and moderate bud mite resistance (Northwoods, Raintree)

Royal Filbert-- European, large nuts, thin shells, pollinate with Barcelona, zones 5-8, best for the East (Miller, Stark)

AMERICAN species *(C. americana)*: most often known as hazelnuts. Native, wild hedgerows grow throughout the northern U.S. and southern Canada. American hazelnuts are usually smaller than the European nut. The American species serves as a host for Eastern filbert blight fungus but is very tolerant of its attack.

American-- bear early, less than 15' tall, pretty ornamental, good nuts, yields better with 2 (Kelly)

HAZELBERTS: a cross between the European filbert and American hazelnut. These combine the large European nut size with American hardiness and early ripening.

Fingerlakes Super Hardy-- large nut, productive, early bearing, hardy, resists aphids and bud mites (Miller)

Gellatly-- early bearing, hardy (Grimo)

Grimo-- productive tree, available grafted, layered or seedling (Grimo, Windmill)

Hambleton-- well-filled nut, available grafted or layered (Windmill)

Turkish Trazel (cross of *C. colurna* and *C. avellana*)-- excellent small shade tree and nut producer, shapely, good flavor, only 20-30' tall, hardy to -25F (Gurney's, Raintree)

NOTES

When buying a filbert or hazelnut, make sure it is intended to be a nut-bearing tree. Many are grown only as ornamentals and may be poor nut bearers. Nuts from grafted or layered trees are generally higher quality than those from seedling trees.

Corylus (several species)   *Betulaceae (Birch)*   Hazelnut or FILBERT

GROWTH CONDITIONS
Height: 20'   Breadth: 15'
Spacing: 15-20' for trees   3-5' for hedges
Pollination: All need cross-pollination.
Chilling Requirement: Medium-high hours
Bearing Age: 2-4 years
Root Depth: Unlike other nut trees, this has no tap root.
pH: 6.5
Site: Full sun in maritime climates. Partial shade in very sunny, hot climates. In the East choose a
        northern, cold exposure to delay premature bloom. Can adapt to clay and sand, but prefers
        deep, fertile, well-drained soil. Must avoid low frost pockets or poorly drained areas.
Water: Medium. Water well in times of bad drought. In maritime climates like the Northwest mature
        trees rarely need watering. Sawdust mulch helps keep moisture in the soil.
Fertilizer: Heavy feeder, but do not fertilize unless foliage is pale and growth is slow. Appropriate
        new growth is 6-9".
Side-dress: Apply compost in late autumn and organic mulch in early spring.
Training: Free-standing-- open center.   Wire-trained-- N/A.
Pruning: To grow a shrub, cut excessive sucker growth yearly. For a tree, prune to establish a central
        leader and basic scaffold, and remove all suckers. Nuts develop on 1-year-old wood, so prune
        lightly every year to stimulate new growth. Make only thinning-out cuts where branches are
        cut back to their base, not in half or stubbed off.

PESTS: blue jay, filbert bud mite, filbertworm, filbert weevil, squirrel
DISEASES: crown gall, Eastern filbert blight, filbert bacterial blight, powdery mildew

HARVEST: Nuts usually turn brown and ripen by late summer, but an immature husk, shaped like a
barely opened daffodil blossom, prevents them from dropping for almost another month. The nut is ripe
when, if pressed, it readily turns in the husk. When ripe, you can either hand harvest the husks, or wait
until nuts drop to the ground and risk competing with the squirrels and birds.

STORAGE REQUIREMENTS: Place hulled nuts in water, and remove rotten and diseased nuts that
float to the top. Dry and cure by spreading nuts in one layer in a cool, dry, well-ventilated place for
several weeks. They're ready for storage when the kernels rattle in the shell, or, when unshelled, the
nutmeat snaps when bent. Avoid big piles of nuts which encourage rot.
Fresh, shelled/unshelled: Temp: 65-70/34-40   Humidity: low   Storage Life: several weeks/months
Frozen, shelled: Temp: frozen   Humidity: N/A   Storage Life: 12+ months

OTHER GROWING NOTES: Filberts, also known as hazelnuts, are unusual because they can be
grown as shrubs, hedgerows, or trees. An ideal size for home growers, they are generally hardy.
However, very early blooming renders them very susceptible to late frosts. In the Northwest, they never
go fully dormant. Filberts tend to bear in alternate years, depending on how much new wood was
produced and how much was pruned out the prior year. In areas that are subject to temperatures of 5F
or lower they do not produce nuts consistently. In the first 2 years protect young tree trunks from
sunscald. Filberts produce numerous suckers that are easily used for propagation and good for coppice
management (see Chestnut). Delicious in baked goods, filberts are also high vitamin and protein snacks.

ALLIES: Some evidence-- none
        Uncertain-- none
COMPANIONS: none
ENEMIES: none

AMERICAN -- Pure strains are rich in pectin, best for jelly, and renowned for a "foxy" flavor (cloying sweet like the Concord) that, if possible, wine-makers avoid. Newer hybrids are good fresh and for wine.

Red

Swensen-- very early, good for Northern states, hardy to -40F with occasional winter injury, for table and wine, good for cold storage, zones 3-7 (NYFT, St.Lawrence, Raintree, Windmill)

Reliance-- early, seedless, fruity, high yields, stores to 3 months, hardy to -10F without protection, resists anthracnose, black rot, powdery & downy mildew, good fresh, zones 4-8 (Burpee, Gurney's, Kelly, Miller, NYFT, Raintree, Stark)

Canadice-- early, seedless, very good flavor, high yields, keeps on vine a long time, very disease resistant, hardy to -15F without protection, for table, jelly, or wine (widely available)

Vanessa-- early, seedless, high quality, vinifera character, hangs in compact clusters, from Vineland Ontario Station, has survived -25F (NYFT, Raintree, Southmeadow, Windmill)

Einset-- midseason, high yields, stores well, resists botrytis, flavor has a hint of strawberries, good fresh or dried as raisins, hardy to -5F, zones 5-8 (NYFT, Raintree)

Saturn-- midseason, excellent flavor, high yields, good fresh or as dessert wine, hardy, disease resistant, hardy to -5F without protection, zones 5-8 (Miller, NYFT, Raintree, Stark)

Catawba-- very late, high vigor, susceptible to mildew, keeps up to 2 months, for wine, juice, jelly and also table, hardy to -10F, zones 5-8 (Burpee, Miller, Southmeadow, Windmill)

White

Himrod-- early, low yields, very vigorous, great for home garden, stores well, excellent fresh flavor, good for raisins, hardy to 0F without protection, zones 5-8 (widely available)

Interlaken-- early, small berries, high yields, excellent flavor fresh, excellent raisins, hardy to +5F without protection, zones 5-8 (Kelly, Miller, NYFT, Raintree, Southmeadow)

Kay Gray-- extremely hardy, medium berry, mild fruity flavor, disease resistant, good fresh, juice, wine, vigorous, hardy to -15F without protection (NYFT, St. Lawrence)

Cayuga-- late, high vigor, moderately susceptible to mildew, for juice & jelly, very high quality wine, hardy to -5F without protection, zones 4-7 (Miller, NYFT)

MUSCADINE *(V. rotundifolia)*-- Indigenous to the American Southeast, these require a warm moist climate and are good for jelly, juice, and wine. They require cross-pollination, so plant two varieties.

Fry-- gold-yellow, large berry, very sweet, vigorous, high yields, good fresh, zones 7-9 (Burpee)

Carlos-- bronze, large berry, self-pollinating, disease resistant, very vigorous, makes sparkling wines, zones 7-9 (Burpee)

HYBRIDS (FRENCH HYBRIDS, AMERICAN-EUROPEAN HYBRIDS)-- These represent an attempt to obtain the best of both worlds: European taste and American hardiness and disease resistance.

Aurore (Seibel 5279)-- gold-pink berry, early, moderate vigor, high yields, for wine, juice, jelly & table, hardy to -10F without protection, zones 6-7 (widely available)

Seibel 9110-- gray-yellow berry, crisp, meaty, delicious table grapes, adherent skins, needs protection from severe winters (Southmeadow)

EUROPEAN and CALIFORNIA *(V. vinifera)*-- Low in pectin, these require a frost-free season of 170-180 days and are not hardy below 10F without protection. Most wines are made from *Vinifera* or the American-European hybrids. Among the many varieties, these are hardiest.

White Riesling-- one of hardiest wine grapes, for cool climates, Zones 5-9 (NYFT, Van Well)

Cabernet Sauvignon-- black, very seedy, for cool climates and long growing season, red wine, cane prune, zones 5-9 (Fowler, Henry Field's, NYFT)

NOTES:

Grape seeds secrete growth hormones within the berry, so commercial growers spray seedless grapes with growth hormones. Homegrown unsprayed seedless grapes will be smaller.

Vitis labrusca (American)   *Vitacae (Grape)*   **GRAPE**

GROWTH CONDITIONS
Height: pruned, 12-20'   unpruned, 50-100'
Spacing: 8' is best, or 7' in shallow soil and 10' in deep soil
Pollination: All are self-fertile with the exception of a few muscadine vines.
Chilling Requirement: None.
Bearing Age: 3-4 years
Root Depth: In deep soil they can easily extend 12-40'.
pH: 6.5-7.0
Site: Best on a 15-degree south-facing (SE or SW) slope.
Water: Low to dry. To harden the vines for winter, don't water much after August.
Fertilizer: Apply compost only at the beginning of the growing season or during blooming. When applied late in the season Nitrogen delays ripening, inhibits coloring, and subjects vines to winter injury if they keep growing too long into the fall. American grapes and hybrids are especially sensitive to N-deficiency in the early spring and during blooming.
Training: Refer to diagrams on page 74. For vigorous vines the less common Geneva double curtain method provides the best aeration, most sun, and high yields. Plant vines down the center, prune each to 2 trunks, and grow trunks to long 6-8' cordons on upper wire. Train the first vine to the front wire, the second to the back wire, and so on. The more common 4-arm Kniffen method provides an attractive privacy screen but shades lower vine parts. For both methods, bury 9' end-posts 3' in the ground. Use heavy galvanized #11 wire.
Pruning: To spur prune European vines consult other sources. Cane prune all others as follows: (1) Cut out water spouts which are shoots on more than 2-year old wood. (2) Remove winter-damaged wood. (3) Cut out last year's fruiting cane. (4) Identify canes receiving the most sun by their darker wood and closely spaced nodes, select the thickest to bear this season's fruit, and cut back to only 8-15 nodes. (5) For each selected fruiting cane, choose a cane nearby as a renewal spur for next year's fruit; cut back to 2 buds. Each year replace the fruiting arm with a cane from a renewal spur, and select new renewal spur for the following year.

PESTS: leafhopper, grape berry moth, Japanese beetle, phylloxera root aphid, plum curculio, mealybug, mite, rose chafer
DISEASES: anthracnose, black rot, botrytis fruit rot, crown gall, downy mildew, leaf spot, powdery mildew, Pierces disease (spread by leafhoppers)

HARVEST: Cut bunches when fruits are fully colored, sweet, slide off easily, and the stems and seeds are brown. Grapes don't ripen further once picked. For raisins, use a hydrometer and harvest when grapes reach 20% soluble solids. Less solids significantly lowers both raisin weight and quality.

STORAGE REQUIREMENTS: Cool to 50F as soon as possible after picking and spread out fruit bunches in single layers. Dry until stems shrivel slightly, then store in trays no more than 4" deep.
Fresh: Temp: 40   Humidity: slightly humid   Storage Life: 2-3 months
Preserved, taste (months): Jelly: good   Freeze: poor   Dry: excellent   Juice: good (12+)

OTHER GROWING NOTES: Grapes vines need well-drained soil and should have at least 20" of topsoil. They don't need very fertile soil because of vigorous, extensive roots; vines that grow more slowly also develop more "character." Plant vines at the same depth as grown in the nursery. Mound soil over the crown to prevent wind damage, except in the West because of possible crown rot. Cut out all but 1 or 2 stems (with 2-3 buds each) for the central trunk. Grape roots prefer warm soil, so mulch with stones or black plastic to raise soil temperature. If vines overbear, thin flowers before berries form.

ALLIES: Some evidence-- blackberries (*Rubus* sp.), Johnson and Sudan grass (see warning in chart).
Uncertain-- chives, hyssop

VERY HARDY (*A. kolomikta*): hardy to zone 3 (-40F), beautiful plants. The male has variegated leaves, and females display some variegation too. Northwoods Nursery brought 7 "Arctic Beauty" varieties back from the Soviet Union in 1987, only one of which is listed below. Fruits are smaller than fuzzy kiwi and are smooth-skinned.

"Arctic Beauty"-- ornamental male with no fruit, good for zones 3-7 (Gurney's)

Krupnopladnaya-- very large fruit, productive, good flavor, 14% sugar, high Vitamin C (Northwoods)

HARDY (*A. arguta*): hardy to zone 4 (-25F), native to northern China. Fruits are smaller than fuzzy kiwi and its smooth skin can be eaten like a grape.

Issai-- self-fertile Japanese variety, ideal for limited spaces, fruit will be larger with pollination although it will then have seeds, zones 5-9 (Burpee, Field's, Hartmann's, Northwoods, Stark)

74-49-- proven vigorous and reliable in Virginia, large fruit, aromatic, sweet (Northwoods)

Ananasnaja-- means pineapple-like in Russian, very sweet fruit with a hint of mint flavor, brought from Belgium to the Northwest, actually a hybrid of Arguta and Kolomikta (Hartmann's, Northwoods, Raintree)

Miller's Kiwi-- sweet, vigorous, hardy, fully rooted plants (Miller)

TENDER or FUZZY KIWI (*A. deliciosa*): native to China, first commercially grown in New Zealand, fuzzy, hardy to zones 8-10 (5-10F), can be grown as far north as the Pacific Northwest and British Columbia, Canada, or cultivated in greenhouses.

Blake-- self-fertile, early ripening, medium fruit, productive (Northwoods, Raintree)

Hayward-- the variety usually found in supermarkets, good for warm areas of maritime Northwest (Northwoods)

Saanichton 12-- large fruit, the hardiest fuzzy variety, same flavor and size of store kiwi, grown on Vancouver Island, British Columbia, Canada for 30+ years (Northwoods, Raintree)

NOTES

One male can fertilize up to eight female vines. Tag them to be sure you always know which is which. Try to buy larger plants as they have a higher survival rate. Otherwise you may want to start small rooted cuttings in 5-gallon containers.

General Female Winter Pruning Guidelines: cut out damaged wood, curled or twining growth, and all wood that has fruited two seasons. Select fruiting arms that have short internodes (less than 2" apart), are 10-14" apart, and well-exposed to sunlight; cut these back to 8 buds.

General Female Summer Pruning Guidelines: select next season's fruiting arms, remove other shoots, cut out erect water shoots, shorten curled or tangled growth. Make sure enough light passes through to cast patterns on the ground below.

General Male Pruning Guidelines: cut back flowering arms after blooming in July to 20-24", and if necessary again in August-September to 29-31". Trim vines in winter.

GROWTH CONDITIONS
Height: Up to 30' long vines
Spacing: 10-20' between plants, 15-20' between rows, male and female within at least 100'
Pollination: Cross-pollination between male and female vines required. 1 male can pollinate 8 females.
Chilling Requirement: Vines benefit from 400-600 hours below 45F
Bearing Age: 3-5 years, except self-pollinating types can bear 1 year after planting
Root Depth: Shallow (which means they're susceptible to crown and root rot in wet areas).
pH: 6.0-6.5
Site: Full sun (minimum 6 hours), except for the *A. kolomikta* which likes partial shade in hot
        climates. Wind protection is important. Prefers rich, fertile soil, but will tolerate heavy soil.
        In any soil, good drainage is imperative. Avoid soggy, low areas. Best spot is to the north of
        a building or tree to delay bud break. Cover vines if frost threatens in spring or fall.
Water: Heavy. Drip irrigation is best. Overhead sprinkling can protect fruit and foliage from frosts.
Fertilizer: Heavy feeder. Apply slow acting organic fertilizers, very thick compost, or well-rotted
        manure in late winter and spring, several inches away from the crown. Don't fertilize past mid-
        June. Kiwi needs high K, and also Mg to prevent K-induced deficiency. Never apply Boron,
        as above-optimum levels can be severely toxic.
Side-dress: Apply twice during the growing season; use only mildly nitrogenous substances.
Training: Requires trellis, arbor, T-bar fence, pergola, wall, or chain-link fence to support fruiting
        vines. Supports for females should be 6' tall, and males 7' tall. Stake when planting.
Pruning: Similar to grapes. Kiwis fruit on the base 6 buds of this season's fruiting shoot off of 1-year-old
        wood. On planting, prune the main stem back to 4-5 buds. The first summer allow
        the vine to grow freely. Cut back females to 6' and males to 7', and remove all but
        2 or 4 strongest cordons for each. The second winter, head back female cordons to
        8-10 buds, and males to 1/2 that length.

PESTS: no significant pests reported in North America
DISEASES: no significant diseases reported in North America

HARVEST: Allow to ripen on the vine until the first signs of softening; fruit should give with a little finger pressure. Clip hardy kiwi with some stem. Snap off fuzzy kiwi, leaving the stem on the vine. Even minor damage causes ethylene production, which prematurely softens other fruit. In dry climates you can let the kiwi dry on the vine; they will become intensely sweet and keep about 6 weeks.

STORAGE REQUIREMENTS: Remove soft, rotten, or shriveled fruit on a regular basis from fresh storage. To freeze, place whole kiwis in plastic bags, or freeze 1/4" unpeeled slices, then pack in plastic bags. To dry, peel the fruit, cut in half, dry at 120F for 2 hours and repeat the next day.
Fresh,whole: Temp: 32   Humidity: 85-95%   Storage Life: 2 months (hardy) 4 months (fuzzy)

OTHER GROWING NOTES: Kiwi is a productive and tasty candidate for the home grower--only if proper attention is paid to site, water, support, and pruning. The buds, young shoots, and fruit of all species, regardless of hardiness, are very frost tender and need to be protected when temperatures fall below 30 degrees for any length of time, in spring or fall. Cover at night to protect from frost damage, or use overhead sprinkling until temperatures surmount 32. Frost-damaged fruit will emit ethylene gas in storage, thereby hastening the softening of other fruits. Kiwi vines can bear 40-50 years. Yield and fruit size is optimized by light pruning and fruit thinning, rather than heavy pruning and no thinning. Thin before flowers open to about 60 fruit/sq.meter.

ALLIES: Some evidence-- none
        Uncertain-- none
COMPANIONS: none
ENEMIES: none

PEACH VARIETIES

YELLOW FLESH

Redhaven-- early, good fresh, frozen & canned, almost fuzzless, requires thinned early, hardy wood and buds, disease resistant, not good for warm winters, 950 hours chill, zones 5-8 (Adams, Fowler, Hilltop, Kelly, NYFT, Sonoma, Southmeadow, Stark)

Compact Redhaven-- same as Redhaven, but semidwarfed to 10', tolerates bacterial spot and leaf curl, 850 hours chill, (Stark, Van Well)

Frost-- midseason, medium fruit, semi-freestone, good flavor, highly resistant to leaf curl, good in Pacific Northwest (Northwoods, Raintree)

Harrow Beauty-- midseason, a beautiful tree and fruit, good fresh, excellent flavor, hardy, medium vigor, very open, spreading, productive, tolerates bacterial spot and brown rot, 850 hours chill (Hilltop, NYFT, Windmill)

Sunhigh-- midseason, large oblong fruit, very good flavor, sweet & melting flesh, susceptible to bacterial spot, 750 hours chill, best in East (Adams, Cumberland, Southmeadow)

Canadian Harmony-- midseason, large fruit, good flavor, some resistance to bacterial spot, good for California and Northwest, 850 hours chill (Adams, Cumberland, Hilltop, Kelly)

Madison-- late midseason, good fresh and canned, sweet, juicy, thin skins, very hardy, vigorous, hardier than Redhaven, tolerates frost during blooming, good bud hardiness, 850 hours chill (Adams, Cumberland, Hilltop, Kelly, NYFT, Stark)

Biscoe-- late, medium fruit, good flavor, well-formed tree, vigorous, productive, highly resistant to bacterial spot, 850 hours chill (Cumberland, Hilltop)

Rio Oso Gem-- late, large fruit, good fresh, frozen & for pies, reported non-browning, large showy flowers, naturally smaller tree, vigorous, 850 hours chill (Adams, Fowler, Hilltop, Sonoma)

Jerseyglo-- late, large fruit, hardy and easy to manage, very resistant to bacterial spot (Hilltop)

Stark Encore™-- very late, medium-large fruit, excellent flavor, very resistant to bacterial leaf spot, buds are cold hardy (Stark)

WHITE FLESH

Babcock-- early, small-medium fruit, very sweet, low acid fruit, requires heavy thinning, good in California (Fowler)

Raritan Rose-- early, large fruit, excellent fresh, firm flesh, tender, juicy, honeysweet, hardy buds, very vigorous, susceptible to brown rot, 950 hours chill, best in East (Adams, Hilltop)

Champion-- midseason, old variety, medium fruit, excellent fresh, extremely tender & juicy flesh, very hardy, vigorous (Hilltop, Miller, Southmeadow)

GENETIC DWARF PEACHES AND NECTARINES

Stark Sensation-- early, 4-6', good fresh, canned, or frozen, good for Midwest, zones 5-8, also zone 4 if potted (Stark)

Nectar Babe-- early, nectarine will grow less than 6', easily grown in pot, keep rain off to avoid peach leaf curl, Honey Babe is best pollinator (Fowler, Raintree)

Honey Babe-- early midseason, 3-5', flesh is yellow, firm, sweet, delicious, for container growing, keep rain off to avoid leaf curl, good in Northwest (Northwoods, Raintree)

Garden Beauty-- midseason, clingstone nectarine, for tub planting (Windmill)

NOTES

Root Stocks: See plum rootstock chart (most are the same). Peaches do best on a peach seedling rootstock, which produces standard trees. Standard trees can be kept small by pruning. Elberta rootstocks are not hardy for the North.

Prunus persica　　　　*Rosaceae (Rose)*　　　　**PEACH**

GROWTH CONDITIONS
Height: dwarf, 4-10'　　standard, 15-20'
Spacing: dwarf, 12-15'　　standard, 15-25'
Pollination: Most self-pollinate, but yields will be higher with cross-pollination.
Chilling Requirement: Most need 600-900 hours below 45.
Bearing Age: 2-3 years
Root Depth: Shallow, over 90% in top 18". Roots won't branch out when planted too deeply.
pH: 6.0-6.5
Site: Full south or south-east exposure, whether or not espaliered. Will not survive on heavy clay
　　　soils. Do not plant on former apricot, cherry, or peach tree sites; when waterlogged, their roots
　　　release hydrogen cyanide that may linger in soil and hinder growth.
Fertilizer: Low N when under three years. Appropriate new growth is 12-15" when young, and 8-
　　　18" when bearing.
Training: Free-standing-- open center　　Wire-trained-- fan, against a south-facing wall
Pruning: Unlike apple, peach bears fruit on 1-year old wood only and should be pruned to encourage
　　　new growth. Cut out crossing branches, those shading each other, intruding on the center, and
　　　winter-damaged. Remove at least one-third of the previous year's growth, or too much fruit
　　　will be set. Every few years cut out some older wood. Cut back upright-growing shoots to
　　　outward-pointing buds.

PESTS: aphid, birds, cherry fruit sawfly, codling moth, gopher, gypsy moth caterpillar, Japanese beetle,
　　　mite, oriental fruit moth, peach tree borers, peach twig borer, plum curculio, root
　　　lesion nematodes, tarnished plant bug, tent caterpillar, weevil, whitefly
DISEASES: bacterial canker, bacterial spot, brown rot, crown gall, cytospora canker, peach leaf curl
　　　curl, scab, verticillium wilt

HARVEST: Pick when fruit is firm, almost ready to eat, and easily slides off the stem by tipping or
twisting. Never pull it directly off or you'll bruise the peach and hasten spoilage. If fruit has a mild case
of brown rot, harvest only those peaches that are infected and dip them in hot water for 7 minutes at
120F, or 3 minutes at 130F, or 2 minutes at 140F. This kills the fungi, won't harm the fruit, and lets you
store them for further ripening.

STORAGE REQUIREMENTS: To freeze the fruit, peel, pit, and cut in halves or slices. Pack with
some honey mixed with lemon or a pectin pack. Peaches don't store well in a root cellar.
Fresh: Temp: 50-70　Humidity: low　　Storage Life: 3-14 days
Preserved, taste (months):　Can: fair　Freeze: good (6+)　Dry: unknown

OTHER GROWING NOTES: Peaches are considered one of the hardest fruits to grow, particularly
for growers who don't use chemical sprays. Plant at about the same depth it was grown in the nursery;
its upper roots should be only a few inches below the soil surface. Thinning is crucial to a good harvest.
After the June drop but before the fruit is 1-1/4" in diameter, thin to (a) 1 fruit per 30-40 leaves, (b)
1 fruit per 10" on early-ripening varieties, or (c) 6-8" on late-ripening varieties. "Cling" varieties are firm,
best for canning, but rarely available to homegrowers. "Freestone" varieties don't can well; their flesh
separates from the pit when ripe and is soft. Peach trees live a mere 8 years in the South and 18 years
in the North, which poor drainage renders shorter in both cases.

ALLIES: Some evidence-- alder, brambles, buckwheat, goldenrod, lamb's-quarters, ragweed, rye mulch,
　　　smartweed, sorghum mulch, strawberry, wheat mulch
　　　Uncertain-- caraway, coriander, dill, garlic, nasturtium, tansy, wildflowers, wormwood, vetch
OTHER: bird control: a border of dogwood, mulberry, or other aromatic fruit, all of which birds prefer
ENEMIES: none

PEAR VARIETIES

EUROPEAN (*Pyrus communis*)
Harrow Delight-- very early, medium-large fruit, juicy, melting, hardy, productive, good fire blight resistance, zones 5-7 (Hilltop, NYFT, Raintree, Rocky Meadow, Stark, Windmill)
Moonglow-- early, Comice seedling, Bartlett type, good fresh, for pies or canned, upright, heavy spurs, hardy, strong pollinator of other pears, vigorous, wide climate tolerance, good fire blight resistant, zones 5-8 (Jung, Miller, Southmeadow, Stark)
Harvest Queen-- early, new Bartlett type (slightly smaller fruit), identical flavor and appearance to Bartlett, very fire blight resistant (Hilltop, NYFT, Windmill)
Collette-- early midseason, very high quality fruit, long bearing for several months, good fresh and canned, hardy to -10 to -15 (Miller, Windmill)
Seckel-- midseason, self-fertile, very small fruit, yellow-green with russet cover, "sugar pear", fresh or canning, keeps well, productive, very hardy, some fire blight resistance, zones 5-8 (widely available)
Orcas-- midseason, large fruit, yellow with red blush, great fresh, canned or dried, extremely productive, scab resistant, good for the Northwest (Raintree)
Comice-- late, Oregon-grown winter pear, large fruit, top flavor, vigorous, some fire blight resistant (or moderate susceptibility), erratic crops, requires storage before ripening, good storage pear. A low chill requirement makes it suitable also for Southern California; it prefers milder climates with less summer heat but is grown commercially in Southern California. Zones 5-9. (widely available)
Beurre Bosc-- late, large pear, brown russet over green or yellow, long-necked, perfumed and melting flesh, excellent keeper, large & vigorous tree can grow up to 25'. Does well in heavy clay soils. Can withstand hot summer temperatures and resists cold winters. (Adams, Kelly, Miller, Raintree, Sonoma, Southmeadow)
Magness-- late, needs pollinator, Comice-Seckel seedling, medium-large fruit, delicious flavor and melting, juicy flesh, slightly russeted, more spreading than most pears, cross-pollinates with Asian varieties, resists fire blight, zones 5-8 (Burpee, Rocky Meadow, Sonoma, Southmeadow, Windmill)

ASIAN (*Pyrus serotina*)-- all are attractive ornamentals
Hosui-- early, medium fruit, golden, juicy and crunchy, excellent flavor like butterscotch, becoming a leading commercial variety in California, resists fire blight, zones 6-9 (Adams, Miller, Raintree, Sonoma, Stark)
Chojuro-- late midseason, medium oblong fruit, brown & russeted, rich aromatic flavor, crisp like apples, can keep until March, medium sized tree, spreading and vigorous, will pollinate with Seckel and Bartlett (Miller, Raintree, Sonoma, Van Well)

NOTES

Root Stock: Quince is the most dwarfing rootstock, isn't as hardy as the pear, increases the tree's susceptibility to fire blight, needs staking, doesn't do well in poorly drained soils, but has some resistance to pear decline and pear root aphids. If fire blight is a problem for you, but you must use quince for achieving the most dwarfed tree, choose varieties that have the highest natural fire blight resistance. One superior root stock, a cross of Old Home and Farmingdale (OHxF), offers resistance to fire blight, pear decline, and better tolerance of heavy, wet soils. For standard trees, the most common rootstock is the Bartlett seedling, which is hardy to winter cold but very susceptible to fire blight, nematodes, pear root aphids and pear decline.

Pyrus communis   *Rosaceae (Rose)*   **PEAR**

GROWTH CONDITIONS
Height: dwarf, 8-15'   semidwarf, 15-20'   standard, 30-40'
Spacing: dwarf, cordon-3' pyramid-5' fan-15' espalier-15'   semidwarf, 20'   standard, 30'
Pollination: All require cross-pollination.
Chilling Requirement: Most need 600-900 hours below 45.
Bearing Age: 2-4 years
Root Depth: Deep
pH: 6.0-6.5
Site: Full south or south-east exposure.
Support Structures: Limb spreaders strengthen joints, encourage earlier blossoming and higher yields.
    More than other fruits, pear branches sag with fruit and may need to be tied up.
Water: Heavy and constant supply; ground irrigation especially important to minimize fire blight.
Fertilizer: Avoid high N. Pears need a lot of boron, so periodically check soil for deficiency.
Training: Free standing-- central leader for Comice & Anjou. Open center for Bartlett, Bosc, those with
    flexible limbs, and those susceptible to fire blight.
    Wire-trained-- all cordons, espalier, stepover, palmettes
Pruning: Cut as little as possible because every cut exposes tissue to fire blight.

PESTS: aphid, apple maggot, cherry fruit fly, codling moth, European apple sawfly, flea beetle, gypsy
    moth, mite, oriental fruit moth, pear psylla, pearslug, plum curculio, tarnished plant
    bug, tent caterpillar, thrips, weevil, whitefly
DISEASES: bitter pit, blossom blast (Boron deficiency), cedar apple rust, crown gall, crown rot,
    cytospora canker, fire blight, pear decline, pear curl, scab

HARVEST: Pick when pears are at least 2" in diameter. Don't allow European varieties to ripen on
the tree as they'll become mealy and coarse. Handle very carefully; although they appear hard, they'll
bruise easily. Asian pears should ripen on the tree.

STORAGE REQUIREMENTS: Some pears require lengthy storage before they begin to ripen, and
some will never ripen if left in cold storage too long. After cold storage, ideal ripening temperature is
60-70F; some pears won't ripen after cold storage if the home temperature is too high. If you wish to
avoid the need for cold storage place pears in a paper bag with ripe apples or pears, for they emit
ethylene gas which stimulates the final stages of fruit ripening.

	Minimum	to	Maximum Storage Life at 30-32F	Max. Storage Life at 40-42F
Anjou	2	to	4-6 months	2-3 months
Bartlett	0	to	1-1/2 months	2-3 weeks
Bosc	0	to	3 - 3-1/2 months	2 - 2-1/2 months
Comice	1	to	2-1/2 - 3 months	1-1/2 - 2 months
Seckel	0	to	3- 3-1/2 months	none

OTHER GROWING NOTES: Pears can tolerate heavy clay soils better than most other fruits. Their
blossoms are fairly frost resistant and won't be injured by temperatures as low as 28F. European pears
don't usually need thinning because of a low "set" ratio, the number of blooms producing fruit. Asian
pears should be thinned to 1 fruit per cluster to avoid overbearing. The higher the temperature right
after blooming, the sooner the fruit will mature, generally in 106-124 days after blooming. Pear trees
are among the longest lived fruit trees, sometimes achieving as much as 200-300 years.

ALLIES: Some evidence-- alder, brambles, buckwheat, rye or sorghum or wheat mulch
    Uncertain-- caraway, coriander, dill, garlic, nasturtium, tansy, wildflowers, wormwood, vetch
ENEMIES: none

PECAN VARIETIES

SOUTH-WEST REGION (arid climates)

Pawnee-- early nut maturity, large nuts, well-filled nut, vigorous with long unbranched limbs that later branch with strong angles, good producer, bears throughout tree, more scab resistant for growing in more northern areas, plant with Posey (Fowler, Nolin River)

Posey-- early nut maturity, good for more northern areas, plant with Pawnee (Nolin River)

Mohawk-- early, large nuts, good flavor, vigorous, upright and spreading, partially self-fertile, replaces Mahan, very good producer. May be good for northern California but may not fill well there. Best in Southwest, zones 7-9 and southern edge of 6. (Fowler, Nolin River, Stark)

Cheyenne-- matures to only 35-45', thin shells, heavy crops at an early age, best pollinated with Stuart, best suited for Southwest but has been grown in the East, zones 7-9 (Stark)

SOUTH-EAST (humid climates)

Candy-- vigorous, prolific, scab resistant (locally available)

Stuart-- high yields, thin-shelled nuts, spreading branches, vigorous, prone to disease, also grows in the West, zones 7-10 (Gurney's, Henry Field's, Stark)

NORTH (short season)-- The "North" refers to the northern part of the pecan growing region such as Indiana, Illinois, Iowa, Missouri, Kentucky, Tennessee, and Kansas. Pecans can be grown further north through southern New England and the Northwest, but they will never produce filled nuts there.

Fisher-- good producer as far north as Scranton, PA area, good flavor, medium nut, good cracker, zones 5-7, grow with Lucas (Grimo, Nolin River)

Lucas-- good medium nut, cracks and fills well, high yields, good as far north as Scranton, PA, grow with Fisher (Nolin River)

Greenriver-- late, very good producer, medium nut, good south of Ohio River as far north as southern IN, IL, and MO, scab resistant, pollinates with Major (Nolin River)

Major-- medium-large nut, large yields, thin shell, easy cracker, scab resistant, pollinates with Greenriver, good in the TN, KY, VA and as far north as southern IN, IL, and MO, zones 6-9 (Henry Field's, Nolin River, Stark)

Starking Hardy Giant-- self-pollinating, yields even after winters of -20F, very large nuts, thin shells, good nut but not heavy bearer, larger yields when cross-pollinated (Stark)

HICAN-- This is a cross between shellbark hickory and pecan, is reputed easier to grow in Northern areas than pecan and is a good ornamental. Its nuts generally favor the hickory flavor. Plant several varieties for full crops. Nolin River carries a bunch of varieties. You may not want to grow Hican's if you have a lot of hickory trees nearby, as hickory weevils are reputed to like Hicans. Also, Hicans productivity may depend on your climate and what you use as a pollinator.

James Hican-- matures to 60', zones 6-8 (Stark)

Burton-- self-pollinating, medium nut, good producer and bears young, thin shell, good for South and Midwest as far north as northern IN, IL, and OH, (Grimo, Nolin River)

NOTES

Look for grafted trees, which will produce sooner than seedling stock.

Carya illinoensis   *Juglandaceae (Walnut)*   **PECAN**

GROWTH CONDITIONS
Height: 75-100'
Spacing: Depends on variety-- 25' x 25' to 70' x 70'
Pollination: Self-fertile, but nuts will be higher quality with cross-pollination.
Chilling Requirement: Most require some chilling but the hours depend on the variety.
Bearing Age: 3-4 years in South, 8-10 years in North
Root Depth: Very deep
pH: 5.8-7.5
Site: Full sun and rich, well drained soil.
Water: Medium, but during drought periods water up to 3-4" per week
Mulch: Avoid sawdust.
Fertilizer: Low N when young.
Side-dress: Apply compost in late winter-early spring.
Training: Free-standing-- central leader   Wire-trained-- N/A
Pruning: at planting cut back 1/3 to 1/2 of the top, about 2-3" above a bud facing the prevailing
          wind. Cut out crowded or crossed branches.

PESTS: aphid, birds, fall webworm, hickory shuckworm, pecan casebearer, pecan weevil, scale, squirrel,
          walnut caterpillar
DISEASES: canker dieback, crown gall, liver spot, pecan bunch, root rot, scab, sunscald

HARVEST: Gather nuts from October to January. As the pecan matures the outer hull splits to expose
the inner nut. As the hull dries the nut tends to fall out to the ground. Most varieties, though, require
their limbs shaken to encourage nut drop. Spread a canvas sheet on the ground to collect the nuts. Don't
start harvest until the hulls on the inner part of the tree split open, which will be last.

STORAGE REQUIREMENTS: Place hulled nuts in water, and remove rotten and diseased nuts that
float to the top. Dry and cure by spreading nuts in one layer in a cool, dry, well-ventilated area. They're
ready for storage when the kernels rattle in the shell, or when unshelled nutmeats snap when bent. Store
unshelled nuts in attics or cool underground cellars, where they'll keep for a year. Store shelled nuts in
plastic bags with holes, or in tightly sealed tin cans lined with paper with a hole punctured in the can
beneath the lid. Shelled nuts can also be stored in the refrigerator or freezer for up to a year.
Fresh: Temp: 34-40   Humidity: dry   Storage Life: 12+ months

OTHER GROWING NOTES: The pecan is a member of the walnut family and is usually cultivated
in mild, warm regions. In order to produce filled nuts, the tree requires a long, hot growing season
averaging 75-85 degrees, averaging a minimum of 1000 Cooling Degree Days, with 140-250 frost-free
days. Midwest states are more suited for nut production than Northeastern states like Connecticut
because, despite being at the same latitude, they usually experience higher summer temperatures. The
four major groups of pecan cultivars are adapted to the Southwest, Southeast, and "North" (see comments
on the previous page). Pecans tend to bear in alternate years. They bloom in late spring and summer.
High humidity at bloom time can hinder pollination, increase disease and, at harvest time, cause nuts to
sprout while still in the husks. In choosing cultivars, note that vigorous growers usually bear heavily, and
trees that break dormancy in late spring will suffer the least frost damage. Also, the smaller the
transplant the less injury to the tap root.

ALLIES: Some evidence-- none
          Uncertain-- none
ENEMIES: none

EUROPEAN -- The sweetest plum. Pollinate with other Europeans, Damsons or Americans.
> **Stanley**-- late midseason, self-fertile, freestone, vigorous, productive, resists bacterial spot, very susceptible to black knot, good fresh, canned, cooked, dried, zones 5-7 (widely available)
> **Green Gage (Reine Claude)**-- late, self-fertile, yellow-green fruit, juicy, very sweet, compact tree, not for warm winters, susceptible to brown rot, good fresh, frozen, canned (widely avail.)
> **Count Althann's Gage**-- late, cling, leading European dessert plum, sweet, juicy, golden flesh resists bacterial spot, moderate resistance to black knot, zones 5-7 (Southmeadow)
> **Pearl**-- late, red-speckled yellow fruit, yellow flesh, extremely sweet, tender & melting flesh, tree is moderately upright, thought unsurpassed by Southmeadow (Rocky Meadow, Southmeadow)

DAMSON *(P. institia)*-- Very small and tart, these are best suited for preserves and cooking.
> **Shropshire Damson (French Damson)**-- late, cling, genetic semidwarf, good for jelly, very resistant to bacterial spot, very susceptible to black knot, productive, vigorous, zones 5-7 (Hilltop, NYFT)

JAPANESE *(P. salicina)*-- Very juicy and soft, these make excellent fresh eating. Some can be canned and cooked. Generally they like warmer climates. Cross with other Japanese or Americans.
> **Shiro**-- early, yellow fruit, hardy, prolific, low tree, moderately resistant to bacterial spot and black knot, susceptible to bacterial canker, leaf scald & brown rot, extremely juicy, excellent sweet flavor, clingstone, good fresh, canned, cooked, zones 5-9 (widely available)
> **Weeping Santa Rosa**-- early, very ornamental, self-fertile, easy to keep at 8' or espaliered, large fruits, rich sweet-tart flavor, good pollinator, low chill (Northwoods, Raintree, Sonoma)
> **Ozark Premier**-- early midseason, red skin, yellow flesh, very tasty, sweet, large fruit, resists bacterial spot, canker & black knot, susceptible to leaf scald & brown rot, zones 5-9 (Adams, Hilltop, Stark)
> **Redheart**-- early midseason, red, juicy, firm flesh, excellent flavor, holds quality canned or frozen, good pollinator, cross with Elephant Heart, zones 5-9 (Hilltop, Stark, Windmill)
> **Burbank**-- midseason, red-purple firm fruit, dwarf, somewhat drooping, needs thinning, hardy, prolific, resists bacterial spot and black knot, susceptible to bacterial canker and brown rot, especially leaf scald, pollinate with Shiro, zones 6-9 (Burpee, Hilltop, Miller, Stark, Windmill)
> **Elephant Heart**-- late, self-fruitful, red, very juicy, good flavor & quality, vigorous, hardy, prolific, cross with Redheart (Fowler, Hilltop, Rocky Meadow, Southmeadow, Windmill)

AMERICAN HYBRID -- Bred especially for Northern areas, these pollinate Americans or Japanese.
> **Toka**-- midseason, very hardy, medium fruit, firm flesh, good fresh (Hilltop, Jung, Windmill)

BEACH *(P. maritima)*-- Good in very poor soil and extremely hardy. Pollinate with other beach.
> **Miller's Beach**-- small shrub or tree, once established can withstand long droughts, extreme cold and most diseases, great for jam and jelly, good windbreak (Miller)

OTHER
> **Pluot**™-- early, a cross of plum and apricot, reputed best tasting new fruit, ripens mid-summer, cross with Japanese, Plumcot or Aprium™ (see apricot), zones 6-9 (Stark, Raintree)

NOTES

Root Stocks: see charts on pages 108-109

Prunus domestica (European)   *Rosaceae (Rose)*   **PLUM**

GROWTH CONDITIONS
Height: dwarf, 3-5'   semidwarf, 14'   standard, 16-30'
Spacing: dwarf, 8-12'   semidwarf, 12-20'   standard, 20-25'
Pollination: European are usually self-pollinating. Japanese need cross-pollination.
Chilling Requirement: European need 700-1000 hours below 45, while Asian need 500-900 hours.
Bearing Age: European, 4-5 years   Japanese, 2-3 years
Root Depth: Depends on rootstock, generally shallow
pH: 6.0-8.0
Site: See Enemies (below). Plums need at least 8 hours. of sun and well-drained soil. European &
       Damson-- heavy loam, and south or south-east exposure. Japanese & Beach-- sandy loam, and
       northern slope or 12-15' north of a building to minimize premature bloom and frost loss.
Water: Medium. Consistent watering is critical. Avoid watering in autumn, except in droughts.
Fertilizer: Low N in first three years. They may need K & Zinc supplements. Appropriate new
       growth for European plums is 16-18" when young, and 10-14" when bearing fruit. Appropriate
       growth for Asian plums is 18-20" when young, and 15-18" when bearing.
Side-dress: Apply in the spring a layer of compost or mixture of well rotted manure and wood ashes.
Training: Free-standing-- open center for Japanese. Central leader or dwarf pyramid for European.
       Wire-trained-- fan.
Pruning: Never prune in the winter. Trees are best pruned only after the tree starts to bear fruit.
       Europeans require little pruning while Japanese require harder pruning. Fruit is on spurs 2-6"
       long that live 5-8 years, so don't prune these.
Support Structures: Forked prop to hold up heavy fruiting branches.

PESTS: aphid, apple maggot, birds, cankerworm, cherry fruit fly, cherry fruit sawfly, European apple
       sawfly, fall webworm, flathead borer, mite, oriental fruit moth, peach tree borers,
       peach twig borer, pearslug, plum curculio, weevil, whitefly
DISEASES: bacterial spot, black knot, brown rot, cherry leaf spot, crown gall, cytospora canker,
       peach leaf curl, powdery mildew, verticillium wilt

HARVEST: Plums turn color 20-30 days before harvest. Pick when the fruit starts to soften and comes
off with a slight twist. Be careful not to injure the spurs. European plums-- for fresh eating, pick when
ripe; for cooking, pick underripe. Japanese plums-- always pick underripe; if allowed to fully ripen on
the tree, they will be mushy and overripe.

STORAGE REQUIREMENTS: Ripen Japanese plums at 60-65F. If not too soft, they can be stacked.
Fresh: Temp: 37-40   Humidity: 90%   Storage Life: 2 weeks
Preserved, taste (months):   Can: good (12+)   Freeze: good (12+)   Dry: good (12+)

OTHER GROWING NOTES: Plums are naturally smaller than apple, pear, or peach trees, and, as
a rule, will grow well wherever pears do. For a stone fruit, plums have an unusual range of flavors, sizes,
and shapes. Japanese plums, now common in the stores, are very juicy, soft, and excellent dessert fruits.
European plums are much sweeter, though, and dry well as prunes. Plum curculio greatly damages
plums. Thin fruit no later than two months after full bloom. For both European and Japanese, allow
only one fruit per spur or cluster. While usually self-thinning, European plums may need to be thinned
to 2-3" apart. Thin Japanese plums, a more vigorous tree, to 4-5" apart. When thinning, destroy all fruit
with the curculio's crescent-shaped egg-laying scar.

ALLIES: Some evidence-- alder, brambles, buckwheat, and rye, sorghum or wheat mulch
       Uncertain-- caraway, coriander, dill, garlic, nasturtium, tansy, wildflowers, wormwood, vetch
ENEMIES: don't plant where following have grown in previous 3 years: cocklebur, eggplant, ground
       cherry, horse nettle, lambs quarters, pepper, pigweed, potato, raspberry, strawberry, tomato,
       weeds in nightshade family

PLUM ROOTSTOCKS *

Unlike apple trees, standard size plum trees are naturally smaller and can be kept small through pruning. Because of this quality a very dwarfing rootstock is not essential for espalier work. Pay attention to variety characteristics, too, as each has a different growing habit. For example, a Japanese plum (naturally more vigorous) might be better on a more dwarfing stock than, say, a European plum. Buy smaller trees when possible because they suffer less transplanting shock; in several years they're more productive and vigorous than a larger transplant.

Most nurseries don't offer an in-house choice of rootstocks; your ability to choose a different rootstock will usually depend on choosing a different nursery. The purpose of these charts is not to help you make an independent decision, but it is to help you conduct an informed discussion with the nursery grower. We urge you to seek the nursery growers' advice on what will be good for your soil, climate, space, and desired variety. We strongly advise that your nursery grower's experience and judgment should prevail.

Names	P. Besseyi (Western Sand Cherry)	P. Tomentosa (Nanking Cherry)	Pixie (P. Domestica)	St. Julien (P. Americana)	Citation	Marianna 2624	Other Notes
Size (% of Standard)	dwarf 20-35%	mini-dwarf 15-25%	dwarf 30-40%	dwarf 70-80%	dwarf 70-75%	semi-dwarf 90%	
Height	3-5'	2-4'	6'	10-15'	14'	16'	
Width	3-5'	2-3'	5'	13'	13'	14'	
Best Soil	loam	loam	loam	sandy loam	sandy loam	clay loam	
Anchorage	poor	poor	good	good	good	good	
Crown Rot	HR	HR	LR	LR	LR	MR	
Oak Root Fungus	--	--	--	S	--	MR	
Nematodes	--	--	MR	--	MR	R	
Crown Gall	--	--	--	--	S	MR	
Bact.Canker	S	S	MR	R	--	HS	
Hardiness	H	H	--	H	--	--	
Mice	--	--	--	S	--	MR	
Precocious	--	VP	P	--	--	--	
Other	Lives less than 8 years.	Lives less than 10 yrs.	Rootstock promotes small fruit.	Good disease resistance. Citation can replace this.	Good disease and pest resistance.		

* We gratefully thank Robert Kourik for permission to reprint information on rootstocks from his book *Designing and Maintaining Your Edible Landscape Naturally* (see Bibliography).

PLUM ROOTSTOCKS, continued

R = Resistant   MR = Moderately Resistant
S = Susceptible   MS = Moderately Susceptible
L = Low Hardiness   H = Hardy   VH = Very Hardy
P = Precocious (early bearing)   VP = Very Precocious

Names	Myrobolan	Myrobolan 29c	Nemagaard (P. Persica)	Bailey (P. Americana)	OTHER NOTES
Size (% of Standard)	standard 100%	standard 100%	augmented 110%	standard 100%	Hilltop says the standard size trees are acceptable for espalier.
Height	18'	18'	20'	18'	
Width	16'	16'	18'	16'	
Best Soil	clay loam	clay loam	clay loam	sandy loam	
Anchorage	excellent	fair	very good	--	
Crown Rot	MR	MR	LR	--	
Oak Root Fungus	MS	MS	S	--	
Nematodes	R	S	R	--	
Crown Gall	MR	HS	S	--	
Bact.Canker	S	S	S	R	
Hardiness	--	--	--	H	
Mice	S	S	MR	--	
Borer	S	S	HS	--	

RASPBERRY VARIETIES

RED *(R. idaeus)*
Heritage-- everbearing, tall canes but usually sturdy enough to not need stakes, medium berry, excellent quality, very hardy, zones (4)5-8 (widely available)
Titan-- early, thornless, firm, sweet and juicy, mild flavor, trellis recommended, high yields, resists diseases and pests, zones 5-7 (Henry Field's, Kelly, Miller, NYFT, Nourse, Stark)
Killearney-- early, large & firm, disease resistant, one of hardiest raspberries, zones 3-8 (Burpee)
Latham-- midseason, large firm berry, excellent flavor, good fresh, frozen, canned, prone to virus so get virus-free, zones (3)4-8 (Gurney's, Henry Field's, Kelly, Miller, Nourse, Rayner, Stark)
Taylor-- midseason, conical large berry, very firm, excellent flavor, good quality, vigorous, hardy (NYFT, Miller, Windmill)
Chilliwack-- midseason, new from British Columbia, excellent for wet sites, resists root rot, large firm berry, very sweet, productive, suited to Northwest (Northwoods, Raintree)

YELLOW *(R. idaeus)*
Golden West-- midseason, large berry, upright canes, vigorous, disease resistant, good fresh, frozen and jam, also pretty ornamental (Raintree)
Fallgold-- everbearing, sweet and juicy berry, vigorous, hardy, zones 4-8 (Burpee, Gurney's, Henry Field's, Jung, Miller, Northwoods, Raintree)

PURPLE (cross of red and black raspberry)
Royalty-- late midseason, juicier than black raspberry, sweeter than Brandywine purple raspberry, high yields, very hardy, resists insects and immune to raspberry aphid that carries mosaic, can be tip-layered but this one is best propagated by suckers, gourmet, good fresh and for jam, zones 4-8 (Jung, Kelly, Miller, Northwoods, NYFT, Nourse, Rayner, Stark, Windmill)

BLACK *(R. occidentalis)*
Bristol-- very early, large firm berry, vigorous upright canes, no staking needed, leading variety in Finger Lakes area, zones 5-8 (Miller, NYFT, Nourse, Rayner, Stark)
Jewel-- very early, large glossy berry, high quality, high yields, not susceptible to any serious disease, only mildly susceptible to mildew, hardy (Kelly, NYFT, Nourse, Rayner)
Cumberland-- midseason, large glossy fruit, excellent flavor, long picking season into fall, very hardy, zones 5-8 (Burpee, Gurney's, Henry Field's, Van Well)

NOTES

Always select certified disease-free stock. Black and purple types are better for preserves.

Propagation: Red & yellow-- by suckers. Black & purple-- by layering. See BLACKBERRY.

Rubus (3 species)   *Rosaceae (Rose)*   **RASPBERRY**

GROWTH CONDITIONS
Height: 5-10'
Spacing: Red & Yellow-- 2-4' in a row (suckers & new canes will fill out row)
      Black and Purple-- 3-4' in hills (no suckers, but need room for branching canes)
Pollination: Self-pollinating.
Chilling Requirement: Most require some chilling, but the amount depends on variety.
Bearing Age: 2 years
Root Depth: 12"
pH: 5.5-7.0
Site: Full sun. Rich loam. Good drainage. East-facing spot sheltered from late afternoon sun. Plant at
      least 300 feet away from any wild brambles, which harbor pests and diseases. Also keep at a
      distance from different types of berries to minimize cross-pollination.
Water: see BLACKBERRY
Mulch: see BLACKBERRY. One gardener with a 60-year patch layers 8-10" of leaf mulch in autumn,
      and some wood ashes in winter to counter leaf acidity. He rarely needs to waters.
Fertilizer: see BLACKBERRY
Training: A trellis is important for disease and pest reduction, quality fruit, and easy harvest. Place
      bottom wire at 2', middle wire at 3', and top wire at 4' for black and purple or 5' for red &
      yellow. Fan out canes and tie with cloth strips.
Pruning: After harvest or in spring, cut out thin, weak, spindly or sick canes, and ones finished bearing.
      Red & yellow-- thin to 8 canes per 3 row-ft, or 4-6" soil per cane. "Topping off" canes lowers
      yields, so don't unless the cane is taller than 6'. Cut out most sucker growth. Everbearers-- cut
      to 5-7 canes per hill. To encourage branching, when primocanes are 18-24" cut off the top 3-4"
      of the cane ("topping off"). In late winter cut lateral branches back to 8-12" long.

PESTS: aphid, birds, caneborer, flea beetle, fungus beetle (in ripe fruits), Japanese beetle, mite,
      raspberry root borer, sap beetle, strawberry weevil, tarnished plant bug, weevil, whitefly
DISEASES: anthracnose, botrytis fruit rot, cane blight, cane gall, crown gall, leaf curl, leaf spot, mosaic,
      rust, powdery mildew, verticillium wilt

HARVEST: When berries slide easily off without pressure, harvest into very small containers so berries on the bottom won't be crushed. After harvest cut floricanes to the ground, and on everbearers cut the tips of primocanes. Burn or destroy all canes for disease control.

STORAGE REQUIREMENTS: Freeze within 2 days of harvest. Spread berries out on cookie sheets and freeze. When rock hard store in heavy freezer bags. Refrigerated they keep 4-7 days.
Preserved, taste (months): Can: excellent as jams (12+) Freeze: excellent (6) Dry: good

OTHER GROWING NOTES: Red raspberries are the hardiest bramble fruit. See notes under BLACKBERRY about yields, rows, floricanes, and primocanes. The "everbearing" raspberry cane bears annually; its floricanes bear a summer crop, and primocanes bear in the fall on their tips. The bottom of the primocane matures to bear the following summer as the floricane. For continuous harvest, try growing biennials for a spring crop and everbearers for a bumper fall crop (see pruning).

ALLIES: Some evidence-- none
      Uncertain-- garlic, rue, tansy
COMPANIONS: See BLACKBERRY
OTHER: Raspberries, unlike most other plants, do tolerate the juglone in black walnut roots.
ENEMIES: Don't plant where nightshade family was grown in last 3 years, due to verticillium wilt.

STRAWBERRY VARIETIES

JUNEBEARERS-- 1 crop per year in late spring or early summer. Usually the highest quality berries.

Earliglow-- early, this sets the standard for all others, medium-large berry, best flavor of all, good fresh, canned, frozen, resistant to red stele, verticillium, leaf spot and leaf scorch, best from North Carolina to New England to Missouri (Burpee, Jung, Miller, Nourse, Rayner)

Surecrop-- early midseason, good choice for beginners, large & firm, good fresh, canned, frozen, very verticillium resistant, resists leaf spot, scorch, red stele and drought, vigorous even in poor soil, good coast to coast, zones 4-8 (Burpee, Henry Field's, Kelly, Miller, Nourse, Rayner, Stark)

Allstar-- midseason, easy to grow, good fresh, frozen, and U-pick, high quality, very hardy, consistent high yields, resists red stele, leaf scorch, powdery mildew, and somewhat verticillium wilt, good in Northeast, mid-Atlantic & west to Missouri (Burpee, Kelly, Miller, Nourse, Rayner)

Catskill-- midseason, very large berry, soft, sweet, good dessert & freezing quality, very resistant to verticillium wilt, good in colder areas of New England to central Pennsylvania to Minnesota (Miller, Nourse, Rayner)

Jewel-- late, new in 1985, very high quality large fruit, good fresh and frozen, hardy, not resistant to red stele or verticillium wilt but low incidence of fruit rots and foliar diseases, good from Nebraska to Maine and south to Maryland and Ohio (Kelly, NYFT, Nourse)

Sparkle-- late, medium berry, good frozen or for preserves, resists red stele and harsh winters, good in Northeast, west to Wisconsin, and Rocky Mountain region (Burpee, Gurney's, Henry Field's, Kelly, Miller, Nourse, Rayner)

Lateglow-- late, medium berry, firm, sweet and aromatic, high yields, strong resistance to red stele and verticillium wilt, tolerates leaf spot, leaf scorch, gray mold and powdery mildew (Burpee, Jung, Nourse, Rayner)

EVERBEARERS-- 2 main crops per year. For only 1 large and late crop pick off all early summer blossoms. The standard everbearer needs 15 or more hours of daylight. A newer breed, however, are "day-neutral" everbearers, which are not supposed to be affected by day length.

Fort Laramie-- large berry, good flavor, tolerates -30F without mulch, pretty in hanging baskets, hardy in mountain states and high plains, also good in Southern states (Field's, Gurney's, Jung, May)

Ozark Beauty-- standard everbearer, large berry, need to keep runners to 2 or 3 to ensure large fruit, good fresh or frozen, extremely productive, good Maine to Missouri and West Coast, wide climate adaptability, zones 4-8 (Field's, Fowler, Gurney's, Jung, Kelly, May, Miller, Stark)

Sequoia-- very large berry, excellent flavor, vigorous, resists many diseases, tolerates some soil alkalinity, good for West coast, can be grown in desert climates as winter annual (Fowler)

Tristar-- "Day Neutral," early and continuous crop through fall at about 6 week intervals, heaviest crop in the fall, medium & firm, good fresh and frozen, very sweet, resists red stele and verticillium, tolerates leaf spot and scorch, can be grown in towers or hanging baskets because runners bloom and bear before rooting, good in Northeast, Midwest, and throughout West, zones 5-8 (Field's, Gurney's, Jung, Northwoods, Nourse, Rayner, Raintree, Stark)

NOTES

Try to buy certified virus-free plants.

Fragaria X Ananassa   *Rosaceae (Rose)*   **STRAWBERRY**

GROWTH CONDITIONS
Height: 8-12"   Breadth: 6-12"
Spacing: 8-15"   Rows: 2 - 5-1/2'
Pollination: Self-fertile.
Chilling Requirement: Most require chilling hours, but the amoung depends on variety.
Bearing Age: Everbearing (including newer "day-neutrals)-- end of first summer planted.
          Junebearing-- 1 yr after planting; in the deep South, fall-plantings may bear in early spring.
Root Depth: Shallow, up to 8".
pH: 5.5-6.8
Site: Good drainage. North-facing sunny slope to delay blossom in areas susceptible to late frost. The
          previous fall prepare beds with 5 lbs manure per 10 sq.ft. and whenever renewing the bed.
Water: Medium
Mulch: Apply 3-4" after ground is frozen hard, remove in spring, and replace in hot weather. Do
          not cover crowns. University studies in New Hampshire show row covers through winter, not
          mulch, produces higher yields. Pull off covers during April bloom (replace if frost is expected).
Fertilizer: Low N. Apply very lightly and often rather than in two heavy feedings.
Thinning: When runners get too prolific for a solid 7-8" spacing, cut off excess runners.

PESTS: aphid, birds, earwig, flea beetle, garden webworm, Japanese & June beetles, mice, mite,
          nematode, pill bug, slug, snail, sap beetle, strawberry beetle, st. crownborer, st.
          leafroller, st. weevil, st. root weevil, tarnished plant bug, white grub, wireworm
DISEASES: anthracnose, botrytis fruit rot, leaf blight, leaf spot, leaf scorch, powdery mildew, red stele,
          root rot, septoria leaf spot, verticillium wilt, walnut bunch, yellows (virus)

HARVEST: Pick all berries as soon as ripe, whether or not damaged, to prevent disease. Handle very
gently to avoid bruising. Berries picked with green caps last longer in storage.

STORAGE REQUIREMENTS: Do not wash or remove green caps.
Can: not good   Freeze: excellent (12+)   Dry: can dry as fruit leather   Jam: excellent (12+)

OTHER GROWING NOTES: Plan about 24 plants to feed a family of 4 strawberry lovers.
Junebearer strawberries yield a single crop in June-July and make lots of runners. Everbearing
strawberries yield a first crop in June-July and a second in late summer-early fall; they require summer
daylight of 15 or more hours (unless it is a newer "day neutral" type). If you suffer late spring frosts,
choose varieties that flower late and tolerate high humidity. When planting, cover all roots but keep the
upper 2/3 of the crown above the soil line. To promote a healthier, more productive plant, deflower all
Junebearers the first year and Everbearers only in their first late-spring flowering time. For a bumper
fall crop, however, you may deflower Everbearers in June every year. Most strawberry plants reproduce
by runners. These can be pinched off to produce larger berries but lower yields, or trained to 7-10" for
a smaller berry but higher yields. Strawberries tend to become less productive each year, so beds are
often renewed by various methods. For a perennial bed, try the "spaced runner system." Space plants
in rows 2-4' apart, train runners to 7-8" apart by pinning them down with clothespins or hairpins. Cut
off excess runners to maintain spacing. In year 2, train runners into the central paths. Immediately after
harvest in year 2 or 3, mow down the original 2 or 3-year old plants, till in several times, spread lots of
compost, till a final time, and mulch with chopped leaves or compost every 2 weeks until fall. Every 2-3
years the pathways and growing beds trade places. U. of Wisconsin studies show enhanced yields when
"Regal" perennial rye grass is grown as a living mulch and mowed to 2-3" two or three times per year.

ALLIES: Some evidence-- none
          Uncertain-- borage, thyme
COMPANIONS: bush beans, lettuce, onion family, sage, spinach
ENEMIES: all *brassicas*

WALNUT VARIETIES

BLACK (*J. nigra*)

Purdue No.1-- superior tree, the only known patented hardwood, from Purdue University, very thin shell, extra large meat size, also excellent for timber, Indiana Walnut Products has a program to buy nuts back from you for cracking (Indiana Walnut Products)

Emma Kay-- an excellent variety, high kernel filling, thin shell, excellent cracking, good flavor, heavy yields, good in the Midwest (Grimo, Nolin River, Saginaw)

Thomas-- oldest grafted black walnut, one of largest nuts, well filled, high quality, very hard thin shells, good cracking, early and heavy yields, good in Northern and Western regions where anthracnose is not a problem, zones 5-9 (Fowler, Gurney's, Grimo, Miller, Saginaw, Stark)

Thomas Myers-- good straight tree for timber and good nuts, heavy bearer, large nuts cracks well, good through zone 8 and as far north as MA, Southern WI and MI (Nolin River)

Weschcke-- good flavor, high yields, one of hardiest black walnuts, pollinates Bicentennial, good for the far North (Grimo, St. Lawrence, Windmill)

Bicentennial-- excellent timber type, nuts as hard as Thomas, large nut, precocious, vigorous, one of hardiest black walnuts, good for the far North (Grimo, St. Lawrence, Saginaw)

PERSIAN (a.k.a. English or Carpathian) (*J. regia*) -- Because they leaf early, Persian walnuts grow best where peach trees don't suffer frost-kill. Carpathian refers to its namesake mountain range in Poland from where many Persian walnuts were imported; now it usually just refers to "hardy" cultivars.

Hansen-- bears young, self-fruitful, thin shell, good flavor, small to medium nut, resists anthracnose and husk maggot, naturally small, hardy, widely planted in the East, considered one of the best, especially good for Great Lakes area (Grimo, Nolin River, Saginaw, Windmill)

Colby-- early maturing, medium nut, thin shell, good flavor, hardy, especially good for Great Lakes area (Grimo, Nolin River)

Champion-- natural dwarf, grows to only 35', thin shell, tasty nut, hardy, zones 5-9 (Stark)

Himalaya-- very hardy, a good quality nut, good for the far North (Grimo, Windmill)

Franquette-- common cultivar in Northwest, tight nut resists worms, medium-large elongated nuts, high quality, thin smooth shells, tree leafs out and blooms late, slow maturing, not hardy in colder parts of Northwest, good for the West and Northwest (Fowler, Northwoods, Raintree)

Spurgeon-- large, flavorful nuts, reliable producer, productive, leafs out late, best cultivar for pockets where late spring frosts are a problem, benefits from pollination by Franquette, good for Northwest (Northwoods, Raintree)

BUTTERNUT (*J. cinerea*): From the Ohio valley and southward choose varieties with "clean foliage" for anthracnose resistance. Increasingly scarce, these offer high quality lumber. Hardy in zones 3-7.

Creighton-- good cracking qualities, medium nut, late vegetating, clean foliage, vigorous, rated number one in Indiana in 1988 (Nolin River, Saginaw)

Kenworthy-- large nut, good flavor, good cracking, vigorous, hardy (Grimo, Windmill)

Loumis "Bountiful"-- self-pollinating, 40-50', mild, thin shell, high yields, zones 4-7 (Stark)

HEARTNUT (*J. sieboldiana*) -- A Japanese ornamental walnut, these grow fast and bear nuts that hang in strings or clumps of 10-15. Its heart-shaped nutmeat is the sweetest of walnuts, with no bitterness, high in protein, and easy to extract. The tree bears even in poor soils.

Heartnut-- grows 40-60', cross-pollinate with Butternut and Buarnut, zones 5-9 (Northwoods, Miller, Stark; Nolin River, Saginaw & Windmill carries specific cultivars)

OTHER

Buarnut or Butterheart (butternut X heartnut)-- disease resistant, nuts are similar to butternut, zones 4-7 (Grimo, Miller, Northwoods, St. Lawrence, Saginaw, Windmill)

NOTES

Juglans regia (Carpathian)   Juglandaceae (Walnut)   **WALNUT**

GROWTH CONDITIONS
Height: 20-80'
Breadth: 20-40'
Spacing: 10'. When 10" in diameter in about 25 years thin to 22-50'.
Pollination: All walnuts require cross-pollination.
Chilling Requirement: All require some chilling hours.
Bearing Age: 3-5 years for nuts, 10-20 years to produce veneer for market.
Root Depth: Very deep.
pH: 5.5-7.0   Persian, 6.0-7.0
Site: Full sun. Don't plant anywhere near vegetable garden or orchard. Deep, well-drained loam.
Water: Medium.
Training: Free-standing-- central leader   Wire-trained-- N/A
Fertilizer: Don't fertilize the first year. In following years apply compost or well-rotted manure. When
          10 years old, apply 1/4 lb boron (borax) in deep bar holes for steady nut production.
Pruning: Unlike most fruit and nut trees, prune in the fall. Don't start until 4-5 years old. Cut out
          dead or diseased wood, and crossed or competing branches.

PESTS: aphid, bluejay, codling moth, fall webworm, mouse, navel orangeworm, squirrel, walnut
          caterpillar, walnut husk fly, walnut maggot
DISEASES: crown gall, walnut anthracnose, walnut blight, walnut bunch

HARVEST: Due to the indelible stains imparted by the husks, always wear gloves. Remove the outer
husks within 1 week of harvest; let dry for several days after which the husks will be easy to remove.
Three methods to de-husk the nut: 1) corn sheller equipped with a flywheel and pulley, driven by 1/4
hp motor, 2) spread a single layer in a wooden trough on a driveway and run a car or tractor over them,
which splits the husk easily, 3) take them to a professional huller.

STORAGE REQUIREMENTS: Rinse off hulled nut shells and place in water. Remove rotten and
diseased nuts that float to the top. Dry and cure by spreading in one layer in a cool, dry, well-ventilated
area. They're ready for storage when the kernels rattle in the shell, in 1-3 weeks, or when unshelled
kernels snap. Store shelled nuts in plastic bags with holes, or in tightly sealed tin cans lined with paper
and with a hole punctured in the can beneath the lid, or freeze. Store unshelled nuts in an unheated shed
over winter, and in spring move them to a cooler place.
Fresh: Temp: 32-36   Humidity: 60-70 %   Storage Life: 1 year
Preserved, taste (months): shelled, frozen: excellent (24)

OTHER GROWING NOTES: Black walnut and butternut roots excrete an acid (juglone) that inhibits
the growth of many plants, so plant far away from vegetables and flowers. Weed control is vital to the
initial years of walnut tree growth. All walnuts benefit from mulching. Walnut trees grown for nut crops
require large crowns, for veneers a straight trunk; to grow for both, veneer requirements prevail, so
prune for straight growth. Carpathian walnuts grow rapidly, about 4-5' per year. Black walnuts, the
largest *Juglans*, bear nuts high in protein and polyunsaturated oils and should be used sparingly in
cooking. Grafted trees usually yield 3-4 times higher kernel filling than seedlings. Butternuts, or white
walnut, are the hardiest *Juglans*, don't require as much water, and also have a rich buttery taste. Buy
as small a tree as possible to minimize injury to the tap root which, in *Juglans*, is very straight and long.
True nut flavor and quality may not emerge for 2-3 years after bearing, so don't judge trees prematurely.

ALLIES: Some evidence-- weedy ground cover
          Uncertain-- none
COMPANIONS: autumn olive, black locust, European alder, soybeans, popcorn (1st few years)
OTHER: Walnuts do better in mixed plantings than in a monoculture walnut grove.
ENEMIES: apple, azalea, tomato (these are particularly sensitive to walnut root acid)

Herbs

Sweet Basil

Chives

Spearmint

Garlic

Dill

Rosemary

Marjoram

Sage

Tarragon

BASIL VARIETIES

GREENHOUSE
Any variety will work.

OUTDOOR
Cinnamon (O. var.)-- similar to sweet basil, cinnamon flavor, from Mexico (widely available)

Dark Opal Basil-- 18", purple-bronze foliage, dark purple flowers, very ornamental, good for seasoning, colors vinegars purple (Fox Hill, Nichols, Richters, Sandy Mush)

Green Ruffles (O. basilicum "green ruffles")-- 24", pretty curly and serrated large leaves (Burpee, Dabney, Richters)

Holy (O. sanctum, purple Tulsi form)-- whole plant has reddish-purple tint, deep, spicy clove scent (Companion Plants, Fox Hill, Sandy Mush)

Lemon (O. citriodorum)-- 12", intense lemon flavor, ideal for tea, compact bush-type (widely available)

Lettuce Leaf (O. basilicum crispum)-- 18", large broad crinkled leaves to 4" long, rich flavor, not as strong as sweet basil (Companion Plants, Nichols, Richters, Sandy Mush, Seeds Blum)

Mammoth Basil (O. basilicum)-- extremely large leaves, sweet fragrance and tasty (Richters)

Mayo/Yaqui Basil (O. basilicum)-- do not grow with other basils if saving seed, good for low desert (Native Seeds)

Mrs. Burns famous Lemon Basil (O. basilicum)-- pure strain, readily self-seeds, plant spring & fall, for low and high desert, some consider superior to other sweet basils (Native Seeds)

Piccolo Verde Fino-- small leaves, intense true basil flavor, slightly minty, favored for pesto because it maintains flavor better after flowering than others (Casa Yerba, Companion Plants, Fox Hill, Richters, Nichols)

Purple Ruffles-- AAS winner, large, very ruffled and fringed leaves, dark purple leaves and pink flowers, beautiful ornamental, also good culinary (Burpee, Fox Hill, Nichols, Richters, Seeds Blum)

Spicy Globe-- great fragrant edging plant and for pots, maintains small mound shape all season, white flowers, good culinary uses (Dabney, Fox Hill, Richters, Seeds Blum)

Sweet Basil (O. basilicum)-- 16", a fast grower, tasty and one of best basil flavors, classic pesto basil (widely available)

Thai-- green leaves with purple flowers and stems, good for Southeast Asian cuisine (Nichols)

NOTES

Basilicum   *Labiatae (Mint)*   **Sweet BASIL**

GROWTH CONDITIONS

Germ.Temp: 75-86   Height: 18-24"
Grow.Temp: Hot   Breadth: 20-30"
pH: 5.5-7.0   Spacing: Intensive: 10-12"   Reg: 12-18"   Rows: 15-25"
Root Depth: 8-12"   Planting Depth: 1/4"
Site: Full sun, protected site
Water: Low, but evenly moist
Fertilizer: Light feeder
Side-dress: Not necessary
Propagation: By seed
First Seed Starting Date:

Days Germ + Days Transplant - Days After LFD = Days Count BACK from LFD
3-9   +   7-14   -   14   = 9 days before LFD
                                                to 4 days after LFD

Last Seed Starting Date:

Days Germ + Days Transplant + Maturity + SDF + Frost Tender = Days BACK from FFD
3-9   +   7-14   + 30-50   + 14 +   14   = 68-101

PESTS: Japanese beetle, slug, snail
DISEASES: botrytis rot, damping off

HARVEST: Pick continuously before the flower buds open. Keep blossoms clipped and pruned in order to encourage continuous bushy growth. Cut in the morning after the dew has dried. Cut the top growth up to 6" below the flower buds or ends. Don't wash the leaves unless necessary, for you'll wash away aromatic oils.

STORAGE REQUIREMENTS: Leaves can be used fresh, dried, or preserved in oil or vinegar. To dry, in a warm, dry, dark place hang bunches of snipped stems with leaves or spread leaves on a wire mesh. When thoroughly dry, strip leaves off stems. Do not crush or grind until you're ready to use. Store in the dark in airtight containers or freezer bags. Some feel basil stored in oil or vinegar is much better than dried. If storing frozen pesto, garlic can get bitter in the freezer so don't add garlic until ready to serve.
Fresh: keep in glass of water at room temperature   Storage Life: 3-5 days (see "Growing Notes")
Freeze: excellent, particularly for making as pesto   Dry: fair-good (relative to fresh basil flavor)

OTHER GROWING NOTES: Basil is an annual warm season herb, very tender to frost and light freezes. It transplants easily and can also be grown easily in a greenhouse. Continuous harvest benefits this herb because pruning fosters a bushier plant. Rosalind Creasy reports that a study by the University of California at Davis recommends never putting basil in the refrigerator. Their study shows that basil will live better if put in a glass of water and kept at room temperature. Basil is one of the more popular herbs for seasoning a wide range of dishes, fresh or dried. In the experience of some culinary experts, dried basil has very little flavor compared with fresh basil. It is, perhaps, hard to compare the flavors of fresh and dried as they are so different and can also give different effects in a dish. No basil lover, however, will ever pass up fresh for dried. There are quite a wide range of basil varieties, from purple to lime green, curly to ruffled-edged leaves, and smooth to hairy leaves. An ingredient in the liqueur Chartreuse, basil varies widely in flavor from the minty to hints of clove and cinnamon.

COMPANIONS: pepper, tomato
OTHER: Basil is said to repel flies, mosquitoes, and to improve growth and flavor of vegetables.
ENEMIES: cucumber, rue, snap beans

GREENHOUSE

Caraway should grow well in the greenhouse if grown in a pot deep enough to accommodate its tap root.

OUTDOOR

The single cultivar of caraway is widely available.

NOTES

Carum carvi   *Umbelliferae (Parsley)*   **CARAWAY**

GROWTH CONDITIONS

Germ.Temp: 70   Height: 2'
Grow.Temp: Warm   Breadth: 12-18"
pH: 5.5-7.0   Spacing: Intensive: 6"   Reg: 12-18"   Rows: 18-24"
Root Depth: Long tap root   Planting Depth: 1/4 - 1/2"
Site: Full sun to light shade
Water: Low, but evenly moist
Fertilizer: Light feeder
Side-dress: Not necessary
Propagation: By seed and cuttings
First Seed Starting Date:

        Days Germ + Days Transplant + Days Before LFD = Days Count BACK from LFD
        17   +   0 (direct)   +   0-7   =   17-24

Last Seed Starting Date:

        Days Germ + Days Transplant + Maturity + SDF + Frost Tender = Days BACK from FFD
        17   +   0 (direct)   +   55   + 14 +   N/A   =   86

PESTS: carrot rust fly
DISEASES: none

HARVEST: When the seeds are brown and before they begin to fall, snip the stalks. Tie in bundles and hang upside down in a warm, dry, airy place. Place paper-lined trays under the stalks to collect falling seeds, or cover with a paper bag and let the seeds drop into the bag. Shaking the stalks may also be necessary to dislodge the seeds. After a few weeks when the fallen seeds are thoroughly dry, store them in an airtight jar.

STORAGE REQUIREMENTS: Store in airtight jars in a cool, dark place.
Freeze: caraway leaf doesn't freeze well   Dry: the seed is excellent dried

OTHER GROWING NOTES: Caraway is a biennial warm season herb, tender to frost and light freezes. It is commonly grown as an annual in most areas of the country, except for Northern California where it apparently won't grow well. Sow it directly as it doesn't transplant well, or transplant while still small. It flowers in the spring and produces seed in its second summer, or in its first summer if sown in the fall. Caraway roots, which are long tap roots, can be eaten like carrots. The leaves can be used in salads, soups, or stews. The oil is used to flavor Kummel, a German & Russian liqueur, as well as Aquavit.

COMPANIONS: coriander, fruit trees, peas
OTHER: Caraway is supposed to be good for loosening the soil, and is reputed to attract beneficial
        insects to fruit trees.
ENEMIES: fennel

GREENHOUSE
All chives grow well in a cool greenhouse or on a windowsill.

OUTDOOR
Chive-- common strain, mild onion flavor, great in salads, soups, potatoes, eggs, and cheese, and fish dishes (widely available)
Curly Chive (Allium senescens var. "glaucum")-- ornamental, not edible, deep pink flowers (Companion Plants)
Garlic Chive (Allium tuberosum)-- mild onion-garlic flavor, broader leaves than common strain, from Japan, pretty white flowers (widely available)
Grolau Chive-- similar to the common strain but developed for indoor growing, excellent in greenhouses, productive when cut continuously, good strong flavor (Nichols)
Mauve Garlic Chive-- same as the garlic chive but with pretty mauve flowers (Richters)
Yellow Garlic Chive-- same as the garlic chive but with light yellow flowers (Richters)

NOTES

Allium schoenoprasum   *Liliaceae (Lily)*   **CHIVE**

GROWTH CONDITIONS

Germ.Temp: 60-70   Height: 6-18"
Grow.Temp: Hot   Breadth: 6-8"
pH: 5.5-7.0   Spacing: Intensive: 6"   Reg: 5-8"   Rows: 12"
Root Depth: Bulb clumps   Planting Depth: 1/4 - 1/2"
Site: Full sun to a little light shade
Water: Average
Fertilizer: Light feeder
Side-dress: Not necessary
Propagation: Division or seed. Divide plant in mid-May every three years into clumps of 6 bulbs
First Seed Starting Date: Chives mature in 50 days, whether or not transplanted.

Days Germ + Days Transplant + Days Before LFD = Days Count BACK from LFD
10-14   +   21-42   +   0   =   31-56

PESTS: none
DISEASES: none

HARVEST: After the plant is 6" tall, cut some blades down to 2" above the ground to encourage plant production. Herbs should be cut in the morning after the dew has dried. Rather than cutting chive tips, cut near the base of the greenery so new tender shoots will emerge. Do not wash the cuttings or aromatic oils will be lost.

STORAGE REQUIREMENTS: Chives are best fresh or frozen, but can be dried. To dry, tie them in small bunches and hang upside down in a warm, dry, dark place. Do not crush or cut up until ready to use. Store the stem whole, if possible. If harvested with the flower, you can store them whole in white vinegar to make a pretty light lavender and mildly flavored vinegar for gifts. Another storage method, recommended by Dr. Alan Gouin as an excellent way of preserving chive flavor, is to layer in a glass jar 1" of kosher salt alternately with 1" of chives. Pack down each layer with a spoon. Use these chives in any dish just as you would fresh chives, but they're reportedly especially good in soups. The brine can also be used to flavor such dishes as soups.
Freeze: excellent   Dry: fair-good

OTHER GROWING NOTES: Chives are a perennial warm season herb, hardy to frost and light freezes. This herb likes rich and well-drained soil. Chives are virtually foolproof since they suffer no diseases or pests. After several years you can divide them for expansion, and in the autumn you can dig up a clump to pot indoors for continuous winter cutting. Chives blossom mid-summer and are an attractive addition to the garden. If allowed to bloom, cut them back after flowering so new shoots will come up in spring. Chives also thrive in a cool greenhouse or on a kitchen windowsill.

COMPANIONS: carrot, celery, grape, peas, rose, and tomato
OTHER: Chives are a putative deterrent to Japanese beetles, black spot on roses, scab on apples, mildew on cucurbits, and aphids on celery, lettuce and peas.
ENEMIES: beans, peas

GREENHOUSE
Coriander grows well in the greenhouse.

OUTDOOR
Chinese Coriander-- especially good for fresh leaf production because it doesn't bolt as quickly (Richters)
Coriander (standard)-- fresh leaves are delicious in salsa and Latin, Indian, Chinese and many other cuisines. The seeds are traditional in curry, chili, and some baked goods, and are a great addition to soups, stews and Indian dishes. Good in all areas, including high and low desert. Self-seeding in warmer climates. (widely available)
Slow-bolt Coriander-- especially good for fresh leaf production because it doesn't go to seed as quickly (Seeds Blum, Shepherd's)
Vietnamese Coriander (Polygonium odoratum)-- not a true coriander, almost identical to native smartweed or knotweed, a perennial in some climates, tastes remarkably similar to true coriander, can be grown indoors with sufficient light (Companion Plants, Richters)

NOTES

Coriandrum sativum   Umbelliferae (Parsley) **Cilantro or CORIANDER**

GROWTH CONDITIONS

Germ.Temp: 50-70   Height: 12-21"
Grow.Temp: Cool   Breadth: 6-12"
pH: 6.0-7.0   Spacing: Intensive: 6-8" Reg: 8-12" Rows: 12-15"
Root Depth: 8-18"   Planting Depth: 1/4 - 1/2"
Site: Full sun to partial shade   Water: average
Fertilizer: Light feeder. N reduces flavor.
Side-dress: Not necessary
Propagation: By seed
First Seed Starting Date:
          Days Germ + Days Transplant + Days Before LFD = Days Count BACK from LFD
          12   +   30   +   7-21   = 49-63
Last Seed Starting Date:
          Days Germ + Days Transplant + Maturity + SDF + Frost Tender = Days BACK from FFD
          6   +   21   +   55   + 14 +   0   = 96

PESTS: carrot rust fly
DISEASES: none

HARVEST: For fresh leaves, snip the stalks with smaller immature leaves for best flavor. Herbs should be cut in the morning after the dew has dried. Cut the top growth up to 6" below the flower buds or ends. Do not wash or aromatic oils will be lost. For seeds, harvest when the whitish seeds and leaves turn brown but before seeds drop. Cut the whole plant.

STORAGE REQUIREMENTS: The leaves store poorly unless preserved in something like salsa, where its flavor can still fade in a day. But coriander seeds keep well in tight jars. To dry seeds, tie the plant upside down in a warm, dry, dark place until the seeds turn brown in several weeks. Place stalks in a paper bag and thresh until all seeds are removed from stems. Sift out seeds from chaff. Another method to finish the drying process is to remove the seeds from stems and dry them in a slow oven (100F) until they turn a light brown. You can smell the difference between properly air-dried or roasted coriander seed and seed that is still green. For best flavor, don't grind the seeds until ready to use. Store seeds in cool, dark place in an airtight jar.
Fresh: put cuttings in glass of water, refrigerate, & refresh water daily   Storage Life: 3-7 days
Freeze: some report excellent for leaf, some report poor   Dry: excellent for seed, poor for leaf

OTHER GROWING NOTES: Coriander is an annual cool season herb, tender to frost and light freezes. In some warmer climates coriander is self-seeding. It grows easily, although it does go to seed quickly when the weather turns hot. For a steady supply of the leaf try sowing in succession every one-two weeks. If you're growing it for seed, you'll need to stake the plant. Put in stakes at the time of sowing or transplanting. Mulch coriander early and heavily to keep weeds down. All parts of the coriander are edible, including the root which tastes like the leaves but with an added nutty flavor. Unlike most herbs, fresh coriander leaf is usually either loved or hated. Make sure your guests can tolerate fresh coriander before including it in a dish. Coriander is supposed to attract useful insects, and coriander honey is apparently famous for its flavor. You can make imitation coriander honey by adding a small amount of coriander oil to clover honey.

COMPANIONS: caraway, eggplant, fruit trees, potato, tomato
OTHER: Coriander is supposed to enhance anise growth. It is also a putative companion to fruit
          trees because it is supposed to attracts beneficial insects.
ENEMIES: none

DILL VARIETIES

GREENHOUSE
Dill grows well in the greenhouse. See "Other Growing Notes," opposite.

OUTDOOR
Aroma Dill-- this offers larger yields and a better aroma (Sandy Mush)

Bouquet Dill-- best grown for dill seeds for pickles and potato salads, a more compact and attractive plant than the common strain (Nichols, Shepherd's)

Dill-- old-fashioned dill, used for dill pickles and sauerkraut (widely available)

Dukat Dill-- best for its fresh leaves, originally from Finland, slow-bolting, flavor is mellow and aromatic, never bitter, excellent with shrimp, fish and cucumbers (Dabney, Shepherd's)

Indian Dill (Anethum sowa)-- seeds used in Indian curries, leaves used in rice and soups, little more bitter than the common strain, smaller plant (Companion Plants, Sandy Mush)

NOTES

Anethum graveolens   *Umbelliferae (Parsley)*   DILL

GROWTH CONDITIONS

Germ.Temp: 50-70
Grow.Temp: Hot
pH: 5.5-6.5
Root Depth: Very long taproot
Site: Full sun, sheltered from wind
Water: Average

Height: 3-4'
Breadth: 24"
Spacing: for leaf, 8-10" for seed, 10-12"   Rows: 18-24"
Planting Depth: 1/4 - 1/2"

Fertilizer: Light feeder. Might need one application of compost or slow release fertilizer.
Side-dress: Not necessary
Propagation: Seed
First Seed Starting Date: Sow every 3 weeks for a continuous supply of leaves.

Days Germ	+	Days Transplant	-	Days After LFD	=	Days Count BACK from LFD
14	+	21-30	-	14	=	21-30

PESTS: carrot rust fly, green fly, parsleyworm, tomato hornworm
DISEASES: none

HARVEST: Cut the tender feathery leaves close to the stem. Herbs should be cut in the morning after the dew has dried. Do not wash or aromatic oils will be lost. Dill foliage has the best flavor before the flower head develops and when used the same day it's cut. If you want to harvest dill seed, let the plant flower and go to seed. Harvest when the lower seeds turn brown and before they scatters. The lower seeds on a head will brown first, while the upper ones can dry inside. Finish drying by tying stems and hanging upside down in a cool, dark, dry place, or place in a paper bag with holes cut in the sides. Sift to remove the seed from chaff.

STORAGE REQUIREMENTS: Fresh dill keeps for up to 3 days in a jar, stems down in water, covered with plastic. It will store for up to 3 months layered with pickling salt in a covered jar in the refrigerator. To use just brush off salt. To freeze, store on the stem in plastic bags. Cut off what you need and return the rest to the freezer. To dry the leaves, spread them over nonmetallic screen in a dark, warm, dry place for several days. Then store in an airtight container. Don't crush or grind until ready to use.
Freeze: good for foliage   Dry: good for foliage, excellent for seeds

OTHER GROWING NOTES: Dill is an annual or perennial warm season herb, very sensitive to light freezes and frost. If it's not grown in a protected spot, make sure you stake it to prevent the wind from knocking over the tall stalks. Dill doesn't transplant easily because of its long taproot, so don't transplant once it grows beyond seedling stage. If it's not planted early enough, seed may not develop until the beginning of the second year. It can be grown in the greenhouse if you provide a container large enough for its roots, at least 6-8" in diameter, and pot it in rich soil. In the garden, if allowed to go to seed without complete harvest, it will reseed itself and grow as a perennial. As a seed it's used primarily for pickling. As dill weed, it's used to flavor sauces, fish, meats, soups, breads, and salads. To keep the best flavor, try snipping the weed with scissors instead of mincing with a knife.

COMPANIONS: all *Brassicas*, fruit trees
OTHER: Some gardeners report that in orchards dill helps attract beneficial wasps, bees and flies that will pollinate blossoms and attack codling moths and tent caterpillars. Others report it may help cabbage by repelling aphids, spider mites, caterpillars. There is, however, no scientific study or proof.
ENEMIES: carrot, fennel (cross-pollinates with dill), tomato

FENNEL VARIETIES

GREENHOUSE
All varieties of fennel should grow well in the greenhouse.

OUTDOORS
Sweet Fennel *(F. vulgare)*: grown primarily for leaves and seeds

Bronze *(F. vulgare dulce* var. *rubrum)*-- pretty coppery leaves, ornamental and flavorful seeds, may tend to be biennial (Burpee, Companion Plants, Nichols, Richters, Seeds Blum, Shepherd's)

Green Leaf-- can be grown for leaves, seeds, and stalks (Cook's)

Red Leaf-- bronze leaves, known for ornamental and culinary uses (Cook's)

Sweet *(F. vulgare dulce)*-- grown primarily for seeds and leaves, but stalks can be eaten as a vegetable, popular in Italy (Companion Plants, Dabney, Fox Hill, Nichols, Richters)

Finnochio or Florence Fennel: best for swollen roots and stalks

Florence *(F. vulgare* var. *azoricum)*-- develops nice crisp, anise-flavored stalks, fall-maturing, usually grown as an annual (Burpee, Dabney, Fox Hill, Richters)

Herald-- high bolt resistance, grow for plump, sweet bulbs (Thompson & Morgan)

Zefa Fino-- good bulbing variety, from Switzerland (Cook's)

NOTES

Foeniculum vulgare   *Umbelliferae (Parsley)*   **FENNEL**

GROWTH CONDITIONS

Germ.Temp: 60-80   Height: up to 4-5' (may need staking)
Grow.Temp: Cool   Breadth: 12-18"
pH: 5.5-7.0   Spacing: slim fennel, 6"   Florence fennel, 10-12"
Root Depth: Tap root   Planting Depth: 1/4" (just barely covered with soil)
Site: Full sun and rich, well-drained soil
Water: Low, but evenly moist. Water in times of drought.
Fertilizer: Light feeder
Side-dress: Not necessary
Propagation: By seed. Division and replant established plants every three years.
First Seed Starting Date:

      Days Germ + Days Transplant + Days Before LFD = Days Count BACK from LFD
      6-17   +   10-28   + 26   = 42-71

Last Seed Starting Date:

      Days Germ + Days Transplant + Maturity + SDF + Frost Tender = Days BACK from FFD
      6-17   +   0 (direct)   + 60-70 + 14 +   14   = 94-115

PESTS: carrot rust fly
DISEASES: none

HARVEST: For leaf clippings, you can start to cut the leaves once the plant is established. For fennel stems and bulbs, wait until the plant begins to bloom, pinch off the blooms, and allow the stems and bulb to fatten several more days. Cut them off at the base and use while fresh. For seeds, allow plant to bloom. When the seeds turn brown, cut off the entire seed head and place in a paper bag. Fennel seeds are very delicate and fall easily from the plant, so be sure to cut seedheads before seeds are blown away. Dry in a warm, dark place for several weeks.

STORAGE REQUIREMENTS: Store seeds and dried leaf clippings in airtight jars in a cool, dark place. Dried leaf clippings do lose their flavor over time. Stems and bulbs can be stored for 1-2 weeks in the refrigerator. You might also peel and store the stems in white vinegar with black pepper corns for use in salads.
Freeze: fennel leaf clippings can be frozen   Dry: the seed is excellent dried

OTHER GROWING NOTES: Fennel is a perennial warm season herb, half-hardy to frost and light freezes. This herb is best sown in succession plantings in the spring, as it tends to bolt in hot summers. For a fall crop, sow in July. If you're growing Florence fennel, renowned for its swollen and tender anise-flavored stalks, mound the soil a little bit around the base to promote more tender, blanched stalks. Fennel stems are a more common culinary item in Europe than in the U.S. They're delicious raw in salads, steamed, sauteed with a little butter and wine, or added to soups, stews and fish dishes. Fennel leaves are thought by some to improve digestion, and fennel tea to have anti-flatulent and calming effects. Fennel seeds are delicious in breads, sausages, pizza and tomato sauce, stews, and fish and chicken dishes.

COMPANIONS: most vegetables
ENEMIES: all beans, caraway, coriander (prevents seeds from forming), dill (cross-pollinates with
        (fennel), pepper, tomato

GARLIC VARIETIES

GREENHOUSE
None, garlic doesn't do well in the greenhouse.

OUTDOOR
Artichoke Garlic-- very early, cloves are layered like artichoke leaves, purple skin, fairly large (Seeds Blum)

California White-- easy to grow, stores like onions, very mild flavor (Henry Field's, Jung)

Elephant Garlic (Allium ampeloprasum)-- milder than regular garlic and about 6 times larger, hardy for fall planting, developed and named by Nichols, bake whole or roast or use fresh in salads and other dishes where a mild garlic is desired (widely available)

Italian Garlic or Rocambole or Serpent Garlic (A. sativum ophioscordon)-- mild garlic flavor, easy to peel, above ground bulblets and below ground bulbs are prized in Europe, the stems bearing the small bulblets are looped (Richters, Sandy Mush, Seeds Blum)

Nichols Silverskin-- noted for its strong flavor, size and easy peeling (Fox Hill, Nichols)

Nichols Top Set-- pungent flavor, harvest medium bulbs at end of season, small bulblets at the top of each plant can be kept for early spring or fall planting (Nichols)

NOTES

Culinary Proverb: "Anything not benefitting from the addition of chocolate will probably benefit from the addition of garlic."

Allium sativum   *Liliaceae (Lily)*   **GARLIC**

GROWTH CONDITIONS

Germ.Temp: 60-80	Height: 1-3'
Grow.Temp: Cool	Breadth: 6-10"
pH: 4.5-8.3	Spacing: Intensive: 3" Reg: 4-6" Rows: 12-15"
Root Depth: Bulbs, 2" - 2'	Planting Depth: 1 - 2", pointed end up

Site: Full sun
Water: Low. For perennial bulbs withhold all water during summer, except in arid, dry areas (see below).
Fertilizer: Light feeder. Use compost and liquid seaweed extract.
Side-dress: Not necessary
Propagation: Usually propagated by cloves (easiest method), though garlic can be started by seeds.
First Clove Starting Date: Cloves can be planted about 6 weeks before the last frost.

Days Germ + Days Transplant + Days Before LFD = Days Count BACK from LFD
7-14   +   0 (direct)   + 14-21   = 28-42

Last Clove Starting Date: cloves can be planted in autumn for harvest in spring

Days Germ + Days Transplant + Maturity + SDF + Frost Tender = Days BACK from FFD
7   +   0 (direct)   + 90   + 14 +   0   = 111

PESTS: nematode
DISEASES: botrytis rot, white rot

HARVEST: Green garlic shoots, a gourmet treat in many places, can be cut from the bulbs going to flower and used like scallions. Garlic bulbs are ready to harvest when the tops turn brown and die back. Do not knock the tops down to hasten harvest. Some research indicates this practice shortens storage life. Withhold water and, in a few days, dig carefully to lift the plants. The tops usually are not strong enough to pull, with the exception of the perennial garlic (see below). Do not bruise bulbs or they'll get moldy and attract insects when stored.

STORAGE REQUIREMENTS: Cure bulbs in the sun for several days to two weeks to harden the skins and dry. To braid, keep the tops on. Otherwise clip off dried leaves and the root bunches. Store in paper bags, net bags, or nylon stockings, tying a knot between each bulb in the stocking.
Fresh: Temp: 32   Humidity: 65-70%   Storage Life: 6-7 months

OTHER GROWING NOTES: Garlic is an annual or perennial cool season crop, hardy to frost and light freezes. Plant cloves in rich, deep, moist well-drained soil in a sunny location. While it can be started from seed, it's easiest to grow from individual cloves. Garlic bulbs mature in an average of 6-10 months. Cloves may be planted in either fall or spring, but fall plantings yield larger bulbs the next summer than spring plantings harvested in the fall. You may have to add compost to the soil before planting. Remove flower buds if they develop. Early cultivars store poorly and have inferior quality.
Perennial Method: One Washington State gardener has a garlic patch that hasn't been planted or plowed for 20 years. His method: when the garlic is about 2' tall, pinch off the seed buds that develop or garlic won't form. Do not water at all during the summer (except in arid, dry climates water regularly). Harvest only the large plants by simply pulling them (no digging necessary). The smaller plants die back and emerge again the following year. After harvest, lightly till the surface with a hand cultivator and uproot weeds. Water well to germinate weed seeds, then cultivate again to get rid of young weeds. In October spread a 3-4" leaf mulch. In spring garlic will grow through the mulch again.

COMPANIONS: beet, *Brassicas*, celery, chamomile, fruit trees, lettuce, raspberry, rose, savory, tomato
OTHER: Garlic spray has been found to have some antifungal powers in controlling downy mildew, cucumber and bean rust, bean anthracnose, early tomato blight, brown rot of stone fruit, leaf spot of cucumber, bacterial blight of beans, and soft-bodied insects such as aphids and leafroller larvae.
ENEMIES: all beans, peas

GREENHOUSE
    Tender varieties can be grown inside.

OUTDOOR
    Hardy English-types
        English Lavender (L.a. or L. vera)-- 3', the hardiest lavender, considered the best for culinary uses, perfumes, soaps and oils, spreading, bushy growth, silvery grey and narrow leaves, light purple flowers, good for northern climates (Companion Plants, Dabney, Nichol, Richters, Sandy Mush)
        Grey Lady (L.a."Grey Lady")-- 18", fast, compact growth, grey foliage, lavender-blue flowers, hardy (Companion Plants, Sandy Mush)
        Jean Davis (L.a."Jean Davis")-- 18", dainty compact mounds, low growth, bluish foliage, pink flowers, very hardy, excellent for borders and formal gardens (Dabney, Sandy Mush)
        Rosy (L.a. "Rosea")-- 18", attractive, compact plant, pink flowers, good for borders and formal gardens (Companion Plants, Richters)
        True Lavender-- 3', very hardy, good for clipped borders (Sandy Mush)
    Tender types -- good for frost-free areas or dig up and pot as a winter house plant.
        French or Fringed Lavender (L. dentata)-- 3', very green toothed leaves, very fragrant foliage, provides more but lower quality oil with camphor-rosemary scent (Companion Plants, Dabney, Richters, Sandy Mush)
        Spanish Lavender (L. stoechas)-- 30", beautiful grey foliage with green overtone, toothed and narrow leaves, aroma is strong, resinous and reminds some of turpentine, flowers bloom nearly all year, light purple flowers, excellent year-round pot plant (Companion Plants, Sandy Mush)
        Spike (L. latifolia)-- coarse, broad leaves, oil is used in soaps, high oil yields (Richters)

NOTES

Lavendula angustifolia   *Labiatae (Mint)*   **LAVENDER**

GROWTH CONDITIONS

Germ.Temp: N/A   Height: 14" - 3'
Grow.Temp: Hot   Breadth: up to 5'
pH: 6.5-7.0   Spacing: Intensive: 2'   Reg: 4-6'   Rows: 6'
Root Depth: Deep   Planting Depth: cover roots properly
Site: Full sun, can be stony, protected from wind
Water: Low
Fertilizer: Light feeder. Lime may be needed to make sure soil is basic enough.
Side-dress: Not necessary
Propagation: Cuttings or seed. Lavender is seldom started from seed because of its long germination
          time. In summer use cuttings 2-3" long from the side shoots. Make sure there is some
          older wood on cutting. Place cuttings in moist, sandy soil in a shaded cold frame 3-4" apart.
          When they're one year old plant in well-drained, dry soil that is protected from severe frost.
          The first year plants should be pruned to keep from flowering and encourage branching.

PESTS: caterpillars
DISEASES: fungal diseases

HARVEST: Don't cut until the second year planted outside. Pick the flowers when in blossom but just
before full bloom, usually in August. On a dry and still day, cut early in the day after the dew has dried.
Cut the top growth up to 6" below the flower spikes. Do not wash them or aromatic oils will be lost.

STORAGE REQUIREMENTS: To dry, tie branches in small bunches and hang upside down in a
warm, dry, dark place. Then remove the flowers from the stems and keep whole in storage.
Dry: excellent, will remain aromatic for a long time

OTHER GROWING NOTES: Lavender is a perennial warm season herb, hardy to frost and light
freezes in Zones 5-8. It likes full sun and light, well-drained soil. Lavender can be grown easily in
containers in the greenhouse or on windowsills, and trained to different forms. Besides serving as a
pretty border plant, dried lavender flowers are touted as a good moth repellant and lavender oil as an
additive to soaps and sachets. For the best oil production lavender needs hot, dry weather from May
through August. Oils have been used for centuries for a wide variety of things from curing lice, repelling
mosquitoes, embalming, to use in porcelain lacquers, varnishes and paints. Lavender is also used to make
a light perfume. Add rose petals, lavender flowers, and jasmine flowers to distilled vinegar, and store
in airtight bottles. In the kitchen lavender flowers and leaves can be used to flavor jellies and vinegars.
Author Rosalind Creasy tells us that in southern France (Provence) lavender is added to herb mixes for
such things as salads. She also raves about lavender ice cream which, in her book *Cooking From The
Garden*, she describes as having a "unique lemony-perfume taste."

COMPANIONS: none
OTHER: Lavender leaves are reputed to repel insects.
ENEMIES: none

GREENHOUSE
Any variety can be grown in a cool greenhouse in the winter, but its flavor will be milder.

OUTDOOR
Golden Marjoram (O. marjorana "Aurea")-- crinkled, yellow-white leaves, attractive border plant, not strongly scented, not good for culinary uses (Companion Plants)
Pot Marjoram (O. onites)-- 12-15", pretty plant, spreads slowly in all directions, attracts bees, profuse blooms in late summer, stronger flavor than true marjoram, hardier than marjoram, larger flowers (Companion Plants, Fox Hill, Nichols)
Sweet or Knot Marjoram-- 12-24", best culinary variety, good in soups, salads, vinegars and Italian, French and Portuguese cuisines, an infusion is said to be good for coughs and sore throats, keeps well on a sunny windowsill through winter, small oval grey-green leaves (widely available)

NOTES

Origanum majorana   *Labiatae (Mint)*   Sweet MARJORAM

GROWTH CONDITIONS

Germ.Temp: 65-75   Height: 1-2'
Grow.Temp: Hot   Breadth: 10-12"
pH: 6.5-7.0   Spacing: Intensive: 6-8"   Reg: 8-10"   Rows: 15"
Root Depth: 6-12"   Planting Depth: 0", tiny seeds need light and should not be covered
Site: Full sun
Water: Low
Fertilizer: Light feeder
Side-dress: Not necessary
Propagation: Seeds, cuttings, root division. If you propagate by seed, either sow seeds directly outside
            after all danger of frost has passed, or start seeds indoors and then transplant in clumps of
            three, spaced 6-8". Germination takes 8-14 days. Pinch back plants before they bloom.
            After the first year, you can divide the plant roots, and pot them for your winter windowsill
            or greenhouse.

PESTS: aphid, spider mite
DISEASES: botrytis rot, damping off, rhizoctonia

HARVEST: Pick marjoram all summer and, if you want, cut it down to 1" above the ground. In the
North don't cut it back severely in the fall as it will weaken the plants. Herbs should be cut in the
morning after the dew has dried. Cut the top growth up to 6" below the flower buds or ends. Do not
wash or aromatic oils will be lost.

STORAGE REQUIREMENTS: To dry, tie the cuttings in small bunches and hang upside down in
a warm, dry, dark place. When dried, remove the leaves from the stems, and store whole. Do not crush
or grind until ready to use. Store in air-tight jars in a dark place.
Freeze: good   Dry: excellent, will retain much of its flavor

OTHER GROWING NOTES: Marjoram is a perennial or annual warm season herb, very tender to
frost and light freezes. It is winter hardy only in the South, zones 9-10, so most gardeners will want to
grow it outdoors as an annual or in pots to bring them indoors through the winter. Marjoram likes full
sun and soil that is light, dry, and well-drained. Also, note marjoram's requirement for very low-acid
soil. This herb has played many roles over the centuries, from medicinal and culinary purposes, aromatic
uses in closets and sachets, to serving as a green wool dye. Don't confuse sweet marjoram with "wild
marjoram" or the perennial oregano (O. vulgare). Sweet marjoram is used for cooking while the "wild
marjoram" is used for medicinal purposes.

COMPANIONS: sage. Marjoram is also alleged to generally improve the flavor of all vegetables.
ENEMIES: cucumber

OREGANO VARIETIES

GREENHOUSE
Any variety will do well in the greenhouse.

OUTDOOR
Compact Oregano (O. compacta Nana)-- 2-3", excellent ground cover in sunny areas, strong flavor, does well in a cool window in winter (Sandy Mush)

Dark Oregano-- 2', excellent seasoning, larger and darker leaves, more upright than standard (Fox Hill, Sandy Mush)

Golden Creeping Oregano (O. var. Aureum)-- 6", decorative golden ground cover, needs winter mulch, very mild oregano flavor (Companion Plants, Dabney, Fox Hill, Richters, Sandy Mush)

Greek Oregano (O. var. hirtum/O. hirtum/O. heracleoticum)-- 18", excellent flavor, white flowers, bright green leaves, good for drying (widely available)

Italian Oregano-- see Thyme, this has a strong oregano flavor but is actually a thyme

Mexican Oregano (Lippia graveolens)-- not a true oregano but listed here for its oregano flavor, often sold in Mexico and the Southwest as true oregano, used in Southwest chili and Mexican dishes, very strong flavor resembling oregano, can be grown into a miniature tree in a greenhouse or bright window (Companion Plants, Dabney, Fox Hill, Richters, Seeds Blum)

Mt. Pima Oregano (Monarda austromontana)-- used as commercial oregano in Mexico, wild plant with an unusual flavor, for low and high desert (Native Seeds)

Oregano Tytthantum (Khirgizstan Oregano)-- 18", excellent flavor, bushy growth, glossy green leaves, pink flowers (Sandy Mush)

Seedless Oregano (O. Viride)-- 18", excellent seasoning, as strong as Greek oregano but sweeter and less biting, leaves resemble sweet marjoram (Companion Plants)

NOTES

Origanum vulgare subs. *hirtum*   *Labiatae (Mint)*   OREGANO

GROWTH CONDITIONS

Germ.Temp: 65-75

Grow.Temp: Hot

pH: 6.5-7.5

Root Depth: Shallow

Site: Full sun

Water: Low

Fertilizer: Light feeder

Side-dress: Not necessary

Height: 12-24"

Breadth: 12"

Spacing: Intensive: 18" Rows: 18-20"

Planting Depth: 0", tiny seeds should not be covered

Propagation: Root division in spring, or cuttings and seeds. The easiest method is to take cuttings in summer and root them in sandy compost. Seeds germinate in about 4 days.

PESTS: aphid, leafminer, spider mite

DISEASES: botrytis rot, fungal disease, rhizoctonia

HARVEST: One gardener claims that a first harvest when the plant is a mere 6" tall fosters bushy growth. When the plant is budding proliferously in June she cuts the plant severely so that only the lower set of leaves remains. The plant reportedly leafs out again in a couple weeks. Then she cuts it back severely again in August. For times of highest oil content for flavor, see Notes below. Generally, herbs should be cut in the morning after the dew has dried. Cut the top growth up to 6" below the flower buds or ends. Do not wash the leaves or aromatic oils will be lost.

STORAGE REQUIREMENTS: To dry, tie the cuttings in small bunches and hang upside down in a warm, dry, dark place. When dried, remove the leaves from the stems, and keep leaves whole for storage. Store in airtight jars in a dark place. Don't crush or grind until ready to use.

Freeze: good   Dry: good

OTHER GROWING NOTES: Oregano is a perennial warm season herb, hardy to frost and light freezes through zone 5. It likes full sun and well-drained, average soil. Flowering doubles the concentration of oil in oregano leaves, so for the strongest flavor don't harvest until the plants start flowering. For non-flowering varieties, harvest in the late spring as the oil concentrations rise steadily in the spring and then decline. Even the late spring peak flavor of these varieties, however, doesn't compare with the oil levels in autumn flowering varieties. So, for the strongest flavored oregano choose a variety that is autumn flowering. Since it's difficult to get a good-flavored oregano, start yours from a cutting or plant that you can taste or that has an established track record. The best is O. heracleoticum.

COMPANIONS: all beans, cucumber, squash

ENEMIES: none

PARSLEY VARIETIES

GREENHOUSE
>   Any variety thrives in a cool greenhouse.

OUTDOOR
>   Plainleaf Group (P. crispum neapolitanum)
>   **Giant Italian**-- 2-3', thick stalks, great in soups, stews, salad (Nichols)
>   **Italian Broad Leaf or Single Italian**-- stronger flavor than the curled, best for drying, flat dark green leaves (Companion Plants, Dabney, Richters)
>   **Plain or Single-leaf Parsley**-- earlier maturing than others, deeply cut, bright green leaves, excellent flavor (Nichols, Richters, Shepherd's)
>   Curled Group (P.crispum)
>   **Decora**-- best for warm climates, hot weather doesn't slow growth, deep green curled leaves, thick leaves, good aroma and flavor (Richters)
>   **Exotica or Forest Green**-- grows vigorously even in cool weather, deep green curled leaves, good aroma and flavor (Nichols, Richters)
>   **Mosscurled**-- standard curly variety, bright green, good aroma and flavor, best for freezing (Companion Plants, Dabney, Nichols, Richters)
>   Hamburg Group (P.crispum tuberosum)
>   **Parsnip Rooted or Hamburg** -- the parsnip-like root of this variety can been added to soups and stews, leaf can be used but its flavor isn't rich (Burpee, Nichols)

NOTES

Petroselinum crispum   *Umbelliferae (Parsley)*   **PARSLEY**

GROWTH CONDITIONS

Germ.Temp: 50-85

Grow.Temp: 60-65

pH: 6.0-7.0

Root Depth: Shallow - 4'

Site: Full sun to partial shade

Water: Low

Fertilizer: Heavy feeder

Height: 12-18"

Breadth: 6-9"

Spacing: Intensive: 4"   Reg: 6-12"   Rows: 12-36"

Planting Depth: 1/4"

Side-dress: 2-3 times during the season apply compost or spray with liquid seaweed.

Propagation: Seed

First Seed Starting Date:

Days Germ + Days Transplant + Days Before LFD = Days Count BACK from LFD

11-42   +   7-14   +   10   = 28-66

Last Seed Starting Date:

Days Germ + Days Transplant + Maturity + SDF + Frost Tender = Days BACK from FFD

11-42   +   7-14   + 63-76 + 14   + 14   = 109-160

PESTS: cabbage looper, carrot rust fly, carrot weevil, nematode, parsleyworm, spider mite

DISEASES: crown rot, septoria leaf spot

HARVEST: Cut as needed. To keep it productive frequently cut back the full length of the outside stems and remove all flower stalks. Herbs should be cut in the morning after the dew has dried. Cut the top growth up to 6" below the flower buds or ends. Do not wash the leaves or aromatic oils will be lost.

STORAGE REQUIREMENTS: To dry, tie the cuttings in small bunches and hang upside down in a warm, dry, dark place. When dried remove the leaves from the stems, and keep whole for storage. The drying job can be finished, if you prefer, in the oven or microwave. Store in airtight jars in a dark place. Don't crush or grind until ready to use.

Freeze: curly parsley does well frozen   Dry: broad leaf Italian is better for drying

OTHER GROWING NOTES: Parsley is a cool season biennial herb, hardy to frost and light freezes. It is notorious for taking a long time to germinate. Several options to speed things along are to soak the seeds overnight or for 48 hours, refrigerate the seeds, freeze the seeds, or pour boiling water over the soil plug before covering it. If you soak the seeds for longer than overnight, change the water twice. Make sure you discard the water, as it will contain some of the germination inhibitor, furanocoumarin. If you let some of the plants go to seed late in the season they may produce seedlings that can be lifted and grown on the windowsill for next year's crop. Parsley is hardy but will usually go to seed in its second year, so it's most often grown as an annual. While some say it's hard to transplant, you can direct sow or transplant it from pots. An excellent source of Vitamin C, iron and minerals, parsley is more than a pretty garnish. It's refreshing flavor is a great addition to soups, salads, sauces and many dishes.

ALLIES: Some evidence-- none

Uncertain-- black salsify, coriander, pennyroyal

COMPANIONS: asparagus, corn, pepper, tomato

ENEMIES: none

GREENHOUSE
Any variety. Rosemary grows beautifully in the greenhouse.

OUTDOOR
Culinary
Common or Upright Rosemary-- over 6', hardy to 15F, the only rosemary good for cooking (Dabney, Nichols, Richters)
Ornamental -- Most can be used for culinary purposes but are better ornamentals.
Arp (R.o. "Arp")-- 5', hardiest cultivar to -10F, grey-green leaves, shrubby, very fragrant, light blue flowers, ornamental (Dabney, Fox Hill)
Benendon Blue or Pine-Scented or Augustissimus-- 2-5', hardy to 20F, very strong pine-like aroma, dark blue sparse flowers, tall, narrow growth habit, used in potpourri, the only non-culinary variety (Companion Plants, Fox Hill, Richters, Sandy Mush)
Blue Boy-- 2', hardy to 20F, smallest habit and leaves of any rosemary, especially suited for indoor growing, good on windowsills and for bonsai, prostrate type, mild fresh fragrance, light blue flowers abundant in summer (Companion Plants, Dabney, Fox Hill)
Creeping or Prostrate Rosemary (R.o. prostratus)-- 6-12", hardy to 20F, excellent for bonsai, espalier, hanging baskets and living wreaths, its long branches twist and curl, short and narrow leaves, mild fragrance, pale blue flowers, blooms almost year round (Companion Plants, Dabney, Sandy Mush)
Joyce deBaggio or Golden Rain-- 5', hardy to 20F, gold-edged leaves, strong fragrance like common rosemary, dark blue sparse flowers, compact, bush, self-branching, very pretty landscape specimen, looks gold from a distance (Companion Plants, Dabney)

NOTES

Rosmarinus officinalis　　*Labiatae (Mint)*　　　**ROSEMARY**

GROWTH CONDITIONS

Germ.Temp: 65-75	Height: 2-6'
Grow.Temp: Hot	Breadth: 12-24"
pH: 6.0-7.0	Spacing: 12-24"
Root Depth: 12-24"	Planting Depth: 1/4"

Site: Full sun, good drainage essential
Water: Low
Fertilizer: Light feeder
Side-dress: 2-3 applications per season of liquid seaweed.
Propagation: Stem-tip cuttings taken in the spring or fall root easily in sandy compost. It's not recommended to propagate from seed because the seeds are unreliable and lose viability rapidly. If you do start from seeds, however, use seeds that are less than two weeks old. Rosemary seeds take a long time to germinate, up to three weeks, so be patient. Make sure the seed pots have excellent drainage, but don't let the soil dry out.

PESTS: in the greenhouse, spider mite and whitefly; outdoors, mealybugs and scale
DISEASES: in humid climates fungal botrytis rot, rhizoctonia

HARVEST: When the plant matures you can harvest it all year. Cut 4" branch tips, but do not remove more than 20 percent of the plant's growth. Herbs should be cut in the morning after the dew has dried. Do not wash them or aromatic oils will be lost.

STORAGE REQUIREMENTS: To dry, tie cuttings in small bunches and hang upside down in a warm, dry, dark place. When dried, remove the leaves from the stems, and keep whole for storage. Store in airtight jars in a dark place. Do not crush or grind until ready to use.

OTHER GROWING NOTES: Rosemary is a perennial warm season herb, very tender to light frost and freezes. It is very tolerant of a wide variety of soil conditions ranging from 4.5 to 8.7 pH, and anywhere from 12-107 inches of water per year. Rosemary likes a sunny location and does not transplant well. If grown from seed, do not harvest for 3 years. It benefits from frequent pruning at any time of year, and can be trained into interesting shapes. Don't hesitate to cut it back severely. "Dr. Rosemary", nurseryman Thomas De Baggio in northern Virginia, recommends that above Zone 8 rosemary be grown in pots year round and brought indoors for the winter as most varieties are hardy to only 15-20F. There is only one variety, "ARP," that is hardy to -10F and can be grown outdoors above zone 8. If you grow "ARP" outside, support its limbs and shield it with burlap in the winter (polyethylene can build up heat underneath), leaving the top open to minimize fungal disease. Overwatering will cause tips to turn brown, followed by all leaves browning and dropping off. For pest problems try a soap-based insecticide or a homemade solution of 5 Tb liquid soap per 1 gallon of water. Spray both tops and bottoms of leaves.

COMPANIONS: all *Brassicas*, beans, carrot, sage
OTHER: Rosemary is alleged to deter bean beetles, cabbage moth, and carrot rust fly.
ENEMIES: cucumber

GREENHOUSE
Any variety. Sage grows well in the greenhouse.

OUTDOOR
Blue or Cleveland Sage (S. clevelandii)-- 3', royal blue flowers, pleasant aroma, good for culinary and potpourris, from Southern California (Companion Plants, Dabney, Fox Hill, Richters)

Clary or Muscatel Sage (S. scleria)-- 2-4', fragrant, very ornamental, masses of white or pink flowers, large, hairy, toothed leaves, used to make Muscatel wine. This variety is said to have medicinal values; an infusion of its seeds is said to be a good eye wash. This grows well in heavy soils. (Companion Plants, Dabney, Fox Hill, Nichols, Sandy Mush, Seeds Blum)

Common or Garden Sage-- 2-3', grey-green pebbly leaves, pale blue flowers, good culinary herb for meat, stuffings, sausage, omelettes, cheese and bean dishes. This variety is said to have medicinal values. (Companion Plants, Dabney, Richters, Sandy Mush)

Golden Sage (S.off. "Aurea")-- 18", hardy to 20F, chartreuse-yellow on edges of dark green leaves, good culinary and border plant, compact growth (Companion Plants, Richters, Sandy Mush)

Pineapple Sage (Salvia elegans)-- 2-4', brilliant red flowers with pineapple scent, attracts hummingbirds, good culinary sage for drinks, chicken, jams and jellies, good indoor plant, needs good light indoors (Companion Plants, Dabney, Richters, Sandy Mush)

Purple Sage (S.off. "purpurea")-- 18", compact, aromatic red-purple foliage, good culinary sage for stuffings, sausage, eggs, soups and stews, needs winter mulch, good in or outdoors in full sun (Companion Plants, Fox Hill, Richters, Sandy Mush)

Tri-color Sage (S.off. "tricolor")-- 2-3', hardy to 20F, variegated white, purple and green leaves, true sage flavor, very showy, excellent border plant where hardy, needs winter mulch (Companion Plants, Fox Hill, Richters, Sandy Mush)

NOTES

A tribute to its reputed ancient medicinal uses: "why should a man die if he has sage in his garden." From the catalogue of Dabney Herbs.

Salvia officinalis   *Labiatae (Mint)*   **SAGE**

GROWTH CONDITIONS

Germ.Temp: 60-70   Height: 12-40"
Grow.Temp: Warm   Breadth: 15-24"
pH: 6.0-7.0   Spacing: Intensive: 18-20" Rows: 3'
Root Depth: Shallow   Planting Depth: 1/4"
Site: Full sun, good drainage essential
Water: Average
Fertilizer: Light feeder
Side-dress: An occasional spray of liquid seaweed will benefit the plant.
Propagation: Layering, stem cuttings, seed. Crowns of old sage plants can rarely be divided successfully, but dividing may work on younger plants. For seeds, start indoors 1-2 months before the last frost or sow directly outdoors 1-2 weeks before the last frost. They germinate in about 21 days. Transplant outdoors about 1 week before the last frost. In the fall take a 4" cutting and root it for planting the following spring.

PESTS: slug, spider mite, spittlebug
DISEASES: powdery mildew, rhizoctonia, verticillium wilt

HARVEST: If you want to keep these plants through winter, in the first year harvest lightly and don't harvest past September. Herbs should be cut in the morning after the dew has dried. Cut the top growth up to 6" below the flower buds or ends. Don't wash the leaves unless necessary or you'll wash away aromatic oils.

STORAGE REQUIREMENTS: To dry, tie cuttings in small bunches and hang upside down in a warm, dry, dark place. When dried, remove the leaves from the stems, and keep whole for storage. Store in airtight jars in a cool, dry, dark place. This herb can also be frozen in airtight containers.

OTHER GROWING NOTES: Sage is a perennial shrub, hardy to -30F if covered. In the North cover with a loose mulch of hay or evergreen boughs. A June-bloomer, sage likes well-drained and moderately rich soil, though it will tolerate poor soil and drought. Sage seeds store and germinate poorly. When started from seed, it takes about two years to grow to a mature size. Most gardeners start sage from cuttings or division, using the outer, newer growth. Some gardeners advise that you replace your sage plants every several years when they become woody and less productive. Sage has putative antibacterial activity and has been used as a natural preservative for meats, poultry and fish. It also supposedly works better as a preservative with rosemary than alone. Distilled sage extracts have been made into antioxidants used recently to increase the shelf-life of foods. Some research also indicates that sage lowers blood sugar in diabetics, and may have estrogenic properties, which some think could explain why folklore says that sage dries up milk. Fresh sage has a lemony and slightly bitter flavor while dried sage has a more musty flavor.

COMPANIONS: all *Brassicas*, cabbage, carrot, marjoram, rosemary, strawberry, tomato
OTHER: Sage can be used to deter cabbage moths and carrot flies.
ENEMIES: cucumber, onion family

TARRAGON VARIETIES

GREENHOUSE

Tarragon does well with 16 hours of light and a 6-week period at 40F.

OUTDOOR

French Tarragon (A. dracunculus var. sativa)-- classical French Tarragon, cannot be grown from seed, best if shaded during hottest part of the day, divide every 4-5 years to maintain flavor, narrow pointed leaves (Burpee, Companion Plants, Fox Hill, Richters, Sandy Mush)

Russian Tarragon (A. dracunculus)-- not recommended, almost flavorless, tarragon seeds are always this variety (widely available)

Tarahumara (Mt. Pima Avis, aka: Mexican Mint Marigold) (*Tagetes lucida*)-- a substitute for tarragon, perennial native to Mexico, used as a tea, wonderful aroma, for low and high desert (Native Seeds)

NOTES

Artemisia dracunculus   *Compositae (Sunflower)*   **TARRAGON**

GROWTH CONDITIONS

Germ.Temp: 75-75	Height: 12-36"
Grow.Temp: Warm	Breadth: 24"
pH: 6.0-7.0	Spacing: Intensive: 18" Reg: 2' Rows:
Root Depth:	Planting Depth: cover roots

Site: Full sun to partial shade
Water: Average
Fertilizer: Light feeder
Side-dress: Not necessary
Propagation: Cuttings, divisions, seed. French tarragon cannot be grown from seed, so if you grow tarragon seeds it is the less aromatic, more common Russian tarragon. To propagate French tarragon, in the early spring take cuttings or divisions and transplant 2' apart.

PESTS: none
DISEASES: downy mildew, powdery mildew, rhizoctonia (root rot)

HARVEST: Begin harvest 6-8 weeks after transplanting outside. The leaves bruise easily, so handle gently. Herbs should be cut in the morning after the dew has dried. Cut the top growth up to 6" below the flower buds or ends. Don't wash or aromatic oils will be lost.

STORAGE REQUIREMENTS: To dry, tie cuttings in small bunches and hang upside down in a warm, dry, dark place. When dried, remove the leaves from the stems, and keep whole for storage. The leaves will brown slightly during the drying process. Do not crush or grind until ready to use. Store in airtight jars in a dark place. Another way to store fresh tarragon is to preserve it in white vinegar, where the flavor is better preserved than when dried, or to freeze the leaves in airtight plastic bags.
Freeze: good (better than dried)   Dry: fair

OTHER GROWING NOTES: Tarragon is an aromatic perennial herb, hardy to frost and light freezes through zone 4. It likes full to partial shade in rich, sandy well-drained loam. The plants should be divided every two or three years for flavor and vigor. All flower stems should be removed to keep the plant productive. Tarragon most often fails from being planted in soil that is too wet or acid. It can be grown in containers in the greenhouse or on a windowsill as long as you ensure good drainage. The only tarragon worth growing is French tarragon, but it is somewhat harder to find than Russian tarragon. Tarragon is an excellent flavor enhancer in vinegars, salad dressings, and chicken, cheese and egg dishes.

COMPANIONS: Tarragon is alleged to enhance the growth of most vegetables.
ENEMIES: none

GREENHOUSE
Any variety does well, but keep foliage dry to prevent rot.

OUTDOOR
Caraway (T. herba-barona)-- 4", rapid spreader, good ground cover and in rock gardens, rose flowers, used for meats, soups and vegetables (Companion Plants, Dabney, Nichols, Richters)
Common, Garden or English (T. vulgaris)-- 14", small upright shrub, source of antiseptic oil Thymol. Common, English and French variations are most often used in cooking and also are excellent bee plants. (Companion Plants, Dabney, Fox Hill, Nichols, Sandy Mush)
Creeping (T. glabrescens)-- 6", main use as a good ground cover, a dense mat with purple flowers, fast spreader, early bloomer (Companion Plants)
English, German or Winter (T. vulgaris var.) -- 8", broad dark green leaves, robust growth habit (Companion Plants, Fox Hill, Richters, Sandy Mush)
French or Summer (T. vulgaris var.)-- 12", greyer and sweeter than the English, needs some winter protection, pink flowers, trim upright plants (Companion Plants, Dabney, Fox Hill, Nichols, Richters, Sandy Mush)
Italian Oregano Thyme-- 10", strong oregano taste and aroma, tender perennial (Companion Plants, Nichols, Sandy Mush)
Lemon and Golden Lemon (T. citriodoratus)-- 12", low-growing with strong lemon scent delicious in teas, or fish and chicken dishes, not as hardy as other thymes, may need winter protection. The Golden Lemon variation has sharply defined yellow edges on leaves and is a beautiful plant. (Companion Plants, Dabney, Fox Hill, Nichols, Richters, Sandy Mush)
Mother-of-Thyme or Creeping (T.praecox subsp. articus)-- 2", beautiful ground cover, good bee plant, rose-purple flowers, dark green leathery leaves, used in formal herb gardens, between stepping stones and on earth benches. Releases fragrance when stepped or sat on. There is a red-flowered and lemon variation of this. (Dabney, Richters, Sandy Mush)
Silver (T. vulgaris "Argenteus")-- 10", somewhat sprawling, striking plant, pretty white margins on green leaves, pale blue flowers, flavor like common or garden thyme, good for edging and hanging baskets (Companion Plants, Dabney, Fox Hill, Richters, Sandy Mush)

NOTES

Thymus vulgaris   *Labiatae (Mint)*   **THYME**

GROWTH CONDITIONS

Germ.Temp: 60-70   Height: 3-12"
Grow.Temp: Warm   Breadth: 18" - 3'
pH: 5.5-7.0   Spacing: 8-12"
Root Depth: 6-10"   Planting Depth: 0 - 1/4"
Site: Full sun to partial shade
Water: Average
Fertilizer: Light feeder
Side-dress: Not necessary
Propagation: Cuttings, divisions, layering, seed. Seeds-- start indoors 2-3 weeks before the last frost,
          keeping seeds dry and uncovered. Layering, divisions, and cuttings-- snip 3" from fresh new
          green growth, place in wet sand, keep moist for two weeks, and transplant when rooted.
          The best time for divisions or cuttings is spring, although they also can be taken through
          early summer.

PESTS: aphid, spider mite
DISEASES: botrytis rot, fungal diseases, rhizoctonia (root rot)

HARVEST: Cut as needed before the plant blossoms in midsummer. Or harvest the entire plant by
cutting it down to 2" above the ground; the plant will grow back before the season ends. The second
harvesting method, however, renders the plant less hardy for the winter. Herbs should be cut in the
morning after the dew has dried. Cut the top growth up to 6" below the flower buds or ends. Do not
wash the leaves or aromatic oils will be lost.

STORAGE REQUIREMENTS: To dry, tie cuttings in small bunches and hang upside down in a
warm, dry, dark place. When dried, remove the leaves from the stems, and keep whole for storage. Do
not crush or grind leaves until ready to use. Store in airtight jars in a dark place or freeze in airtight
containers.
Freeze: fair   Dried: excellent

OTHER GROWING NOTES: Thyme is a perennial herb, hardy to frost and light freezes through
zones 5-9. It likes full sun and does well in light and dry to stony, poor soils. Good drainage is always
essential or the plant will be susceptible to fungal diseases. Keep it sheltered from cold winds. It may
not survive severe winters unless covered or heavily mulched. The plant may become woody and
straggly in two to three years. Either replace it or try cutting back three-fourths of the new growth
during the growing season to rejuvenate it and keep it bushy. French thyme is difficult to propagate by
cuttings, but can be accomplished by the following method. Prune the plant severely in mid-June, and
take small 1/2" to 1" softwood cuttings in mid-July. Root the cuttings in a sand bed, and cover the bed
with a milky white plastic "tent" about 6-8" above the top of the cuttings. Mist the cuttings once a day
at mid-day.

COMPANIONS: all *Brassicas*, eggplant, potato, strawberry, tomato
OTHER: may repel cabbageworm and whitefly
ENEMIES: cucumber

Macro & Micro Destructive Agents:
Organic Remedies

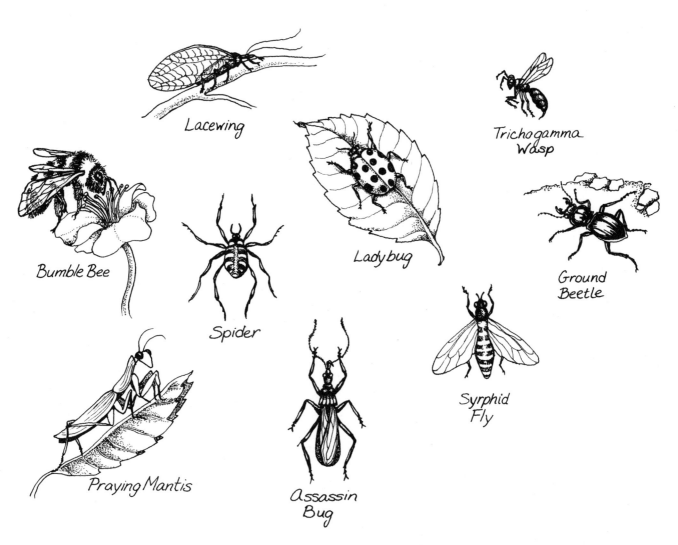

Lacewing

Trichogamma Wasp

Bumble Bee

Spider

Ladybug

Ground Beetle

Syrphid Fly

Praying Mantis

Assassin Bug

Some Beneficial Insects

SOME BENEFICIAL INSECTS

(Others Are Mentioned In The Text)

Assassin Bugs — Eat immature insects.

Bumble Bees — Pollinate blossoms, from which fruits and vegetables develop. One of Nature's best helpers for our food supply.

Ground Beetles — Eat caterpillars, cutworms, some species of slugs and snails, and soft-bodied larvae.

Lacewing Wasps — Eat aphids, corn earworms, mealybugs, mites, leafhopper nymphs, thrips, caterpillar eggs, scales, and whiteflies.

Ladybugs — Eat aphids, mealybugs and small insects. Different species of ladybugs prefer different insects.

Praying Mantis — Eat aphids and small insects.

Syrphid Flies (Hover flies, Flower flies) — Eat aphids, leafhoppers, mealybugs, mites, scales, and small insects.

Spiders — Eat insects and other pests.

Wasps, parasitoid (non-stinging)

    Braconids — Parasitize aphids, larvae of moths, butterflies, and many beetles.

    Chalcid — Parasitize aphids, mealybugs, scales, and larvae of beetles, moths, butterflies.

    Ichneumonid — Parasitize moth and butterfly larvae.

    Pediobius foveolatus — Parasitize Mexican bean beetle larvae.

    Trichogramma — Parasitize and eat eggs of the corn borer, cabbage looper, codling moth and many caterpillars.

MACRO AND MICRO DESTRUCTIVE AGENTS

Organic Remedies

"An Ounce Of Prevention..."

Prevention and a self-sustaining balanced ecosystem are the organic gardener's most important tools to minimize diseases. Without preventive measures, the advantages of organic gardening quickly diminish. Just like with people, in plants preventive medicine means adopting a holistic approach *from the beginning*. Some diseases and insects can be minimized by breaking the pest cycle through proper garden siting, crop rotation, intercropping, and soil maintenance. Other pests can be minimized by ensuring good plant nutrition, because healthy plants are less susceptible to attack.

Realistic expectations are intrinsic to this holistic approach. False expectations can lead to ghost gardens gone to seed or to habitual quick chemical fixes. Abandon at the outset the idea of picture-perfect produce. Even a healthy garden with an advantageous balance between predators and prey will suffer some damage through the growing season.

As garden steward, your role is to determine the severity of the damage, factors promoting the damage, and decide what action--if any--is worth taking. Damage does not necessarily mean lower yields. Most plants can lose up to 20 percent of their foliage and still match yields of those with no foliage loss. If you can identify an imbalance, then you might be able to take long-term remedies. Events seemingly out of your control, such as unusually prolonged wet periods that promote fungus, might be addressed over the long-term by improving soil drainage and ventilation. In the short-term, however, often the best single remedy is to prevent further garden contamination: remove and destroy the infected plants.

An organic garden is an object of sentiment, not sentimentality. It may be hard to trash a plant you lovingly nurtured and nourished. But the needs of the whole garden can outweigh the needs of the one plant. In order to make a plant grow that is weak, diseased, or unsuitable for your micro-environment, the remedy may be more deleterious to you and your garden than the benefits warrant. Outdoors, where nature's balancing act prevails, a philosophical embrace of imperfection and a "tough love" policy toward diseased plants are both critical.

A garden in its totality, from microorganisms in the soil to the birds, resembles more the acquisition of a pet than a sofa. A garden is like a complex living organism that takes time to understand. Several years may be needed to build a productive soil and resident population of beneficial organisms. It also takes time to learn which varieties are suited to your micro-environment. A neighbor one-mile up the road may have perfect conditions for your favorite tomato, but you may not be able to grow it well because of micro-environment variations.

If you can learn to accept some imperfections, some diseases, some insects, and some failures, then your garden can be a continual source of nutritive food, relaxation, and pleasure.

DEFENSIVE STRATEGIC PLANNING

"Don't Be An Attractive Target"
"A Healthy Body, By Definition, Is Less Susceptible To Disease"
"Don't Let The Nose Of The Camel In The Tent Because The Rest Of the Body May Soon Follow"

Garden Location: In any garden, this is perhaps the key step toward preventing plant disease.

Direct Sun. Choose a location that receives bright sunlight most of the day--**especially morning sun** in humid areas, so that dew will dry as rapidly as possible. This will help minimize growth and spread of fungal and bacterial pathogens.

Good Drainage. Choose a garden site that drains well. If it doesn't already drain well, mix into your soil materials that will improve the drainage such as humus and sand. This is important so that the plant roots don't become water-logged and, therefore, oxygen-starved and severely stressed. Poor drainage also increases your chances of root rots and various soil-borne diseases.

Soil Condition: Soil is "alive," full of organisms large and small. Your role as caretaker is to encourage a healthy diversity of organisms and nutrients. One of the best guidelines in organic gardening is to "feed the soil, not the plants."

Healthy Soil will help you grow healthy plants. Practically, this means avoid dumping large quantities of chemical fertilizers on your soil. Although they may help plant growth temporarily, they can kill beneficial soil organisms, such as earthworms, and in the long run can deplete the soil. Earthworms, for example, are a major way to feed the soil and thereby promote healthy plant growth. See page 8 for more information on earthworms. As steward, then, you can enrich your garden soil by the following:

- **Import earthworms,** if your soil doesn't already have them.
- **Enrich your soil** with peat humus, compost, composted manure and, for clay soil, sand. All of these are available from many suppliers listed in Section 8.
- **Minimize tilling depth**. After the initial tilling, double-digging, or other preparation of your garden bed, don't till more than a few inches deep (unless absolutely necessary)--to avoid killing or disturbing earthworms and other soil organisms. There are a few exceptions to this rule, which are noted in the animal pest charts.
- **Avoid soil compaction**. Don't walk on your garden soil, if possible. Some gardeners lay 6-12" of straw to avoid compaction where heavy machinery is needed.
- **Sow cover crops** after harvest to replenish the soil. Sow a legume or grass cover crop, such as cowpeas or winter rye. These help retain soil moisture, improve soil texture, and organic matter; legumes will also return nitrogen to the soil.
- **Use raised beds** where possible, because they automatically help you achieve multiple goals, such as good drainage, minimal soil compaction, and aeration. Contained raised beds also help minimize disease organism spread by keeping it localized to the infected bed. See page 11 for more information on raised beds.
- **Solarize garden soil** if your garden develops a soil-borne disease problem. Solarization is accomplished by creating a kind of mini-hothouse to raise soil temperature to 130-140F for several days. Temperatures higher than this will kill beneficial organisms. There are different methods, depending on how large and deep an area you wish to solarize. An easy way to solarize your soil is to loosen the soil in mid-summer, thoroughly drench it with water, let it sit overnight, cover with 4-mil thick clear plastic, stretch the plastic tight, and seal the edges with rocks or soil. Let the soil heat up for 4-6 weeks. Then remove plastic and plant as usual. Consult sources in the Bibliography for other methods.
- **Pasteurize potting soil** in extensive greenhouse operations, and to start seeds in flats, pots,

or other containers. Otherwise use unpasteurized soil mix. Also, pasteurization may not be necessary if you use potting soil taken from uncultivated areas or fields growing grains or forage. An easy way to pasteurize is to place a 1 to 1-1/2" layer of soil in shallow pans, and bake for 1 hour at 220F. Or cover with foil, stick in a meat thermometer so it doesn't touch the bottoms or sides, and bake at 350F until soil temperature reaches 180F. Turn off the heat and let the soil remain in the oven another 30 minutes. Store soil in tightly sealed plastic bags.

Plant Location and Selection: Consider your garden plot a place to encourage *diversity* of life, large and small. The soil is alive with microbial organisms, many of them disease pathogens. One of the best ways to minimize these pathogens is to interrupt or discourage their life-cycle. The following practices will help you achieve this goal.

- **Rotate your crops.** At a minimum, plant the same vegetable in the same soil site only once every other year (a 2-year rotation). If possible, routinely rotate on a 3-8 year basis. The same soil site is defined as a radius of 10 feet from where the vegetable is planted. So rotation can occur within the same growing bed as long as it is at least 10 feet away from where it was the previous year.
- **Intercrop.** Try to avoid "monocrops"--crops of, say, just corn or beans. Space and time permitting, if you want to grow a large amount of one vegetable, try to plant it in several different places or break up a large patch with plantings of another vegetable. Intercropping discourages some pests from having an easy feast on their favorite food. Also, certain vegetables may grow better in one spot than another, so experimentation with placement could be helpful.
- **Test different varieties** of the same crop. Each variety of a particular vegetable has slightly different growing habits and different disease and insect resistance. One variety may thrive where another dies. The more varieties you try the higher intrinsic resistance your garden has to wide-spread disease and insect damage. Over time you will identify the varieties that fare best in your particular microclimate.
- **Encourage good air circulation** by giving each plant adequate space to grow to maturity. Prune trees and canes annually to prevent overcrowding limbs and branches. In some cases you may need to remove trees if they've become too crowded.
- **Select varieties resistant or tolerant** to the problems specific to your climate, whether fungal, bacterial, viral, or insect. Your extension agent or local organic association should be able to tell you what the predominant pest problems are in your area. For some diseases, selecting resistant varieties is the only prevention and remedy.
- **Buy certified** disease-free seed or plants whenever possible. For certain Eastern-predominant diseases, buying seed grown West of the Rockies is an important preventive measure.

Second Line Of Defense Against Macro And Micro Destructive Agents:

GOOD TACTICS

"A Stitch In Time Saves Nine"
"If It Ain't Broke, Don't Fix It"

Most of the following defensive actions are *also organic remedies* for a host of different disease or animal pests. If you adopt these practices *at the outset*, your need for the rest of this section will be minimal. Some steps may be free, some inexpensive, some more expensive. Do what you can, when you can, choosing options that are congruent with your goals. A purple martin house, for example, may cost $150 because its construction is complex. But it will last twenty years and greatly reduce your need for any insecticidal spray, chemical or organic. A bluebird or bat house, by contrast, can be easily built of scrap lumber or bought for a small price and, in sufficient numbers, may accomplish the same goal.

Plant Maintenance: These steps are critical for prevention. They also, as a group, are the most common and important *remedies* for disease or insect damage. If you do experience disease or insect problems, go over this list and, if there is a step not already taken, implement it as a remedy.

- **Avoid deep planting** where fungal root rot (rhizoctonia) is a problem. This will encourage early emergence of seedlings and give them a better chance of survival.
- **Water from below** by some form of irrigation. A cheap method is to use gallon-size plastic jugs, cut out the bottoms, lodge the necks upside down in the soil, place at intervals appropriate to the plants' needs, and fill with water. More expensive methods include soaker and emitter tubes. Watering from below helps prevent and remedy fungal disease by discouraging its growth and minimizing its spread through water droplets. It also is more efficient, with less evaporative loss.
- **Water before noon** to let the plants dry off in the middle of the day, before nightfall. This, too, discourages fungal growth.
- **Don't work around or touch wet plants.** Diseases are frequently spread by human hands and tools, so this preventive measure is standard cultivation practice.
- **Don't touch healthy plants after working with diseased plants**, for reasons given above.
- **Avoid high Nitrogen fertilizers** which not only can harm soil organisms, but can push the plant to put its energy into leafy growth not fruits.
- **Feed the soil with compost.** For some diseases a major remedy is to spread 1 inch or more of compost through the garden. See page 9 for more information.
- **Mulch** is another occasional remedy to fungal, bacterial, and certain insect pest problems. Apply several inches of mulch in the spring and 4 to 6 inches in autumn, after harvest (see Fall Cultivation below). For more information on mulch see page 13.
- **Control weeds** in and around the garden. Weeds can harbor insect and disease pests. If you weed regularly in the early summer months, you should not experience a severe weed problem through the rest of the season. Removing perennial weeds and thistles within 100 yards of the garden is considered a remedy for several diseases.
- **Remove rotting or dead leaves, stalks, weeds and plants**, which can be a breeding ground for pests. Clean the garden of fall leaves, too, even though you may not be growing any fall crops.
- **Remove piles of wood, garden debris,** or other potential breeding grounds for pests to a spot away from the garden.
- **Don't allow large stagnant pools of water.** Small bird baths and running water are not a problem.
- **Mow grass in orchards** where the grass is potential breeding ground. One "natural" orchard plan involves planting companion grasses or plants that attract beneficial insects, and allowing them to naturalize. Most orchards, however, are surrounded by orchard grass, and this should be kept mowed to discourage pests.
- **Disinfect tools** periodically, even if there's no sign of disease. When working with diseased plants, always disinfect tools between pruning cuts.
- **Shade plants in extremely hot weather**, if they wilt continuously, with a shading material such as cheesecloth. If they wilt one day, that doesn't mean they will die the next. But don't be afraid to shade your plants. Recent NASA studies indicate that plants integrate light over time, and that long sunny summer days provide more light than they require. If plants are wilting from heat stress, also make sure they receive adequate water.
- **Protect plants from freezes** with any light material whenever a freeze is anticipated. Even newspaper will work.
- **Harvest fruits and vegetables promptly when ripe.** Allowing fruits and vegetables to stay on the stem too long promotes certain diseases.
- **After harvest, immediately remove plants.** Don't allow harvested plants to just sit in the garden. Either remove them and, if not diseased, add them to the compost pile. Or, where appropriate, work them back into the soil.

- **Fall cultivation**. After plants have been harvested and the garden cleaned of plant debris, leave the soil completely bare for a few days. For normal purposes cultivate the soil no more than 3 inches. For certain insect pest problems, cultivate the soil to a depth of 6 to 8 inches to expose eggs and larvae for birds and other predators. Two weeks later lightly cultivate the soil a second time with a rake, this time only 2 inches deep. Leave bare for a few more days. Then plant a cover crop, or apply a layer of winter mulch 4 to 6 inches deep.

- **At all times, remove and destroy infected or diseased leaves, canes, or the entire plant when necessary.** For some disease and insect pests, removing the infected leaves may be sufficient. For other pests, which may be systemic, removing the affected leaves may not be sufficient. If all other measures above and below fail to control the problem you may need to resort to various sprays--whether simple home remedies, insecticidal soaps, or more harsh remedies such as the copper-based fungicides and botanical sprays.

Helpful Supports And Devices:
These devices may seem unnecessary, but they can make the difference between the presence or absence of a problem. In some cases, they are recommended as remedies to specific disease or animal pests.

- **Trellises, stakes, A-frames, tepees** and other forms of plant support accomplish multiple goals. Not only do they minimize growing space, but they promote better light penetration and air circulation, both of which help minimize disease. Further, these supports make it much easier to prune and harvest. Use such supports for vegetables like tomatoes, pole beans, peas, cucumbers, melons, and squash. Melons and large squash can be supported on trellises with something like panty hose. If grown on the ground melons should at a minimum be raised off the soil with something like steel cans or plastic containers to minimize rot. Cane fruit, such as blackberries, raspberries, and grapes are also grown effectively when trellised.

- **Row covers** are helpful throughout the growing season. In spring and fall they will keep your crops warm and protected from frost, prolonging your season. In spring and summer, they are an easy and effective protection against insect attack. Before applying row covers, however, make sure that harmful insects are not trapped underneath. Row covers are usually a light-weight woven material, such as polyester or polyvinyl alcohol, that allows in air, light, and water, and requires no supports. An additional item to keep the beds warm under row covers are simple plastic jugs, filled with water and spaced every few feet. These absorb heat during the day and radiate the stored heat through the night.

- **Wire cages, stakes, and water-based white paint** are critical aids to saplings. The wire cages provide an effective barrier against animals. When planting the sapling, install a 1/2 to 1/4" hardware cloth around the trunk, extending 4" below ground to prevent rodents from burrowing under and rising 18-24" above ground to prevent rabbit damage (especially in winter months). Make sure the wire is spaced a couple of inches away from the trunk to allow for growth. For trees on dwarf root stock characterized by poor anchorage, place a 4 to 6 foot stake close to the trunk before filling the planting hole with soil, and attach with special ties that permit growth and flexing. Tree trunks can be painted anytime, but if done while young this will help prevent sunscald or winter injury--a condition promoted by sunny winter days and resulting in cracks or cankers.

- **Electrical fences or other barriers** against large animals, such as deer, are almost essential in rural areas. Many a gardener has fallen asleep to a prospering garden and awaked to find devastation. Many gardeners initially feel the problem doesn't warrant the expense, only to change their mind once their entire garden, flowers and vegetables alike, are wiped out in short order. For suggestions on different types of barriers, see the remedies for deer in the animal pest chart.

Attract Beneficial Animals:
Birds, bats, bees, predatory and parasitic wasps, ladybugs--these are just a few of the beneficial animals that are critical in a self-sustaining garden. Beneficial animals are one of your easiest ways to prevent both animal and disease pests, because animal pests can spread diseases. They save you both money and time (and time is money). To attract beneficial insects, plant

herbs, flowers, and clovers around the borders of your garden. For more information on beneficials, see pages 9-10 and also page 150.

In the beginning your ecosystem may not contain all of the beneficial animals that you want or need. You may, then, want to import beneficial insects to fight the problem. Such a practice is part of *Integrated Pest Management* (IPM), a relatively new concept in crop management. IPM relies extensively, but not exclusively, on precisely timed releases of beneficial insects to fight pest problems. Backyard gardeners who don't have the opportunity or inclination to investigate the proper timing or method of releasing purchased beneficial insects shouldn't bother with this remedy, because their money will most likely be wasted. If, however, you wish to experiment and can follow through on the timed releases then importation of beneficials can be an effective remedy. Beneficial insects are listed, where applicable, in the animal pest chart, and suppliers can be found in Section 8. We urge you to consult the supplier and follow instructions on both quantity and timing to ensure success.

Some purists, however, feel that the importation of beneficial insects disrupts the development of a balanced local ecosystem. This argument has some merit. Some beneficials, however, can be self-limiting; when their food source dies, they die. Ideally, a self-sustaining garden should not need imported help, but you may decide to resort to imported beneficials for acute infestations. The decision really depends on your individual goals and, as discussed previously, the amount of damage you're willing to tolerate. Most important, if the first and second lines of defense are implemented, the probability of extensive damage to any single crop or crop variety is low.

Third Line Of Defense Against Macro And Micro Destructive Agents:

IDENTIFY THE PROBLEM

"If you hear hoofbeats look for horses, not zebras."

Identification may seem an improbable defensive action, yet it is absolutely vital. When you see water spots on your ceiling, you don't immediately go to the time and expense of replacing your roof; it may be a simple problem of condensation due to inadequate ventilation of the roof rafters. When you develop a fever, you also don't immediately resort to penicillin. Similarly, when plants get sick, it is essential to accurately diagnose the problem before you take any action. What you may think initially is a fungus may be a simple problem of something like inadequate phosphorous.

The most common garden problems are frequently the most simple to fix: over or under watering, inadequate nutrients, inadequate drainage, inadequate ventilation. Take the time, then, to examine the problem carefully.

The remainder of this section on disease and animal pests is intended primarily to help you narrow down the possible causes of your plant problem, and to help you conduct informed discussions with professionals. If you wish to experiment with your garden, and do not have an investment in saving every plant, maximizing yields, or obtaining picture-perfect produce, then the following guidelines and remedies can be a source of fun, discovery, and learning. If you are a market gardener with an investment in yields--quality and quantity--then it is vital to obtain an accurate diagnosis from a professional before implementing a remedy. Advice and soil tests from extension agents are free.

Regular Monitoring: Perhaps the most important guideline is to monitor your garden daily, if you have time, or at least weekly. Then act quickly to prevent a pest or disease from becoming a problem, starting with the most benign methods of control, which are also usually the easiest and least expensive. These might include the simplest, such as handpicking, trapping, or spraying the plants with a strong jets of water to clear off the bugs. Work your way up from there to stronger methods, such as biological predators. If the problem becomes very serious, you might try stronger controls like botanical insecticides--but use them sparingly and as a last resort (see WARNING under Botanicals). The key is to find which control in your garden is the most effective but also the most benign.

Systematic Examination Of The Environment: Before attempting diagnosis, you must first learn how to observe. First, take a general accounting of the plant and determine the parts that are affected. The following are just a few examples of what you might look for.

Leaves: look at the edges (margins), veins, top side, and bottom side. Notice wilting, general coloration and distortion (curling, crinkling), holes, spots, eggs, insects.

Blossoms and fruits: look at the petals, blossom end of the fruit, and skin. Notice spots, discolorations, decay, cuts, holes, premature drop, lack of fruit setting, eggs, insects.

Stems or bark: examine from the soil level to the top, even slightly below soil level. Notice cuts, cracks or splits in the tissue, blisters, growths (cankers or galls), discoloration, wilting, stunting, twisting, spindly growth, sticky coating, gummy exudate, spots, eggs, insects.

Roots and surrounding soil (if the plant is sufficiently diseased that you wish to dig it up): examine the length and breadth of main roots and root hairs. Notice nodules, knots, decay, underdevelopment, twisting or distortions, eggs, cocoons, insects.

Start With The Basics, Not "Zebras": After examining the plant and its environment, the first thing to do is consider the basics, not the esoteric. Start with the most common garden problems--water, nutrients, drainage, air circulation--even if insects or disease are clearly present. Many pests will not attack a plant unless it is already weakened and stressed.   Before reaching for the fungicide, check to see if the roots are too wet and compacted to get oxygen. Global garden destruction can be due to animals, such as deer and rodents. And global garden sickness can be caused by acid rain, pollution, or smog--modern afflictions we often forget in diagnosis.

Problem	Symptoms	Tools And Remedies
WATER **Too Much**	The soil around the stem is soaked. Mold, moss, or fungus may be growing on top of the soil. Other symptoms include wilting, yellowing, and dead leaf margins.	**Diagnostic Tools**: Why guess? Buy a simple moisture meter to find out whether the root medium is too wet or dry. Buy a rain gauge and mount it where it can be easily checked.
Too Little	Plants wilt due to loss of tissue turgor, which is maintained by water pressure. Leaves may eventually brown and die. With prolonged water shortage, growth is stunted.	**Remedies:** Earthworms Compost Do the obvious--let the root medium dry out, or provide more water.
WALNUT WILT	Roots of black walnut and butternut trees secrete an acid (juglone) that is toxic to tomato, potato, pea, cabbage, pear, apple, sour cherry, and others. The plants can suddenly wilt and die. Their vascular systems brown, which may cause a false diagnosis of Fusarium or Verticillium wilts.	**Diagnostic Tools**: If affected plants are growing near a black walnut or butternut tree, the acid from the tree roots is most likely the problem. **Remedies:** Remove the trees, or plant the garden farther away from the tree than the height of the tree.

Problem	Symptoms	Tools And Remedies
NITROGEN (N) **Too Little**	Slow growth. Lighter green leaf color, followed by yellowing tips usually starting at the bottom of the plant. Leaf undersides may become blue-purple. Eventually plant becomes spindly, and older leaves drop. Fruits are small and pale before ripening, and overly colored when ripe. Where: widespread.	**Diagnostic Tools:** Soil test kits are widely available. **Remedies:** Earthworms Compost (slow-release) Foliar spray of diluted fish emulsion or other liquid fertilizer Fish meal (slow release) Composted manure (slow release) Hoof & horn meal (slow release) Cottonseed meal (medium-release) Blood meal (fast-release)
Too Much	Lush, green foliage. Little or no fruit, because the plant is putting all of its energy into growth. Where: usually due to an excess of fast-acting fertilizer.	**Avoid:** Urea, the various nitrates, ammonium phosphate.
PHOSPHOROUS (P) **Too Little**	Leaf undersides turn blue-red, first in spots then expanding to entire leaf. Darkened leaves develop a blue-green tinge. Green crops have reddish-purple color in stems and leaf veins. Fruiting crops are leafy, with fruits setting and maturing late, if at all. Where: widespread, except in the Northwest. Most severe in the Southeast from the Gulf to NC.	**Diagnostic Tools:** Soil test kits are widely available. **Remedies:** Earthworms Compost Bone meal (slow release) Soft phosphate (even slower release) Phosphate rock (very slow release) **Avoid:** Phosphoric acid, superphosphates, and highly soluble compounds.
POTASSIUM (K) **Too Little**	Leaves at the plant base turn a grayish-green. Leaf edges yellow, brown, or blacken, and curl downward. Black spots appear along leaf veins. New leaves curl and crinkle. Flowers and fruit are small and inferior. Stems are hard and woody. Plant and roots are stunted. Leaves may turn bronze, yellow-brown, or mildly bluish. Where: most common East of the Mississippi, in coastal fog areas, and is most severe in parts of TX through FL, and north to VA.	**Diagnostic Tools:** Soil test kits. **Remedies:** Earthworms Compost Greensand (very slow release) Crushed granite (very slow release) Rock potash (slow release) Kelp meal (medium release) Wood ash (fast release, caustic) Feldspar dust **Avoid:** Potassium chloride.

Problem	Symptoms	Tools And Remedies
MAGNESIUM (Mg) **Too Little**	Lower, older leaves yellow between the leaf veins and eventually turn dark brown. Leaves get brittle and curl upward. Fruit matures late. Symptoms usually in late season. Where: acidic soils, leached, sandy soils, or soils high in K and Ca.	**Diagnostic Tools**: Soil and pH tests. **Remedies:** Earthworms Compost Seaweed meal Liquid seaweed (foliar spray)
CALCIUM (Ca) **Too Little**	Newer, upper leaves turn dark green, sometimes curl upward, and leaf edges yellow. Fruits develop water-soaked decaying spots at the blossom end. Examples: Blossom End Rot in tomato, lettuce Tip Burn, celery Black Heart, and Baldwin Spot in apple and pear flesh (brown spots under the skin and bitter flesh). Where: acidic, leached, or very dry soils.	**Diagnostic Tools**: Soil and pH tests. **Remedies:** Earthworms Compost Ground limestone (slow release) Ground oyster shells (slow release) Crumbled egg shells (slow release) Avoid high Nitrogen and Potassium fertilizers Avoid: Quick lime, slake lime, hydrated lime.
BORON (B) **Too Little**	Bushy growth from lower stems. Newer shoots curl inward, turn dark, and die. Young leaves turn purple-black. Leaf ribs get brittle. Fruit develops cracks or dry spots. Where: eastern U.S., especially in alkaline soils.	**Diagnostic Tools**: Soil and pH tests. **Remedies:** Granite dust (slow release) Rock phosphate (slow release) Liquid kelp foliar spray (fast acting) Boric acid spray on newly opened fruit blossoms (.02 lb: 1 gallon water)
IRON (Fe) **Too Little**	Similar to N-deficiency, but leaf yellowing is between the veins and starts first on upper, not lower, leaves. Where: often in soils with pH above 6.8.	**Diagnostic Tools**: Soil and pH tests. **Remedies:** Compost Bring soil pH below 6.8 Add peat moss manure (lowers pH) Glauconite (source of Fe) Greensand (source of Fe)
ACID SOIL **pH below 6.0**	Nitrogen, Phosphorous, and other nutrient deficiencies will appear because an acid medium makes them less biologically available. The plant will perform poorly and exhibit multiple symptoms.	**Diagnostic Tools**: Soil and pH tests. **Remedies:** Earthworms Compost Ground dolomitic limestone (slow

Problem	Symptoms	Tools And Remedies
ACID SOIL (continued)	Excess Aluminum and Manganese, because an acid medium makes these more biologically available.	release, contains Mg & Ca) Ground calcitic limestone (slow release, no Mg & Ca) Wood ashes (fast release, caustic) Organic material, because lime speeds decomposition of organic matter.
	Where: where acid rain falls, especially in the Northeast.	
ALKALINE SOIL **pH above 7.0**	Micronutrient deficiencies. Poor plant performance.	**Diagnostic Tools**: Soil and pH tests. **Remedies:** Earthworms Compost, and other organic materials Gypsum (Calcium Sulphate) Aluminum Sulphate Powdered Sulphur
DRAINAGE		**Diagnostic Tools**: Dig a gallon-size hole, fill with water, let it drain, fill a second time with water and time how long it takes to drain. More than 8 hours indicates poor drainage.
Too much	Sandy soils will not retain water sufficiently.	
Too little	Long-standing puddles. Slowly-melting snow.	**Remedies For Both Conditions**: Earthworms Compost or other organic matter helps soil retain and drain water.
POOR VENTILATION	Plants wilt due to heat stress. Dew dries very slowly. Mold, moss, mildew, and other symptoms of too much moisture.	**Remedies:** Stake plants, or use some support structure to keep plant erect. Prune trees and plants. Remove suckers between stem crotches. If necessary, if the garden is too crowded, remove weakest, smallest, or least desired plants.

Micro And Macro Destructive Agents: Micro destructive agents are called micro because they cannot be seen by the naked human eye. These include fungi, bacteria, and viruses. By contrast, macro destructive agents are those you can visibly see and identify, from whiteflies to deer.

Identification of macro pests is therefore much easier and in most cases is possible without the aid of a professional. Micro pests are another matter. A definitive diagnosis of most microscopic organisms cannot be made without specialized training and sometimes tests. The difficulty is compounded by the fact that microscopic organisms share numerous symptoms. Several broad differences do exist. A fungus infection can frequently result in mold growth, while a symptom of bacteria can be bad smelling plant parts. A virus is often symptomized by mottled coloring in the leaves. These differences are not reliable for diagnosis, however, because they don't always accompany the disease. As a result, when a definitive diagnosis is necessary, you should consult a trained professional.

The Blue-Cheese Syndrome: A garden is much like blue cheese, which contains about 13 critical microorganisms to produce its distinctive taste and texture. In blue cheese, about half are fungal, half bacterial. Similarly, every garden contains a wide variety of micro and macro organisms, all acting and interacting to produce a particular condition of health or poor health. In the advanced stages of disease, therefore, there is probably no such thing as a "pure" infection by a single organism or even a single family of organisms. Disease is usually promoted by a host of factors, from nutrients to microbial activity. Once a plant is weakened it can be attacked by several different organisms simultaneously.

The good news is that some organic remedies are broad-spectrum, or will help attenuate different types of diseases. Many of these remedies are also the same good preventive practices mentioned above--such as ensuring good soil drainage or watering from below to prevent further contamination through water droplets. One of the most basic broad-spectrum "remedies" is to remove and destroy diseased leaves, fruit, branches, or plants. The lesson here is that once the basics have been ruled out, and disease has been ruled in, a thorough and accurate diagnosis of the major pathogens responsible for the disease may not be necessary if the broad-spectrum remedies work.

Differential diagnosis is important, however, when insect vectors play a role, for the insects then can be controlled. A differential diagnosis is also especially critical any time the gardener wants to use remedies specific to a particular disease, such as a botanical, mineral, or other chemical sprays. Finally, a large-scale or commercial gardener who has constraints far beyond that of the backyard gardener usually must seek professional help with diagnosis before implementing remedies.

The following is a *broad outline* of micro and macro pest symptoms, promoting factors, and remedies. It is not a definitive list of symptoms and remedies, nor is it a substitute for professional advice or textbooks. A single plant may exhibit only one or multiple symptoms. As with everything, you will find occasional exceptions to the promoting factors and remedies.

Remember, most remedies listed below are also the same good *preventive* garden practices discussed above in the First and Second Lines of Defense.

Destructive Agent	Symptoms	Promoting Factors And Remedies
FUNGAL DISEASES	Fungal-specific symptom: Mold on any plant part. Mold can be fuzzy, flat, or colored. Spots (on leaves, stems or bark, or fruit and flowers): watery, soft, sunken, dry, shriveled, colored. Leaves: yellowed, wilted, fallen, defoliation, curled, wrinkled. Fruit: shriveled, misshapen. Flowers: spots, discolored petals. Stems: rot (decay), sunken areas, girdling, watery blisters and other types of cankers, cracks, dark	**Promoting factors**: usually fostered and spread by prolonged periods of rain, moisture, dew, humidity. Spread by tools, gardeners, wind, sometimes seeds and insects. Can be soil-borne, and harbored in plant debris. Some fungal pathogens can live up to 15 years in the soil. **Immediate Remedies:** Remove and destroy diseased plants, or parts of plants. Water from below. Don't touch plants when wet, to avoid spreading disease. Disinfect hands after working with diseased plants. Disinfect tools between cuts.

Destructive Agent	Symptoms	Promoting Factors And Remedies

FUNGAL DISEASES (continued)	swellings.
	
	Roots: rot (decay), discoloration, knots, cankers.
		Improve ventilation.
		Keep orchard grass mowed.
		For some fungal problems, you can spray with copper-based fungicides, Bordeaux mixture, sulfur, or lime-sulfur. Never use sulfur on apricots or *cucurbits*, which are sensitive to sulfur and will be injured. Copper can kill earthworms.
		For certain fruit tree fungi, follow a spray program starting in spring when the tree is dormant, such as that recommended by Necessary Trading Company (see Section 8).
		Find out which spray is appropriate for the disease.
		
		Long range Remedies:
		Earthworms.
		Compost.
		Use long crop rotations of 3-5 years for all the fungal wilts.
		Plant in a well-drained area.
		Select resistant varieties.
		Where recommended, hot water seed treatment:
		    Brassicas--place seeds in water at 122F for 25 minutes.
		    Solanaceae--122F for 30 minutes.
		    Celery--118F for 30 minutes.
		For fruit trees, paint trunk and lower limbs to reduce cold injury, because disease spreads through injury.
		Don't prune trees until bud swell, because disease may spread through dead buds and bark cuts.
		Prune limbs or canes 4" below the infection (cankers, galls), and disinfect tools between cuts.
		Increase organic matter in soil to discourage wilts.
		Store harvested produce in well-ventilated, cool, dry areas.
		Solarize garden soil, if feasible.

BACTERIAL DISEASES	Bacteria-specific symptoms: bad smells associated with fruit, roots,	**Promoting Factors:** Usually spread by rain and some beetles (e.g.

Destructive Agent	Symptoms	Promoting Factors And Remedies

BACTERIAL DISEASES (continued)	stems, or leaves.
	
	Spots (on leaves, stems and bark): sunken, raised, water-soaked, tissue may drop out of spots leaving holes.
	
	Leaves: yellowed, curled, wilted, stunted.
	
	Fruit: slimy, spots.
	
	Blossoms: withered, dead.
	
	Stems: lesions, wilted, blackened, dead, wart-like growth, oozing.
	
	Roots: soft, slimy.
		cucumber beetles, flea beetles).
		
		Immediate Remedies:
		Remove and destroy infected plants.
		Disinfect tools.
		Don't touch plants when wet.
		Clean cultivation.
		For trees, prune out infected parts, disinfect tools between cuts, and destroy removed parts.
		Where severe, remove and destroy tree. If feasible, solarize soil.
		Where recommended, (usually fruit trees) spray with a copper-sulfur blend. (This can kill earthworms.)
		Where recommended, (usually on vegetables) apply micronized sulfur.
		
		Long Range Remedies:
		Earthworms.
		Compost.
		Plant Resistant varieties.
		Crop rotation.
		Hot water seed treatment:
		    Carrots--122F for 10 minutes.
		    Solanaceae--122F for 25 minutes.
		In the East, use seed grown West of the Rockies (free of bacterial blight).
		Improve soil drainage.

VIRAL DISEASES	Virus-specific symptoms: mottled coloring in leaves. Leaves: mottled coloring, misshapen growth, yellowing, curling downwards, crinkling, unusual narrow, pointed, or fernlike leaves, veins may disappear. Fruits: misshapen, premature ripening. Blossoms or flowers: misshapen, underdeveloped, not very many. Stems: stunted, twisted,	**Promoting Factors:** Usually spread by insect or human vectors (e.g. aphids, cucumber beetles, grasshoppers, leafhoppers, thrips, smokers for tobacco mosaic, human hands, and tools). **Immediate Remedies:** Control insect vector. Disinfect tools and hands before working with plants. Remove and destroy infected plants, or parts of plants. Clean cultivation. **Long Range Remedies:** Earthworms.

Destructive Agent	Symptoms	Promoting Factors And Remedies
VIRAL DISEASES (continued)	misshapen.	Compost. Plant resistant varieties. Remove weeds that harbor insect vectors. Plant in wind-protected areas, to minimize aphid contamination. Use closer spacing where leafhoppers are a problem.
INSECT PESTS	Visible presence of insect (but those that suck plant juices are harder to spot). Leaves: chewed or ragged holes, defoliation, tunnels, blotches, skeletonization, wilting, webbing, leaf drop, eggs on upper or lower leaf sides. Fruit: small, round or other shaped holes, premature drop. Flowers: malformed. Stems and bark: holes or sunken area, severed, weak, stunted or distorted, wilted. Roots: malformed, poorly developed, eaten, decay in storage.	**Immediate Remedies:** Handpick. Remove and destroy eggs. Traps, most are insect-specific. Mulch where appropriate. Remove and destroy heavily infested plants. Clean cultivation. Where appropriate, apply sprays of insecticidal soaps, oils, etc. **Long Range Remedies:** Earthworms. Compost. Plant resistant varieties. Use row covers before pest emerges. Fall cultivation. Encourage insect-eating birds and other beneficial animals. Solarize soil, if feasible.

Become Familiar With Specific Remedies For Micro And Macro Pests: The following are a list of common remedies used against micro and macro pests. To minimize repetition, the charts refer to these remedies in shorthand. Please refer back to these explanations when using the charts. Suppliers for these remedies are listed in Section 8.

WARNING: "What goes up must come down." Remember that substances that may damage insects above the soil may also damage beneficial organisms in the soil. Such remedies may be treating the plant at the expense of the ecosystem. Wherever possible we have noted the possible effects remedies may have on beneficial organisms above and in the soil.

Some perspective may be important. Most garden vegetable plants last for a year, while the soil takes years to build into a healthy medium. If you drive out beneficial organisms in order to get rid of a bad pest problem in one year, and if you harm the soil in the process, then it is a distinct possibility your garden the following year will have even more problems, requiring even more remedial measures. This is the kind of vicious cycle that leads to open-field hydroponics, discussed in Section 2.

While there may be times you wish to use these remedies to save some plants, we urge you to do so with consideration for the soil. This means applying the remedy in the smallest effective quantities, and in the smallest area necessary for control. Massive preventive spraying is not usually necessary or recommended for the backyard gardener. Commercial growers and orchardists may have no choice at the moment, but the backyard gardener usually does.

Bacillus thuringiensis (Bt): Something akin to the "wonder drug" of organic growing, Bt is a bacterium that was discovered in 1901. It comes in powder form that is biodegradable and is alleged to be so safe that it can be sprayed or dusted right up to the day of harvest. It works by paralyzing the insect's gut. Bt specifically kills leaf-eating caterpillars and leaves unharmed other insects, animals and birds. Now new strains of Bt are being isolated which target specific larvae, such as the new M-One™ that attacks Colorado potato beetle larvae.

WARNING: As with any "antibiotic," legitimate concern exists that exclusive or immoderate use of Bt's will foster Bt-resistant pests in future generations. In fact, such resistance has already been confirmed in at least one moth pest. Many specialists, however, believe that if such problems develop new strains of Bt can be developed to conquer the newly resistant pests. This argument, of course, was the very same as that used by pharmaceutical companies about new forms of penicillin to combat penicillin-resistant bacteria. What is generally not realized is that, although new forms of penicillin were successfully developed, the toxicity to humans of the newer penicillins exceeded the original by 10 to 12 times. The allergic responses to the original penicillin was less than 1% and "improved penicillins" run up to 10 to 20% *severe* allergic responses. As a consequence, non-commercial growers may decide, like us, not to use Bt, or if necessary to use it only as a last resort.

Beneficial nematodes: Unlike the various nematodes that cause damage, beneficial nematodes such as *Neoplectana carpocapsae* are a fast and totally safe control for various pests. A number of species and varieties of beneficial nematodes exist. As juvenile-stage microscopic organisms, these parasites inject the insect with bacteria that kills the host within 24 hours. They don't harm humans, plants, pets, birds, earthworms, honeybees, or beneficial insects. A self-limiting control, they seek out soil grubs (young phase of certain insects), feed, reproduce and, when their food supply is exhausted, die. Only effective in the juvenile stage, these nematodes can be stored in the refrigerator for up to 2 months.

Beneficial nematodes must be applied at sufficient rates to be effective, about 50,000 per foot of standard row or per square foot in raised beds. Numerous destructive pests are susceptible to these nematodes, including borers, weevils, cutworms, cucumber beetles, and even gypsy moths. One quart is sufficient for about 50 square feet and sells for about $5. Just sprinkle the mixture where the pests are a problem. Also, one source suggests their use in compost heaps to eradicate harmful larvae.

Beneficial insects and plants: Beneficial insects are attracted to flowering *umbelliferae*, such as dill and carrots in their second year, yarrow, sweet cicely, and fennel. The Henry Doubleday Research Association in Coventry, England has shown that the following beneficial insects are attracted to the noted plants:

Hover fly-- pot marigolds, *Nemophilia*, bush morning glory, poached-egg plant *(Limnanthes douglasii)*.

Parasitic wasps and flies-- yarrow *(Achillea)*, flowering fennel and carrots, angelica.

Lacewings and parasitic wasps-- mustard.

For more information on beneficials, please see the first page of this section and also Section 2.

Botanical controls: These are insecticides that are derived from naturally occurring sources, and are considered "organic" by many people because of their alleged lack of persistence in the environment. Botanicals are also generally thought to be relatively safe for birds, pets, humans and other wildlife. Some of the new synthesized chemicals, however, which are not considered organic, seem to be more gentle on beneficial insects in and above the soil than some of these older "organic" sprays. Minerals, such as copper, are not strictly speaking botanicals, but they are included under this rubric for easy reference.

WARNING: No insecticide--botanicals included--should be used unless your crops have suffered significant damage. Regardless how safe the insecticide is reputed, the introduction of botanical poisons, minerals, or other substances alters your garden's natural system of checks and balances. Rotenone and pyrethrins can kill beneficial organisms in and above the soil just as easily as the pests you're trying to eradicate. Ryania and sabadilla are somewhat less treacherous to beneficial insects. "Significant damage" is a matter of personal interpretation. But bear in mind that most plants can lose up to 20 percent of their foliage and still produce yields that equal plants with no foliage loss.

Even when significant damage occurs, you might consider the size of the area you will need to spray and the value of your crop, compared to the potential damage to the ecology of the rest of your garden.

At all times insecticides and fungicides should be used as an absolute *last resort*, after all other methods have failed. When used, apply the botanical control to just the leaves, plants, or areas that are affected, and at the minimal concentrations necessary to do the job.

For more information, see headings below on Copper, Pyrethrum, Rotenone, Ryania, and Sabadilla.

Bug juice: Considered an "old home remedy," this may or may not be effective. It is thought that some insects may release a pheromone upon death to warn their brethren away. But this practice might also help spread disease to other plants. If you wish to try this experimentally, capture 1/2 cup of the pest, crush, and liquefy with 2 cups of water. Strain to remove particles for spraying. Do not use a household blender. Use an old blender jar, or mortar and pestle specifically for garden use. Spray both sides of leaves and stems.

Clean cultivation: See "Plant Maintenance" (page 154). Generally, clean cultivation means you should remove and destroy all infected plants or parts of plants, clean out weeds, dead and rotting vegetation, piles of junk, and plants that are finished bearing. Destroy diseased plants by burning (where permitted), burial, or some other appropriate means. Don't allow stagnant pools of water or piles of brush, lumber, or stones to occur near the garden. Don't work around or touch wet plants, particularly when diseased. And don't add diseased plant material to compost piles.

Copper (see WARNING in Botanical Controls, above): Copper is usually considered a fungicide, and can be dusted, sprayed, or combined with other substances, such as rotenone. It is an effective control of fungal and bacterial diseases such as anthracnose, all blights, downy and powdery mildews, leaf spot, rust, fire blight, scab, and brown rot. The main problem with using copper in a self-sustaining garden is that it has been shown to kill earthworms through drips and fallen leaves. For a more detailed discussion of the effects of copper and other substances on earthworms, see *The Earthworm Book* by Jerry Minnich (listed in Bibliography).

Crop rotation: At a minimum, plant the same vegetable in the same soil site only once every other year, a 2-year basis. Some diseases require a longer minimum rotation. The same soil site is defined as a radius of 10 feet from where the vegetable is planted. So rotation could occur within the same growing bed as long as it is at least 10 feet away from where it was the previous year or where refuse from the planting occurs. If possible, routinely rotate on a 3-5 year basis.

Diatomaceous Earth: This is an insect remedy with very low toxicity. It is a hydrophilic (water-loving) form of silicon dioxide (sand) that rapidly takes up water. Harvested from riverbeds, it is made of petrified skeletons of water-dwelling microorganisms known as Diatoms. It works by desiccating insects.

Apply a dusting of diatomaceous earth after a light rain, dew, or after lightly spraying plants with water. Dust all plant surfaces, starting from the base and moving upward. You can also spray diatomaceous earth in a weak insecticidal soap solution (1/4 lb D.E.: 5 gallons water: 1 tsp insecticidal soap), which will help the spray adhere to plant surfaces. Fruit trees can be painted with the the same solution. Whether dusted or sprayed, reapply after rainfall.

D.E. is effective against most soft-bodied insects (aphids, mites, slugs, etc.), but may also work with some beetles and weevils.

Fall cultivation: Leave the soil completely bare for a few days. Cultivate soil to a depth of 6-8 inches to expose eggs and larvae for birds and other predators. Two weeks later lightly cultivate the soil a second time with a rake, this time only 2 inches deep. Leave bare for a few more days. Then plant a cover crop, or apply a layer of winter mulch 4-6 inches deep.

Garlic spray: This falls into the category of old-home remedies, which means it may or may not work for you. Garlic has been found to have some antifungal properties (see the chart on Garlic), but the methods of extraction and quantities necessary haven't been widely tested. This spray should be treated as experimental. See "Hot pepper spray," below, for ideas on how to prepare garlic spray.

WARNING: Earthworms will not eat onion family plants, so this spray could drive them away from the area sprayed.

Handpick: This is often the most effective control. Use gloves at all times to prevent allergic reactions. To kill bugs, drop them into soapy water, boiling water, or water that has some insecticidal soap in it. Small amounts of kerosene or oil will work, but are harder to dispose in an ecologically safe way.

Horticultural Oil: The two horticultural grades of oil work by suffocating mature insects, larvae and eggs. The older and heavier grade of horticultural oil, sometimes called dormant oil, is applied to fruit trees in early spring or fall while the trees are still dormant. If applied to large areas of plant foliage oil can severely injure or kill the plant by clogging leaf pores, thereby preventing respiration. The newer and lighter grades of horticultural oil sometimes called superior horticultural oil, is less injurious to some plants because it evaporates more quickly. They can be used up to one month before harvest, as long as soil moisture is adequate, relative humidity favors evaporation, and the plant is relatively healthy. Woody ornamentals are most likely to tolerate this oil in their foliage state. To test whether a plant will tolerate the superior oil, spray it on a few leaves. In several days leaf tips and margins will yellow if the plant is damaged by the oil. Horticultural oils are considered relatively safe to humans and other warm-blooded animals, and to beneficial insects.

Hot pepper spray: Red peppers have been shown to contain an active ingredient called *capsaicin* that repels onion fly maggots when as little as 1 milligram was sprinkled around the plant base. It is also thought to be effective against other insects as well. It apparently does not work well in monocultures, but works well in gardens with a variety of plants where insects have a choice of feeding sites. Capsaicin kills nerve fibers in mammals, so it may be effective against insect pests by affecting their nervous system. Capsaicin is available commercially.

WARNING: The effects of capsaicin on beneficial insects and earthworms are not well-known.

The following are two recipes to try.

(1) Chop, or grind, or blend hot peppers. Mix 1/2 cup of ground hot peppers with 2 cups of water. Strain to remove particles.

(2) An effective recipe from Dr. Carl Totemeier, horticulturist: Mix 2 tablespoons garlic powder, 1-2 tablespoons tabasco sauce or Louisiana hot sauce, dash of liquid dish washing detergent, and 2 cups of water. Because of the soap, this spray will tend to stick better to the leaves and bugs. Dr. Totemeier says it works well against many soft-bodied insects such as aphids, white fly, mealy bug, and most larvae (except that of gypsy moth).

Spray the plant twice, 2-3 days apart. The spray must physically contact the pest in order to affect it. Pepper spray will usually repel, not kill, the bugs.

Hot water seed treatment: Place seeds in a cheesecloth bag and put this bag in water at the designated temperature. Stir continuously, and add hot water periodically, to keep water temperature even. Don't pour hot water directly on the seeds. When finished, remove the seeds and immerse in cold water. Drain and dry.

Insecticidal soap spray: This is not the same thing as homemade soap; it is not effective for household cleaning. Insecticidal soap is based on fatty acid salts that penetrate insect cell membranes. They work best on soft-bodied insects such as aphids, mealybugs, mites, and whiteflies. It biodegrades in 2-14 days, and the residue on the plant is considered ineffective once dry.

Insecticidal soaps are specifically formulated to attack only harmful pests and, unless specified, are not harmful to pets, humans, or most beneficial insects. In fact, they have been used in conjunction with beneficials such as *Encarsia formosa* and ladybug larvae. Insecticidal soaps are better for plants than household soap sprays because they usually won't burn plant leaves, they don't have the additional ingredients of household soaps, and the active ingredients (fatty acid salts) are present in known quantities. Any phytotoxic symptoms will appear within the first 48 hours of spraying; so if you're unsure whether the soap will burn or injure a plant, test it on just a few leaves and wait for 2 days to see if wilting, yellowing, or other symptoms of burn appear.

Insecticidal soap only works on contact, so it must be sprayed directly on the pest. Spray only those areas affected by the pest, not the entire patch of plants, and not even necessarily the entire plant. This is called spot spraying. Coat all sides of infested plant surfaces.

Insecticidal soap is generally not very effective against hard-bodied insects, but the addition of isopropyl alcohol increases its effectiveness because it is carried by the alcohol through the pest's protective coating to its body. Add 1/2 Cup isopropyl alcohol to every 4 Cups of insecticidal soap. Some commercial insecticidal soaps already come mixed with some alcohol, even though they may not advertise this fact.

Don't spray insecticidal soap at temperatures over 90F or in the full sun. Don't spray newly rooted cuttings, new transplants, or blooming fruit and nut trees. It's best to spray in the early morning. Rinse all soap residues off any plant that begins to wilt in the first few hours after spraying.

Pyrethrum (see WARNING in Botanical Controls, above): A botanical poison derived from the pyrethrum flower, a member of the chrysanthemum family. This is considered a "knock-out" insecticide, although considered safe for warm-blooded animals and relatively safe for honeybees and ladybug larvae (only because it degrades within 6 hours in temperatures over 55F). It works by paralyzing the insect, although the insect may revive if it receives less than a lethal dose. Use this one with extra special caution; if possible, use ryania or sabadilla before using pyrethrum. Spray at dusk when honeybees are less active, and don't spray at all if a heavy dew is expected. The foliar spray is considered less harmful to bees than the dust application.

Rotenone (see WARNING in Botanical Controls, above): A botanical poison refined from the root of a tropical plant. It can also be found in the roots (5% concentration) of a native weed, Devil's shoestring (*Tephrasis virginiana*), which Native American's have used as a fish poison. It is used at two concentrations, 1% for the more easily killed insects, and 5% for the more difficult bugs. It kills beneficial insects just as easily as harmful insects, and is extremely toxic to fish. If possible, use ryania or sabadilla before using rotenone. It degrades within 3-7 days in the presence of light and oxygen.

Row covers: Row covers are an extremely effective prevention against egg-laying insects. They are made of light-weight material that lets in air, light, and water. Cover your transplants immediately or when specified for pest emergence times. Seal edges to the ground and leave on all season, unless otherwise noted. Allow extra material sufficient for growth of the tallest plant covered. For plants that need pollination, such as most cucumbers, you can lift the edges of the row covers during bloom time, 2 hours in the early morning twice per week. This is all the time bees and other pollinators need to do their good work. Then secure the edges again until harvest time.

Note: Do not use row covers if the pest was seen in that spot the previous season and it overwinters or lays eggs in the soil. Also, row covers usually raise the temperature underneath, which is helpful for extending your growing season in spring and fall. If you plan to keep them through the warm season, however, especially if you live in southern growing zones, the temperature rise may not be beneficial to plants that don't tolerate heat well. Tufbel™ is reputed to be one of the best row covers. Suppliers listed in Section 8 offer various row covers.

Ryania (see WARNING in Botanical Controls, above): A botanical poison refined from the South American ryania shrub. As a contact and stomach poison, it controls pests by making them extremely sick. It is considered safe to humans and other warm-blooded animals and plants. It is also considered less toxic to beneficial insects, including honeybees than other botanical controls. The foliar spray is less harmful to bees than the dust application. Ryania degrades quickly, so it can be used close to harvest.

Sabadilla (see WARNING in Botanical Controls, above): A botanical poison derived from the seeds of a South American lily. A very old insecticide dating back to the 16th century, sabadilla is somewhat less harmful to beneficial insects than other botanicals, except honeybees are vulnerable to it. Applied as a dust, humans and pets can experience irritated mucous membranes and sneezing fits.

Soap spray (homemade): This is not the same thing as insecticidal soap sprays (see above). Tests of various types of household sprays show different levels of effectiveness against bugs and different levels of burning plant leaves. Start off with 2-3 tablespoons of soap per gallon of water; never use more than 4 tablespoons as it will burn the plant leaves. Test different soaps to determine which brand and concentration doesn't burn the leaves. Another option is to rinse the plant 1-2 hours after you sprayed; this should avoid harming the plant but still affect the insects. Avoid soaps that are dyed or perfumed. Soap flakes, though harder to prepare, seem to cause the least damage to plants. Some liquid dishwashing soaps are mild enough to be left on the plant without rinsing. Soap spray is a contact insecticide (see Insecticidal soap above).

   WARNING: Unless you are absolutely sure the home soaps are biodegradable, they may do more harm than good when sprayed widely. Spot spraying should not be a problem. Commercial manufacturers may label a kitchen soap "biodegradable," but the question is under what conditions and in how many years? Their label may be appropriate for a septic tank, but whether it will biodegrade rapidly in the soil should be checked out with the manufacturer. When in doubt, use an insecticidal soap which is designed to biodegrade rapidly and target specific pests.

Soap and lime spray: Mix agricultural lime at the rate of 1/4 to 1/2 Cup per gallon of water. Add 2-3 Tb of insecticidal soap per gallon. The soap helps the lime adhere to insect bodies. The lime can dry out very small insects, kill some small insects and mites, and can irritate adults. Test the spray first on a small area of the plant, as some have adverse reactions to these materials. Wait several days before judging the results and spraying the remainder of the plant. As with other soap sprays, you should spot spray to avoid harming beneficial insects.

Stem collar: These are used as a physical barrier to crawling pests. Use wax paper cups, which don't fall apart easily in rain, or other impenetrable material such as cardboard or tar paper. To prepare the cups cut a hole in the bottom for the stem, and slits radiating out from the hole to permit stem growth. Place inverted around the base of the stem. Sink the edges at least 1 inch into the soil. For other materials simply cut a 3-4 inch collar, push it 1 inch into the soil, and fasten the sides closed securely. Toilet paper tubes work fine and eventually disintegrate.

Sticky bands: Sticky bands are wrapped around tree trunks to trap larvae, egg-laying females, or other pests. Use wide cotton batting, burlap, or heavy paper, usually at least 6" wide. Place about chest height. Over this tie a 6-12" piece of tar paper coated with Tanglefoot™, or a mixture of pine tar and molasses, or a mixture of resin and oil. Wrap around the trunk and secure with wire or a tie. Renew the sticky substance periodically. If trapping larvae, remove the bands and destroy the larvae once a week in warm weather, or every two weeks in cool weather. If trapping a crawling insect not bearing or laying eggs (e.g. aphids), clean as necessary and renew the sticky substance.

Sticky balls: These traps may be best as an early warning device to detect the presence of pests in sufficient numbers to require other action. Usually red, these balls are hung in trees as both early warning and control devices. As a monitoring device, count pests trapped every 2-3 days and recoat the ball every 2 weeks. As a pest control, use 1-4 balls per tree, depending on the tree size, clean and recoat as needed, and remove all balls after 4 weeks to avoid catching too many beneficial insects.

Sticky traps: These traps may be best as an early warning device to detect the presence of pests in sufficient numbers to require other action. For monitoring, count pests trapped every 2-3 days and recoat every 2 weeks. These traps are usually yellow or white boards about 8 x 10 inches, coated with a sticky substance such as Tangle Trap™ or petroleum jelly. Do not use motor oil, recommended by some, because it will interfere with the proper color. Place them adjacent to susceptible plants. Don't place them above plants. Clean and recoat as needed. Try not to use these more than 3 to 4 weeks at a time to avoid capturing more beneficial insects than necessary. In a greenhouse, place the traps at the canopy height of the plants.

Traps: Traps are an easy, non-toxic way to monitor and control many different insects. They usually use pheromones and visual colors to attract the specific bug. Monitoring is useful to determine when the insect emerges, where it comes from, and how many are present--before resorting to chemical remedies. Generally, traps are a safe and cost effective tool for a self-sustaining garden. Traps are available for such insects as slugs, Japanese beetles, codling moth, gypsy moth, oriental fruit moth, corn earworm, cherry fruit fly and husk fly, apple maggot (see "Sticky Balls"), some scales, and more.

SOME CAVEATS: Some traps that are not pheromone-specific can capture some beneficial insects and consequently shouldn't be left out longer than recommended. Some pheromone traps that work over long distances may actually attract more of the insect to your garden. Some pheromone traps are best suited to large commercial operations. Before investing in traps, consult your supplier on its advisability for your particular situation and whether it is best placed in or away from the garden.

Identify The Specific Micro And Macro Pests: Don't be discouraged by the following charts on disease, insect and animal pests. Most diseases should not be a problem if you rotate crops, destroy diseased material from garden areas, use resistant varieties, and start with pathogen-free transplants. As for insects, most gardens experience a very small number, usually no more than three to five major pests. Proper controls adopted in a timely fashion should minimize major threats to your crops. Also, remember that plants can lose up to 20 percent of their foliage and still produce yields that equal plants with no foliage loss.

Only when you have made a positive identification of the microscopic destructive agent should you use remedies specific to the disease. Specific disease remedies, such as botanical sprays, are generally more injurious to the ecosystem than broad-spectrum remedies listed above in the Second Line of Defense. An application of a special remedy that doesn't target the disease is not only a waste of money and time, but potentially harmful to the plant and ecosystem. An anti-bacterial spray, for example, when used inappropriately could feasibly wipe out the beneficial bacteria above and in the soil. These balances in and above the soil take time to build, and should not be sacrificed lightly. If you are ready to spray or use some other pest-specific remedy, it's worth the time to first consult a textbook, extension agent, or other professional to ensure correct identification of the pest.

Prevention is by far the best approach to both disease and insect control, but it is most critical with diseases. Post-infection remedies for specific macro pests are often more varied and usually include some easy, non-toxic methods that don't harm beneficials above or in the soil.

In our compilation we tried to avoid, or at least minimize, controls that might be difficult to administer, could potentially harm the earthworms and soil microorganisms, or could cause ecological imbalances in future years. Not everyone, however, agrees on the use of certain substances. Whenever in doubt, we have tried to err on the safe side.

Founded in 1985, the Organic Foods Production Association of North America (OFPANA) is actively involved in trying to establish which substances are or are not safe. It has established criteria, which are still evolving, to certify growers as "organic." Its guidelines classify numerous chemical and other substances as permitted, regulated, or prohibited. A copy of the guidelines can be ordered for $12.50 (1990 price) from the OFPANA Office, P.O. Box 1078, Greenfield, MA, 01301. In Section 8 you can find a list of state organizations that are establishing guidelines on the local level.

MICRO PESTS: DISEASES

Criteria For Selection: Diseases mentioned in the plant entries were included below only if they met the following criteria: (1) Remedies exist above and beyond those listed in the previous discussion. Diseases that can be controlled by steps mentioned in the First through Third Lines of Defense are not listed to avoid unnecessary repetition. (2) Insects are known to spread the disease organism, meaning that the disease may be attenuated by controlling the insect. (3) The disease organism is especially virulent and the plants need to be removed immediately.

Pathogens: Diseases in different plants may share the same common name (e.g. Bacterial Wilt) but they are often caused by different pathogens. Consequently the "same" disease may have distinct symptoms in different plants. To make matters more difficult, sometimes even the same pathogen will cause different symptoms in different species. To simplify matters for the backyard gardener, we group diseases by their common names and describe the different symptoms, where possible.

Remedies: To avoid repetition below, remember not to work with plants when wet, and to practice clean cultivation as described on page 166. These are both helpful remedies with many diseases.

WARNING: Diseases are much more difficult than insect pests to diagnose accurately. This chart is included primarily to indicate how serious a problem disease identification may be, given the similar symptoms shared by a wide variety of diseases, and to help you conduct a more informed discussion with professionals. It is not intended to be a final diagnostic tool. Before you use botanical or other sprays, or institute large-scale or costly remedies, it is vital that you achieve an accurate diagnosis. The following precautions are strongly urged. If attempting diagnosis on your own, read the descriptions for all possible diseases listed in the plant entry; don't just stop at the first one that seems to match the symptoms of your plant. Because this chart presents a selection of diseases, consult other texts listed in the Bibliography. When in doubt, take a plant sample to a local professional to obtain a diagnosis.

Disease	Description	Organic Remedy
Armillaria Root Rot (aka: Honey mushroom, Mushroom root rot, Oak root fungus, Shoestring fungus) Fruit trees Nut trees Ornamentals	Fungus: White, fan-shaped fungus appears between the bark and wood. Lower trunk decays. Crown is girdled by fungus. Mushrooms appear in autumn around the plant base. Roots rot and die slowly. If stressed by other factors, the tree will die suddenly. Fungus spreads underground 1 foot at a time. Where: Western states, Atlantic coast, all of FL, and Gulf coast. Worst in heavy, poorly drained soils.	1. In mild cases, remove the soil around rotted trunk areas. Cut out dead tissue. Let trunk dry out through the summer and replace soil when a freeze approaches. 2. In severe cases, remove the plant, stump, and, if possible, the roots.

Disease	Description	Organic Remedy
Asparagus Rust Asparagus	Fungus: Leaves and stems develop orange-red spots or blisters which, in time, burst open with orange-red spores. Tops yellow and die prematurely. Spread by wind and spores. Where: Widespread. Worst in moist seasons.	1. Cut, remove and destroy affected tops. 2. Do not start new plantings next to old plantings. 3. Destroy wild asparagus. 4. See #3-5 under BEAN RUST.
Aster Yellows	see YELLOWS	see YELLOWS
Bacterial Canker (aka: Bacteral Blast, and Bacterial Gummosis) Almond Apricot Blueberry Cherry Peach Tomato	Bacteria: Almond, Apricot, Peach--Small purple spots develop on leaves, black spots on fruits, and cankers on twigs. Cherry-- Leaves wilt and die. Cracks and stems may ooze in spring and fall. Limbs may die. Blueberry-- Stems develop reddish-brown to black cankers, and nearby buds die. Plants eventually die. Tomato-- Oldest leaves turn downward first, leaflets curl and shrivel. Only one side may be affected. A stem cut lengthwise may reveal discoloration of creamy white to reddish brown. Young infected fruits are stunted and distorted. Fruits may develop small, white round spots. Transmitted by wind, rain, infected seeds, and debris. It enters through skin wounds. Where: Widespread, especially in cool, windy, moist weather.	1. Tomato-- Hot water seed treatment at 122F for 25 minutes. 2. Tomato-- Plant resistant varieties or certified seed. 3. Tomato-- Rotate crops. 4. Trees-- Prune immediately. Between cuts disinfect tools and hands. If uncontrollable by pruning, destroy tree.
Bacterial Wilt (aka in corn: Stewart's Disease) Beans Corn *Cucurbits* Eggplant Tomato *continued*	Bacteria: Beans-- Seedlings usually die before 3" tall. Mature vines wilt, especially mid-day, and die. *Cucurbits*-- Plants wilt rapidly and, even while green, can die. Cut stems produce oozy strings. This bacteria blocks the plant's vascular system. Corn-- Plants may wilt, and leaves can develop long water-soaked or pale yellow streaks. A cut in the lower stem oozes yellowish droplets that can be drawn out into fine, small threads. Tomato-- Plants wilt and die rapidly, starting with young leaves first. Lower foliage may yellow slightly. A lengthwise stem cut	1. Corn and *cucurbits*-- control the insect vector (see Description). 2. Immediately remove and destroy infected plants. 3. Beans and tomato-- plant only certified wilt-free seeds. Rotate crops on a 4-5 year basis. Fumigate soil 4. Plant resistant varieties.

Disease	Description	Organic Remedy
Bacterial Wilt, *ctd.*	reveals an oozy gray-brown core. Transmitted in beans by seeds, in *cucurbits* by both cucumber beetles, in corn by the corn flea beetle. The pathogen affecting beans and tomatoes overwinters in debris. Where: Corn-- Central, South, & East. *Solanaceae*-- South. *Cucurbits*-- Northeast & North Central states. Some wilts are fostered by moist soil and soil temperatures above 75F.	
Bean Rust Beans	Fungus: Leaf undersides develop small, red-orange to brown blisters full of spores. Leaves yellow, dry, and drop prematurely. Spores are spread by wind and water. Where: Eastern seaboard and irrigated areas in the West. Fostered by relative high humidity for 8-10 days.	1. Don't reuse vine stakes. 2. Use long crop rotations. 3. If necessary, apply a sulfur spray every 7-10 days until 1 month before harvest. 4. Use heavy mulch and drip, not overhead, irrigation to minimize spreading it through splashing. 5. Select resistant varieties.
Black Heart Celery Potato	Environmental: Celery-- A low calcium-potassium ratio causes spreading brown water-soaked areas on leaves. Potato-- Low oxygen levels at the tuber center cause purple, black or gray areas. Where: Widespread, but rare in the Northwest and North Central states.	1. Celery-- Make sure the soil contains adequate calcium. 2. Potato-- Improve soil drainage to reduce chances of it recurring. Don't leave potatoes in or on very hot soil (over 90F).
Black Knot Apricot Cherry Plum	Fungus: Coal black, hard swellings appear on twigs and limbs. Growths develop in late summer as olive green, then blacken. They can be 2-4 times the thickness of the branch. Limbs weaken. Trees die slowly. The disease is detected the year after infection. Spread by wind and rain. Harbored in the tree knots. Where: East of the Mississippi.	1. Cut off all twigs and branches at least 4 inches below swellings. Destroy cuttings. Cover wounds with paint or wax. 2. Remove all infected wild cherry and plum. 3. Where significant damage is expected spray with a lime-sulfur or Bordeaux mix at the first bud stage. 4. Plant resistant varieties.
Blotch Disease (aka: Sooty Blotch) *continued*	Fungus: Only skins are affected. Fruits are still edible. Mottled, irregular shaped spots (up to 1/4") appear. "Cloudy fruit" has spots	1. Scrub citrus fruit skins. 2. Peel skins off other fruits in order to eat.

Disease	Description	Organic Remedy
Blotch Disease, *ctd.* Apple Citrus Pear	that run together. Where: East, Central, and Southern states to the Gulf.	3. Prune and space trees for better air circulation. 4. Prune and destroy infected twigs.
Canker Dieback Apple Pecan	Fungus: Apple-- Watery blisters on bark. Oval dead patches (1"-1') may become sunken. Eventually leaves yellow. Apple and Pecan-- Branches wilt and die from the tip down. Where: Widespread. For apples, especially a problem in moist springs and early falls. For pecans, may be caused by inadequate water in winter or heavy soils with poor drainage.	1. Avoid wounding tree trunks and stems. 2. Cut off infected branches well below infection. 3. For small cankers gouge out with sharp knife and treat with tree paint or Bordeaux paste. Disinfect tools between cuts. 4. Destroy all pruned matter. 5. Pecan--ensure adequate drainage in hardpan soils, and deep watering in sandy soils.
Cedar Apple Rust Apple Pear	Fungus: Light yellow spots on leaves become bright orange spots. Fruits may also develop spots. Cedar Apple Rust has a 2-year life cycle. Transmitted by wind and rain by spores from red cedars and junipers. Where: East and Central states, and AK.	1. Remove all red cedars, junipers, wild apple, and ornamental apples within 300 yards. OR plant a windbreak between the disease hosts and apple trees. 2. See #3-5 under BEAN RUST. (Copper may be used, but can harm earthworms.)
Celery Mosaic Celery	Virus: Leaves turn yellow and mottled green. Stalks are stunted, twisted and narrow.	1. Control aphids. 2. Destroy infected plants.
Cherry Leaf Spot and Plum Leaf Spot (aka: Yellow Leaf in cherry) Cherry Plum	Fungus: Purple spots on leaves, followed by bright yellow foliage. Spots often drop out of leaves, followed by defoliation. Heavy fruit drop in plums. Very damaging. Harbored in debris and spread by wind. Where: East of Rockies, and particularly bad in warm, wet conditions.	1. Destroy fallen leaves and fruit. Pinch off infected leaves. 2. A spray of wettable sulfur from petal fall to harvest is virtually the only control. 3. Fall cultivation of soil, no more than 2 inches, reduces spore spread.
Common Mosaic Beans *continued*	Virus: Severely stunted plants with few pods. Mottled green, elongated leaves crinkle and curl downwards at the edges. Infection occurs usually near bloom time. Plants eventually die. Spread by aphids and gardeners.	1. Control aphids. 2. Destroy infected plants, no matter how mildly affected. 3. Remove all perennial weeds within 150 feet of the garden. 4. Plant resistant varieties.

Disease	Description	Organic Remedy
Common Mosaic, *ctd*.	Overwinters in perennial weeds like Canadian thistle. Where: Widespread.	
Cottony Rot (aka: Pink Rot and Watery Soft Rot in cabbage, White Mold in beans) Beans Cabbage Celery Lettuce	Fungus: General-- White mold develops, and small, hard black bodies form on or within the mold. Beans-- Stems develop water-soaked spots, then branches and leaves. White mold develops in these spots. Cabbage and Lettuce-- Stem and leaves near ground become water-soaked, leaves wilt, and plant collapses. White mold grows on the head. Celery-- White, cottony growth appears at stalk base. Stalks rot and taste bitter. Spread by the small black bodies, which can survive in soil for up to 10 years. Where: Widespread. Most common in cool, moist conditions.	1. Remove and destroy infected plants, if possible before black bodies form. 2. Plant in well-drained soil. Raised beds will help greatly. 3. Beans and celery-- Where flood irrigation is feasible, usually in muck or sandy soil, flood the growing area for 4-8 weeks, or alternate flooding and drying, which kills the black bodies. 4. Rotate with immune or resistant crops such as beets, onion, spinach, peanuts, corn, cereals, and grasses. Avoid successive plantings of beans, celery, lettuce, or cabbage.
Crown Gall Almond Apple Apricot Blackberry Blueberry Cherry Filbert Grape Peach Pear Pecan Plum Raspberry Walnut	Bacteria: Fruit trees and brambles weaken and produce small, poor fruit. Galls are swellings that circle roots and crowns, and sometimes are several inches in diameter. Galls can be spongy or hard. Plants can survive for many years but are very susceptible to other stresses. Transmitted through wounds in the roots, crowns, and stems by tools and soil water. Where: Widespread.	1. Brambles-- Destroy canes and plants with symptoms. 2. Trees-- Prune galls and treat with tree surgeon's paint or a bactericidal paint. Cover with soil after painting. Destroy infected portions. Disinfect hands and tools between cuts. 3. Remove badly infected trees, trunks, and roots. Destroy. Don't plant another susceptible tree there for 3-5 years. 4. Propagate fruit trees only by budding. 5. Select resistant rootstocks. 6. Use Gall-trol™ or Norbac 84-C™ at planting (competitive bacteria). 7. Ensure good soil drainage.
Crown Rot	see SOUTHERN BLIGHT	see SOUTHERN BLIGHT
Crown Rot *continued*	Fungus: Late in the season 1 or more branches turn reddish. Leaves turn yellow	1. Rake soil away from tree crown and, if necessary,

Disease	Description	Organic Remedy
Crown Rot, *ctd.* Almond Apple Cherry Pear	or brown, and wilt. Dead bark tissue appears at the soil line, with sunken and sometimes girdling cankers. Like collar rots and damping off, this fungus attacks at or below the soil surface. Where: Widespread where trunks are wet at the soil line.	expose upper roots. This improves air circulation and may correct the problem. 2. Avoid standing water or continuous wet conditions around the trunk. 3. Allow soil to dry out thoroughly between watering. 4. Avoid deep planting of new young trees.

Cucumber Mosaic
(aka: CMV, Mosaic)
(aka in spinach:
  Yellows)
 	
  Cucurbits
  Lettuce
  Pepper
  Potato
  Raspberry
  Spinach
  Tomato
	Virus: General-- Yellow-green mottling and curled foliage. Plants are weak, stunted, may have few blossoms, poor fruit, and may die. Fruits are misshapen and mottled. Distorted leaves are common.
	Pepper & Tomato-- Older leaves look like oak leaves and develop large yellowish ringspots. Affected leaves can drop prematurely. Fruits develop concentric rings and solid circular spots, first yellow then brown. Fruits flatten and roots are stunted.
	Potato-- Tubers may develop brown spots, and the plant yellows and dies.
	Raspberry-- Dry, seedless, crumbly fruit. Canes may droop, blacken, and die.
	Cucurbits-- Leaf margins can curl downward, and cucumbers and summer squash fruits become mottled yellow-green.
	
	Spread by aphids (*cucurbits*, lettuce, pepper, tomato) striped or spotted cucumber beetles (*cucurbits*), and gardeners. It overwinters in many perennial weeds.
	
	Where: Widespread.
		1. Control appropriate insect vector (aphids or cucumber beetles). See description. Apply row covers until blossom time to prevent aphids and cucumber beetles.
		2. Remove and destroy infected plants and, if severe, surrounding plants.
		3. Remove all perennial weeds within 150 feet of the garden.
		4. Plant resistant varieties.

Curly Dwarf Artichoke	Virus: Stunted plants. Spread by aphids and leafhoppers. Where: Pacific coast and southern coast of TX.	1. Control aphids and leafhoppers. 2. Remove and destroy all infected plants. 3. Remove all milk thistle and other nearby weeds.
Curly Top (CTV) (aka: Western Yellow Blight in tomato) *continued*	Virus: General-- Stunted plants have numerous small leaves that pucker, crinkle, curl, and yellow. Fruits are few, dwarfed, or may ripen prematurely. Beans-- Leaves also are darker green.	1. Control beet leafhoppers. 2. Apply row covers until blossom time to reduce leafhoppers. 3. Prune and destroy infected

Disease	Description	Organic Remedy
Curly Top, *ctd.* Beans Beet *Cucurbits* Pepper Spinach Tomato	Young plants may die, but older plants usually survive. Plant produces few or dwarfed pods, and looks bushy. *Cucurbits*-- Leaves can also be mottled. Tomato-- Branches are also very erect, leaflet veins turn purple, and plant turns a dull yellow. Spread by beet leafhoppers. Where: Widespread.	parts of plants immediately. If serious, remove and destroy all infected plants and all nearby plants. 4. Grow tomatoes away from beets, spinach, melons or other leafhopper hosts. Also space them closely to discourage leafhoppers. 5. Select resistant varieties.
Enation Mosaic (aka: Pea Virus I, Leaf Enation) Pea	Virus: Young leaves become mottled. Leaf undersides develop small outgrowths known as enations. Vine tips become misshapen and internodal distance shortens. Stunted plants have few, if any, pods. Pods may have yellow seeds. Extremely damaging. Spread primarily by aphids, and overwinters in various clovers, vetch, and alfalfa. Where: Widespread, but particularly a problem in the Northwest.	1. Control aphids. 2. Plant early to avoid high aphid populations. 3. Select resistant varieties.
Fire Blight Apple Pear	Bacteria: Infected shoots turn brown and black, as though scorched by fire. Lesions may ooze orange-brown liquid. Blossoms wither and die. Reddish, water-soaked lesions develop on bark. Spread by aphids, psylla, bees, and rain. Enters through blossoms or new growth. Where: Widespread, particularly in areas of high humidity, dew, and rain. Bacteria remain dormant through the winter inside cankers.	1. Control aphids and psylla. 2. Remove and destroy all suckers and infected branches. Cut at least 12 inches below point of visible wilt. After each cut disinfect tool in bleach solution (1:4 dilution). In winter, repeat and treat cuts with asphalt-based dressing. 3. Keep orchard grass mowed. 4. Avoid heavy pruning or high nitrogen fertilizer. Both stimulate rapid twig growth. 5. Check soil acidity. The more acid the soil, the more prone to fire blight. 6. If significant damage occurs, spray with a copper-sulfur blend labeled for fire blight. 7. Plant resistant varieties.
Fusarium Wilt *continued*	Fungus: General--Yellowing, stunting, and wilting (often rapid). Lower leaves may wilt first. Plants usually die, but seedlings can	1. Remove and destroy infected plants. 2. Ensure good soil drainage.

Disease	Description	Organic Remedy
Fusarium Wilt, *ctd.* (aka: Fusarium Yellows, or Yellows) Asparagus *Brassicas* Celery Lettuce Melon Peas Potato Spinach Sweet Potato Tomato Turnip Watermelon	die quickly. In some plants, a sliced lower stem may reveal discoloration originating from the roots. Celery-- Ribs also redden. Muskmelon-- One side of the vine develops a water-soaked yellow streak near the soil line, which darkens to brown. Potato-- In storage, blue or white swellings may develop on brown decayed areas. Spread by water, and tools, and seeds. It can live in soil for 20 years. Likes warm, dry weather. Where: Widespread, but mostly East of the Rockies. Worst in the South in light, sandy soil, and in dry weather with temperatures of 60-90F. Temperatures above 90F retard the disease.	3. Don't plant susceptible crops for 8 years where fusarium was last seen. Rotate crops on a regular basis as a preventive measure, too. 4. Solarize garden soil, where possible. Sterilize potting soil. 5. Select resistant varieties. This is one of the best controls. 6. Asparagus-- Use seed labeled as treated with a Clorox solution (available in NJ).
Leaf Blight (aka: Bacterial Blight) Carrot	Bacteria: Carrot-- Spots on seedling leaves start out yellow-white. In time they turn brown and look water-soaked. Where: AZ, IA, ID, MI, NY, OR, WI.	1. Hot water seed treatment: 126F for 25 minutes. 2. Plant disease-free seed. 3. At harvest remove and destroy carrot tops. 4. Rotate on a 2-3 year basis.
Oak Wilt Chestnut Oak	Fungus: Water-soaked spots form on leaves usually along and tip and margin. Leaves turn brown and fall off. Symptoms start in the top of the tree then move to the trunk, which will develop short, bulging, vertical splits in the bark. A very serious disease in Chinese chestnut. White oak is a major reservoir for the fungus but tolerates the disease better. Where: States bordering the Mississippi, west to OK, KS, NE, and east to PA, and south to all states in the Appalachian mountains.	1. Once this disease is identified, immediately cut and destroy tree. Remove the stump and major roots. 2. The fungus is thought to enter through wounds that penetrate the tree bark. So you might try dressing wounds with a fungicide or tree paint as soon as they are spotted.
Orange Rust Blackberry Raspberry *continued*	Fungus: Yellow spots appear on both sides of leaves in early spring. In several weeks the leaf underside ruptures with masses of orange-red powdery spores. Spread by wind. Overwinters in plant stems and roots.	1. Remove and destroy all infected canes, roots, suckers, and all infected wild berries within 500 yards. 2. Mulch heavily with straw and leaf mold. 3. Apply lots of compost in

Disease	Description	Organic Remedy
Orange Rust, *ctd.*	Where: Widespread.	autumn with extra P & K. (Low P & K encourages rust.) 4. Select resistant varieties.
Pear Decline Pear	Mycoplasma: Transmitted by the pear psylla. Especially affects those on oriental rootstocks. Tree weakens and slowly dies.	1. Control pear psylla. 2. Use only *P. communis* rootstock.
Pecan Bunch Pecan	Mycoplasma: Symptoms are similar to WALNUT BUNCH. Where: AS, KS, LA, GA, MS, MO, NM, OK, TX	See controls for WALNUT BUNCH.
Phytophthera cinnamomi Blueberry (Highbush)	Fungus: Leaves yellow. Leaf margins brown, wilt, and fall off. Stunted growth. You may also see a "flag" branch on an otherwise healthy-looking bush (the branch is dead with dried leaves still attached). Lives indefinitely in all soil types, except perhaps sand. Most prevalent in wet soils with poor drainage. Where: Emerges in hot, moist conditions, especially in FL, GA, AS.	1. Best prevention is to grow plants in raised beds to ensure good drainage. 2. Avoid stressing the plant with under or over-fertilization or over-watering. 3. Cut down the infected part of the bush all the way to the ground, remove, and destroy.
Psyllid Yellows Potato Tomato	Toxic substance released by tomato psyllid: Potato-- Young leaves yellow or redden, brown, and die. Sprouts emerge on young tubers and form new tubers, creating eventually a chain or deformed tubers. Tomato-- Older leaves get thick and curl upward. Young leaves turn yellow with purple veins. Plant is dwarfed and spindly. Developed fruit is soft. If the plant is attacked while young no fruit will appear.	1. Clear away Chinese lantern and ground cherries, both of which are hosts. 2. Control the tomato psyllid. Garlic spray might work.
Scab (many different strains) Almond Apple Apricot Beet Cucumber *continued*	Fungus: Symptoms vary in different plants. The disease develops rapidly at 70F. Beet & Potato-- Ugly corky, wart-like lesions on the outside of roots. Tubers are still edible if damaged areas are removed. *Cucurbits*-- Leaves develop water-soaked spots and can wilt. Stems can develop small cankers. Immature fruit develop gray concave spots which darken, become deeper,	1. Remove and destroy all diseased leaves, plants, and fruit. Mow under trees. 2. Beets and potatoes-- Lower soil pH to below 5.5. 3. Fruit trees-- Spray or dust with sulfur 3 weeks after petal drop, and repeat 2 weeks later. 4. Pecans-- Remove all leaves, shucks, and dead leaves. Burn,

Disease	Description	Organic Remedy
Scab, *ctd.*	and develop a velvety green mold.	if legal. Hot composting methods will destroy the organism. 5. Ensure good drainage. 6. All vegetable crops-- Rotate on a 3-year basis at minimum. 7. Melons-- Ensure full sun by planting in a sunny location. 8. Plant soybeans in infested soil and turn under. 9. Select resistant varieties.
Melon Peach Pecan Potato Pumpkin Squash Watermelon	Fruit trees--When fruit is half-grown, small greenish dark spots eventually turn brown. Branches and twigs may develop yellow-brown spots. Fruit can crack. Pecan-- In spring when leaves unfold, irregular, olive-brown to black spots appear, usually on leaf undersides. Concave spots appear on nuts. Nuts and leaves drop prematurely. Spread among fruit and nut trees primarily by wind. Overwinters in fallen leaves and dead twigs. Dry soil favors this fungus, so keep soil moist but not soggy. Where: Widespread, particularly in the humid Southeast. Fostered by humidity.	
Smut (different strains) Corn Onion	Fungus: Corn-- Stunted or misshapen stalks. Smut develops anywhere on the leaves, stalks, ears, or tassels. Ugly white or gray galls are covered with a shiny milky membrane that ruptures and releases more black spores. Onions-- Black spots on leaves or bulbs. Cracks that contain black powder appear on the sides of spots. Onion seedlings may die in a month. If not infected by the time its first true leaves appear, the seedling will usually escape this disease. Where: Most likely to occur in a hot dry seasons and dry springs followed by a wet spell. Spores survive for years. Onion-- prevalent in Northern states.	1. Corn--Remove and destroy smut balls before they break. If severe, remove and destroy infected plants. Remove all stalks in fall. Control corn borers when tassels first appear to reduce injury. 2. Avoid manure fertilizer, which may contain spores. 3. Rotate crops on a 3-year basis at a minimum. 4. Select disease-resistant corn and disease-free onion sets. 5. If you can produce it reliably, you might try selling young corn smut to specialty restaurants; it's become a gourmet item in some areas.
Southern Blight (*Sclerotium rolfsii*) (aka: Crown Rot, *Sclerotium* Root Rot, Southern Wilt) Artichoke Beans Okra *continued*	Fungus: Leaves yellow, wilt, and drop, starting at the bottom, followed by vine wilt and death. White mold grows on the stem at or near the soil line. The white mold may harden and crust over. Round, yellow, tan or dark brown bodies the size of mustard seeds appear on lower stems and on soil, and may develop this white mold growth. Some fruits and roots develop round lesions. Storage rot may occur in	1. In warm climates, immediately dig up infected plants and destroy. In cool climates above 38 degrees latitude some suggest this disease may not need controls. 2. Black plastic mulch is reported by Auburn U. in Alabama to help control this disease, and is an easier control than soil solarization.

Disease	Description	Organic Remedy
Southern Blight, *ctd.* Peanuts Pepper Soybeans Tomato Watermelon Known to infect 200 plant species	cabbage, squash, potato and sweet potato. This fungus can spread over the soil to other plants. It oerwinters 2-3" below the soil line in the mustard seed-like bodies. Where: Prevalent in Southern states below 38 degrees latitude, coast to coast. This fungus prefers warm soil (80F or higher), moisture, and sandy soils low in Nitrogen.	3. After harvest plow in the plant stubbles deeply. 4. Rotate crops, and don't plant susceptible vegetables near each other. 5. Solarize soil. 6. Use wide spacing. 7. Plant early where there is a history of Southern Blight.
Southern Wilt	see SOUTHERN BLIGHT	see SOUTHERN BLIGHT
Spotted Wilt Tomato	Virus: Leaves develop small orange spots. Older leaves brown and die. Plant is stunted. Green fruits can develop yellow spots that develop concentric zones of brown, green, pink, or red shading. Transmitted almost entirely by thrips. Where: Widespread.	1. Control thrips. Use a reflective mulch such as aluminum foil or black plastic sprayed with aluminum. 2. Grow 2 plants per pot and set out together. Only a maximum number of plants per given area get infected, so yields can be kept high.
Stewart's Disease	See BACTERIAL WILT	see BACTERIAL WILT
Sunscald (aka: Winter Injury) Apple Cherry Onion Pecan Pepper Tomato	Environmental: The SW side of the plant warms during the day, then cells rupture during cold nights. Vegetables develop white or yellow wrinkled areas. Onions get bleached and slippery tissue during curing. Fruit tree bark darkens and splits open in long cracks or cankers. Where: Widespread. Dark tree bark is the most susceptible. Worst in drought years with cold, sunny, winter days.	1. Fruit trees-- Shade bark by covering with burlap, or apply a white interior latex paint. 2. Vegetables-- Keep as much foliage as possible to shade fruit, so don't prune suckers at the plant base. If necessary, prune above the first group of leaves above fruit. 3. Onions-- Don't cure in the direct sun.
Tobacco Mosaic (TMV) Eggplant Pepper Tomato	Virus: Misshapen leaves in young plants. Dark green mottled leaves tend to be pointed or fernlike, can curl and wrinkle, and have a grayish coloring. In the final disease stage leaves drop, branches die, fruits yellow and wrinkle. Very difficult to control. Spread by tools and hands (especially smoker's). Virus is known to live in cured tobacco for up to 25 years. Where: Widespread.	1. Never smoke near plants, and have smokers scrub hands before touching plants. 2. Destroy infected and nearby plants. Clear nearby perennial weeds. 3. Disinfect all tools. 4. Spray infected seedlings with skim milk or reconstituted powdered milk solution. Spray until seedlings are dripping. 5. Select resistant varieties.

Disease	Description	Organic Remedy
Walnut Bunch (aka: Witch's Broom, Brooming Disease) Strawberry Walnut	Mycoplasma: Walnut-- Lateral buds don't remain dormant, but produce bushy, densely packed shoots and undersized leaves, often two weeks earlier than healthy branches. Few nuts are produced. Nuts are shriveled, soft-shelled, poorly developed and have dark kernels. Diseased shoots enter dormancy in fall very late. Strawberry-- symptoms are on shoots only. On swollen stems deformed shoots are bush and "broom-like." Occurs on woodlands borders and where balsam fir is present. Where: Northeast and Midwest.	1. Walnut-- Remove all diseased branches. This can be an effective control. Make cuts well back from the infected area. Disinfect tools. 2. Walnut-- Propagate only from disease-free trees. 3. Strawberry-- Remove all infected berries and plants. 4. Strawberry-- Eliminate nearby balsam firs.
Western Yellow Blight	See CURLY TOP	See CURLY TOP
Winter Injury	see SUNSCALD	see SUNSCALD
Yellows	Fungus: see FUSARIUM WILT	see FUSARIUM WILT
Yellows Beet Celery (similar virus) Spinach	Virus: Leaves yellow, starting at tips and margins. Outer and middle leaves can get thick and brittle. Stunted plants and roots. Spread by aphids. Where: CA, OR, WA, UT, CO, MI, NB, OH, MD, VA.	1. Control aphids. Use a reflective mulch such as black plastic sprayed with aluminum. 2. Don't plant winter spinach near beets. 3. Plant vegetables in protected areas to minimize aphids spreading by wind.
Yellows (aka: Aster Yellows) Broccoli Carrot Celery Lettuce Onion Tomato Strawberry	Mycoplasma: Young leaves yellow. Topgrowth is yellow and bushy like witches' broom. Older leaves my become distorted. Carrot tops turn reddish-brown in mid to late season. Flowers may be absent, green, underdeveloped, misshapen, or fail to produce seed or fruit. Immature leaves are narrow and dwarfed. Stunted plants. Sterile seeds. Vegetables ripen prematurely. Yields and quality are severely affected. Spread by leafhoppers, particularly the six-spotted leafhopper. Where: Widespread, but particularly destructive in the West, where it affects over 200 plant species.	1. Control leafhoppers. Eradicate weeds to destroy leafhopper eggs, especially early in the season. 2. Immediately remove and destroy infected plants and plant residues. 3. Plant tolerant varieties.

MACRO PESTS: INSECTS AND ANIMALS

Clean cultivation: To avoid repetition below, clean cultivation and sanitation practices are assumed (see pages 166 and 154). Both are an important prevention and remedy for many diseases and insects.

Damage not requiring control: For chewing pests, plants can tolerate up to 20% defoliation without significant loss in yield or quality. This doesn't include plants whose leaves are the product such as in spinach or cabbage.

Remedies: The use of aluminum foil mulch for prolonged periods could possibly lead to leaching out of aluminum into the soil. If you're planning on leaving the mulch on for long periods, consider a substitute like black plastic sprayed with reflective aluminum paint.

Allies: Please check the Ally Chart (Section 7) because an alleged ally may help only one of the crops. Also, remember that an ally may effectively deter one insect pest but can potentially attract others.

* Indicates the plants most frequently attacked by the insect.

\# Indicates remedies that should be used experimentally, as their effectiveness may depend on the severity of the problem and on your method of application. Most haven't been formally tested.

Macro Pest	*Description*	*Organic Remedy*
Aphid (many sp.) Many herbs Most fruits Most vegetables	Foliage curls, puckers, or yellows. Plants can be stunted or distorted. Cottony masses may appear on twigs of trees and shrubs. Presence of sticky "honeydew" which attracts ants and supports black, sooty mold. Aphids of different species suck leaves, fruit, stems, bark and roots. Tiny (1/16-1/8") soft-bodied insects are pear shaped, and can be brown, black, pink, white or green. They have long antennae and 2 tube-like projections from the rear, and may have wings. Aphids transmit many viral diseases. The phylloxera aphid attacks grapes and nearly wiped out the French wine industry in the 1800's.	1. This may be a symptom of too much Nitrogen or pruning. Check for the presence of aphids. 2. Use row covers. 3. Control aphids and ants, which carry aphid eggs, with sticky bands, sticky yellow traps, or yellow pans filled with soapy water. 4. Keep grass mowed around garden. 5. A reflective mulch such as aluminum foil repels them. 6. \# Homemade Sprays: A. Forceful water jets 2-3 times per day. B. Bug juice. C. Garlic, onion or pepper. D. Oxalic acid from leaves of rhubarb or spinach (boil 1 lb. of leaves 30 minutes in 1 quart water, strain, cool, and add a touch of soap (not detergent). E. Tomato or potato leaf juice. 7. Other sprays: A. Light or Superior Horticultural Oil (3% solution), applied
continued		

Macro Pest	Description	Organic Remedy

Aphid, *ctd.*

Where: Widespread. 20 or more generations per year. The phylloxera aphid is primarily a problem in the West (e.g., California and Arizona) where European vines are grown.

in the plant's dormant or active phase. B. Insecticidal soap. C. Strong lime solution spray. Make sure all sprays contact the aphids.
8. Dust with Diatomaceous Earth to dry up aphids, or with calcium to control ants.
9. Fall cultivation.
10. Rotate crops (more effective with root-feeding species).
11. Biological controls: Larvae and adults of the green lacewing and ladybug. Syrphid fly larvae, minute pirate bug, damsel bugs, big-eyed bugs.
12. Botanical controls: Sabadilla dust, Rotenone (1% solution), Pyrethrin.
13. Allies (see chart): Anise, broccoli, chives, clover, coriander, cover crops of rye and vetch, fennel, French beans, garlic, lambs's quarters, nasturtium, onion family, tansy.

Apple Maggot

* Apple
  Blueberry
  Cherry
  Pear
  Plum

Slight cavities and holes indicate eggs are present. Brown streaks on fruit skins. Premature fruit drop. After fruit falls or is picked, flesh becomes brown pulpy mess. Very damaging.

Small (1/4") white-yellowish worms hatch in mid to late summer. They create winding brown tunnels as they feed inside fruit. Once the fruit falls, larvae emerge to pupate in the soil.

The adult is a small black fly with yellow legs, a striped abdomen, and zigzag black markings on its wings. Females lay eggs in puncture wounds in fruit.

Monitor trap: Mix 2 tsp ammonia, 1/4 tsp soap flakes, and 1 quart water. Hang in jars on the sunny side of trees, shoulder high. 10 jars per orchard should give good picture. Count flies every 2-3 days.

Where: Northeast, West to the Dakotas, and South to AS and GA. 1-2 generations per year.

1. Red sticky balls. Hang these on perimeter trees at shoulder height, with about 4 balls per tree.
2. # Make a control trap of 1 part molasses/9 parts water, add yeast, and pour into wide-mouthed jars. When fermentation bubbling subsides, hang jars in trees.
3. Remove and destroy badly infested fruit or feed to animals. Drop mildly damaged fruit into water to kill maggots; these are okay for cider.
4. Fall cultivation.
5. Biological Controls: Beneficial nematodes, applied in late summer to early fall.
6. Botanical Controls: Rotenone (5% solution).

Macro Pest	Description	Organic Remedy
Asparagus Beetle Asparagus	Defoliation. Misshapen spears. Adult beetles eat leaves, fruit, and spears. The small (1/4") metallic blue-black beetle, with 3 yellow-orange squares on each side of back, lays dark shiny eggs the size of specks on leaves and spears. Eggs develop into orange larvae with black heads and legs, then green-gray grubs with dark heads. Beetles overwinter in garden trash. Where: Widespread, but rare in the Pacific coastal areas, Southwest, FL, and TX. 2 generations per year in cold areas, 3-5 in warm areas.	1. Use row covers. 2. Harvest regularly in the spring. 3. Vacuum adults off ferns. Immediately empty bag and destroy bugs, or they can crawl back out. 4. Fall cultivation to destroy overwintering pests. 5. In autumn let chickens in the garden to eat beetles. 6. Biological controls: Encourage birds, and import ladybugs, chalcid and trichogramma wasps, and *Encarsia formosa*. 8. Botanical controls: Ryania, Rotenone (1% solution). 9. Allies (see chart): Basil, parsley, marigold, nasturtium, tomato. Also, beetle allegedly dislikes bone meal.
Bean Jassid	see POTATO LEAFHOPPER	see POTATO LEAFHOPPER
Bean Leaf Beetle * Beans Pea	Holes in leaves, particularly young seedlings. Adult beetles feed on leaf undersides and on seedling stems. Larvae attack roots, but usually don't affect the plant. Not a frequent pest. The adult is a small (1/4") reddish-tan beetle with 3-4 black spots on each side of its back. It lays eggs in the soil at the base of seedlings. Larvae, slender and white, feed on roots. Where: Primarily Southeast. 1-2 generations per year.	1. Same controls as MEXICAN BEAN BEETLE. 2. Biological controls: Ladybugs and lacewings eat the eggs. Beneficial nematodes, mixed into seed furrow and in mulch, may kill larvae and emerging adults. 3. Botanical controls: Rotenone (1% solution).

Beet Leafhopper
(aka: Whitefly in the West)
 	
* Beet
* Bean
  Cucumber
  Flowers
  Spinach
  Squash
  Tomato
	This leafhopper spreads curly top virus. Symptoms of curly top are raised leaf veins, stunted plants, small, wartlike bumps on the leaf undersides, and curled, brittle leaves.
	
	For a description of this and other leafhoppers, see LEAFHOPPER.
	
	Where: West of Missouri and Illinois, except not in coastal fog areas. Up to 3 generations per year.
		1. See LEAFHOPPER controls.

Macro Pest	Description	Organic Remedy
Birds Fruits Nuts Many Vegetables	Can be major pests of all fruits and berries, and corn and peas. Where: Everywhere.	1. Trees-- Netting must be held out away from the tree by supports. Otherwise they peck through the netting. Secure the netting tight around the bottom. For more complete protection you can use cheesecloth, which is harder to peck through. 2. Growing beds-- Use row covers over corn and peas. 3. # Corn seed-- Spread lime down seed rows. Plant corn seeds deeper than usual, or mulch heavily. Erect several taut strands of black thread or fishing line over each seed row. Or start seeds inside and transplant once established. 4. Mature corn-- When silks brown, tie small rubber bands over each ear. 5. Construct growing boxes that are screened on all sides. 6. For berries and other large plants, erect around the plant a Tepee structure out of lumber or poles, and drape netting over it. 7. # Strawberries-- Paint large nuts red and place in the strawberry patch before fruit has ripened. Some gardeners report birds tire of pecking at "berries" before the real thing ripens. 8. # Scare-eye balloons have been reported effective. 9. # Mulberry and elderberry trees offer berries in the fall that birds eat before anything else. Mulberry grows rapidly to a breadth of 50-60'. 10. # Use noise-making devices to scare birds away. One gardener reported that talk shows with human voices worked best.
Blackb'y Sawfly Blackberry	Rolled and webbed leaves. Adults are small wasp-like flies with 2 pairs of transparent wings hooked to each other. They lay white eggs on leaf undersides in May. Blue-green larvae (3/4") roll leaves closed with webs and feed inside the webs through July. They then drop to the ground to pupate in the soil.	1. Use sticky traps to catch adults. 2. Handpick eggs and larvae in spring. 3. Botanical controls: Rotenone (1% solution), Pyrethrin.

Macro Pest	Description	Organic Remedy
Blister Beetle	see STRIPED BLISTER BEETLE	see STRIPED BLISTER BEETLE
Boxelder Bug Almond Ash * Boxelder * Maple	Damaged foliage and twigs. Medium-sized (1/2") bugs suck plant juices. They look like squash bugs, but are brown with red markings. Nymphs are bright red. Where: Wherever boxelders grow.	1. Remove any nearby female boxelder trees. 2. Insecticidal soap spray, though this isn't a very effective control of hard-bodied insects.
Br. Almond Mite	See MITE	See MITE
Cabbage Butterfly	see IMPORTED CABBAGE WORM	see IMPORTED CABBAGE WORM
Cabbage Looper Beans * Brassicas Celery Lettuce Parsley Peas Potato Radish Spinach Tomato	Ragged holes in leaves. Seedlings can be destroyed. Worms bore into the heads of all cabbage family plants. This large (1-1/2") pale green worm with light stripes down its back doubles up or "loops" as it crawls. It hides under leaves in hot, dry weather. The worm overwinters as a green or brown pupa in a thin cocoon attached to a plant leaf. The adult moth (1-1/2") is night-flying, brownish, and has 1 silver spot in middle of each forewing. It lays greenish-white round eggs, singly, on leaves. Eggs hatch in 2 weeks and the looper feeds for 3-4 weeks. Monitor: Use pheromone traps to monitor population levels of adult moths, starting soon after planting. Where: Widespread. 4 or more generations per year. Note: Spray only when it is cool and damp, and when you see that loopers are not hiding under leaves.	1. Use row covers all season. 2. Handpick loopers. 3. Plant spring crops to avoid the cabbage looper peak. 4. Stagger planting dates to avoid entire crop susceptibility. 5. # Hot pepper spray. 6. Spray with soap and lime, or dust wet plant with lime. 7. In the deep South, practice a thorough fall cultivation and also rotate crops on 3 to 5 year basis. This insect doesn't overwinter in the North, so these steps aren't necessary. 8. Make viral insecticide from loopers infected with nuclear polyhedrosis virus (NPV). Loopers are chalky white, sluggish or half-dead, may be on top of leaves or hanging from undersides. They turn black and liquefy within days. Capture 3 and make bug juice. Spray from 3 bugs covers 1/4 acre. Loopers take 3-6 days to die, but 1 spray can last entire season. 9. Encourage predators such as toads, bluebirds, chickadees, robins and sparrows. 10. Biological controls: Bt, applied every 2 weeks until heads form (broccoli, cabbage, etc.). Lacewings and trichogramma wasp. 14. Botanical controls: Sabadilla, Rotenone (1% solution), Pyrethrin. 15. Allies (see chart): Dill, garlic, hyssop, mint, nasturtium, onion family, sage, and thyme.

Macro Pest	Description	Organic Remedy

Cabbage Maggot
 	
* *Brassicas*
  Peas
  Radish
  (Late Spring)
  Turnip
	Seedlings wilt and die. Stems are riddled with brown, slimy tunnels. Stunted, off-color plants. The maggot transmits both bacterial soft spot and black leg.
	
	The adult resembles a housefly, but is half the size and has bristly hairs. They emerge from underground cocoons in spring at cherry blossom time, in early summer, or in autumn. It lays eggs on plant stems near the soil line or in cracks in the soil.
	
	The small (1/3"), white, legless worm with a blunt end attacks stems below the soil line. To overwinter, maggots pupate 1-5" deep in the soil and emerge on the first warm spring day. In season, each life cycle takes about 6-7 weeks.
	
	Monitor: Yellow sticky traps are a good early warning device for adults. Also, take a scoop of soil from the plant base, place in water, and count the eggs that float to the top to determine the extent of the problem.
	
	Where: Widespread, particularly in Western and Northern U.S. It thrives in cool, moist weather. Numerous generations per year.
		1. Use row covers in early season.
		2. # Maggots don't like alkaline environment. Circle plants with a mixture of lime and wood ashes, moistened to prevent blowing, or Diatomaceous Earth. Replenish after rain. Mix wood ashes into the surrounding soil. Do not replenish more than 1 or 2 times; continued use of wood ashes raises the pH excessively by its addition of potassium.
		3. Use a 12" square of tar or black paper to prevent larvae from entering the soil.
		4. Plant very early spring or in fall to avoid maggot peak in May-early June.
		6. Biological controls: Beneficial nematodes are effective when applied before planting.
		7. Allies (see chart): Clover, garlic, onion family, radish, sage and wormwood.

Cabbage Moth	See IMPORTED CABBAGE W.	See IMPORTED CABBAGE W.
Cabbageworm (aka: Cross-striped Cabbageworm) Cabbage	See Imported Cabbage Worm for symptoms. New worms are gray with large round heads. Mature worms (2/3") are green to blue-gray with long dark hairs and at least 3 distinct black bands across each segment. The adult moth is small, pale yellow with mottled brown on its forewings. Where: Widespread.	Same controls as IMPORTED CABBAGE WORM

Macro Pest	Description	Organic Remedy
Caneborer (aka: Rednecked Cane Borer) Blackberry Raspberry	Large cigar-shaped swellings on canes. Where cane joints swell the cane may break off and die. Blue-black beetles (1/3") with coppery red thorax appear in May, and lay eggs in June in cane bark near a ragged or eaten leaf. Flat-headed larvae bore into canes and cause swellings or galls in late July-August. Cut open galls to find creamy white grubs. Where: Northeast, and other types in other parts of the U.S.	1. Cut out all canes with swellings and burn or destroy.
Cankerworm, Fall & Spring (aka: Inchworm, Measuring Worm) Apricot * Apple Cherry Elm Maple Oak Plum	Skeletonized leaves. Few mature fruit. Trees may look scorched when damaged by the spring variety. Defoliation may occur 2-3 years in a row. Small worms (1") are green, brown or black, have a yellow-brown stripe down their back, and drop from trees on silky threads when ready to pupate. They pupate 1-4" deep in the ground in cocoons near the trees. Male adults are grayish moths. Females are wingless. In the spring they lay brownish-gray eggs in masses on tree trunks or branches, or in the fall brown-purple egg masses beneath the bark. Eggs hatch in 4-6 months. Where: Widespread. The fall variety is worst in early spring in CA, CO, UT, and Northern U.S. The spring variety is worst in the East, CO, CA.	1. Use sticky bands from October to December, and again in February, to catch wingless females crawling up trees to lay eggs. Renew sticky substance periodically. 2. Encourage predators such as bluebirds, chickadees and nuthatches. 3. Spray Horticultural Oil before leaves bud in spring. 4. Biological controls: Trichogramma wasps work on spring species. Chalcid wasps. Bt, applied every 2 weeks from the end of blossom time to 1 month later. 5. Botanical controls: Sabadilla.
Carrot Rust Fly Caraway Carrot Celery Coriander Dill *continued*	Stunted plants. Leaves wilt and turn yellow. Soft rot bacteria in the carrot. Small (1/3"), yellow-white larvae burrow into roots and make rusty-colored tunnels.	1. Use row covers all season. 2. Fall cultivation and early spring cultivation disrupts overwintering maggots. 3. Rotate crops. 4. Avoid early planting. Plant all target crops after maggot peak. 5. Yellow sticky traps. British

Macro Pest	Description	Organic Remedy
Carrot Rust Fly, *ctd.* Fennel Parsley Parsnip	The adult fly is slender, shiny green, and lays eggs at the plant crown in late spring. Where: Widespread, but mostly a problem in Northern and Pacific Northwest states. Several generations per year.	horticulturists have shown these traps are most effective for this pest when placed at a 45-degree angle. 6. # Sow seeds with used tea leaves. 7. # Spread wood ashes (moistened to prevent blowing), pulverized wormwood, or rock phosphate around the plant crown to repel egg-laying. 8. Allies (see chart): Black salsify (oyster plant), coriander, lettuce, onion family, pennyroyal, rosemary, and sage.
Carrot Weevil Beet * Carrot Celery Parsley Parsnip	Zigzag tunnels in the tops and roots of plants. Defoliation. Small (1/3"), pale, legless, brown-headed worms tunnel into roots and celery hearts. The tiny (1/5") dark brown, hardshelled adult is snout-nosed, and overwinters in garden litter and hedgerows. Where: East of the Rockies. 2-3 generations per year.	1. Use row covers all season. 2. Fall cultivation. 3. Rotate crops. 4. Encourage chickadees, bluebirds, juncos, and warblers. 5. Biological controls: Beneficial nematodes when plants are very small. 6. Botanical controls: Sabadilla, Rotenone (5% solution).
Carrotworm	see PARSLEYWORM	see PARSLEYWORM
Celery Leaftier (aka: Greenhouse Leaftier) * Celery Kale Many more	Holes in leaves and stalks. Leaves folded and tied together with webs. Medium (3/4"), pale green- yellow worms, with white stripe down the length of their backs, eat a host of vegetables. They web foliage together as they feed, and eventually pupate in silky cocoons inside webs. The adult is a small (3/4"), brown nocturnal moth. It lays eggs that look like fish scales on leaf undersides. They can do great damage, but don't usually appear in large numbers. Where: Widespread, but worst in the Northeast and Southern California. Most destructive in greenhouses. 5-6 generations per year in warm areas, 7-8 in greenhouses.	1. Handpick and destroy pests. Also pick damaged or rolled leaves where leaftier may be hiding inside.

Macro Pest	Description	Organic Remedy
Celeryworm	see PARSLEYWORM	see PARSLEYWORM
Cherry Fruit Fly Cherry Pear Plum	Small, disfigured fruit. Premature fruit drop. Rotten flesh with maggots feeding inside. These black fruit flies resemble small houseflies, with yellow margins on the thorax and 2 white crossbands on the abdomen. They emerge in early June and feed for 7-10 days by sucking sap. They then lay eggs in developing fruit through small slits. The maggots are yellow or white small worms with 2 dark hooks on their mouth. They feed inside fruit, then drop to the ground and pupate for 6 months 2-3" deep in the soil. Pupae overwinter in the soil. Monitor: Use sticky red balls or pheromone traps to monitor populations levels. Where: Widespread, except in the Southwest and Florida.	1. Fall cultivation after the first several frosts will expose pupae to predators. 2. See remedies #1-3 for APPLE MAGGOT. 3. Biological controls: Braconid wasps.
Cherry Fruit Sawfly Apricot Cherry Peach Plum	Fruits shrivel and drop. Small (1/8") adult wasp-like flies have 2 pairs of transparent wings hooked together and yellow appendages. Small (1/4") larvae are white with brown heads. They bore into young fruit and feed on seeds. They exit fallen fruit to pupate and overwinter in silken cocoons in the ground. Where: Pacific coast.	1. Shallow 2" cultivation around trees to expose pupae. 2. See controls for BLACKBERRY SAWFLY.
Cherry Fruitworm Cherry continued	Rotten flesh with larvae feeding inside. Can be very damaging. The small, gray adult moth lays single eggs on cherries in May-June. Small (3/8") pinkish larvae hatch in 10 days and bore into fruit where they feed.	1. Biological controls: Bt, sprayed in the first week of June.

Macro Pest	Description	Organic Remedy
Cherry Fruitworm, ctd.	They overwinter in the stubs of pruned branches or in bark crevices. They are distinguished from the cherry fruit fly maggot by their black head and caterpillar-like body. Where: CO, and North and West of CO. 1 generation per year.	
Cherry Slug	see PEARSLUG	see PEARSLUG
Chestnut Weevil (aka: Snout Weevil) Chestnut	The adult (5/16-1/2") has a very long snout (proboscis), as long or longer than its body. It emerges from April-August, and in August deposits eggs into the bur through a tiny hole. Larvae feed on kernel tissue for 3-5 weeks, sometimes hollowing out the interior, then leave the nut. Larvae are legless, white, plump, and curved like a crescent moon. Mature larvae overwinter 3-6" below ground. Where: Wherever Asian Chestnuts are grown. This pest completes a life-cycle in 1-2 years.	1. Collect all fallen nuts every day and immerse in hot water (122F) for 45 minutes to kill all larvae. This prevents larvae from entering the soil and continuing the cycle. 2. Plant away from woods or forest from which squirrels and other rodents can bring in infested nuts. 3. Fall cultivation. Also, chickens can help clean up larvae.
Click Beetle	see WIREWORM	see WIREWORM
Codling Moth Almond * Apple Apricot Cherry Peach Pear Walnut (English) continued	Holes and tunnels in fruit, with brown fecal material at the core and a brown mound at the hole opening. Sometimes cocoons in bark crevices. Large (1") larvae is white tinged with pink, with a brown head, and has a voracious appetite. Adult moths (3/4") are gray-brown with dark brown markings on lacy forewings, fringed back wings, and dark brown edging on all wings. They lay flat white eggs, singly, on twigs on upper leaf surfaces. Eggs hatch in 6-20 days, and larvae tunnel into and out of fruit. Pupae overwinter in tough cocoons in cracks in loose bark, fences, buildings, or	1. In spring, band tree trunks with several thicknesses of 6" wide corrugated cardboard. Exposed ridges must be at least 3/16" wide and must face tree. This gives larvae place to spin cocoons when they leave fruit. Remove and kill larvae once a week in warm weather, once every 2 weeks in cool weather. Continue through harvest. Burn cardboard. 2. Use sticky bands to catch larvae. 3. # Make a trap for larvae of 2 parts vinegar/1 part molasses in wide-mouth jar. Hang 3 to 4 per tree, 8" below limb. Clean and replenish daily. 4. In spring, scrape off all loose rough bark from trunk and limbs. Catch scrapings and destroy. Seal pruning wounds. 5. Apply soap and lime or fish oil

Macro Pest	Description	Organic Remedy
Codling Moth, *ctd.*	garden debris. Monitor: Use pheromone traps to determine population levels. More than 5 moths per trap per week indicates that controls may be needed. Where: Widespread. 2 generations per year; the first generation attacks immature fruit, the second attacks mature fruit.	spray to entire tree before leaves appear in late winter, and, later, to tree trunk and base weekly. 6. Apply Horticultural Oil spray before buds open. Be sure to cover all surfaces of the tree. 7. Encourage woodpeckers in the winter with 1 suet per tree. 8. Biological controls: 2 or 3 sprays of Bt, applied 3 to 4 days apart at peak egg laying time, is very effective. Three timed releases of trichogramma wasps, first at petal fall, then 3-8 weeks later, and 5-8 weeks later in early fall, is also helpful. Beneficial nematodes can help most when sprayed on wet tree trunks and nearby soil in late winter. 9. Pheromone-based mating disruption devices should be commercially available soon, but may not be effective in small orchards. 10. Botanical controls: Ryania, Sabadilla, Pyrethrin. 11. Allies (see chart): Cover crops of the buckwheat, clover and daisy family, dill, garlic, wormwood.
Colorado Potato Beetle * Eggplant Pepper * Potato * Tomato *continued*	Skeletonized leaves and complete defoliation. Adults and larvae chew foliage. Small (1/3"), yellow hardshelled beetles have orange heads with black dots and black stripes down their backs. They lay bright yellow eggs on leaf undersides. Eggs hatch in 4-9 days and become plump red larvae with black spots and black heads. Where: Widespread, but mostly a problem in the Eastern U.S. Rarely a problem in Southern CA through TX, LA, and GA. 1-3 generations per year.	1. Use row covers in early season. 2. Handpick immediately, when sighted, and crush adults and egg masses. Very effective control. 3. Apply thick organic mulch to impede the movement of overwintered adults to plants. Beetles walk more than fly during early season. Potatoes can be started in thick mulch above ground. 4. Fall cultivation. 5. Where different potato and tomato varieties are grown, resistant varieties will be less susceptible. If only one resistant variety is grown, however, even this will be consumed. All eggplants are susceptible. 6. Timed plantings to avoid beetles. Plant potatoes as early as possible to allow sufficient plant growth to withstand attack of overwintered adults. 7. Foliar spray of fish wastes was shown by U. of Maine studies to repel

Macro Pest	Description	Organic Remedy
Colorado Potato Beetle, *ctd*.		these bugs. They used Biostar™. 8. A recent U. of Delaware study showed that ground tansy, diluted 1:100 (leaf to water weight ratio), used as a foliar spray dramatically reduced bug feeding. 10. # Garlic, onion and pepper sprays, applied directly on beetles, are irritants. 11. Foliar sprays of hydrogen peroxide (1 Tb: 1 gallon water) applied directly on active adults provide fair control. Do not apply in direct sunlight in the heat of the day. 12. A dusting of Diatomaceous Earth dries out beetles. Soap and lime spray is also thought to dry out beetles, but generally soap is not effective against hard-bodied insects. 13. In the fall let chickens into garden to eat beetles and larvae. 14. Encourage predators like songbirds, toads and ground beetles. 15. Biological controls: Ladybugs, lacewings & *Edovum puttleri* eat the eggs. Beneficial nematodes. Two-spotted stink bug *(Perillus bioculatus)*. New Bt strains (M-One™, Trident, Foil) are very effective if applied in the larval stage. Once the larvae are too big Bt doesn't help much. 16. Botanical controls: Sabadilla, Rotenone (5% solution). 17. Allies (see chart): Beans, catnip, coriander, dead nettle, eggplant, flax, horseradish, nasturtium, onion family and tansy. Since beans are allegedly noxious to this bug, and potatoes repel Mexican bean beetle, they might be companions.
Corn Borer	see EUROPEAN CORN B.	see EUROPEAN CORN BORER
Corn Earworm (aka: Vetchworm, Cotton Bollworm, Tomato Fruitworm, Tobacco Budworm) *continued*	Ragged holes in tender leaves. Eaten tassels and damaged pods or developing fruits. Chewed silk and damp castings near the silk. Damaged kernels, often at the ear tip. Extremely destructive. Large (1-1/2 to 2") light yellow,	1. Mineral oil, applied just inside the tip of each ear, suffocates the worms. Apply only after silk has wilted and started to brown at the tip, or pollination will be incomplete. Use 1/2 medicine dropper per small ear, 3/4 of a dropper per large ear. You might add red pepper to the oil to see if it

Macro Pest	Description	Organic Remedy
Corn Earworm, *ctd.* Beans * Corn, sweet Pea Peanut Pepper Potato Squash Tomato	green, red or brown caterpillars, striped, with "spines" at bands, feed first on leaves and corn silk. They feed on kernels and exit through the husk to pupate. Feeding lasts about 1 month, when they drop to the ground and pupate 3-5" deep in the soil. The adult (1-1/2") grayish brown moth feeds on flower nectar. It lays 500-3,000 tiny, single, ribbed, dirty white eggs on host plants. This pest is most numerous 2-3 weeks after a full moon. Some say corn should ideally silk during the full moon. Its numbers are reduced by cold winters and wet summers. Where: Widespread, but primarily a problem in South and Central states. 2-3 generations per year.	increases the effectiveness. Apply two or more applications of oil, spaced at 2 week intervals. 2. Fall cultivation. Also in spring cultivate the top 2 inches of soil. 3. Handpick worms after silks brown. 4. Time plantings to avoid worms. In Northern states, early plantings that silk before mid-July often avoid attack. 5. Plant resistant varieties with tight husks. Or clip husks tighter with clothespins. 6. The USDA recently showed petunia leaves contain a natural repellant. 7. Spray light or superior Horticultural Oil (2-3% solution). Bt added to the oil spray will increase its effectiveness. 8. Biological controls: Minute pirate bugs. Lacewings. Trichogramma wasps and Tachinid flies lay eggs in the moth eggs and prevent hatching. Inject beneficial nematodes into infested ears; they seek out and kill worms in 24 hours. Bt can be applied to borers before they move into the stalks. Then wettable Bt, applied every 10-14 days, is effective. 9. Botanical controls: Ryania, Rotenone (1% solution), Pyrethrin. Use pheromone traps to identify moth flight paths before spraying. Spray moths before they lay eggs. 10. Allies (see chart): Corn, marigold, and soybeans.
Corn Maggot (aka: Seedcorn Maggot) Beans * Corn, sweet Peas	Damaged seeds that fail to sprout. Poor, stunted plants. Small (1/4") yellow-white larvae, with long heads tapering to point, tunnel into larger vegetable seeds. The adult is a small gray-brown fly that lays eggs in April through May in the soil and on seeds and seedlings. Where: Widespread. 3-5 generations per year. Worst injury is early in cold, wet soil high in organic matter.	1. Delay planting until soil is warm. Avoid planting early in soils high in organic matter and manure. 2. Plant seeds in shallow furrows to speed emergence. 3. If damage is heavy, replant immediately. Seeds will germinate before the next generation of adults emerge. 4. Allies (see chart): Rye.

Macro Pest	Description	Organic Remedy
Corn Rootworm (Northern & Western) Corn, sweet	Weak plants with damaged silks and brown tunnels in the roots. Adult yellow-green beetles are small (1/4") and emerge in late July-August. They feed on corn silks and other plants. They lay eggs in the ground in late summer near corn roots. Eggs hatch in late spring. Small (1/2") narrow, wrinkled white worms with brown heads feed only on corn and burrow through corn roots. Where: The Western variety is active in the upper Midwest, and East to PA and MD. The Northern variety is active in NY to KS and SD. 1 generation per year.	1. Crop rotation. If beetles are found feeding on silks then plant sweet corn in a different location next year.
Corn Rootworm (Southern)	see CUCUMBER BEETLE (Spotted)	see CUCUMBER BEETLE
Cucumber Beetles, Striped & Spotted (Spotted, aka: Southern Corn Rootworm) Asparagus * Beans, early * Corn, sweet * Cucumber Eggplant * Muskmelon Peas Potato * Pumpkin * Squash Tomato * Watermelon Some fruit trees continued	Both types eat stems and leaves of cucurbits before the first true leaves emerge. Spotted beetles also eat flowers and fruit. Adults transmit bacterial wilt of cucurbits, brown rot in stone fruit, cucumber mosaic and wilt. Larvae feed on the root system. Small (1/3"), thin white larvae with brown heads and brown ends feed for 2-6 weeks on roots and underground stems. Heavy larvae populations can reduce plant vigor and damage melon rind surfaces next to the ground. Adults of both types are small (1/4") with black heads and yellow or yellow-green backs. Striped beetles have 3 black stripes down the back. Spotted beetles have 11-12 black spots scattered across the back. Both lay yellow-orange eggs in the soil near host plants. Beetles tend to congregate on one leaf or plant, so it may be possible to remove a selected plant and destroy large quantities.	1. Use row covers from sowing or transplanting to bloom. Lift edges during bloom time for 2 hours in early morning only twice per week to allow pollination. Then secure edges again until harvest. 2. Vacuum adults with a Dustbuster vacuum at dusk. Empty into a plastic bag immediately, or they'll crawl out. 3. Select resistant varieties. 4. Transplant strong seedlings. 5. Fall cultivation. 6. # Circle plants with a 3-4" wide trench, 3" deep. Fill with wood ashes, moistened to prevent blowing. Don't get on plants. 7. Handpick beetles. 8. Apply thick mulch. 9. Lime is thought to dry out these beetles. Apply soap and lime spray directly on beetles, or lime dust (hydrated or plasterer's lime), or spray an equal mixture of wood ashes and hydrated lime mixed in water. Soap alone isn't very effective against hard-bodied insects.

Macro Pest	Description	Organic Remedy
Cucumber Beetles, *ctd*.	Midsummer adults feed on upper plant parts, while autumn adults feed on fruits, then weeds and trees. Striped adults are the most destructive and eat mostly *cucurbits*. Break a cucumber plant stem, put it back together, pull it back apart and see if strings like pizza cheese form. If so, it has bacterial wilt. This test is not so easy with other *cucurbits*. Where: Widespread East of the Rockies, but most serious in the South and where soils are heavy. 1 generation per year in cold areas, 2 in warm climates.	10. # Spray of hot pepper and garlic. 11. # Sprinkle onion skins over plants. 12. Time plantings to avoid bugs. 13. # Plant zucchini or yellow squash to trap early infestations. 14. Encourage song birds. 15. Biological controls: Lacewings and ladybugs eat eggs. To kill adults, apply beneficial nematodes in the seed furrows, around roots, and in mulch. 16. Botanical controls: Sabadilla, Rotenone (1% solution), Pyrethrin. 17. Allies (see chart): Broccoli, catnip, corn, goldenrod, marigold, nasturtium, onion skins, radish, rue, tansy.
Cutworm All Beans *Brassicas* Corn, sweet Cucumber Eggplant Lettuce Melon (seedlings) Peanut Peas Pepper Potato Radish Tomato All seedlings	Severed stems, straight across, at or below soil surface. Plants wilt and collapse. Buds, leaves and fruit may also be eaten by the variegated cutworm. Large (1-2") soft-bodied larvae are gray or brownish larvae with bristles. They curl into a circle when disturbed. They feed at night for several weeks and burrow into the soil during the day. The last generation overwinters as naked brown pupae in the soil. Adults are night-flying moths with ragged blotches like paint drips on their wings. They lay egg masses on leaves, tree trunks, fences and buildings. Eggs hatch in 2-10 days. Where: Widespread. Up to 5 generations per year.	1. Stem collars. 2. Plant transplants inside 1/2 gallon milk cartons, with bottoms cut out and rim about 1" out of the soil. 3. Diatomaceous Earth sprinkle around the base of each plant, and worked slightly into the soil, is very effective. 4. # Sprinkle cornmeal or bran, 1/2 teaspoon per plant, around stem in a circle leading away from the stem. Worms eat this and die. 5. # Make a trap of equal parts of sawdust (pine is best) and bran, add molasses and a little water. At dusk sprinkle several spoonfuls near plants. The sticky goo clings to their bodies and dries, making them food for prey. 6. # Create barriers by making a 3-4" wide trench, 2-3" deep. Fill with wood ashes, moistened to prevent blowing, crushed egg shells, oak leaves, or the mixture in #4. 7. Fall cultivation. Following fall cultivation, allow chickens into the garden to clean out exposed pests. 8. Handpick at night with light. 9. Encourage birds and toads. 10. U. of British Columbia student Greg Salloum claims cutworms will starve before eating plants treated with extracts of pineapple weed or sage

continued

Macro Pest	Description	Organic Remedy
Cutworm, *ctd.*		brush. 11. Biological controls: Apply beneficial nematodes at a rate of 50,000 per plant. Apply Bt. Lacewing, braconid, and trichogramma wasps. Tachinid flies. 12. Allies (see chart): Shepherd's purse and tansy.

Deer
 	
Azaleas
Fruit trees
Holly
Juniper
Roses
Saplings
Vegetables
	Large quadruped mammal. They have two large and two small toes on each foot, a distinct print.
	
	Where: Widespread.
		1. Fences: Serious deer fences need to be electrified with 7 strands, at 8, 16, 24, 40, 50 and 60".
		   A second alternate is to use a one-wire electric fence but only if you bait the fence.
		   All electrified fences work best if baited. Bait with attached pieces of aluminum foil smeared with peanut butter; this attracts deer, shocks them, and trains them to stay away.
		   An effective non-electric fence is two 4' high fences spaced 5' apart, with bare ground between. Deer aren't broad jumpers and realize that, once they get into the middle section, there isn't enough room to clear the second fence.
		   A alternate non-electric is a fence inclined horizontally. Research at the Institute of Ecosystem Studies, New York Botanical Garden, in Millbrook, NY, shows that deer won't jump a horizontal fence.
		2. # Tie bags with 1 oz. of human or dog hair, dried blood meal, or fish heads, to orchard trees and along perimeters of melon and sweet potato patches. This allegedly provides protection for 10 months.
		3. # Make a spray of 2 egg yolks in 1 quart of water. Spray fruit tree foliage. One farmer claims trees weren't bothered the entire season.
		4. # Lay chicken wire squares wherever find deer droppings. Deer will avoid.
		5. # Hanging soap in outer tree limbs is reported by some to work. Some suggest Camay, some Safeguard, some say any brand will work. Be warned, however, that groundhogs love soap.

continued

Macro Pest	Description	Organic Remedy
Deer, *ctd*.		6. The product Hinder™ reputedly works when sprayed on leaves and branches. 7. Maintain dogs to keep deer away. 8. # Use automated blinking lights at night to keep them away. 9. # Old, smelly shoes are reputed to be effective deterrents when placed around the garden perimeter.
Diamondback Moth *Brassicas*	Small holes in outer leaves. Usually a minor pest. Small (1/3") green-yellow larvae with black hairs chews leaves. When disturbed it wriggles and drops to ground. Gray-brown adult moth (3/4") has fringed back wings, with a diamond that shows when the wings are at rest. Where: Widespread.	1. Apply soap and lime spray directly on worms. Also before harvest spray 3 days in a row to kill new worms. 2. # Southernwood is herbal repellant. 3. Biological controls: Lacewings and Trichogramma wasps. 4. Botanical controls: Sabadilla. Rotenone and Pyrethrum work against larvae. 5. Allies (see chart): Cabbage, tomato.
Earwig Bean, seedling Beet, seedling Cabbage, chinese * Celery * Corn, sweet Flowers Lettuce * Potato * Strawberry	As a beneficial, it can scavenge larvae, slow-moving bugs and aphids. As a pest, it feeds on soft plant tissue such as foliage, flowers and corn silks. It can be particularly damaging to seedlings. Symptoms are round holes in the middle of leaves. Nocturnal slender brown beetle-like insect (3/4") with sharp pincers at its tail. It usually crawls, but can fly if it takes off from a high place. Hides under and in things during the day. Where: Widespread, but primarily a pest in the West, particularly the San Francisco Bay area and Northern California areas.	1. Probably best left alone in areas where they're not a serious problem. 2. In areas where they're a serious problem, trap and kill. Good trap locations are moist, tight areas where they spend the day. Try rolled-up moistened newspapers, rolls of moistened corrugated cardboard, or bamboo. Collect and dispose of pests in the morning. 3. If very bad, use commercial earwig bait.
Eelworm	see NEMATODE	see NEMATODE
European Apple Sawfly Apple *continued*	Premature fruit drop. Brown scars on fruit skin. Small wasp-like adult flies are brown and yellow with 2 pairs of transparent	1. Clean up fallen fruit and destroy larvae by placing them in a sealed black bag in a sunny location. 2. Botanical controls: Ryania. Rotenone (1% solution), applied at

Macro Pest	Description	Organic Remedy
European Apple Sawfly, *ctd.*	wings hooked together. They emerge at blossom time.	petal fall and again 1 week later.
Pear Plum	Larvae are white worms with 7 forelegs that bore into fruit and leave chocolate-colored sawdust on the fruit surface. Worms then drop to the ground where they pupate through the winter in the ground. Where: CT, MA, NJ, NY, RI. 1 generation per year.	
European Corn Borer (aka: Corn Borer) Beans, green Chard * Corn, sweet Pepper Potato Tomato	Broken tassels and bent stalks. Sawdust castings outside small holes. This pest bores into ears and feeds on kernels at both tips and butt ends. It bores into the stem and fruit parts of pepper, potato, and green beans. It can attack the stems, foliage, and fruits of over 260 different plants. Extremely destructive. The gray-pink or flesh colored caterpillar (1") has brown spots on each segment and a dark brown head. The adult night-flying yellowish moth (1/2") has dark wavy bands across its wings, and lays clumps of white eggs on leaf undersides. Eggs hatch in up to 1 week. Larvae overwinter in corn stubble. Pupae are reddish brown grubs. Monitor: Use blacklight traps to monitor populations before spraying moths. Catches of more than 5 moths per night warrant sprays applied every 4-5 days, starting at full tassel. Where: Widespread, except the Southwest and far West. 1-3 generations per year, depending on the climate.	1. Remove and destroy all plant debris. 2. Fall cultivation destroys larvae. Plants must be destroyed and turned under at least 1" beneath the soil line. 3. Avoid early plantings which are more susceptible to larvae attack. 4. Handpick by slitting damaged tassels and removing borer. 5. Plant resistant varieties. Small stemmed, early season types are less tolerant of borer injury. 6. Cover ears with pantyhose. 7. Encourage predators such as toads, downy woodpeckers, phoebes, swallows. 8. Biological controls: Trichogramma wasps parasitize eggs. Braconid wasps. Tachinid flies. Ladybugs and lacewings eat the eggs. Release Trichogramma when adults are first caught in a monitoring trap. Bt is also effective. 9. Botanical control: Ryania, Sabadilla, Rotenone (1% solution), Pyrethrin. 10. Apply Bt and botanical controls at tassel emergence if moth activity is high. Repeat sprays every 4-5 days until silks turn brown. 11. Allies (see chart): Clover, peanuts.
European Red Mite	see MITE	see MITE

Macro Pest	Description	Organic Remedy
Fall Armyworm & Spring Armyworm Beans * Corn, sweet Cabbage	Chewed leaves, stems and buds. The fall species also bores into ears and feeds on kernels; it can be very destructive to late plantings. The spring species is a large (1-1/2") tan, brown, or green caterpillar found early in the season in the whorl leaves of corn. The fall armyworms has 3 light yellow hairline stripes from head to tail, and on each side a dark stripe below which is a wavy yellow stripe marked with red. Heads have a prominent V or Y. Both species usually feed on cloudy days and at night, but the fall species also feeds during the day. The adult gray moth of the spring species has one yellow or white spot on each forewing. Each lays up to 2,000 eggs on corn and grasses. Eggs hatch in 7 days, and the cycle continues. Further generations feed through late summer. Where: The spring species is widespread, but most serious in warm climates where there is more generation turnover. The fall species overwinters in the South and migrates to Northern states every year in June-July. 3-6 generations per year.	1. Encourage natural predators such as birds, toads, and ground beetles. Skunks also prey on these, but you may not want to attract them. 2. # In case of a serious problem, dig a steep trench around the garden. Armyworms will be trapped inside and can be destroyed by burning kerosene. 3. # Alternate rows of corn with sunflowers to discourage population movement. 4. Biological controls: Lacewings, ladybugs, and other insect predators eat eggs and young larvae. The new Hh strain of beneficial nematodes (*Neoplectana carpocapsae*) is effective against the larval stage. Ichneumon and braconid wasps. Tachinid flies. Bt is effective against the larvae.
Fall Webworm Fruit trees Pecan *continued*	Large silken tents or nests on ends of branches. Tents include foliage, unlike tentworms. Very damaging. Trees can be stripped and die. This yellowish caterpillar (1-1/4"), has long, light brown or whitish hairs, a dark stripe down its back, and is dotted with small black spots. It builds gray cocoons in secluded sites, fences, bark, or garden debris. White or green eggs are layered in clusters of 200-500 on leaf undersides. Adult white moths, with black or brown spotted wings, emerge in	1. Cut off and destroy nests. Burn where permitted. Otherwise destroy nests by putting them in boiling water or water laced with insecticidal soap (kerosene is toxic to the soil and difficult to dispose of safely). Pick off leaves with eggs and destroy. 2. Biological controls: Trichogramma wasps eat eggs. Bt is also effective.

Macro Pest	Description	Organic Remedy
Fall Webworm, *ctd.*	spring and late summer. Where: Widespread. 2 generations per year.	
Filbert Bud Mite Filbert	Buds swell through the summer and fall to 2-3 times their normal size. They will be easily recognized by December, with thousands of mites feeding per bud. Swollen buds open, dry, and drop prematurely in the spring. Yields are seriously diminished. Tiny mites migrate before bud fall in the spring to newly developing buds. Where: Widespread.	1. Plant resistant cultivars. This is the best control. 2. Early spring aphid foliar sprays may help. 3. You might try pruning out infested buds in early winter.
Filbert Weevil (aka: Hazelnut Weevil) Filbert Western Oak	Deformed green shells. Hollowed out kernels and shells. Small (1/4-3/8") adult beetle is light brownish-yellow with a long snout about half the length of its body. It emerges May-June and lays eggs in late June-early July in the green shell. White larvae feed first on the green shell then on the kernel. They exit through a small holes and drop to the ground where they overwinter 2-8" below the soil surface. Where: Throughout U.S.	1. Similar to CHESTNUT WEEVIL and PLUM CURCULIO.
Filbertworm Almond Chestnut Filbert Oak Persian Walnut	Small holes in the chestnut. Small (1/2" long) adult moth varies in appearance. Its forewings are reddish brown, with a broad coppery band down the center. Larvae (1/2") are white with yellowish heads. They feed on nut kernels. Larvae overwinter in cocoons on the ground and pupate in spring. Where: Throughout the U.S.	1. Early harvest of nuts and immediate destruction of infested nuts. 2. See your extension agent for further help.

Macro Pest	Description	Organic Remedy
Flathead Borer (aka: Flathead Appletree Borer) Apple Ash Beech Boxelder Dogwood Fruit trees Hickory Maple Oak Pecan Many trees	Sunken areas in the bark, which indicate feeding tunnels, are filled with a dry powdery substance known as frass, a mixture of droppings and sawdust. Minor foliage damage. The bark turns dark and may exude sap. Sunny sides of the tree are attacked most. Adults (1/2") are dark bronze beetles with a metallic sheen, and are usually found on the warm side of trees where they lay yellow, wrinkled eggs in cracks in the bark of unhealthy or injured trees. May and June are worst times. Eggs develop into long (1-1/4") yellow-white, U-shaped larvae that have swollen areas just in back of their heads. They bore tunnels into the tree. Where: Widespread, but particularly in the South & Midwest. Oak is a prime target in the West. Maple and fruit trees are prime targets in the East. 1 generation per year.	1. Shade the trunks of young trees with some kind of shield. 2. Protect newly transplanted trees by wrapping with burlap or cardboard from the soil to the lower branches. Or cover with a thick coat of white exterior latex paint. 3. Keep young trees pruned to a low profile. 4. Seal wounds with tree paint. 5. Encourage predators such as crows, wasps, woodpeckers, predatory beetles and vireos.
Flea Beetle (many sp.) (aka: Corn Flea Beetle, Potato Flea Beetle) Beans *Brassicas* Corn Eggplant Lettuce Muskmelon Pepper Potato Radish Spinach Tomato Watermelon Sweet Potato *continued*	Numerous small holes in leaves in early summer. Worst after mild winters and cool, wet springs. Adults transmit Stewart's Wilt to sweet corn and Early Blight to potatoes. These tiny (1/6") dark brown or black beetles jump when disturbed. They can have white or yellow markings. Adults lay eggs in the soil and enjoy the sun. The larvae feed on plant roots and can also damage tubers. Flea beetles stop feeding and hide in wet weather. Monitor: Use white sticky traps for an early warning device.	1. Use row covers. (Pantyhose can be used over small cabbages.) 2. Plant as late as possible. 3. Seed thickly until the danger of infestation is past. 4. Attach sticky bands around the base of wintering plants. 5. Use yellow sticky traps for control. 6. Frequent fall and spring cultivation will expose eggs to predators. 7. # Sprinkle wood ashes, moistened to prevent blowing, around the plant base. Or mix equal parts of wood ashes and lime in small containers and place around the plants. 8. A dusting of Diatomaceous Earth dries up beetles. 9. Vacuum with Dustbuster vacuum. Empty immediately into plastic bag. 10. # Plant after a spring trap crop of radish or pak choi.

Macro Pest	Description	Organic Remedy
Flea Beetle, *ctd.*	Where: Widespread. Usually 2 generations per year.	11. # Sprinkle crushed elderberry or tomato leaves on vulnerable plants. 12. # Mulch with chopped clover. 13. # Companion plant with cover crops of clover or annual ryegrass to reduce populations. 14. # Interplant with shading crops. 15. # Hot pepper or garlic spray. 16. Biological control: Apply beneficial nematodes in mulch or seed furrows. 17. Botanical control: Sabadilla, Rotenone (1% solution), Pyrethrin. 18. Allies (see chart): Candytuft, catnip, mint, shepherd's purse, tansy, tomato, and more.
Fruit Tree Leafroller	see LEAFROLLER	see LEAFROLLER
Gall Wasp Chestnut	Vegetative buds and shoots growth is hindered by galls. Buds are turned into 1/3-1/2" rose-colored balls which often hang onto the branch for several years. Buds may have some parts of leaf or stem growth. Trees lose vigor and may die. The small (1/8") adult wasp emerges in late May-early June and lays eggs inside buds. Eggs hatch in late July and larvae begin to grow. Larvae overwinter inside the bud. Where: Southeast, particularly Georgia. 1 generation per year.	1. Prune and destroy infested shoots.
Garden Symphylan or "Centipede" Asparagus Cucumber Lettuce Radish Tomato	Stunted plants that slowly die. Destroyed root hairs. This pest is not a true centipede, which is beneficial and grows to 3" long. Small (1/4") white worm-like creature with 12 pairs of legs thrives in damp soil, leaf mold, and manure piles. It feeds on root hairs. It burrows down after harvest 12" into the soil where it lays clusters of white spherical eggs. Where: Warm climates and greenhouses. Particularly damaging to asparagus in CA.	1. Inspect soil. 2 or more of these pests per shovel means you can expect damage. Avoid planting where you find damaging populations. 2. Pasteurize potting soil. 3. Solarize outdoor growing beds, where possible. 4. In California, flood asparagus field for 3 weeks in late December-early January to a depth of 1-3 feet.

Macro Pest	Description	Organic Remedy
Garden Webworm * Beans Beet * Corn, sweet * Pea * Strawberry	Holes in leaves and stems. Folded leaves held together with fine webs. Defoliation. Tan-brown moths (1"), with gray markings, appear in spring and lay clusters of eggs on the leaves of host plants. Caterpillars (1") are greenish with small dark spots and hairy. They hatch, feed, and spin webs for shelter. When disturbed they drop to the ground or hide inside silken tubular shelters on the ground. They feed for about 1 month before pupating. The last generation overwinters in the soil in the pupal phase. Where: Widespread, but only serious in parts of the South and Midwest. Several generations per year.	1. Cut off and destroy webbed branches. 2. Handpick caterpillars. 3. Remove infested leaves and stems. 4. Crush worms inside silken tubes on the ground. 5. Botanical control: Dust with Rotenone as a last resort, or use a Rotenone/ Pyrethrin mix.
Gopher and Groundhog Flowers Fruit trees Vegetables	Burrows and chewed vegetation. Fan or crescent-shaped mounds of dirt next to holes. Gophers eat the roots of vegetables, fruit trees and grasses. They also dine on bulbs and tubers. Unlike groundhogs, gophers can't climb fences and, unlike the solitary mole, they invade in numbers. Where: Widespread.	1. Trapping or shooting are the only sure controls. Determine all openings to the tunnel system, then fumigate. 2. For gophers, place 1/4" hardware cloth 2' down into the soil and extending above ground 1'. 3. # Gophers don't like scilla bulbs (also known as squills). These spring flowering bulbs are minimal care and are best for borders or rock gardens. 4. # Plant favorite foods, e.g. alfalfa and clover, at a distance. 5. # Place empty narrow-mouth bottles in hole. Wind vibrating in bottles repels gophers, groundhogs, and moles. 6. # Dog manure placed in their holes is also reported to drive them away. 7. The product Hinder™ is reputed to repel groundhogs. Spray on foliage, borders, and animal paths.
Grape Berry Moth Grape *continued*	Young grapes are webbed together, fail to mature, brown, and fall to the ground. Adult moths emerge in late spring	1. 1 month before harvest (late summer) hoe around grape vines. Create a wide, flat ridge to seed with a winter cover crop. 2. Turn under any cocoons on the soil

Macro Pest	Description	Organic Remedy
Grape Berry Moth, *ctd.*	and lay flat round eggs on stems, flowers, and grapes. Larvae pupate in cocoons attached to bark, in debris, or in fallen leaves. Where: Northeastern states, west to WI and NB, south to LA and AL. 2 generations per year.	surface. Water well to compact the soil and seal in the cocoons where they'll be smothered.
Grasshopper (aka: Locust) All plants	Chewed leaves and stems. Defoliation. The large (1-2") brown, gray, yellow or green heavy-shelled adult has large hind legs, big jaws, and antennae. It lays eggs in weeds or soil. Grasshoppers can pollute well water and reservoirs. Larvae overwinter in the soil. Where: Primarily in grassland areas, particularly in dry seasons.	1. Repeated fall cultivation. 2. Use row covers. 3. Encourage natural predators like birds, cats, chickens, field mice, skunks, snakes, spiders, squirrels, and toads. Also, blister beetle larvae prey on grasshopper eggs, so unless they're a pest themselves, leave these alone. If numerous, they can eat up to 40-60% of the area's grasshopper eggs. 4. # Fill a jar with a mixture of molasses and water. Bury it up to its mouth in the soil. Clean and refresh as needed. 5. Spray insecticidal soap, mixed wi beneficial nematodes, directly on t grasshopper. Apply in evening hours. Soap, alone, is not very effective against hard-bodied insects. You can also try mixing in hot peppers. 6. Biological control: Preying mantis. *Nosema locustae*, a beneficial protozoan often sold as "Grasshopper Attack," controls most grasshopper species. It must be applied in early spring, before grasshoppers grow to more than 3/4", or they won't eat enough for it to be effective. It will last several years, and its effects are greatest the summer following its application.
Greenhouse Leaftier	see CELERY LEAFTIER	see CELERY LEAFTIER

Gypsy Moth
  Apple
  Apricot
  Basswood
  Birch
  Linden
continued
	Rapid defoliation. Masses of worms feeding. Large holes in leaves. No tents. Defoliation in 2 successive years may kill deciduous trees.
	
	This hairy gray or brown caterpillar (1/16 - 2") has 5 pairs of blue and 6
		1. August-April: To destroy egg masses, paint with creosote or drop into water laced with insecticidal soap. (Kerosene is toxic to the soil and difficult to dispose of safely.)
		2. Late April-early June: Attach a 12" wide burlap strip to tree, about chest

Macro Pest	Description	Organic Remedy
Gypsy Moth, *ctd.* Oak Peach Pear Willow	pairs of red spots. Larvae crawl to top of trees and dangle on silky threads to be blown to another tree. When more mature (2-1/2") they hide in daylight and feed at night. The adult female white moth doesn't fly, but lays tan eggs in 1" long masses on trunks, branches, and under rocks. The adult male moth is large (1-1/2") and brown. Adults live less than 2 weeks. Larvae pupate and overwinter in dark cocoons or tie themselves to a branch with silken threads. Where: Primarily in the East, but moving South and West. 1 generation per year. Worst attacks follow a dry fall and warm spring.	height, by draping it over a string. Caterpillars will hide under the cloth during the day. Every afternoon, using gloves, sweep worms into soapy water. 3. Late April-early June: Apply sticky bands. Remove in mid-July. 4. Fall: Check lawn furniture, wood piles, walls, and outbuildings for egg masses. Also check all vehicles for egg masses to avoid transporting eggs to new areas. Destroy all egg masses. 5. Use gypsy moth pheromone traps to monitor populations and to control. 6. Biological controls: Bt is effective when applied every 10-14 days starting in April and continuing through mid-June until the caterpillars are 1" long. Trichogramma and chalcid wasps provide limited control. Lacewings, tachinid flies, predaceous ground beetles, white-footed mice can all help. Also try *Glyptapanteles Flavicoxis* and *Cotesia Melanoscelus*. Use beneficial nematodes at the tree base to prevent migration. 7. Botanical controls: Ryania, Pyrethrin.
Harlequin Bug (aka: Cabbage bug, Calicoback, Terrapin fire bug) * *Brassicas* Eggplant Radish	Wilting plants, especially seedlings. Yellowish or black spots on leaves. White blotches. Very destructive. This small (1/4"), flat and shield-shaped bug has a shiny black and red-orange back. It sucks leaf juices and smells bad. The adult female lays 2 neat rows of black-ringed white eggs on leaf undersides. Eggs hatch in 4-7 days. Nymphs suck leaf juices, causing leaf blotches. The adult overwinters in cabbage stalks. Where: Southern half of the U.S., from coast to coast. Several generations per year.	1. Handpick adults and eggs and destroy. 2. Insecticidal soap. Lace the spray with isopropyl alcohol, which helps it penetrate the shells of hard-bodied insects. Soap, alone, is not very effective against hard-bodied insects. 3. Fall cultivation. 4. # Mustard greens or turnips can be used as trap crops. 5. # In spring, place old cabbage leaves in the garden to attract the bugs. Destroy them when collected. 6. Biological control: Praying mantis might help. 7. Botanical control: Sabadilla, Rotenone (5% solution), Pyrethrin.
Hickory Shuckworm *continued*	Premature nut drop, poor quality kernels, dark-stained spots on shells.	1. Blacklight traps can reduce populations (1 per 3 trees).

Macro Pest	Description	Organic Remedy
Hickory Shuckworm, *ctd.* Hickory Pecan	Very damaging. Large (2/3") caterpillars are cream-colored with brownish heads. They overwinter in shucks on the ground or in the tree. Small (1/2") dark brown-black adult moths emerge when nuts begin to develop and continue emerging throughout the summer. They lay eggs on foliage and nuts. Where: Eastern Canada and U.S., south to FL, west to MO, OK and TX. 1-4 generations per year.	2. Collect all prematurely dropped nuts, and at harvest all shucks. If legal, burn. Otherwise destroy larvae by dropping shucks and nuts in water laced with insecticidal soap or boiling water. (Kerosene is toxic to the soil and difficult to dispose of.) 3. Biological control: Trichogramma wasp-- release 2-3 times per season (mid-April, 2 weeks later, and again 2 weeks later).
Imported Cabbage Worm, Moth and Butterfly * *Brassicas* Radish	Huge ragged holes in leaves with bits of green excrement. Tunnels inside broccoli, cabbage and cauliflower heads. This large (1-1/4") velvety smooth worm, light to bright green, has 1 yellow stripe down its back. It feeds on foliage and pupates by suspending itself by silken threads from plants or objects. The adult (2") is a day-flying white-pale yellow butterfly, with grayish tips and 3-4 black spots on each wing. Butterflies drop hundreds of single light yellow-green eggs on leaf undersides, which hatch in 4-8 days. Where: Widespread. 3-6 generations per year.	1. Use row covers all season. Also try nylon stockings over cabbage heads. Nylon stretches, allows sun, air, and water through but keeps out the butterfly. 2. # Sprinkle damp leaves with rye flour. Worms eat this, bloat, then die. 3. Handpick worms in early morning. Handpick eggs off the undersides of leaves every few days. 4. Fall cultivation, repeated again in the spring. 5. Any green mulch deters this moth. 6. Make the same insecticide as #8 under CABBAGE LOOPER. 7. Use butterfly nets to catch moths; each one caught means 200-300 worms destroyed. 9. Encourage bluebirds, chickadees, English sparrows. 10. Biological control: Bt, applied every 10-14 days until heads form, is effective. Lacewings. Trichogramma and braconid wasps. 11. Botanical control: Sabadilla. 12. Allies (see chart): Celery, dill, garlic, hyssop, mint, onion, rosemary, sage, tansy, thyme, tomato, & more.
Inchworm	see CANKERWORM	see CANKERWORM
Japanese Beetle *continued*	Lacy, skeletonized leaves. Beetles also feed on fruit and corn silk.	1. Handpick in early morning by shaking tree limbs or branches. Catch

Macro Pest	Description	Organic Remedy

Japanese Beetle, *ctd*.

Asparagus
Basil
* Beans
* Corn, sweet
* Grape
Grasses
Okra
Onion
Peach
Potato
Raspberry
Rhubarb
* Roses
Tomato
* Most fruit trees

Grubs feed on grass roots.

This medium-large (1/2") beetle is shiny metallic green with copper-brown wings. The adult lays eggs in the soil, and eats and flies only during daylight, often up to 5 miles.

The grub, similar to our native white grub, is gray-white with a dark brown head and 2 rows of spines. It's smaller, about 1", and lies curled in the soil. It overwinters deep in the soil.

Where: Mostly in the East, but this beetle is slowly moving further West. Eradication near Sacramento, CA was attempted in the early 60's. 1 generation per year.

them on a sheet spread on ground. Drop bugs into water laced with insecticidal soap. (Kerosene is toxic to the soil and difficult to dispose of.)
2. High soil pH discourages grubs.
3. # Make a bait of water, sugar, mashed fruit and yeast. Place on the periphery, not middle, of the garden in sunny spots at least 1' off ground. Strain out beetles every evening.
4. Use commercially available yellow pheromone traps. Place at a distance from the crop so that existing beetles won't be attracted to the crop, and to prevent new beetles from other areas from being drawn in.
5. Encourage starlings, the only bird to eat adult beetles. Other birds eat the grubs.
6. Time plantings to avoid beetle peak.
7. Four o'clocks (*Mirabilis*), larkspur, and geraniums all poison the beetle. These are good interplantings.
8. # Try trap crops of African marigold, borage, evening primrose, *mirabilis* (Four o'clocks), soybeans, white roses, white and pastel zinnias.
9. Biological controls: Apply beneficial nematodes at a rate of 50,000 per sq.ft. of lawn to prevent chewing damage. *Bacillus popilliae*, or milky spore disease, can be applied to lawns and orchard grasses. It attacks grubs and is effective for 15-20 years after just one application.
10. Botanical controls: Rotenone (5% solution), Pyrethrin.
11. Allies (see chart): Catnip, chives, garlic, rue and tansy.

June Beetle (aka: May Beetle)

Corn, sweet
Potato
Strawberry

continued

Damaged leaves of berry plants (adult feeding). Sudden wilting, especially in May or June, and roots and underground stems are chewed or severed (grub feeding).

Night flying adults are large brown beetles. They emerge in May-June. They lay eggs in midsummer (see White Grub). White grubs, slightly

1. see WHITE GRUB controls.
2. Handpick beetles and drop into water laced with insecticidal soap. (Kerosene is toxic to the soil and difficult to dispose of.)
3. Shake beetles from the tree or shrub early in the morning while they're sluggish, and let fall onto a sheet beneath. Collect and destroy beetles.
4. Encourage birds.

Macro Pest	Description	Organic Remedy
June Beetle, *ctd.*	larger than the Japanese beetle grub, feed for 2 years before pupating. Where: Serious damage in Midwest and South. 1 emergence per year.	5. Botanical controls: Rotenone (5% solution).
Lace Bug (many sp.) (Eggplant Lace Bug) Eggplant Potato Tomato	Pale, discolored (bronzed) and curled leaves. Plants may die. Leaves may be dotted with dark, shiny droppings. Nymphs and adults suck plant juices from leaves and stems. They feed in groups on leaf undersides. Small adults lay black eggs on leaf undersides in either fall or spring. Eggs hatch in spring. Brown-black nymphs start feeding immediately. Adults overwinter in garden trash. Where: Southern half of the United States, from coast to coast.	1. Check for eggs every 7-10 days, and destroy all egg clusters. 2. Insecticidal soap spray.
Leaf Beetle	see BEAN LEAF BEETLE	see BEAN LEAF BEETLE
Leaf-footed Bug Almond * Bean Nuts * Potato * Tomato	Chewed leaves in vegetables. In almond there may be poorly developed misshapen nuts or premature nut drop. This large (3/4") bug resembles the squash bug, but its hind legs are expanded and look like leaves. It is dark brown with a yellow band across its body. When handled it emits a distinctive odor. Adults lay barrel-shaped eggs on leaves of host plants. Nymphs look like adults. Adults hibernate in winter, especially in thistle, and emerge in early summer. Where: Widespread, but primarily a problem in the South and westward to AZ. 1 generation per year.	1. Handpick and destroy bugs. 2. Handpick and destroy eggs. 3. Botanical control: Sabadilla.
Leafhopper (many sp.) *continued*	White or yellow mottled, curled leaves die and drop. Excreted honeydew attracts ants and supports black sooty mold. Leafhoppers transmit Curly Top, where mature	1. Use row covers in early spring. 2. Avoid planting, if possible, in wide open space. 3. Insecticidal soap spray. If the infestation is bad, add isopropyl alcohol

Macro Pest	Description	Organic Remedy
Leafhopper, *ctd.* (Beet Leafhopper is known as Whitefly in the West) Asters Beans Beet Carrot Celery Chard Citrus Corn Eggplant Fruit trees Grape Lettuce Potato Raspberry Rhubarb Rose Spinach Squash Tomato	leaves roll upward, turn yellow with purple veins, and become stiff and brittle. Especially damaging in potatoes due to decreased yields. Nymphs suck plant juices. Small (1/4-1/3"), green, brown or yellow slender bugs suck juices from leaves, stems and buds. Nymphs move sideways. The beet leafhopper (1/3") is yellow-green, jumps quickly into the air, and looks like a whitefly. The potato leafhopper (1/3") is green with white spots. The six-spotted leafhopper (1/8") is yellowish with 6 black spots. Adults lay eggs in early spring on leaf undersides. The second generation of eggs, two weeks later, may be laid in plant stems. Adults overwinter in garden trash and weeds. Where: Widespread. For specific regions, see beet and potato leafhoppers. 1-5 generations per year.	to the spray. 4. Sprinkle Diatomaceous Earth or wood ashes, moistened to prevent blowing, around the plant base. Both will dry out leafhoppers. 5. Remove weeds and afflicted plants. 6. Fall cultivation. 7. A reflective mulch such as aluminum foil will repel them. 8. Keep beets and spinach far from tomatoes. Also avoid planting carrots, asters, and lettuce together if your garden has a problem with the 6-spotted leafhopper. 9. Plant resistant varieties. 10. # Black-lights trap adults. 11. # Boil 1 lb. tobacco in 1 gallon of water, strain, and use as a spray. 12. Encourage song birds. 13. Biological control: Lacewings eat the eggs. 14. Botanical control: Sabadilla, Rotenone (5% solution), Pyrethrin. 15. Allies (see chart): Beans, blackberry, clover, goosegrass, red sprangletop, rye and vetch. Geraniums and petunias allegedly repel leafhoppers.
Leaf Miner (many sp: the one described to the right is the Spinach species.) Beans Beet greens Blackberry Cabbage Chard Chestnut Lamb's Quarters Lettuce Oregano Pepper Radish Spinach Swiss chard Turnip	White-brown tunnels or blotches on leaves. Yellowed, blistered, or curled leaves. Stem damage below the soil surface. Leafminers are disease vectors for black leg and soft rot. Larvae (1/3") are pale green or whitish. They mine between the upper and lower edges of leaves, causing a scorched, blotched, and blistered appearance. Adults are tiny (1/6-1/4") black or gray flies that lay eggs on leaf undersides. Eggs are tiny, white, and lined up in groups of 4-5. If hatched, the leaf will have a grayish blister. Where: Widespread. Several generations per year.	1. Use row covers. 2. Cut out the infested parts of leaves with grayish blisters. 3. Remove all lamb's quarters unless used as trap crop. 4. Handpick and destroy eggs. 5. Plant fall crops to avoid the insect. 6. Rotate crops. 7. Apply superior Horticultural Oil. 8. Encourage the chickadee, purple finch, robin. 9. Controls are usually not warranted on the chestnut. 10. Biological control: Beneficial nematodes give some control. Ladybugs and lacewings may eat leafminer eggs.

Macro Pest	Description	Organic Remedy
Leafroller (aka: Fruit tree leafroller) Apple and Other Fruit Trees	Rolled leaves with fine webbing that holds the leaves shut. Chewed fruit, leaves, and buds. Small (3/4") green caterpillars usually have dark heads. They feed for about 4 weeks then spin webs around leaves and sometimes fruit. They pupate in these rolled leaves. The adult is a light brown moth that lays eggs with a camouflage coating in clusters of 30-100 in mid-summer on twigs and bark. Eggs overwinter and hatch into caterpillars in spring. Monitor: Use pheromone traps to monitor moth populations and to know when to spray to prevent egg-laying. Where: Widespread, but most damage occurs in Northern U.S. and Southern Canada. 1 generation per year.	1. Handpick eggs in the winter. 2. Spray light or superior Horticultural Oil in early spring before buds appear. 3. Predators: Trichogramma wasps will eat the caterpillars. 4. Biological control: Dipel Bt is an effective control. Be sure to spray inside the rolled leaf. 5. Botanical control: Rotenone (5% solution).
Locust	see GRASSHOPPER	see GRASSHOPPER
Mealy Bug Fruit trees Greenhouses Houseplants Rosemary Vegetables	Cotton tufts on the leaf underside. Honeydew excretions attract ants and supports black sooty mold. Dwarfed plants. Wilt. Premature fruit drop. These minuscule bugs suck plant sap. They lay tiny, yellow, smooth eggs where leaves join the stem. Where: Widespread, but particularly a problem in warm climates. Numerous generations (each cycle takes 1 month).	1. Strong water jets directed at the undersides of leaves. 2. Destroy mealybugs with cotton swabs dipped in alcohol. 3. Spray light or superior Horticultural Oil before buds appear, to smother eggs. 4. Insecticidal soap spray, especially in the early spring dormant stage. 5. Use sticky bands to trap ants. 6. Biological controls: Green lacewings. *Crytolaemus* ladybug (Australian and uncommon) is a predator and also works in the greenhouse. *Pauridia* parasites prey on bugs.
Measuring Worm	see CANKERWORM	see CANKERWORM
Mexican Bean Beetle * Beans *continued*	Lacy, skeletonized leaves. Pods and stems are eaten in bad infestations. Orange-yellow fuzzy larvae (1/3") are longer than the adult, and attach	1. Handpick and destroy beetles, larvae, and egg clusters. 2. Use row covers. 3. A reflective mulch like aluminum foil will repel them.

Macro Pest	Description	Organic Remedy
Mexican Bean Beetle, *ctd.* Kale Squash	themselves to leaves, usually on the underside, or inside a curled leaf. The small (1/4") copper, round-backed adult beetle, with 16 black spots in 3 horizontal rows on its back, looks like an orange ladybug. The female adult lays orange-yellow eggs in groups of 40-60 on leaves. Eggs hatch in 5-14 days. Most beans can tolerate 10-20% defoliation (more prior to bloom) without loss in yields. Where: Widespread, but particularly a problem in the East and Southwest. 2 generations per year in cold climates, and 3-5 in warmer regions.	4. # A spray of crushed turnips with corn oil. 5. # Spray cedar sawdust or chips boiled in water. 6. Fall: Pull up infested plants as soon as the main harvest is over but while pests are still present. Stuff vines in a plastic bag, tie, and leave in sun for 10-14 days to kill the bugs. 7. Fall cultivation. 8. Early planting. 9. Encourage insect-eating birds. 10. Biological controls: Spined soldier bug is excellent control. Predatory mites. *Pediobius foveolatus* wasps parasitize larvae, are excellent controls, but expensive. 11. Botanical controls: Rotenone (1% solution), Pyrethrins. 12. Allies (see chart): Garlic, marigold, nasturtium, petunia, potatoes, rosemary and savory.
Millipede Lettuce Root Vegetables Roses Seeds	Ragged holes in stems and roots, especially seedlings. Fungal disease may be present. This is a caterpillar-like worm (1/2 - 1"), with a hard-shelled body divided into multiple segments and with 30-400 pairs of legs. It moves slowly by contracting and stretching, feeds at night on decaying vegetation, and sometimes transmits diseases. It lays sticky sacs of hundreds of eggs on or in the soil in summer. Adults live 1 to 7 years. Where: Widespread, but most damaging in the South and West. 1 generation per year.	1. Peat compost is more hostile to millipedes than other types such as leaf or manure compost. 2. Place window-screen wire under plants.
Mite (many sp.) Apple Apricot Asparagus Beans Blackberry *continued*	Yellowed, dry leaves, with yellow or red spots or blotches and small white dots. Veins yellow or turn reddish-brown first. Fine webbing between leaves and across undersides. Poorly developed fruit that drops early. Mites suck chlorophyll out of plants	1. Spray forceful jets of water in early morning, 3 days in a row or every other day 3 times. 2. Spray insecticidal soap at least 3 times, every 5-7 days. 3. # Mix 1/4 lb of glue in a gallon of water. Let stand overnight. Spray on twigs and leaves. When dried it will

Macro Pest	Description	Organic Remedy
Mite, *ctd.* Blueberry Brassicas Celery Chestnut Cucumber Eggplant Grape Herbs Muskmelon Peach Peanut Pepper Raspberry Strawberry	and inject toxins. They can lower chlorophyll by as much as 35 percent. They are worst in hot, dry conditions. Mites are very tiny red, green, yellow, black, or brown arachnids that are difficult to see without a magnifying lens. Some are beneficial. Females lay numerous eggs on webbing under leaves. Mites overwinter in the soil. To detect, hold a white paper underneath and tap the leaves to see if mites, the size of salt grains, are dislodged. Where: Widespread. Many types exist only in specific locales, but general characteristics remain the same. Up to 17 generations per year. Each life cycle takes 7-14 days.	flake off, taking trapped mites with it. Spray 3 times, every 7-10 days. 4. Vacuum plants with Dustbuster vacuum. Empty bag immediately into plastic bag or mites will crawl back out. 5. Fruit trees-- high Nitrogen fertilizers can increase mite populations, so avoid. 6. Spray fruit trees with Horticultural Oil spray late in the dormant period, right at bud break, when mite eggs are most vulnerable. 7. Ensure adequate water. 8. Biological controls: Predatory mites are good outdoors and in greenhouses. Green lacewings and ladybugs feed on the mites. 9. Botanical controls: Sabadilla, Pyrethrins (apply twice, 3-4 days apart). 11. Allies (see chart): Alder, bramble berries, coriander, dill, rye mulch, sorghum mulch, wheat mulch.
Mole Many vegetables	Extensive tunnels. Main runways are usually 6-10" below ground with frequent mounds of soil heaped above ground. Moles are solitary, unlike gophers. They tunnel extensively, often using each tunnel only once. They eat grubs and beetles, which isn't bad, but also feed on earthworms--their favorite food. Their tunnels can harm the root systems of young plants. Where: Throughout U.S., but a major problem in the West.	1. The best control is traps. Set traps at the first sign of tunnels. This can be anytime in most Western states. In cooler climates, this will be in spring. Determine which runs are active before setting traps by stepping lightly on them, mark the spots, and check again in 2 days. If spots are raised, the tunnel is active. Spear or harpoon-type traps are considered the easiest to use. 2. # Plant 4 or 5 poisonous castor bean plants (*Euphobia lathyris*), also known as "mole plants", nearby. Note: This plant can become a pest itself in areas of the West and South. It is also poisonous to humans. 3. # Scatter red pepper or tobacco dust to repel moles. 4. # Wearing gloves to prevent human scent, place Juicy Fruit™ gum in tunnels. Moles are alleged to love it, eat it, and die from it. 5. Control grubs, food for moles. 6. See #4 under GOPHER.
Mouse (many sp.) *continued*	Chewed tree trunks at ground level. Gnawed roots (by pine mice). In	1. At planting install around tree trunks hardware cloth girdles 6" in diameter

Macro Pest	Description	Organic Remedy
Mouse, *ctd.* Apple Fruit Trees Greenhouses Onion, storage Strawberry	strawberry beds, you may find nests in mulch and destroyed roots. The house mouse is uniformly gray. The vole, or field mouse, is white-bellied with gray-brown fur on top. The deer mouse, or white-footed mouse, resembles the vole but has white feet. Mice will move into mole tunnels and feed on crop roots. Where: Widespread.	and 18" high. Set them at least 6" into the soil, preferably in coarse gravel. 2. Remove protective cover for mice by removing all vegetation within a 3' radius of trunk. In winter, pull mulch at least 6" away from tree trunks. Keep grass mowed. 3. For strawberries, wait to mulch until mice have made winter homes elsewhere, when the ground has developed a frosty crust. 4. Make gravel barriers around garden plots, at least 6-8" deep and 12" or more wide. This prevents rodents from tunneling and, if kept free of weeds, from crossing the area. 5. Encourage owls and snakes. 6. Don't mulch perennials until a few frosts have occurred. 7. # Sprinkle mint leaves in garden. 8. Allies (see chart): Wormwood.
Navel Orangeworm Almond * Citrus Walnut	Worms burrow into fruit and nuts on the tree and in storage. Worms are yellow or dark gray with dark heads. They pupate in cocoons within the fruit. The gray adult moth has crescent-shaped dots along its outer margins. Where: Southwest and California.	1. Clean orchard sanitation. 2. Early harvest. 3. Nuts can be fumigated before storage with methyl bromide. 4. Remove and destroy nuts left on the tree in winter. 5. Biological controls: *Goniozus legneri* and *Pentalitomastix plethoricus* both parasitize the pupae. Release them in early spring or after harvest.
Nematode (many sp.) (aka: Roundworm, Eelworm) Apple Beans Carrot Celery Cucumber Dill Eggplant (in South) Garlic *continued*	Malformed flowers, leaves, stems, and roots. Stunted, yellowing leaves. Leaves may wilt during the day. Dwarfed plants, with poorly developed roots, leaves, and flowers. Dieback. Root-knot nematodes cause galls, knots, or branched root crops. Lesion nematodes cause root fungal infections and lesions on roots. Nematodes are blind and usually microscopic. Not all are harmful, and some are beneficial (see page 165). Where: Widespread, especially in warm areas and areas with sandy or	1. Plant resistant varieties. 2. Solarize soil. 3. Increase soil organic matter. Heavy mulch or compost is one of the best deterrents. Compost is host to saprophytic nematodes and predacious fungi that destroy harmful nematodes. Compost also releases fatty acids toxic to nematodes. Leaf mold compost is especially effective, particularly pine needles, rye and timothy grasses. 4. Disinfect tools used in infected soil. 5. Long crop rotation. 6. A fertilizer mixture of 70% fish emulsion and 30% yucca extract (Pent-A-Vane™) reduces nematodes.

Macro Pest	Description	Organic Remedy
Nematode, *ctd.* Mustard Okra Onion Parsley Peas Potato Raspberry Strawberry Sw.Potato Tomato Many others	loamy soils. Not very common in clay soils. The eggs of some nematode species remain viable in the soil for years.	7. Kelp meal and crab shell meal (chitin) stimulate beneficial fungi that prey on nematodes. Dig these into the soil 1 month before planting to reduce populations. 8. # Sprinkle an emulsion of 1 part corn oil: 10 parts water. 9. White and black mustard exude oil hostile to nematodes. 10. Cover crops of barley, castor bean, corn, cotton, joint vetch, millet, rye, sesame or wheat reduce populations. All plants must be turned under to be effective. Winter rye, when tilled under in spring, produces an organic acid toxic to nematodes. Note: The only rye that will control nematodes is cereal rye (*Secale cereale*). 11. Plant tomatoes near asparagus. Asparagus roots are toxic to tomato nematodes. 12. A solution of water hyacinth leaves or flowers macerated in water (1:3 on a weight basis) has been shown to kill nematodes (1989 study by botanists in India). Also, tomato and eggplant roots soaked in this solution for 80 minutes prior to plantings grew 3 times faster than unsoaked controls. 13. Allies (see chart): Asparagus, barley, corn, garlic, hairy indigo, marigold (*Tagetes* sp.), mustard (white or black). Note: Research shows that marigolds suppress root lesion nematodes for 3 years when planted in the entire infested area for a full season. Spot plantings are not as effective, and may reduce yields of nearby crops. See Ally Chart.
Nut Curculio Chestnut Oak	Premature nut drop. Circular cavities in nuts and shells. The small (3/16") adult is black with reddish brown blotches, with a long curved long snout of curculios. It emerges May-June, occasionally feeds on foliage, and deposits eggs when the bur cracks to expose the nut.	1. Same controls as for the PLUM CURCULIO. 2. Drop infected nuts into water to kill larvae.

continued

Macro Pest	Description	Organic Remedy
Nut Curculio, *ctd.*	Larvae feed on nut kernels for about 3 weeks then emerge through small (1/16") holes. Where: Southeast. 1 generation per year.	
Onion Eelworm	See NEMATODES	See NEMATODES
Onion Fly Maggot (aka: Onion Maggot) * Onion Radish	Rotting bulbs in storage. Destroyed seedlings. Faded and wilted leaves. Lower stems of onion near the bulb are damaged or destroyed. Worse damage than that caused by the cabbage maggot. This is a small (1/3"), legless, white worm that tapers to a point at the head. It feeds on stems and bulbs. The adult fly resembles a hairy housefly. It lays eggs at the base of plants, near the bulb or neck, or in the bulb. Where: Particularly Northern and coastal regions, where cool, wet weather abounds. 3 generations per year. The last generation attacks harvest and storage onions.	1. Avoid planting in rows and close spacing. This discourages maggot movement between plants. 2. Red onions are the least vulnerable, followed by yellow then white varieties. 3. Sprinkle Diatomaceous Earth around the plant base, and work slightly into the soil. If this isn't available, then sprinkle wood ashes, moistened to prevent blowing, near the base of the plants. 4. Don't store damaged bulbs. 5. Encourage robins and starlings. 6. Biological controls: Beneficial nematodes.

Oriental Fruit Moth
 	
* Apple
* Peach
  Pear
  Plum
  Quince
 	
continued
	Wormy fruit. Terminals of rapidly growing shoots wilt, turn brown in a few days, and die. Gummy exudate. Holes in fruit and in fruit stems.
	
	These small larvae (1/2") are yellow-pink with brown heads, and are very active. When small they tunnel into tender shoots and later enter fruit through the stem end. They don't tunnel to the core of apples, but in peaches feed close to the pit. On the outside fruit may not look damaged. Larvae emerge from fruit and pupate in silken cocoons attached to tree trunks, weeds, or garden debris.
	
	The adult moth (1/2") is gray, and lays white eggs on leaves and twigs.
		1. If this is a consistent pest, plant early-ripening cultivars to starve the last generation.
		2. Prune trees annually to avoid dense growth.
		3. Plant early maturing varieties of peach and apricot.
		4. Inspect tree trunks and destroy all cocoons.
		5. Pheromone-based mating disruption lures are commercially available but may not be effective in small orchards.
		6. Biological Controls: Import the Braconid wasp *Macrocentrus ancylivorus and release according to instructions from supplier.*
		7. Botanical Controls: Ryania, Rotenone, Pyrethrins.
		8. Allies (see chart): Goldenrod, lamb's

Macro Pest	Description	Organic Remedy
Oriental Fruit Moth, *ctd*.	Monitor: Pheromone traps are available for early detection. Captures exceeding 5-10 moths per trap per week warrants control action. Where: East of the Mississippi and Upper Northwest. Several generations per year.	quarters, strawberries.
Parsleyworm (aka: Carrotworm, Celeryworm Black Swallowtail) * Carrot Celery Celeriac Dill * Parsley Parsnip	Chewed leaves, often down to bare stems. Damage is usually minor because of low populations. This long (2") stunning green worm has a yellow-dotted black band across each segment. It emits a sweet odor and projects 2 orange horns when disturbed. The adult is the familiar black swallowtail butterfly. Its large black forewings (3-4" across) have 2 rows of parallel yellow spots. Its rear wings have a blue row of spots with 1 orange spot. Adults lay white eggs on leaves which hatch in 10 days. Where: East of the Rockies, and a similar species West of the Rockies. Several generations per year.	1. Handpick in early morning. 2. Encourage song birds. 3. Biological controls: Lacewing larvae. Parasitic wasps.
Peach Tree Borer, Greater Apricot Cherry Nectarine * Peach Plum *continued*	Brown gummy sawdust (frass) on the bark, usually near the ground. Very damaging. Trees can die. Large (1-1/4") yellow-white larvae have dark brown heads. They feed under the bark at or below the soil surface all winter. The highest they'll usually go is about 12" above the soil. Adult moths (1") are blue, clear-winged, and look like wasps. They emerge in the North in July-August, and in the South in August-September. They lay brown-gray eggs at the trunk base in late summer to fall. Where: Where vulnerable plants are	1. Insert stiff wires into holes to kill larvae. Do NOT remove gummy exudate, which helps to seal wounds. 2. Use sticky bands, from 2" below the soil line to 6" above. Destroy and replace the bands each week. 3. Tobacco dust ring: Encircle the trunk with a piece of tin, 2" away from the bark. In mid-May fill with tobacco dust. Repeat every year. 4. # Tie soft soap around the trunk from the soil line up to the crotch. Soap drips repel moths and larvae. 5. In the near future pheromone dispensers should be available. These confuse males and stop mating, but may not be effective in small orchards. 6. Encourage birds. 7. Biological Controls: Spray or inject

Macro Pest	Description	Organic Remedy
Greater Peach Tree Borer, *ctd.*	grown, particularly in Eastern states and the lower half of the U.S. from coast to coast. 1 generation per year.	beneficial nematodes into the holes. Spray Bt every 10 days or syringe it into the holes. 8. Allies (see chart): Garlic.

Peach Tree Borer, Lesser
 	
    Apricot
    Cherry
    Nectarine
* Peach
    Plum
	Same symptoms as Greater Peach Tree Borer, but damage is in upper limbs. They invade through wounds created by such things as winter injury, pruning, and cankers.
	
	Where: Same as Greater Peach Tree Borer, but 2-3 generations per year.
		1. See #1, 5, 6, and 7 for the Greater Peach Tree Borer.
		2. Take measures to minimize winter injury (see Sunscald on page 181), pruning wounds, or other entry sites.
		3. Use sticky bands on affected limbs Destroy and replace bands each week.

Peach Twig Borer
 	
    Almond
    Apricot
* Peach
    Plum
	Red-brown masses of chewed bark in twig crotches. Infested fruit late in the season.
	
	Small (less than 1/2") red-brown larvae construct cocoons under curled edges of bark. The adult is a small (1/2") steel-gray moth.
	
	Where: Widespread, but very damaging on the West coast. 3-4 generations per year.
		1. Increase organic matter in soil.
		2. See #2 for Lesser Peach Borer.
		3. See #1, 4, 5, and 6 for the Greater Peach Tree Borer.
		4. Pheromone traps are available that catch males (not the same as mating-disruption lures). These can be used to monitor population levels and, in small areas, to help control populations.
		4. Spray dormant lime-sulfur spray (diluted 1:15) before the pink stage and after petal fall.

Pear Psylla Pear *continued*	Yellow leaves. Leaf drop. Low vigor. Honeydew excretion attracts yellow jackets and ants and supports black soot mold. Blackened leaves and fruit. Scarred and malformed fruit. Nymphs and adults suck plant juices, and can transmit fire blight and pear decline. Very damaging. Nymphs are very tiny and yellow, green or light brown. They feed on the top sides of leaves until only the veins remain. Adults are tiny (1/10"), light brown to dark orange-red, and have clear wings. Before buds open, adults lay tiny yellowish-orange eggs in cracks and crevices, in the base of terminal buds, and in old leaf scars. Also check tender growing tips of the highest shoots. Nymphs hatch in 2-4 weeks. Most hatch by petal fall.	1. Spray Insecticidal soap, in high pressure, as soon as females emerge and when leaf buds are just beginning to turn green. Continue through season as needed. 2. Dust tree and leaves with limestone. 3. Destroy all debris, which harbors the eggs. Adults and eggs spend winter on or near tree. 4. Spray light Horticultural Oil in the fall, and again in spring at the green tip stage, continuing every 7 days until larvae emerge. 5. Plant tolerant varieties. (Bartlett and D'Anjou are the most susceptible). 6. Botanical control: Rotenone (5% solution).

Macro Pest	Description	Organic Remedy
Pear Psylla, *ctd.*	Where: Eastern (East of Mississippi) and Northwestern states. There are 3-5 generations per year.	
Pearslug (aka: Cherryslug) Apple Cherry * Pear Plum	Pink-brown patches on upper surface of leaves. Lacy skeletonized leaves. Defoliation. Streaks of chocolate covered sawdust on apples. Larvae (1/2") are dark green-orange, covered with slime, tadpole-shaped, and look like small slugs with large heads. Larvae feed for 2-3 weeks on upper leaf surfaces. Larvae in apples feed just under fruit skin until about 1/3 grown, then bore through the fruit. After feeding they drop to the ground to pupate. The adult is a small black and yellow sawfly, little larger than a housefly, with 2 sets of transparent wings hooked together. At bloom time the adult emerges from cocoons in the soil. The sawfly inserts its eggs into leaves or into the skin of fruit. Where: Widespread. 2 generations per year.	1. Shallow cultivation, no more than 2" deep, at the tree base right before full bloom. This exposes cocoons to predators. 2. # Dust trees with wood ashes, slightly moistened to prevent blowing, which will dry out larvae and kill them. Wash trees with water after 5 days. 3. Pick up fallen fruit every day. 4. Botanical control: A pyrethrin/rotenone/ryania blend.
Pecan Casebearer Pecan	Small cocoons at the base of the bud indicate overwintering larvae. Tunneled shoots. Eaten nuts in the early maturation phase. Trees will experience little damage, but nut yields are reduced. This small (1/2") caterpillar is olive gray to jade green with a yellow-brown head. When buds open, caterpillars feed on buds and shoots. Adult moths emerge when the nut forms. They lay single light-colored eggs on the blossom end of the nut. Larvae then feed on developing nuts. Where: Wherever pecans are grown. 2 generations in Northern climates, 4 generations in Southern climates.	1. Blacklight traps (1 per every 3 trees) will reduce populations. 2. Collect all prematurely dropped nuts, and at harvest all shucks. If legal, burn. Or otherwise destroy in hot water or water laced with insecticidal soap. (Kerosene is toxic to the soil and difficult to dispose.) 3. Biological control: Trichogramma wasps-- release 2-3 times per season (in mid-April, 2 weeks later, and again in 2 weeks.)

Macro Pest	Description	Organic Remedy
Pecan Weevil Hickory Pecan	Premature nut drop and hollowed kernels. Similar to the Chestnut Weevil. The adult (3/4") is light brown and, as it ages, may become dark brown. It's snout is needle-thin and can be as long as its body. Adults feed on husks and young nuts. Grubs are white with reddish-brown heads. They feed on kernels, emerge, and pupate in "cells" as much as 12" below the soil surface. Adults may not emerge for 2-3 years. Where: Wherever pecan and hickory are grown. 1 emergence per year.	1. Same controls as for Chestnut Weevil and Plum Curculio. 2. Burlap bands wrapped around trees. (See "Sticky Bands" at beginning of this section).
Phylloxera Aphid	See APHID	See APHID
Pickleworm Cucumber Melon Squash	Holes in buds, blossoms and fruits of most *cucurbits*. Masses of rotting green excrement. This medium (3/4") caterpillar is green or copperish. The first generation emerges midsummer. Damage is worst late in the season when the broods are largest. The adult nocturnal moth is yellowish. It lays eggs that develop into small caterpillars that are pale yellow with black dots. These change color as they mature. Where: Primarily in the Southeast and Gulf states, particularly Florida and Louisiana. 3-4 generations per year.	1. Plant susceptible crops as early as possible to avoid pest. 2. Destroy all plant debris after harvest. 3. Cultivate the soil deeply in early fall, after harvest. 4. Plant resistant varieties. 5. Botanical control: Rotenone (5% solution) at petal fall, and every 10-14 days through September.
Pill Bug (aka: Roly-poly)	See SOW BUG. Unlike sow bugs, pill bugs roll up into tight balls about the size of a pea.	See SOW BUG
Plum Curculio Apple Apricot *continued*	Eaten leaves and petals. Crescent shaped cavities in fruits. Sap exudate from apple fruit dries to a white crust. Misshapen fruit. Premature fruit drop. Brown rot disease.	1. Hang white sticky traps (8" x 10") in trees at chest height for both monitoring and control. Use several per tree. Remove after 3 to 4 weeks. 2. Starting at blossom time, everyday

Macro Pest	Description	Organic Remedy
Plum Curculio, *ctd.* Blueberry Cherry Peach Pear * Plum	This small (1/4") dark brown beetle, has a long down-curving snout and 4 humps on its back. It emerges at blossom time when temperatures climb above 70F. When disturbed it folds its legs and drops to the ground. It lays eggs in crescent shape fruit wound. Grubs are gray-white with brown heads and curled bodies. They feed at the fruit center for 2 weeks and emerge only after fruit falls to ground. They pupate in the ground. Adults take about 1 month to emerge. Where: East of the Rockies. 1-2 generations per year.	in the early morning spread a sheet or tarp under the tree and knock branches with a padded board or pole. Shake collected beetles into a bucket of water laced with insecticidal soap. (Kerosene is toxic to the soil and difficult to dispose.) 3. Remove all diseased and fallen fruit immediately. Destroy larvae by burning fruit or burying in the middle of a hot compost pile. 4. Keep trees pruned. Curculios dislike direct sun. 5. Encourage the chickadee, bluebird, and purple martin. Domestic fowl will also eat these insects.
Plume Moth Artichoke	Irregular holes in stems, foliage, and bud scales. Small worms are on bud scales and new foliage. Damage is year-round, but worst in the spring. Larvae bore into the fruit, blemish the scales, and tunnel into the heart. Nocturnal adult brown moths (1") have plumed wings and fly near the plant. They lay eggs on leaf undersides. Where: Pacific and Texas coasts.	1. Pick and destroy all wormy buds. 2. Remove and destroy all plant debris in the fall. 3. Remove all nearby thistles. 4. Biological controls: Bt is effective.
Potato Bug	see COLORADO POTATO BEETLE	see COLORADO POTATO BEETLE
Potato Flea Beetle	see FLEA BEETLE	see FLEA BEETLE
Potato Leafhopper (aka: Bean jassid) * Apple Beans (South) Peanut * Potato (East and South)	See LEAFHOPPER. This leafhopper causes "hopperburn:" a triangular brown spot appears at leaf tips, leaf tips curl, yellow, and become brittle. Reduced yields in potatoes. Where: Primarily in the East and South. It migrates South for winter, and returns North in spring to feed first on apples then potatoes. 2 generations in Mid-Atlantic states.	1. See LEAFHOPPER. 2. # Potato leafhoppers are said to be trapped by black fluorescent lamps.

Macro Pest	Description	Organic Remedy
Potato Tuberworm (aka: Tuber Moth) Eggplant * Potato Tomato	Wilted shoots and stems. Dieback. The gray-brown adult moth is small with narrow wings. It lays eggs on the leaf undersides or in tubers. Larvae (3/4") are pink-white with brown heads. They tunnel into stems and leaves. They pupate on the ground in cocoons covered with soil, and can emerge in storage to pupate. Where: In the South from coast to coast, and Northward to WA, CO, VA, and MD. Worst in hot, dry years. 5-6 generations per year.	1. Plant as early as possible. 2. Keep soil well cultivated and deeply tilled. 3. Cut and destroy infested vines before harvesting. 4. Destroy all infested potatoes. 5. Screen storage areas and keep storage area cool and dark. (Darkness discourages moth activity.)
Rabbit Bean Carrot Lettuce Pea Strawberry Tulip shoots Bark of fruit trees	A small white or gray mammal with long ears and short tail that travels primarily by hopping. Rabbits will eat vegetables, herbs, flowers, and chew on young fruit trees. Where: Widespread.	1. # Sprinkle any of the following around plants: Blood meal, moistened wood ashes, ground hot peppers, chili or garlic powder, crushed mint leaves, blood meal, talcum powder. Replenish frequently, especially after rain. You can also sprinkle black pepper right on the plants, which gives rabbits sneezing fits and keeps them away. 2. Cover seedlings with plastic milk jugs that have their bottoms cut out. Anchor them well in the soil, and keep the cap off for ventilation. This can also be used as a season extender in the spring. 3. # Place old smelly leather shoes on the garden periphery. 4. # Place fake snakes near garden. 5. Wrap base of fruit trees with hardware cloth. 6. Set rabbit traps. 7. Encourage owls and sparrow hawks with nest boxes. 8. The product Hinder™ is reputed to be an effective repellant. Spray on foliage, borders and animal paths. When painted on bark it is also supposed to prevent tree girdling by rabbits. 9. Fine-woven fences are effective deterrents. 10. # Garlic, marigold and onion are said to deter rabbits.

Macro Pest	Description	Organic Remedy
Raspberry Caneborer Blackberry Raspberry	Sudden wilting of tips. 2 rows of punctures about 1" apart. Medium-sized (1/2") adult is a long-horned black and yellow beetle. It lays 1 egg between a double row of punctures on the stem near the cane tip. A small worm hatches and burrows 1-2" deep near the base of the cane to hibernate. This is a major cane pest. Where: Kansas and eastward. 1 generation per year.	1. Cut off cane tips 6" below the puncture marks, and burn or destroy. 2. Botanical control: Rotenone (1% solution). Apply 2 treatments 7 days apart, timed to coincide with adult emergence during June. Consult your county Extension agent for the local adult activity period.
Raspberry Root Borer (aka: Raspberry Crown Borer Blackberry Raspberry	Wilting and dying canes in early summer, usually when berries are ripening. Stunted plants. Larvae are small, white, and hibernate at the soil level near canes. They tunnel into cane crowns and bases. The adult moth has clear-wings and a black body with 4 yellow bands. Where: Eastern U.S. 1 generation.	1. Cut out infected canes below the soil line.
Raspberry Sawfly	similar to BLACKBERRY SAWFLY	see BLACKBERRY SAWFLY
Rednecked Cane Borer	see CANEBORER	see CANEBORER
Root Fly and Root Maggot	see CORN and CABBAGE MAGGOTS	see CORN and CABBAGE MAGGOTS
Rose Chafer (aka: Rose Bug) * Grape Peony * Rose Other fruits and flowers continued	Chewed foliage. Destroyed grass roots. This slender adult beetle (1/3-1/2") is tan, with a reddish-brown head and long spiny, slightly hairy, legs. It emerges in late May-early June and feeds for 3-4 weeks, attacking flowers first, then fruit blossoms and newly set fruit. It lays eggs in the soil which hatch in 1-2 weeks. Larvae (3/4") feed on grass roots, then pupate 10-16" deep in the soil.	1. Handpick adults. 2. Cheesecloth fences, stretched higher than the plants, will deter the beetle as it doesn't fly over barriers. 3. Do not allow chickens to clean garden because these beetles are poisonous to chickens. 4. Ohio State U. research shows commercially available white traps are most effective with this pest, and that no chemical attractants are necessary.

Macro Pest	Description	Organic Remedy
Rose Chafer, *ctd.*	Where: East of the Rockies, primarily a pest in sandy soils and North of New York City. 1 generation.	
Roundworm	see NEMATODE	see NEMATODE
Sap Beetle (many sp.) (aka: Corn Sap Beetle, Strawberry Sap Beetle) Corn Strawberry Raspberry	Brown hollowed-out kernels at the corn ear tip. Sometimes individual damaged kernels are scattered throughout. Round cavities eaten straight into ripe strawberries. Feeding injury between the raspberry and stem. Injury predisposes small fruit to secondary rot organisms. This small (3/16") black, oblong beetle invades ears through the silk channel or via holes in the husk caused by other pests. This is often associated with corn borer or corn earworm damage. A smaller, brown oval beetle attacks small fruit. White maggot-like larvae eat inside kernels and infested fruit. They scatter when exposed to light. Where: widespread.	1. Clean and complete harvesting of small fruit and removal of damaged, diseased and overripe berries helps to reduce populations. 2. Deep plowing in fall or early spring reduces overwintering populations of the corn sap beetle. 3. Destroy alternate food sources, such as old vegetable crops beyond harvest. 4. Same controls as for CORN EARWORM, except 3, 4, 6, and 7. The same predators of corn earworm feed on sap beetle eggs and larvae, but the parasites listed are more specific.
Scale (many sp.) Fruit trees Nut trees Shrubs *continued*	Small spots of reddened tissue on leaves or branches. Fine dusty ash. Hard bumps on fruit. Dead twigs or branches. Limbs lose vigor, leaves yellow, and the plant dies, usually from the top down. Honeydew excretions support black fungus and attract ants. Scales are extremely small, and suck plant nutrients from bark, leaves, and fruit. You may see the insect's "armor," which is either a part of its body or, in some species is made up of old skeletons and a waxy coating that shields them from attacks. This armor may look like flaky, crusty parts of the bark. The immature insect (1/16") crawls to a feeding spot where it stays for	1. Spray Insecticidal soap. 2. Apply Horticultural oil spray late in the spring, right at bud break. One spray should be sufficient. 3. # Glue dissolved in water is an effective spray. See #3 under MITES. 4. Scrape scale off plants or touch them with a an alcohol-soaked cotton swab. Repeat every 3 or 4 days until scale falls off. 5. Biological controls: Use *Comperiella bifasciata* for yellow scale, the Chalcid wasp *A. luteolus* for soft scale in California, *A. melinus* for red scale, the *Metaphycus helvolus* wasp for softscale or black scale, the *Vedalia* ladybug for cottony cushion scale, and the *Chilococorus nigritis* ladybug for all scales.

Macro Pest	Description	Organic Remedy
Scale, *ctd*.	the remainder of its life. Ants carry scales from plant to plant. Where: Different species occur throughout U.S. 1-3 or more generations per year.	
Seedcorn Maggot	see CORN MAGGOT	see CORN MAGGOT
Skipjack	see WIREWORM	see WIREWORM

Slug (many sp.) & Snail
 	
  Artichoke
  Asparagus
  Basil
  Beans
  Brassicas
  Celeriac
  Chard
  Celery
  Cucumber
  Eggplant
  Greens
  Lettuce
  Onion
  Peas
  Pepper
   (seedling)
  Sage
  Squash
  Strawberry
  Most fruit trees
	Large, ragged holes in leaves, fruits and stems, starting at plant bottom. Trails of slime on leaves and soil.
	
	Slugs are large (1/2 - 10" long), slimy worm-like creatures that resemble snails without shells. They are mollusks but have no outer protective shells. Their eyes are at the tip of 2 tentacles. They come in all colors, brown, gray, purple, black, white, yellow, and can be spotted. They feed mostly from 2 hours after sundown to 2 hours before sunrise. Females lay clusters of 25 oval white eggs in damp soil, which hatch in about 1 month.
	
	Snails, also in the mollusk family, have hard shells and scrape small holes in foliage as they feed and lay masses of eggs. Eggs are large (1/8") and are like clusters of white pearls. Snails can go dormant in periods of drought or low food supply.
	
	Where: Widespread, but they rank as a top pest, if not number one, in the West. They thrive in temperatures below 75F.
		1. Remove all garden debris.
		2. Cultivation or spading in spring or times of drought will help destroy dormant slugs and eggs.
		3. # Place stale beer in shallow pans, the lip of which must be at ground level. Replace every day and after rain, and dispose of dead slugs. Because they're attracted to the yeast, even more effective is 1 tsp of dry yeast in about 1/4 C of water. Where slugs are too numerous for this solution (e.g. in the West), try other traps below.
		4. # Board trap: Set a wide board about 1" off the ground in an infested area. This provides daytime shelter for them and easy collection for you.
		5. # Gutter trap: Set aluminum gutter around the beds and coat with ivory soap. The slugs will get trapped in this. Empty and kill them regularly.
		6. Seedlings: Keep seedlings covered until they're 6" high, particularly pea seedlings. Try plastic jugs with the bottoms cut out, anchored firmly in the soil, with the caps off for ventilation. Make sure no slugs are inside.
		7. Asparagus: Plant crowns in wire baskets anchored several inches down in the ground.
		8. Barriers to raised beds:
		(a) strips of aluminum screening about 3" high, pushed about 1" into the soil. Bend top of the screen outward, away from bed, and remove 2 strands from the edge so it's rough.
		(b) a 2" strip of copper flashing tacked around the outside of beds, 1" from top

continued

Macro Pest	Description	Organic Remedy
Slug & Snail, *ctd.*		of bed. This carries a minor electric charge that repels slugs. Copper bands around tree trunks works similarly. Snail Barr™ is available commercially. (c) crushed eggshells around plants. (d) strips of hardware cloth tacked onto top edges of bed, extending 2" above edge. Make sure there are sharp points along the top edge. 9. Sprinkle Diatomaceous Earth around the plant base and work slightly into the soil. If not available, sprinkle wood ashes around the plant base. Avoid getting on plants. 10. Don't apply mulch until soil has warmed to 75F, which is warmer than slugs like. 11. Destroy all eggs. Find them under rocks, pots and boards. 12. # Use the weed Plantain as a trap crop, but first be sure it doesn't itself become a pest in your area. 13. # Spray with wormwood tea. 14. Encourage predators such as birds, ducks, lightening bug larvae, ground beetles, turtles, salamanders, grass and garter snakes. Ducks have a voracious appetite for these pests. 15. Biological control: Predatory snail, *Ruminia decollata*, will feed on brown garden snails. They can't be shipped to most places like Northern California or the Northwest. It kills native snails. 16. Allies (see chart): Fennel, garlic and rosemary.
Southern Corn Rootworm	see CUCUMBER BEETLE	see CUCUMBER BEETLE
Sow Bug (aka: Dooryard Sow Bug) Seedlings *continued*	Chewed seedlings, stems, and roots. See also **PILL BUG**. These bugs are crustaceans. They are small (1/4-1/2") oval, hump-backed bugs with 14 legs. Sow bugs scurry when disturbed and generally hide under leaves and debris. The Pill bug will roll itself into a ball for protection.	1. Apply wood ashes or an oak leaf mulch. 2. Water plants with a very weak lime solution. Mix 2 lbs per 5 gallons, and let sit for 24 hours before using. 3. # Bait with 1/2 potato placed cut-side down on the soil surface. In the morning collect and kill bugs. 4. Botanical control: If the problem is severe, Rotenone (1% solution).

Macro Pest	Description	Organic Remedy
Sow Bug, *ctd.*	Where: Widespread. Common in gardens, but not usually a severe problem. 1 generation per year.	
Spider Mite	see MITE	see MITE
Spinach Flea Beetle	see FLEA BEETLE	see FLEA BEETLE
Spittlebug (many sp.) (aka: Froghopper) Corn Many Others	Foamy masses ("frog spit"), usually at stem joints. Faded, wilted, curled, or discolored leaves. Stunted, weakened, and sometimes distorted plants. Adults (1/3") are dull brown, gray or black, sometimes with yellow markings. They hop and look like short, fat leafhoppers. They lay eggs in plant stems, and in grasses between the stem and leaf sheath. The foam covers the eggs, which overwinter. In spring when nymphs hatch they produce even more froth for protection. Adults and nymphs suck plant juices from leaves and stems. Where: Widespread, but worst in the Northeast, Oregon, and high humidity regions. 1 or more generations.	1. Many species are not a serious problem, so you may want to leave them alone. 2. If seriously damaging, cut out plant parts with "spittle" or simply remove the foamy mass. Destroy egg masses or nymphs contained inside.
Spotted Asparagus Beetle * Asparagus Aster * *Cucurbits* Zinnia	Defoliation and misshapen fruit. It usually appears in July. This slender reddish brown-orange beetle has 6 black spots on each side of its back. It lays single greenish eggs on leaves, which develop into orange larvae in 1-2 weeks. Larvae bore into the berry and eat seeds and pulp, then pupate in the soil. Where: East of the Mississippi. 1 generation per year.	1. Handpick in the morning when the beetle can't fly due to cool temperatures. 2. see also ASPARAGUS BEETLE
Squash Bug Cucumber Muskmelon * Pumpkin * Squash *continued*	Rapidly wilting leaves dry up and then turn black. No fruit development. These medium (5/8"), brown-black bugs feed by sucking plant sap and injecting toxins. When crushed at any	1. Use row covers. When female blossoms (fruit blooms) open, lift edges of covers for only 2 hours in the early morning, only twice a week, until blossoms drop. This permits pollination. 2. Handpick bugs.

Macro Pest	Description	Organic Remedy
Squash Bug, *ctd.* Watermelon	age they emit a foul odor. They like moist, protected areas and hide in deep, loose mulch like hay or straw, as well as in debris or under boards. They lay clusters of yellow, red, or brown eggs on the undersides of leaves along the central vein. Eggs hatch in 7-14 days. Young bugs have red heads and bright green bodies that turn to gray as they mature. Bugs overwinter under vines, in boards, buildings and under dead leaves. Where: Widespread. 1 generation per year.	3. # Sprinkle a barrier of wood ashes, moistened to prevent blowing, around the plant base. Don't get ashes on the plant. Periodically renew. 4. In the fall leave a few immature squash on the ground to attract the remaining bugs. Destroy squash when covered with bugs. 5. Trellised plants are less susceptible to this bug. 6. Pull vulnerable plants as soon as they finish bearing, place in a large plastic bag, tie securely, and place in direct sun for 1 to 2 weeks. This destroys all eggs. 7. Spray insecticidal soap, laced with isopropyl alcohol to help it penetrate the shell. Soap, however, is not very effective against hard-bodied insects. 8. Time plantings to avoid bug. 9. Rotate crops. 10. Use heavy mulch materials. 11. # Place boards in garden where they will hide and be easy to catch. 12. Plant resistant varieties. 13. Encourage birds. 14. Biological control: Praying mantises eat eggs and nymphs. Tachinid flies are natural predators. 15. Botanical control: Sabadilla, Rotenone (1% solution). 16. Allies (see chart): Borage, catnip, marigold, mint, nasturtium, radish and tansy.
Squash Vine Borer Cucumber Gourds Muskmelon Pumpkin Squash *continued*	Sudden wilting of plant parts. Moist yellow sawdust-like material (frass) outside small holes near the plant base. This long (1") dirty-white worm, with brown head and legs, bores into stems where it feeds for 4-6 weeks. It overwinters 1-2" below the soil surface. The adult wasp-like moth (1-1/2") has clear copper-green forewings, transparent rear wings, and rings on its abdomen colored red, copper, and	1. Use row covers. When female blossoms (fruit blooms) open, lift cover edges twice a week, for only 2 hours in early morning, until blossoms drop. This permits pollination. 2. # Reflective mulch such as aluminum foil will repel them. 3. Stem collars can prevent egg-laying. 4. If not grown on a trellis, pinch off the young plant's growing tip to cause multistemming. For trailing squash stems, bury every fifth leaf node to encourage rooting. When one part becomes infested cut it off and remove. Leave other sections to grow.

Macro Pest	Description	Organic Remedy
Squash Vine Borer, *ctd.*	black. It lays rows or clusters of individual tiny, longish, brown or red eggs near the plant base on the main stem. Where: East of the Rockies. 1 generation per year in the North, and 2 generations per year in the Southern and Gulf states.	Mound soil over vines up to blossoms. 6. Slit stem vertically to remove and destroy borers. Mound soil around the slit stem to encourage new rooting. Remove and destroy damaged stems. 7. Handpick the eggs. 8. # Sprinkle wood ashes, crushed black pepper, or real camphor around plants to deter borer. 9. Time planting to avoid borer. In the North plant a second crop in mid-summer to avoid borer feeding. 10. Plant resistant varieties. 11. Remove plants as soon as they finish bearing, place in a plastic bag, tie securely, and place in direct sun for 1-2 weeks to destroy borers and eggs. 12. Biological controls: Inject beneficial nematodes into infected vines at 4" intervals over bottom 3' of vine, using 5,000 nematodes per injection. Also use in mulch around vines. Bt is another effective control; inject it into the vine after the first blossoms and again in 10 days. Clean syringe between injections. Trichogramma wasps attack borer eggs. Lacewings are also predators. 13. Allies (see chart): Borage, nasturtium, radish (plant radishes around the plant base).
Squirrel Fruit Nuts Seeds	The symptoms of squirrels are obvious -- you'll see the squirrel digging in your garden, or scurrying in and around the bottom of your fruit and nut trees. They steal seeds, fruit and nuts. Where: Widespread.	1. You can try hanging mothballs in mesh bags in fruit and nut trees to repel them. 2. # Try mixing 1 tsp of pepper with 1 lb of corn seed, before planting corn. 3. Gather fruits and nuts every day. You may need to harvest fruit slightly underripe, for they can clean out every single ripe fruit in one night.
Stink Bug (many sp.) * Beans Cabbage * Cucumber Mustard *continued*	Tiny holes in leaves and stems, particularly in new growth. Holes are surrounded by milky spots. Stunted, distorted, and weak plants. Adults and nymphs suck sap. The medium-sized (1/3 - 3/4") adult is an ugly gray, brown, green, or	1. Main control is to keep the garden well weeded. 2. Insecticidal soap sprays must be laced with isopropyl alcohol to help penetrate the bug's outer shell. Soap alone, however, is not very effective against hard-bodied insects. 3. Hand pick and destroy.

Macro Pest	Description	Organic Remedy
Stink Bug, *ctd.* Okra * Pepper Snapdragon * Tomato	black. Its back is shaped like a shield. It emits a very unpleasant odor when touched or frightened. Adults lay eggs on plants in mid-spring, and hibernate in debris. Some stink bugs prey on the Colorado Potato Beetle. Where: Widespread, many different species. 1-4 generations per year.	4. Botanical control: Sabadilla, Rotenone (1% solution), Pyrethrins.
Strawberry Clipper	see STRAWBERRY WEEVIL	see STRAWBERRY WEEVIL
Strawberry Crown Borer Strawberry	Stunted or weakened plants. Chewed leaves and stems. Small yellow grubs bore into strawberry roots and crowns, and turn pink the longer they feed. The small (1/5") adult brown snout-nosed beetle has reddish patches on its wings. It feeds on stems and leaves. Adults overwinter just below soil surface, and lay eggs in spring in shallow holes in the crown at the base of leaf stalks. Where: East of the Rockies, particularly in KY, TN, and AS. 1 generation per year.	1. If a patch is infested with crown borer, plant new strawberries at least 300 yards away from the area. Beetles can't fly and won't migrate. 2. Pull and destroy plants that show damage. Replacement plants can be established immediately. 3. Make sure plants are healthy and are fed with compost. Healthy plants can usually tolerate these beetles. 4. Allies (see chart): Borage.
Strawberry Leaf Roller Strawberry	Rolled-up leaves. Skeletonized leaves that turn brown. Withered and deformed fruit. Yellow-green-brown larvae (1/2") feed inside rolled leaves. Small (1/2") adult moths, gray to reddish brown, emerge in May to lay eggs on leaf undersides. Where: Northern U.S., LA, AS, and AK. 2 or more generations per year.	1. For minor infestations, remove and burn leaves. 2. For larger infestations, mow or cut plants off 1" above the crowns. Burn or destroy plants. 3. See also controls for LEAF ROLLER.
Strawberry Weevil or Clipper Brambles Strawberry *continued*	Holes in blossom buds and severed stems. These small (1/10") reddish-brown beetles, with black snouts, feed at night and hide in daylight. Females	1. Remove and destroy all stems hanging by threads. These carry the eggs. 2. Remove mulch, maintain open-canopy beds, and renovate immediately after harvest to discourage new adults.

Macro Pest	Description	Organic Remedy
Strawberry Weevil, ctd.	lay eggs in buds, then sever them. Small white grubs feed inside severed buds and emerge after fruit is picked in July. Where: Northern U.S. 1 generation per year.	3. Plant late-bearing strawberries. 4. Biological controls: Beneficial nematodes are effective control, especially the new Hh strain. 5. Botanical control: Sabadilla, Rotenone (5% solution), and Pyrethrins (apply 2 treatments 7-10 days apart, starting at early bud development.) 6. Allies (see chart): Borage.
Strawberry Root Weevils (many sp.) Strawberry	Adults eat notches into leaves. Larvae eat roots and crown, which weaken, stunts, and eventually kills the plants. Beetles are small to large (1/12"-1"), shiny brown, gray to black. Females lay eggs on the soil surface in spring. Small, white to pinkish, thick-bodied, legless curved grubs feed on roots and then hibernate in soil. Where: Northern U.S. 1 generation.	1. Remove and destroy plants showing damage. 2. Planting annual crops can, in some areas, help avoid weevil damage. 3. Botanical controls: Generally ineffective because of the difficulty in timing sprays to coincide with adult emergence.
Striped Blister Beetle All vegetables	Eaten blossoms, chewed foliage, eaten fruit. Human skin that contacts a crushed beetle will blister. Slender adult beetles (1/2") are black with a yellow stripes. They swarm in huge numbers and can destroy everything in sight. They lay eggs in the soil which hatch midsummer. Other blister beetles may be less damaging. Larvae are heavy-jawed, burrow in the soil, and eat grasshopper eggs. They become hard-shelled as pseudopupa, and remain dormant for under 1 year up to 2 years. Where: East of the Rockies. 1 generation per year.	1. Handpick with gloves to protect skin. 2. Use row covers or netting. 3. Botanical controls: Rotenone dust.
Striped Flea Beetle	see FLEA BEETLE	see FLEA BEETLE
Tarnished Plant Bug Beans continued	Deformed, dwarfed flowers, beans, strawberry, and peaches. Wilted and discolored celery stems. Deformed roots. Black terminal shoots. Pitting	1. Remove all sites of hibernation. 2. Use row covers. 3. Use white sticky traps. 4. Spray insecticidal soap weekly in the

Macro Pest	Description	Organic Remedy
Tarnished Plant Bug, *ctd.* Celery Most vegetables Peach Pear Raspberry Strawberry (This bug attacks more plants than any other insect. 328 hosts have been recorded.)	and black spots on buds, tips, and fruit. Fireblight. Small (1/4") highly mobile adults suck juice from young shoots and buds. They inject a poisonous substance into plant tissue and can spread fireblight. Generally brownish and oval, this insect can have mottled yellow, brown, and black triangles on each side of its back. It lays light yellow, long, curved eggs inside stems, tips, and leaves. Adults hibernate through winter under stones, tree bark, garden trash, or in clover and alfalfa. Nymphs are green-yellow with black dots on the abdomen and thorax. Where: Widespread. Several generations per year.	early morning, though this is not very effective against hard-bodied insects. 5. Biological control: Try beneficial nematodes in the fall to kill overwintering forms. 6. Botanical control: Sabadilla, Rotenone (5% solution), Pyrethrins (in 3 applications 2-3 days apart). Spray in the early morning when bugs are sluggish.
Tent Caterpillar (aka: Eastern Tent Caterpillar, Apple Tree Caterpillar) * Apple Cherry Peach Pear	Woven tent-like nests, full of caterpillars, in tree forks. Defoliation. Large (2") caterpillars are black, hairy, with white and blue markings and a white stripe down the back. They feed in daylight outside the tent on leaves. Adults (1-1/4") are red-brown moths. Females lay egg masses in a band around twigs, and cover them with a foamy substance that dries to a dark shiny brown, hard finish. Eggs hatch the following spring. Where: East of the Rockies. A similar species exists in California. 1 generation per year. Worst infestations come in 10-year cycles.	1. Destroy nests by hand. Wearing gloves, in early morning pull down nests and kill caterpillars by crushing or dropping into a bucket of water laced with insecticidal soap. (Kerosene is toxic to the soil and difficult to dispose.) 2. Use sticky burlap bands. Remove pests daily. 3. In winter, cut off twigs with egg masses and burn. Also look on fences and buildings for eggs. 4. Remove nearby wild cherry trees. 5. Attract Baltimore orioles, bluebirds, digger wasps and chickadees. 6. Biological controls: Bt, sprayed every 10-14 days. 7. Botanical controls: Pyrethrins. 8. Allies (see chart): Dill.
Thrips (many sp.) Beans Corn Onion *continued*	Damaged blossoms, especially those colored white and yellow. Buds turn brown. Whitened, scarred, desiccated leaves and fruit. Pale, silvery leaves eventually die. Dark fecal pellets.	1. Immediately remove infested buds and flowers. 2. # A reflective mulch like aluminum foil is reported to repel them. 3. Control weeds. 4. Spray insecticidal soap.

Macro Pest	Description	Organic Remedy
Thrips, *ctd.* Peanut Pear Squash Tomato	Tiny (1/25") straw-colored or black slender insects with 2 pairs of slender wings edged with hairs. Nymphs and adults both suck plant juices and scrape and sting the plant. They transmit spotted wilt to tomatoes. Adults insert eggs inside leaves, stems and fruit. Eggs hatch in 1 week. Where: Widespread. 5-8 generations per year.	5. Spray a hard jet of water in early morning, 3 days in a row. 6. Dust with Diatomaceous Earth. 7. # Garlic or onion sprays. 8. Spray light Horticultural Oil in the morning, twice, 3-4 days apart. 9. Ensure sufficient water supply. 10. Rotate crops. 11. Biological control: Predatory mites (*Amblyseiulus mackenseii* and *Euseius tularensis*). Green lacewing larvae, ladybugs, and predatory thrips, prey on thrips. Beneficial nematodes may work in soil control in the greenhouse. 12. Botanical control: Rotenone (5% solution), Pyrethrins. A mix might work best. Sulfur and tobacco dusts also work. 13. Allies (see chart): Carrots, corn.
Tobacco Hornworm (aka: Southern Hornworm) Eggplant Pepper Tomato	Virtually same as TOMATO HORNWORM, except this worm has a red horn. Where: Worst in the Gulf states and on ornamentals in California.	1. Same controls as Tomato Hornworm.
Tomato Fruitworm	see CORN EARWORM	see CORN EARWORM
Tomato Hornworm Dill * Eggplant * Pepper * Potato * Tomato *continued*	Holes in leaves and fruit. Dark droppings on leaves. Defoliation. This very large (3-4") green worm has white bars down both sides and a black or green horn at its tail end. The large (4-5") adult moth emerges in May-June, and is sometimes called the Hawk or Hummingbird Moth. It has long narrow gray wings, yellow spots on its abdomen, flies at dusk, and feeds like a hummingbird. It lays single green-yellow eggs on leaf undersides. Pupae (2") emerge and overwinter 3-4" under the soil in a hard-shelled cocoon. Where: Widespread. There is 1 generation per year in the North, and	1. Handpick larvae and eggs. Look for green droppings under the plant. 2. Do not pick worms with cocoons on their backs. Eggs of the Braconid wasp, a predator, are in the cocoons. If you see these, make the same NPV control spray as under CORN EARWORM. Also, do not pick eggs with dark streaks, which means they're parasitized by the Trichogramma wasp. 3. # Apply hot pepper or soap and lime sprays directly on worms. 4. Encourage birds. 5. # Blacklight traps and bug zappers are effective against the adult. But these kill beneficial insects, too. 6. Fall cultivation. 7. Biological controls: Lacewings, braconid and trichogramma wasps, and ladybugs attack the eggs. Release at

Macro Pest	Description	Organic Remedy
Tomato Hornworm, *ctd.*	2 per year in South.	first sign of adults laying eggs. Bt (berliner/kurstake strain), sprayed every 10-14 days, is very effective. 8. Botanical controls: Rotenone (1% solution), Pyrethrins. 9. Allies (see chart): Borage and dill (both used as trap crops), and opal basil and marigold.
Vine Borer	see SQUASH VINE BORER	see SQUASH VINE BORER
Vole (Field Mouse)	see MOUSE	see MOUSE
Walnut Caterpillar Hickory Pecan Walnut	Defoliation, usually in large branches first. Black walnuts are prime targets. This black caterpillar (2"), with long white hairs, lifts its head and tail when disturbed. At night they gather at branch bases. Pupae overwinter 1-3" below the soil surface. Adult moths emerge in spring. They are dark tan with 4 brown transverse lines on their forewings. They lay clusters of eggs on leaf undersides. Where: Eastern U.S. south to FL, and west to TX and WI. 1 generation per year in Northern climates, 2 generations in Southern climates.	1. In late evening brush congregating caterpillars into water laced with insecticidal soap. (Kerosene is toxic to the soil and difficult to dispose.) 2. Spray with dormant Horticultural Oil. Make sure all parts of the tree are covered.
Walnut Husk Fly and Maggot Peach (in West) Walnut	Dark liquid stain over the walnut shell, and sometimes the kernels. This is a by-product of larvae feeding. Kernels may be off-taste. Small larvae feed on the outer husk, then drop to the ground. Pupae hibernate under the trees in the ground in hard brown cases. Adult flies, the size of houseflies, emerge in mid-summer. They are brown with yellow stripes across their backs, and have transparent wings. Females lay eggs inside husks. Where: Various species throughout the U.S. 1 generation per year.	1. Destroy worms in infested nuts by dropping husks into a pail of water. Remove dead maggots when removing the husk. 2. Fall cultivation. 3. Plant late-maturing cultivars in eastern U.S.. 4. For large orchard sprays, consult your extension agent or *Nut Tree Culture in North America* (see Bibliography.)

Macro Pest	Description	Organic Remedy
Webworm, Garden	see GARDEN WEBWORM	see GARDEN WEBWORM
Weevil (many sp.) Apple Beans Blueberry *Brassicas* Carrot Celeriac Cherry Peach Pear Peas Pepper Plum Raspberry Strawberry Sw. Potato	Zigzag paths in roots, fruit, stems. This is a family of hard-shelled, snout-nosed, tear-shaped small beetles. Usually brown or black, they feed at night and hide during the day. Small, white larvae feed inside fruit, stems, or roots. Adults usually lay eggs on the plant, sometimes inside. Bean and pea weevil larvae feed in young seed, and emerge when beans are in storage. They can do extensive damage in storage. Where: Widespread. Usually 1 generation per year.	1. Heat beans and peas before storing: Beans at 135F for 3-4 hours, peas at 120-130F for 5-6 hours. Store in a cool, dry place. 2. Clean cultivation is essential. 3. Deep cultivation exposes larvae. 4. Pea weevil: Plant crops early. 5. Sweet potato weevil: Rotate crops, and use certified disease-free slips. 6. *Brassicas:* Rotate crops. 7. Try dusting with lime when the leaves are wet or dew-covered. 8. Encourage song birds. 9. See also controls under CARROT WEEVIL, PLUM CURCULIO, STRAWBERRY CLIPPER and ROOT WEEVIL. 10. Biological controls: Beneficial nematodes are helpful when applied in early spring near planting time. 11. Botanical controls: Sabadilla, Rotenone (5% solution), Pyrethrins. 12. Allies (see chart): Radish, summer savory and tansy.
Whitefly Greenhouses Most fruits Most vegetables Rosemary	Leaves yellow and die. Black fungus. Honeydew excretions coat leaves and support black fungus. Tiny (1/16") insects with white wings suck plant juices from the undersides of leaves, stems, and buds. They lay groups of yellow, conical eggs on leaf undersides. Nymphs hatch in 4-12 days and are legless white crawlers. Where: Widespread. Several generations per year.	1. Spray insecticidal soap, every 2-3 days for 2 weeks. 2. Use sticky yellow traps. In greenhouses place them at plant canopy height and shake plants. 3. Mix 1 C alcohol, 1/2 tsp Volck oil or insecticidal soap, and 1 quart water. Spray twice, 1 week apart, to the point of runoff. This suffocates whiteflies but doesn't harm plants. 4. Use forceful water jet sprays, in early morning, at least 3 days in a row. 5. # Hot pepper and garlic sprays. 6. Check phosphorous and magnesium levels. Whitefly may be a sign of a deficiency. Magnesium may be applied by mixing 1/2 C Epsom salts in 1 gallon water, and thoroughly soaking soil with solution. 7. Increase air circulation. 8. # Marigold root secretion is alleged to be absorbed by nearby vegetables and repel whiteflies.

continued

Macro Pest	Description	Organic Remedy
Whitefly, *ctd.*		9. Biological controls: Ladybugs and green lacewings. Trichogramma and chalcid parasitic wasps. Whitefly parasites, *Encarsia formosa*, can be used in greenhouses. 10. Botanical controls: Ryania, Pyrethrins. 11. Allies (see chart): Mint, nasturtium, thyme and wormwood.
White-fringed Beetle Virtually all vegetation	Severed roots. Chewed lower stems, root tissue, tubers. Plants yellow, wilt, and die. Extremely damaging. Larvae (1/2") are yellow-white, curved, legless, and emerge in May, with the greatest numbers in June-July. They feed for 2-5 months, and may travel 1/4 to 3/4 mile. They overwinter in the top 9" of the soil, and pupate in spring. Adult beetles (1/2") are brownish-gray with broad, short snouts, have short pale hairs all over, and non-functional wings banded with white. They feed in large numbers. Where: Southeast (FL, AL, AS, GA, KY, LA, MS, SC, NC, TN, VA), but are moving north and have been seen in NJ. 1-4 generations per year.	1. Large-scale government quarantine and eradication measures have eliminated this in some areas, but home gardeners have limited methods of dealing with it. If you experience this pest, notify your extension agent. They should be alerted to the movement of this pest and may be able to help you with control measures. 2. Deep spading in spring can help destroy overwintering grubs. 3. Dig very steep-sided ditches, 1' deep, to trap crawling beetles. Capture and destroy.

White Grub
(larvae of June and Japanese Beetles)
 	
  Apple, young
  Blackberry
* Corn
* Grain roots
* Lawns
  Onion
* Potato
* Strawberry
	Sudden wilting, especially in early summer. See JUNE BEETLE.
	
	Medium to large (3/4 to 1-1/2") plump, white, curved worms have brown heads and several legs near the head. They feed on plant roots. The adult is usually either the May or June beetle.
	
	Where: Widespread. It takes them 10 months to several years to complete one life cycle. 1 emergence per year.
		1. Fall and spring cultivation.
		2. Don't plant susceptible crops on areas just converted from untilled sod, as grubs will come up through the grass.
		3. Allow chickens to pick over garden following fall and spring cultivations.
		4. Encourage birds.
		5. Biological controls: Beneficial nematodes in spring or early summer, as mulch or dressing. Milky spore disease, which takes a few years to spread enough to be effective.

Wireworm (many sp.) *continued*	Plants wilt and die. Damaged roots. Thin and patchy crops.	1. Frequent fall and spring cultivation to expose worms to predators, at least once a week.

Macro Pest	Description	Organic Remedy
Wireworm, *ctd.* * Beans Cabbage * Carrot Celeriac * Corn * Lettuce Melon * Onion Pea * Potato * Strawberry Sw.Potato Turnip	Large (1-1/2"), slender, fairly hard-shelled worms, with only 3 pairs of legs near the head, feed underground. They do not curl up when disturbed. They core into roots, bulbs, and germinating seeds. Corn, grasses, and potatoes may be badly damaged. The adult beetle is also known as the Click beetle or Skipjack. It flips into the air with a clicking sound when placed on its back. It can't fly well or long. The egg-adult cycle takes 3 years, 2 of them the larvae feeding phase. Where: Widespread, but particularly a problem in poorly drained soil or recently sod soil. Overlapping generations are present at all times.	2. Don't grow a garden over grass sod. Plow or till soil once every week for 4-6 weeks in the fall before beginning your garden. 3. # Alfalfa is said to repel wireworms. White mustard and buckwheat are alleged to repel wireworms. Clover and timothy (and other grass hays) are said by some to repel worms, by others to attract them. Perhaps these might be tried as a trap crop, away from your garden. 4. # Potato trap: Cut potato in half, spear with a stick, and bury 1 to 4" in soil, with stick as a handle above ground. Set 3 to 10' apart. Pull potatoes in 2 to 5 days. Destroy potato and all worms. Some gardeners reported capturing 15-20 worms in one potato. 5. # Put milkweed juice on the soil around affected plants. This supposedly repels worms. 6. Biological control: Apply beneficial nematodes 2 months before planting. 7. Allies (see chart): Alfalfa, clover. (Note: see #3 above).
Woolly Aphid	See APHID	see APHID

NOTES:

Allies & Companions

What They Might Do
How and Where They Do It

Allies are supposed to actively repel insects, or enhance growth or flavor of the target plant. Companions, by contrast, are supposed to share space and growing habits well, but do not necessarily play an active role in pest protection or growth. Allies can be and are considered companions, but companions are not necessarily allies.

This chart tells what plants the allies are supposed to help, what they do (repel insects, aid growth, etc.), how they do it (e.g. visual masking), and where, if available, the data was gathered. Some sources say there is evidence for an ally working, but fail to mention the nature of the evidence. In all such cases, we have listed the ally as "uncertain." Evidence to some people might be a one-time occurrence, whereas others may have a more rigorous, scientific approach. Unfortunately, we couldn't divine who was who. For cross-reference, most target plants are listed as companions in the growing chart of the ally plant.

Be aware of the controversy over allies and companions. Efforts to test these claims scientifically with proper controls are few, and results are often difficult to interpret. For example, a specific species of marigolds was shown in field trials to repel nematodes, but only in mass plantings. In small quantities planted next to the target crop they actually decreased yields. As a result, we've tried to include references to as many of the scientific trials as possible, including those where a putative ally carried with it some negative effects. Also, it is important to realize that an ally may effectively deter an insect pest but at the same time may attract other insect pests.

Companion planting should be approached with skepticism, a healthy experimental attitude, and curiosity. Conduct your own trials, as the success of allies and companions depends greatly on your microclimate, soil conditions, and cropping history, to name just a few variables. All references to specific mechanisms of action, when associated with a specific testing site, are from Robert Kourik's book, *Designing and Maintaining Your Edible Landscape Naturally* (see Bibliography). For further information on the original articles consult his book.

KEY:

AH = provides alternate host plant
AW = provides alternate host for parasitic wasps
CM = masking by chemical repellant confuses pest
P = attracts beneficial parasites
PI = physical interference so pest can't reach target
Pred = attracts beneficial predators
PW = attracts beneficial parasitic wasps

VM = visual masking
TR = roots excrete toxic substances
* = best described in original article
Temp. = temperate climate
Some Evidence = some scientific trials, but sources specify where
Uncertain = no scientific evidence

ALLY	TARGET	Target Pest and Benefits	How/Where
Alder	Fruit Trees	Red Spider Mite	Pred, UK
Alfalfa	Barley	Aphid	Pred, Czech.
	Corn	Wireworm	uncertain
Anise	Most Vegetables	Aphid	uncertain
Asparagus	Some Vegetables	Nematodes: asparagus roots contain a toxin in the roots effective against some strains	uncertain
Barley, cover crop	Many Vegetables	reduces Nematode populations	uncertain
	Soybean	Soybean pests	Pred, VA
Basil	Asparagus	Asparagus beetle, improves growth	uncertain
	Most Vegetables	Flies, and improves growth & flavor	uncertain
	Tomato	growth & flavor	uncertain
	Tomato	(Opal basil) Tomato Hornworm	uncertain
Enemies:	Cabbage	lowered yield of cabbage yields	uncertain
	Snap Beans	caused higher incidence of whiteflies	uncertain
Beans			
Beans, French	Bruss.Sprouts	Aphid	PI, England
All Beans	Corn	Leaf Beetle, Leafhopper, and	Pred/ PI,
	Corn	Fall Armyworm	tropics
	Cucumber	adds nutrients	uncertain
Beans, green	Eggplant	Colorado Potato Beetle	uncertain
All Beans	Potato	repels insects	uncertain
Snap Beans	Potato	Colorado Potato Beetle, Leafhopper (NB: may reduce potato yield)	uncertain
Bee Balm (Monarda didyma)	Tomato	improves growth & flavor	uncertain
Beet	Onion	improves growth	uncertain
Blackberry	Grape	Leafhopper (Pierces disease)	AW, temp.
Black Salsify (Oyster Plant)	Various vegetables	Carrot Rust Fly	uncertain
Borage (use as a trap crop)	Squash	Squash Vine borer, growth & flavor	uncertain
	Strawberry	Strawb.Crown borer, growth & flavor	uncertain
	Tomato	Tomato Hornworm, growth & flavor	uncertain
Bramble Berries (e.g. Raspberry)	Fruit trees	Red Spider Mite	Pred, England
Brassicas	Peas	Root Rot (Rhizoctonia)	uncertain

ALLY	TARGET	Target Pest and Benefits	How/Where
Broccoli	Cucumber	Striped Cucumber Beetle	PI, MI
	Beet, sugar	Green Peach Aphid	PW, WA
Buckwheat, cov.crop	Fruit trees	Codling Moth	P
Cabbage	Celery	repels insects	uncertain
	Tomato	Flea Beetle	CM, temperate
	Tomato	Diamondback Moth	CM, tropics
Candytuft	*Brassicas*	Flea Beetle	CM, NY
Caraway	Fruit Trees	attracts beneficial insects	uncertain
	Gardens	loosens soils	uncertain
	Onion	Thrips, and improves growth	VM, Africa
	Peas	improves growth	uncertain
	Pepper	improves growth	uncertain
Catnip	Beans	Flea Beetle (plant in borders) (NB: may increase whiteflies on snap beans)	uncertain
	Broccoli	Cabbageworm, Flea Beetle (NB: some evidence catnip increases Cabbageworms and lowers cabbage yield)	uncertain
	Cucumber	Cucumber Beetles	uncertain
	Pepper	Green Peach Aphid (NB: catnip may compete with pepper)	uncertain
	Potato	Colorado Potato Beetle	uncertain
	Squash	Squash Bug (NB: squash may not grow as large)	uncertain
	All Vegetables	Aphid, Flea Beetle, Japanese Beetle	uncertain
Celery	*Brassicas*	Cabbageworm	uncertain
	Beans	improves growth	uncertain
Chamomile	*Brassicas*	improves growth & flavor	uncertain
	Onion	improves growth & flavor	uncertain
Chervil	Radish	improves growth & flavor	uncertain
Chive	Carrot	improves growth & flavor	uncertain
	Celery	Aphid	uncertain
	Lettuce	Aphid	uncertain
	Peas	Aphid	uncertain
	All Vegetables	Japanese Beetle	uncertain
Clover, red	Barley	Aphid	Pred, Czech.
white	Bruss.Sprouts	Aphid, Cabbage Butterfly & Root Fly	VM, England
unspecified	Bruss.Sprouts	Aphid	PI, England
red & white	Cabbage & Caulif.	Aphid, Imported Cabbage Butterfly	PI & Pred,
unspecified	Cabbage	Cabbage Root Fly	Pred, Ireland
continued			

ALLY	TARGET	Target Pest and Benefits	How/Where
Clover, *ctd.*			
unspecified	Corn	Corn Borer	PI, England
unspecified	Fruit trees	Aphid, Codling moth	P
unspecified	Fruit trees	reduces Leafhopper population	uncertain
New Zeal. white	Oats	Fruit Fly	PI, England
Dutch white	Turnip	Cabbage Root Maggot	CM, PA
unspecified	Many Vegetables	repels Wireworm	uncertain

Note: Clover can also attract leafhoppers which will then damage susceptible crops

ALLY	TARGET	Target Pest and Benefits	How/Where
Coriander	All Fruit trees	attracts beneficial insects	uncertain
	Eggplant	Colorado Potato Beetle	uncertain
	Potato	Colorado Potato Beetle	uncertain
	Tomato	Colorado Potato Beetle	uncertain
	Many Vegetables	Aphid, Spider Mite	uncertain
	Various Vegetables	Carrot Rust Fly	uncertain
Corn	Beans	improves growth	uncertain
	Cucumber	Striped Cucumber Beetle	PI, MI
	Cucurbits	improves growth	uncertain
	Peanut	Corn Borer	VM, temp.
	Pumpkin	improves growth	uncertain
	Soybean	Corn Earworm	PW, GA
	Squash	Cucumber Beetle	PI, tropics
	Squash	Western Flower Thrips	Pred, CA
	Many Vegetables	Nematode (plant corn as cover crop)	uncertain
Corn spurry (*Spergula arvensis*)	Cauliflower	Aphid, Flea Beetle, Cabbage Looper	Pred, CA
Cover grass	Bruss.Sprouts	Aphid	PI, England
Cucumber	Radish	repels insects	uncertain
Dead Nettle (*Lamium* genus)	Potato	Colorado Potato Beetle	uncertain
		improves growth & flavor	uncertain
Dill	*Brassicas*	Cabbage Looper, Imported Cabbageworm	uncertain
	Brassicas	improves growth & vigor	uncertain
	Cabbage	Spider Mite, Caterpillars	uncertain
	Fruit trees	Codling Moth, Tent Caterpillar	uncertain
	Tomato	Tomato Hornworm (use dill as trap crop)	uncertain
Eggplant	Potato	Colorado Potato Beetle (trap crop)	uncertain
Fennel	Most Vegetables	Aphid	uncertain
Flax	Carrot	improves growth & flavor	uncertain
	Onion	Colorado Potato Beetle	uncertain
	Onion	improves growth & flavor	uncertain

ALLY	TARGET	Target Pest and Benefits	How/Where
Garlic	Beet	improves growth & flavor	uncertain
	Brassicas	Cabbage Looper, Maggot, and Worm	uncertain
	Brassicas	improves growth & flavor	uncertain
	Celery	Aphid	uncertain
	Fruit trees	Codling Moth	uncertain
	Lettuce	Aphid	uncertain
	Peach tree	Peach Borer	uncertain
	Raspberry	improves growth & health	uncertain
	Rose	improves growth & health	uncertain
	Many Vegetables	Japanese Beetle, Mexican Bean Beetle, Nematodes, Slug and Snail	uncertain
Garlic spray	Many Vegetables	Bean Anthracnose, Bean Bacterial Blight, Brown Rot of stone fruit, Downy Mildew, Cucumber & Bean Rust, Cucumber Leaf Spot, Tomato Blight, and Soft-bodied Insects (especially when mixed with Tobacco Juice)	uncertain
Goldenrod	Peach tree	Oriental Fruit Moth	*, temp.
	Various Vegetables	Cucumber Beetles	uncertain
Goosegrass (*Eleusine indica*)	Beans	Leafhopper	CM, tropics
Hairy Indigo	Various Vegetables	Nematodes	uncertain
Horseradish	Potato	Potato Bug (plant in patch corner)	uncertain
Hyssop	Cabbage	Cabbage Looper, Moth & Worm	uncertain
	Grape	increases yields	uncertain
Johnson Grass (*Sorghum halepense*)	Grape	Pacific Mite	Pred, temp.
	Grape	Williamette Mite	Pred, CA

Caution: While this grass may help with these mites, one Arkansas grower noted that it killed his vines. So you may want to make sure the grass is not allowed close to the vines.

ALLY	TARGET	Target Pest and Benefits	How/Where
Lamb's Quarters	Collards	Green Peach Aphid	Pred, Ohio
	Cauliflower	Imported Cabbage Butterfly	Pred, CA
	Peach tree	Oriental Fruit Moth	*, temp.
Lettuce	Carrot	Carrot Rust Fly	uncertain
	Radish	improves growth	uncertain
Marigold (*Tagetes* sp.)	Asparagus	Asparagus Beetle	uncertain
	Beans	Mexican Bean Beetle	uncertain
	Eggplant	Nematode	TR, CT
	Lima Bean	Mexican Bean Beetle	uncertain
	Lima Bean	Nematode	TR, CT
continued	Rose	Aphid	uncertain

ALLY	TARGET	Target Pest and Benefits	How/Where
Marigold, *ctd.*			
	Squash	Beetles, Nematode	uncertain
	Tomato	Aphid, Tomato Hornworm	uncertain
	Many Vegetables	Cabbage Maggot	uncertain

NOTE: Research at the Connecticut Agricultural Experiment Station has shown that small French (*Tagetes patula* L.) and large African (*T. erecta* L.) marigolds suppress meadow, or root lesion, nematodes for up to 3 years and one or more other nematodes for 1 or more years. Marigolds are effective when rotated, or grown in the entire infested area for a full season. Interplanting is not as effective, and can reduce crop yields, but some beneficial nematicide effects may be seen the following year. To reduce competetition, interplant marigolds 2 or more weeks after other plants. Two theories exist on how marigolds work: (1) they produce a chemical from their roots that kills nematodes, and (2) they do not serve as a host to nematodes and, in the absence of a host, the nematode population dies.

ALLY	TARGET	Target Pest and Benefits	How/Where
Marjoram	Vegetables	improves flavor	uncertain

ALLY	TARGET	Target Pest and Benefits	How/Where
Mint	*Brassicas*	Cabbage Looper, Moth, and Worm	uncertain
	Brassicas	improves growth & flavor	uncertain
	Broccoli	Ants	uncertain
	Peas	improves growth & flavor	uncertain
	Squash	Squash Bug	uncertain
	Tomato	improves growth & flavor	uncertain
	Many vegetables	Whitefly	uncertain

ALLY	TARGET	Target Pest and Benefits	How/Where
Mirabilis (Four O'Clocks)		trap crop for Japanese beetles	uncertain

ALLY	TARGET	Target Pest and Benefits	How/Where
Mustard (white or black)	Many vegetables	Nematodes	uncertain

ALLY	TARGET	Target Pest and Benefits	How/Where
Nasturtium	Asparagus	Carrot Rust Fly	uncertain
	Beans	Mexican Bean Beetle	uncertain
	Brassicas	Aphid, Beetles	uncertain
	Brassicas	Cabbage Looper and Worm	uncertain
	Celery	Aphid	uncertain
	Cucumber	Aphid, Cucumber Beetles	uncertain
	Fruit trees	general protection (under tree)	uncertain
	Pepper	Green Peach Aphid	uncertain
	Potato	Colorado Potato Beetle	uncertain
	Radish	general protection	uncertain
	Squash	beetles, Squash Bug	uncertain
	Many Vegetables	Whitefly	uncertain

Note: Nasturtiums can get totally covered with aphids, so they must be used as a trap crop to be effective.

ALLY	TARGET	Target Pest and Benefits	How/Where
Onion family	Beet	insects	uncertain
	Brassicas	Cabbage Looper, Maggot Worm	uncertain
	Carrot	Carrot Rust Fly	CM, UK/Africa
	Potato	Colorado Potato Beetle	uncertain
	Swiss Chard	improves growth	uncertain
	Many Vegetables	Aphid	uncertain

ALLY	TARGET	Target Pest and Benefits	How/Where
Oregano	Beans	improves flavor & growth	uncertain
	Cucumber	deters pests	uncertain
	Squash	general pest protection	uncertain
Parsley	Asparagus	Asparagus Beetle, helps growth	uncertain
	Tomato	improves growth	uncertain
Peas	Carrot, Corn	improves growth & flavor by adding nutrients to the soil	uncertain
	Turnip	improves growth	uncertain
Pennyroyal	Various Vegetables	Carrot Rust Fly	uncertain
Phacelia sp.(herbs)	Apple	Aphid, San Jose Scale	PW, USSR
Pigweed (*Amaranthus* sp.)	Collards	Green Peach Aphid (*A.retroflexus*)	Pred, Ohio
	Corn	Fall Armyworm (*A.hybridus*)	Pred & PW,FL
	Corn, Onion, & Potato	brings nutrients to soil surface where available to plants	uncertain
Potato	Beans	Mexican Bean Beetle	uncertain
	Corn	repels insects	uncertain
	Eggplant	use as trap plant	uncertain
Radish	*Brassicas*	Cabbage Maggot	uncertain
	Cucumber	Striped Cucumber Beetle	uncertain
	Lettuce	improves growth	uncertain
	Squash	Squash Bug & Vine Borer (use radish as a trap crop)	uncertain
	Sweet Potato	Sweet Potato Weevil	uncertain
Ragweed	Collards	Flea Beetle	CM, NY
giant	Corn	Corn Borer	AH, Canada
normal	Peach tree	Oriental Fruit Moth	AW, VA
	Peach tree	Oriental Fruit Moth	*, temperate
Red Sprangletop (*Leptochioa filliformis*)	Beans	Leafhopper	CM, tropics
Rosemary	*Brassicas*	Cabbage Moth, repels insects	uncertain
	Carrot	Carrot Rust Fly, repels insects	uncertain
	Many Vegetables	Slug, Snail	uncertain
Rue	Cucumber	Cucumber Beetles	uncertain
	Rose	Japanese Beetle	uncertain
	Raspberry	Japanese Beetle	uncertain
	Many Vegetables	Flea Beetle	uncertain

ALLY	TARGET	Target Pest and Benefits	How/Where
Rye, cover crop	Fruit trees	Aphid	Pred
	Fruit trees	Leafhopper	uncertain
	Many Vegetables	Nematode (turn cover crop under)	TR
	Soybean	Seedcorn Maggot	PI, Ohio
Rye, mulch	Fruit trees	European Red Mite	Pred, MI
Sage	*Brassicas*	Cabbage Looper, Maggot, Moth & Worm	uncertain
	Carrot	Carrot Rust Fly, improves growth	uncertain
	Marjoram	improves growth	uncertain
	Strawberry	improves growth	uncertain
	Tomato	improves growth	uncertain
Savory, Summer	Beans	Mexican Bean Beetle, growth & flavor	uncertain
	Onion	improves growth & flavor	uncertain
	Sweet Potato	Sweet Potato Weevil	uncertain
Shepherd's Purse	*Brassicas*	Flea Beetle	CM, NY
	Corn	Black Cutworm	PW, IL
Smartweed	Peach tree	Oriental Fruit Moth	*, temperate
Sorghum, cov.crop mulch	Cow pea	Leaf Beetle	CM, temperate
	Fruit trees	European Red Mite	Pred, MI
Southern Wood	Cabbage	Cabbage Moth	uncertain
Soybeans	Corn	Corn Earworm	Pred, FL
	Corn	Cinch Bug	uncertain
Strawberry	Peach tree	Oriental Fruit Moth	Pred,temp.
	Spinach	improves growth	uncertain
Sudan Grass	Grape	Williamette Mite	Pred, CA

Caution: While this grass may help with this mite, one Arkansas grower noted that Johnson grass killed his vines. So you may want to make sure the grass is not allowed close to the vines.

ALLY	TARGET	Target Pest and Benefits	How/Where
Sweet Potato	Corn	Leaf Beetle	PW, Tropics
Tansy	*Brassicas*	Cabbageworm, Cutworm (NB: some evidence tansy increases Cabbageworms)	uncertain
	Cucumber	Ants, Cucumber Beetles, Squash Bug	uncertain
	Fruit Trees	Ants, Aphid, Japanese Beetle	uncertain
	Potato	Colorado Potato Beetle	uncertain
	Raspberry	Ants, Japanese Beetle	uncertain
	Squash	Squash Bug (NB: squash plants may be smaller)	uncertain
	Sweet Potato	Sweet Potato Weevil	uncertain
	All Vegetables	Flea Beetle, Japanese Beetle	uncertain

ALLY	TARGET	Target Pest and Benefits	How/Where
Thyme	*Brassicas*	Cabbage Looper & Worm, insects (NB: may lower cabbage yields)	uncertain
	Strawberry	worms	uncertain
	Many Vegetables	Whitefly (NB: in beans may cause higher Whitefly population)	uncertain
Tomato	Asparagus	Asparagus Beetle	uncertain
	Brassicas	Imported Cabbage Butterfly	uncertain
	Cabbage	Diamondback Moth	*, tropics
	Collards	Flea Beetle	CM, NY
Turnip	Peas	improves growth	uncertain
Vetch	Fruit Trees	Aphid	uncertain
Weedy Ground Cover	Apple	Tent Caterpillars	PW, Canada
	Apple	Codling Moth	PW, Canada
	Bruss.Sprouts	Cabbage Butterfly & Worm	Pred, England
	Collards	Flea Beetle	VM, NY
	Collards	Cabbage Aphid	PW, CA
	Mung Bean	Beanfly	PI, Temperate
	Walnut	Walnut Aphid	AW, CA
Wheat, cover crop	Soybean	Soybean pests	Pred, VA
	Many Vegetables	Nematode	uncertain
Wheat, mulch	Fruit Trees	European Spider Mite	Pred, MI
Wildflowers	Fruit Trees	attracts beneficial insects	uncertain
Wormseed mustard	*Brassicas*	Flea Beetle	CM, NY
Wormwood	*Brassicas*	Cabbage Maggot	uncertain
	Fruit Trees	Codling Moth	uncertain
	Many Vegetables	Mice, Whitefly	uncertain
(pulverized)	Carrot	Carrot Rust Fly	uncertain

NOTES:

References & Resources

ANNOTATED BIBLIOGRAPHY

Magazines

American Vegetable Grower. Meister Publishing Co., 37841 Euclid Avenue, Willoughby, OH, 44094.
  A monthly magazine covering new trends in commercial growing. One section covers greenhouse production.

Fine Gardening. Taunton Press, Inc., Newtown, CT, 06470.
  A relatively new bimonthly magazine that stands out as a star. This is a collector's magazine to be savored, like all other Taunton Press publications. At least one or two articles per issue on edibles (vegetables, fruits, or herbs) are balanced with articles on landscaping, ornamentals, insects, diseases, and gardening methods. These are among the best researched and informative articles in popular journals. The photographs are superb.

Harrowsmith Country Living. Camden House Publishing, Inc., Ferry Road, Charlotte, VT, 05445.
  A bimonthly magazine of Canadian origin that covers country gardening, home building and current issues with a clear bent toward ecological responsibility. Good photography and excellent articles.

HortIdeas. Gregory and Patricia Y. Williams, Route 1, Box 302, Black Lick Road, Gravel Switch, KY, 40328.
  A great monthly newsletter that abstracts the best and latest gardening research from both popular and technical journals. An excellent way of keeping up on the latest advances, cultivars, tools, methods and much more.

Mother Earth News. Mother Earth News Partners, 105 Stoney Mountain Road, Hendersonville, NC, 28791.
  A bimonthly magazine that covers different aspects of country living, including one section on gardening. One of the oldest "homesteading" magazines, it has evolved greatly over the years from a "how-to," semi-technical magazine to a more slick, general interest periodical.

National Gardening. National Gardening Association, 180 Flynn Avenue, Burlington, VT, 05401.
  A monthly magazine that covers all aspects of gardening, and provides up-to-date information on NGA projects as well as how to participate in them. Good explanatory photographs accompany informative articles.

The New Farm, Magazine of Regenerative Agriculture. Regenerative Agriculture Association, 222 Main Street, Emmaus, PA, 18098.

Seven issues per year cover growing techniques and issues oriented primarily to the larger scale farmer, but which also may be of interest to the backyard gardener. Great for future-thinking growers.

Rodale's Organic Gardening. Rodale Press Inc., 33 East Minor Street, Emmaus, PA, 18049.

A monthly magazine covering all aspects of organic gardening as well as the results of gardening trials and experiments conducted by the Rodale Research Center. This has long been the most popular monthly, and with its new glossy and slick format it promises to draw in even larger readership. There is still at least one good article on food crops in each issue, balanced with others on ornamentals, machine tools, and methodologies.

Sunset: The Magazine of Western Living. Lane Publishing Co., Menlo Park, CA, 94025.

This hefty monthly features a regular section on Western gardening and landscaping, which includes the coastal areas eastward to Colorado and southward through the desert areas. Highly recommended for Western gardeners.

Books

GENERAL GARDENING AND VEGETABLE GROWING

Appelhof, Mary. *Worms Eat My Garbage: How to set up and maintain a worm composting system.* Kalamazoo, MI: Flower Press, 1982.

A small, very easy to read paperback. Appelhof tells you all you need to know about how to grow earthworms without much effort. Not as complete as Minnich's book, but most people don't need the detail that Minnich offers.

Ball, Jeff. *The Self-Sufficient Suburban Garden: A step-by-step planning and management guide to backyard food production.* Emmaus, PA: Rodale Press, 1983.

An excellent book for novice gardeners, enjoyable, practical, and informative.
Useful Charts: (1) How Much To Plant; (2) Seed-Starting Tips; (3) Planting Guide; (4) Interplanting Guide; (5) Companion Planting; (6) Succession Planting; (7) Growing Guide; (8) Food Storage Options; and more.

Ball, Jeff. *Jeff Ball's 60-Minute Garden: One hour a week is all it takes to garden successfully.* Emmaus, PA: Rodale Press, 1985:

One of our favorite books, not only because its goal of low-time gardening matches ours, but because it is so well written and fun to read. Practical, informative, and easy to follow. Diagrams of useful garden tools, such as a compost sifter, with shopping lists and instructions.
Useful Diagrams and Construction Plans: (1) Boxed Bed With PVC Foundations; (2) Tunnels; (3) Trellis and Orchard Fence; (4) Compost Bin and Sifter; (5) Seedling Box; (6) Garden Sink; (7) Birdhouse Design.

Bartholomew, Mel. *Square Foot Gardening.* Emmaus, PA: Rodale Press, 1981.

Another fun book, good for both novice and experienced gardeners, based on the PBS television series. The square foot method is an interesting, practical method of intensive gardening, in some ways more formulaic (and therefore easier) than French intensive. The back of the book contains cultural notes on vegetables and, of course, square foot spacing rules for each vegetable.

Best Ways To Improve Your Soil. Emmaus, PA: Rodale Press, 1987.
> A small, inexpensive booklet packed with information. Very useful.
> *Useful Charts:* (1) Soil Types; (2) Cover Crop Planting Guide; (3) Composting Materials; (4) Nutrient Profiles of Common Organic Amendments.

Bubel, Nancy. *The New Seed-Starters Handbook.* Emmaus, PA: Rodale Press, 1988.
> For the person who wants an in-depth discussion of how to get your plants off to a good start, Bubel covers everything from germinating to transplanting. Also one of the few books that tells you how to save your own seeds. The last third of the book is devoted to cultural briefs on how to start from seed vegetables, fruits, herbs, and--more unusual--flowers, wildflowers, trees, and shrubs.
> *Useful Charts:* (1) Soil Deficiency: Symptoms & Treatment. Many more.

Creasy, Rosalind. *The Complete Book of Edible Landscaping: home landscaping with food-bearing plants and resource-saving techniques.* San Francisco, CA: Sierra Club, 1982.
> An excellent book on how to make your garden an attractive landscape, and your landscape into an attractive garden. Useful to all gardeners. Major principles of edible landscaping are covered in this timely book. Creay also covers gardening techniques, culture, hygiene, diseases and insects.
> *Useful Charts:* The last half of the book is a very useful "encyclopedia" of fruit, vegetable, herb, and nut culture. Includes varieties and sources.

Creasy, Rosalind. *Cooking From The Garden.* San Francisco, CA: Sierra Club, 1988.
> A true gem that is filled with valuable growing information and visual beauty. Creasy creates and explores specialty gardens of different nationalities, traditions, colors and flavors. In the process she shares a wealth of information on varieties known for such things as color, flavor, and heirloom history. Mouth-watering recipes accompany every section, including such wonders as violet vichyssoise and lavender ice cream. To top it off, she includes an encyclopedia at the end on how to grow each type of vegetable.

Encyclopedia of Organic Gardening, New Revised Edition. Emmaus, PA: Rodale Press, 1978.
> A good general reference book to supplement or be supplemented by others, this covers to a greater or lesser degree every plant one might be curious about. It also covers general topics such as fertilizer, fruit cultivation, landscaping, and much more.
> *Useful Charts:* (1) Planting Dates (gives dates based on average LFD); (2) Shrubs: Recommended Shrubs For The Home Grounds; (3) Straw: Mineral Value of Straws; (4) Trace Elements: Chart On Signs Of Deficiency and Accumulator Plants; (5) Wild Plants, Edible; more.

Fukuoka, Masanobu. *The One-Straw Revolution: An Introduction to Natural Farming.* Emmaus, PA: Rodale Press, 1978.
> Now considered a classic on the subject, this book discusses the importance and methods of no-till cultivation. Some of the methods may not be generally applicable, however, because they're designed for a mild Japanese climate.

Gardening: The Complete Guide to Growing America's Favorite Fruits and Vegetables. National Gardening Association, Addison-Wesley Publishing Company, Inc., 1986.
> For novice and advanced gardeners, this book discusses how to plan and prepare the garden site. It also provides cultural information for individual vegetables and fruits.

Hamilton, Geoff. *The Organic Garden Book: The Complete Guide To Growing Flowers, Fruit and Vegetables Naturally.* New York: Crown Publishers, 1987.
> Excellent color photographs, some of the best we've seen, and diagrams, are what make this

book special. The photographs cover everything from different soil types to how to harvest different vegetables. This book also contains excellent pictures of the different methods of training fruit trees. It also provides good cultural notes.

Useful Charts: At the back of the book, a good list of gardening activities is broken down by season and type of garden (ornamental, fruit, vegetable, greenhouse).

Hirshberg, Gary and Tracy Calvan, editors. *Gardening For All Seasons: A Complete Guide to Producing Food at Home 12 Months of the Year.* Andover, MA: The New Alchemy Institute, Brick House Publishing, 1983.

We've found this book useful for its charts, tables, and cultural notes on vegetables.

Useful Charts: (1) Varieties Of Vegetables For Greenhouse Growing; (2) pH Preference Of Vegetables, Fruits, Flowers and Grains; (3) Disease-Resistant Plant Varieties; (4) Insect-Resistant Plant Varieties; (5) Insect-Repellant Plant Varieties; (6) Companion Planting Guide; (7) Planting Table; (8) Chart Of Nitrogen, Phosphorous and Potassium Components Of Organic Materials; (9) Plants That Attract Birds.

Hunt, Marjorie B. and Brenda Bortz. *High-Yield Gardening: How to get more from your garden space and more from your gardening season.* Emmaus, PA: Rodale Press, 1986.

Chock full of useful suggestions for increasing your garden yield, this is a good general book for both beginning and experienced gardeners.

Useful Charts: (1) Cultural Notes, presented alphabetically by plant; (2) Soil Type; (3) Cover Crop Planting Guide, (4) Composting Materials; (5) Nutrient Profiles of Common Organic Materials; (5) Survey of Raised Beds; (6) High-Yield Low-Space Versions of Popular Vegetables; (7) High-Yielding Varieties for Vertical Growing; (8) Garden Time-Savers; (9) Critical Times For Watering; (10) Succession planting (11) Traditional Companions; (12) Space-Efficient Root Patterns; more.

Jeavons, John. *How To Grow More Vegetables.* Berkeley, CA: Ten Speed Press, 1982.

An excellent discussion on the importance and methods of French intensive raised-bed gardening. Jeavons is well known for advocating high-yield, intensive techniques. Here's a good, detailed description on how to double-dig.

Useful Charts: (1) 4-Year Garden Plan; (2) Companion Plants; (3) Growing Data on Vegetables, Fruits, Grains; (4) Fertilizers and Their Components.

Knott, James Edward. Lorenz, Oscar A. and Donald N. Maynard, editors. *Knott's Handbook for Vegetable Growers, 3rd Edition.* New York: John Wiley & Sons, 1988.

A professional's resource book and authority on all aspects of vegetable growing. Just when you thought you had a handle on the issues involved in vegetable growing, this book can be both a humbling and stimulating experience. Covers everything from hydroponic solutions to irrigation rates. A small ringbinder, it's easy to carry around and fun to browse through for both trivia and essentials. Since this book's purpose is useful charts, we can list only a few of the ones that might be appropriate for the non-professional. Page numbers for the charts are given because they're a bit hard to find.

Useful Charts: (1) Composition of Fresh Raw Vegetables, 23-28; (2) Diagnosis and Correction of Transplant Disorders, 46; (3) Soil Temperature Conditions for Germination, 71; (4) Days Required for Seedling Emergence, 74; (5) Composition of Organic Material, 101; (6) A Key to Nutrient-Deficiency Symptoms, 162; (7) Practical Soil Moisture Interpretation Chart, 170; (8) Disease Control for Vegetables, 257; (9) Insect Control for Vegetables, 272.

Kourik, Robert. *Designing and Maintaining Your Edible Landscape Naturally.* Santa Rosa, CA: Metamorphic Press, 1986.

For the novice and experienced gardener, this is a must reading on edible landscaping, the gardening wave of the future. Unusual, informative, and fun, Kourik's book discusses everything from aesthetics to specific gardening techniques--how to plan gardens, the pros and cons of tillage, how to prune, and much more.

Useful Charts: (1) Companion Planting Research Summaries; (2) Intercropping for Pest Reduction; (3) Green Manure Plants; (4) Dynamic Accumulators; (5) Seven-Step Rotation for Fertility; (6) Multi-purpose Edibles; (7) Soil Indicators (plants); (8) Ripening Dates for Fruit & Nut Varieties; (9) Series of Charts on Fruit Tree Rootstocks; (10) Disease-Resistant Trees; and more.

Larkcom, Joy. *The Salad Garden.* New York: Viking Press, 1984.
A fun book for those interested in salad greens and cooking.

Make Compost in 14 Days. Emmaus, PA: Rodale Press, 1982.
A small, inexpensive booklet with interesting ideas on different methods of composting.

Minnich, Jerry. *The Earthworm Book.* Emmaus, PA: Rodale Press, 1977.
The best book we've found on the subject, this covers everything you might want or need to know about earthworm cultivation. It explains the important benefits of earthworms in your garden and how to grow them easily on a small scale.

Organic Gardening's Soil First Aid Manual. Emmaus, PA: Rodale Press, 1982.
A small paperback, this is a useful collection of short articles by different people on ways to improve your soil. Interesting and good background material.

Poincelot, Raymond P. *No-Dig, No-Weed Gardening.* Emmaus, PA: Rodale Press, 1986.
An excellent discussion of the benefits of not tilling the soil and how to maintain such a garden. Useful cultural notes on vegetables and flowers.

Raymond, Dick. *Down-to-Earth Vegetable Gardening Know-How.* Charlotte, VT: Garden Way Publishing, 1975.
A book full of useful charts and graphs. Page numbers for the charts are given because of the potential difficulty of locating them.
Useful Charts: (1) Green Manures, 90; (2) Plant Diseases, 68; (3) Herbs, 97; (4) Garden Planning Charts and Plans; (5) Planning Chart, including Amounts To Plant, 150.

Raymond, Dick. *Joy of Gardening.* Troy, NY: Garden Way Inc., 1982.
A good book on garden preparation, maintenance, and culture of vegetables and fruits. Good photographs. Good discussion of cover crops.
Useful Charts: (1) Vegetable Planting Guide, useful to us especially for planning amounts to plant; (2) Detailed First Frost Date In The Fall Map of the U.S.; (3) Mulching Guide, comparing advantages and disadvantages of different mulch types.

Reilly, Ann. *Park's Success With Seeds.* Greenwood, S.C.: Park Seed Co., 1978.
A guide to how to start most species from seed.

Rogers, Marc. *Garden Way Publishing's Growing & Saving Vegetable Seeds.* Pownal, VT: Garden Way Publishing, 1978.
A small paperback, this is an easy guidebook to saving seeds. It presents general principles and specifics for each vegetable.

Sunset Books and *Sunset* magazine editors. *Sunset Western Garden Book.* Menlo Park, CA: Lane Publishing, 1988.

Often considered the Western gardener's bible, this book covers all growing areas West of the Rockies. Among other goodies it includes a plant selection guide for different growing conditions, and a huge encyclopedia of over 6,000 plants. A great book.

Thomson, Bob. *The New Victory Garden.* Little, Brown & Co, 1987.
Based on the popular PBS television series, this book emphasizes how to achieve the maximum yield per unit of effort. Perhaps the most unique aspect of this book is its monthly guide on what to do for each vegetable. There is also a short but good section on fruit cultivation, as well as interesting chapters on cider-making and bird feeders.
Useful Charts: Sample page of a gardening journal.

Whealy, Kent, ed. *The Garden Seed Inventory.* Decorah, Iowa: Seed Saver Publications, 1988.
As the Director of the Seed Savers Exchange, Whealy compiles a complete listing of all (over 5,000) non-hybrid varieties offered by over 200 seed companies. Each entry describes the variety, provides synonyms, provides a range of maturity dates and lists all known sources. Known by some as the seed savers bible.

Other books with information on General Gardening and Vegetable Growing:
Smith, see under Greenhouses.
Wolfe, see under Greenhouses.
Foster, Catharine O. *Building Healthy Gardens: A safe & natural approach,* Revised edition. Troy, NY: Garden Way Inc., 1989.

FRUITS AND NUTS

Best Methods For Growing Fruits and Berries. Emmaus, PA: Rodale Press, 1981.
A small booklet, this provides good discussions of individual fruit cultures.

Bilderback, Diane E. and Dorothy Hinshaw Patent. *Backyard Fruits & Berries: How To Grow Them Better Than Ever.* Emmaus, PA: Rodale Press, 1984.
An goood, very thorough book on fruit culture. Fun and informative.

Hill, Lewis. *Fruits and Berries For The Home Garden.* Pownal, VT: Garden Way Publishing, Storey Communications, Inc., 1977.
A good book on all aspects of fruit culture. Both entertaining and informative, Lewis goes the extra mile to explain the why's and hows behind so many orchard practices.

Hill, Lewis. *Pruning Simplified, Updated Edition.* Pownal, VT: Garden Way Publishing, Storey Communications, Inc., 1986.
A great guide on how to prune everything from evergreens and ornamentals to fruit and nut trees. Useful illustrations of before-and-after proper pruning.

James, Jr., Theodore. *How To Grow Fruit, Berries, and Nuts in the Midwest and East.* Tuscon, AZ: HP Books, Fisher Publishing Co, 1983. (Also available for other regions.)
A very good thin paperback on fruit and nut culture, with excellent pictures on planting, pruning, and grafting.

Jaynes, Richard A., editor. *Nut Tree Culture in North America.* Hamden, CT: Northern Nut Growers Association, Inc., 1979.
The only current standard reference on nut culture, this book is essential for anyone interested in growing nut trees. Jaynes has the experts cover all aspects of growing nut trees in detail.

Page, Stephen and Joe Smillie. *The Orchard Almanac: A Spraysaver Guide*. Rockport, ME: Spraysaver Publications, 1986.

> An excellent small handbook on fruit culture with a special emphasis on how to control insects and diseases organically. An excellent presentation of what to do on a monthly basis.
> *Useful Charts:* Good charts at the end of the book on rootstocks, fertilizers, and sprays.

Southwick, Lawrence. *Planting Your Dwarf Fruit Orchard*. Pownal, VT: Garden Way Publishing, 1979.

> A good introduction to planting and pruning fruit trees, this booklet also has a nice glossary of pruning terms.

Other books with information on Fruits, Nuts, and Pruning:

> Baumgardt, John Philip. *How To Prune Almost Everything*.
> New York: Quill, 1982.
> Creasy, see under Landscaping.
> *Encyclopedia of Organic Gardening, see under General.*
> Hamilton, see under General.
> Kourik, see under General. Note his charts on rootstocks, disease resistant fruits, ripening dates, and excellent section on pruning.
> Thomson, see under General.

HERBS

Garland, Sarah. *The Herb Garden*. New York: Penguin Books, 1985.

> Comprehensive coverage of how to grow fragrant herbs for culinary and other purposes.

Hutson, Lucinda. *The Herb Garden Cookbook*. Texas Monthly Press, 1987.

> A good book on how to grow and how to cook with herbs, including many recipes. Particularly useful information for Southwestern gardeners.

Kowalchik, Claire & William H. Hylton, editors. *Rodale's Illustrated Encyclopedia of Herbs*. Emmaus, PA: Rodale Press, 1987.

> Hands down the best and most complete book we've seen on herbs, covering everything from herb culture to how to use herbs for healing.
> *Useful Charts:* (1) Companion Planting; (2) A Sampling of Dangerous Herbs; (3) A Sampling of Herbs for Dyeing; (4) Herb Pests; (5) Herb Diseases; and more.

Shaudys, Phyllis V. *The Pleasure of herbs: A Month-by-Month Guide to Growing, Using and Enjoying Herbs*. Charlotte, VT: Garden Way Publishing, 1986.

> Each month presents a new set of fun projects, from seed-starting, herbal gifts, to creating culinary herbal delights. Cultural information, gardening techniques, and multiple ideas on how to store and use herbs, all are covered. Also included is a brief encyclopedia of herbs.

Other books with information on Herbs:

> Bubel, see under General.
> Creasy, see under Landscaping.
> *Encyclopedia of Organic Gardening, see under General.*

INSECTS AND DISEASES

Ball, Jeff. Rodale's Garden Problem Solver: Vegetables, Fruits, Herbs. Emmaus, PA: Rodale Press, 1988.
> A good book specifically on organic disease and insect control for major plants. Very easy to use. You can problem solve by plants, or by the specific insect or disease.

Carr, Anna, compiler. *A Gardener's Guide to Common Insect Pests.* Emmaus, PA: Rodale Press, reprint 1989.
> An excellent small, inexpensive booklet with great color photos of insects, and short descriptions of their habits and natural controls.

Cravens, Richard H and the Editors of Time-Life Books. *The Time-Life Encyclopedia of Gardening: Pests and Diseases.* Alexandria, VA: Time-Life Books, 1977.
> A good background book on pests, identification, habits, and regions affected. Nice illustrations.

Healthy Garden Handbook. Mother Earth News. New York: Simon & Schuster, Inc., 1989.
> A good guide on organic insect and disease control, this book discusses general methods of maintaining a healthy garden, and specific pest remedies. It offers excellent color photographs of plant allies, diseases, and all developmental phases of pests. A garden remedy section troubleshoots problems you may encounter with each vegetable.
> *Useful Charts:* (1) Insect peak emergence times.

MacNab, A.A., and A.F. Sherf, and J.K. Springer. *Identifying Diseases of Vegetables.* University Park, PA: Pennsylvania State University, 1983.
> Over 200 top notch photographs of the most common diseases in vegetables. Excellent for field identification of vegetable crop diseases.

Shepherd's Purse Organic Pest Control Handbook. Summertown, TN: Pest Publications, Book Publishing Co., 1987.
> A small useful booklet with good color drawings of insects, and notes on their biological, cultural, and acute control. Suppliers of beneficial insects are listed.

Sherf, Arden F. and Alan A. MacNab. *Vegetable Diseases and Their Control, 2nd Edition.* New York: John Wiley & Sons,, Inc., 1986.
> A professional's textbook on vegetable diseases. Each disease is covered by a detailed description of symptoms, cause, disease cycle, and control. Controls are not limited to organic methods.

Smith, Miranda and Ana Carr, *Rodale's Garden Insect, Disease & Weed Identification Guide.* Emmaus, Pa: Rodale Press, 1988.
> An excellent field guide to insects and diseases, with 97 photos for identification.

Steiner, M.Y. and D.P. Elliot. *Biological Pest Management For Interior Plantscapes, 2nd Edition.* Vegreville, AB. Alberta Environmental Centre, 1987.
> A excellent short booklet on major greenhouse insects and their cultural, biological and chemical control. Describes for each insect the damage, occurrence, appearance, and life history.
> *Useful Charts:* (1) Minor Pest Problems and Their Control; (2) Summary of Primary Predators and Parasites of Major Plant Pests; (3) Reported Toxicity of Common Greenhouse Pesticides to Various Biological Control Agents; (4) Suppliers of Biological Control Agents.

Westcott, Cynthia. *The Gardener's Bug Book.* Garden City, NJ: Doubleday & Co., Inc., 1964.

An incredibly thorough listing and description of all insects, with their latin names and common names, habits, regions found in, and life cycles. The remedies listed, however, are outdated and sometimes even prohibited. Great for helping identification.

Yepsen, Jr., Roger, editor. *The Encyclopedia of Natural Insect & Disease Control.* Emmaus, PA: Rodale Press, 1984.
An excellent reference covering major insects and diseases. Excellent color photos. Page numbers for the charts are given because of the potential difficulty of locating them.
Useful Charts: (1) Insect & Disease Resistant Vegetable Varieties, 346; (2) Insect Emergence Times, divided into 16 zones, 399.

Other books with information on Pest and Disease Control:
Encyclopedia of Organic Gardening, see under General.
Hirshberg, see under General.
Kourik, see under General.
Lorenz, see under General.
Raymond, both books, see under General.

HARVEST AND STORAGE

Bubel, Mike and Nancy. *Root Cellaring, The Simple No-Processing Way to Store Fruits and Vegetables.* Emmaus, PA: Rodale Press, 1979.
The only reference book we know on root cellars that is thoroughly researched by investigating what has and hasn't worked over the years. Many other books are pure theory; this one isn't. Many useful diagrams.

Organic Gardening Harvest Book. Emmaus, PA: Rodale Press, 1975.
A small, inexpensive booklet with good information on different methods of harvesting vegetables and fruits.
Useful Charts: (1) Guide for Drying Vegetables (Times and Temps); (2) Selection and Preparation of Vegetables for Freezing.

Stoner, Carol Hupping, editor. *Stocking Up: How To Preserve the Foods You Grow, Naturally.* Emmaus, PA: Rodale Press, 1977 and 1988.
An excellent guide to freezing, canning, drying, and other methods of saving the harvest.
Useful Charts: Timetable for Processing Fruits, Tomatoes, and Pickled Vegetables in Boiling-Water Bath.

GREENHOUSES

Ball, Vic, ed. *Ball Red Book: Greenhouse Growing, 14th edition.* Reston, VA: Prentice Hall, Reston Publishing Co., 1985.
A reference book on greenhouse structures, tools, methods, insect control, mechanization, and computerization. Half the book is devoted to greenhouse culture of flowers, shrubs, and a few vegetables. Essential for all commercial greenhouse growers.

Smith, Miranda. *Greenhouse Gardening.* Emmaus, PA: Rodale Press, 1985.
This book covers everything from greenhouse design, soils, fertilizers, insects and diseases, to vegetable varieties.

Wolfe, Delores. *Growing Food In Solar Greenhouses: A month by month guide to raising vegetables, fruits and herbs under glass.* Garden City, NJ: Doubleday & Company, Inc., 1981.
> The monthly schedule covers such things as micro-climates, raising animals in the greenhouse, container growing, propagation, diseases and insects. Fun and informative.

Other books on greenhouses:
> See Hamilton, under General.
> See Hirshberg, under General.
> See Steiner and Elliot, under Insects and Diseases.

LANDSCAPING

Allen, Oliver E. *Gardening with the New Small Plants: A Complete Guide to Growing Dwarf and Miniature Shrubs, Flowers, Trees and Vegetables.* Boston, MA: Houghton Mifflin Co, 1987.
> An excellent introduction to and discussion of small plants--whether in or out of rock gardens. The author suggests specific species and varieties of shrubs, flowers, trees and vegetables, as well as sources of availability.

Leighton, Phebe and Calvin Simonds. *The New American Landscape Gardener: A Guide to Beautiful Backyards and Sensational Surroundings.* Emmaus, PA: Rodale Press, 1987.
> The many charts of both edible and non-edible plants for different scapes makes this a helpful aide in landscaping. General design principles and design flaws are discussed in-depth. Very readable. *Useful Charts:* (1) Plants For Meadows; (2) Plants For a Sunspot; (3) Plants For a Rock Garden; (4) Plants For a Winter Landscape; (5) Plants For a Water Garden; (6) Plants For a Wildlife Garden; (7) Plants For a Woodswalk

Smyser, Carol A. *Nature's Design: A Practical Guide To Natural Landscaping.* Emmaus, PA: Rodale Press, 1982.
> How to make a contour map, how to assess the impact of water on your property, how to analyze your soil, climate conditions, and natural plant and wildlife habitats. A very interesting and thought-provoking book, bursting with useful diagrams and pictures. A large section of the book is devoted to landscape construction, including how to find native plants, and propagation techniques.
> *Useful Charts:* (1) How To Evaluate Your Landscape in Terms of Energy Efficiency and Environmental Impact; (2) Plant Selection Charts for 10 Ecoregions, listing the appropriate trees, shrubs and forbs with their habitat, growth characteristics and any notable qualities; (3) Functional Uses of Plants; (4) Aesthetic Uses of Plants; (5) Landscape Pest Primer; (6) Plant Associations That Attract Wildlife, divided into regions; (7) Build A Better Birdhouse, includes all pertinent information that might be needed for 12 different birds; (8) A Gardener's Avian Friends, covering pests they eat and plants for food and shelter, broken down by region.

Wirth, Thomas. *Victory Garden Landscape Guide.* Little, Brown & Co., 1984.
> A fun and useful month-by-month guide on landscaping. Wirth offers interesting and useful ideas and charts on everything concerning landscaping, from terraces and patios to fruit trees. He divides each month into 4 categories: (1) Landscaping Opportunities, (2) Plants For a Purpose, (3) Materials & Construction, (4) Plants By Design.

Other Books With Information on Landscaping:
> *Creasy, see under General.*
> *Encyclopedia of Organic Gardening,* see under General.
> Kourik, see under General.

SEED COMPANIES AND NURSERIES

Abundant Life Seed Foundation
P.O. Box 772
Port Townsend, WA 98368
(206) 385-5660
  Good selection of vegetables, small grains, herbs and flowers. Organic, untreated, open-pollinated seeds.

Adams County Nursery
P.O. Box 108
Aspers, PA 17304
(717) 677-8105
  A large selection of fruit varieties for commercial and home growers, on a number of different rootstocks.

Bountiful Gardens
Ecology Action
19550 Walker Road
Willits, CA 95490
  A non-profit organization that sponsors educational programs, and offers a good selection of untreated, open-pollinated seeds for vegetables, herbs, flowers, green manures, and grains.

W. Atlee Burpee Seed Co.
Warminster, PA 18974
(215) 674-9633 Fax: (215) 674-4170
  Conventional vegetables, fruits, herbs and flowers.

Casa Yerba
3459 Days Creek Rd.
Days Creek, OR 97429
  Organically grown herb plants and seeds.

Companion Plants
7247 N. Coolville Ridge Rd
Athens, OH 45701
(614) 592-4643
  $2 for catalog. Huge selection of herbs for culinary, medicinal and other purposes.

The Cook's Garden
P.O. Box 65
Londonberry, VT 05148
(802) 824-3400
Fax: (802) 824-3027
  Large selection of vegetable seeds for outdoor, coldframe and greenhouse culture, especially lettuce. Untreated, organic, open-pollinated seeds.

Cumberland Valley Nurseries, Inc.
P.O. Box 471
McMinnville, TN 37110
(800) 492-0022
Local (615) 668-4153
  Fruit trees, with an unusually extensive collection of peach trees.

Dabney Herbs
P.O. Box 22061
Louisville, KY 40222
(502) 893-5198
  $2 for catalog. Herbs for all purposes.

Earl May Seed &
Nursery Co.
208 No. Elm Street
Shenandoah, IA 51603
(800) 831-4193
  Vegetables, flowers, shrubs and fruit trees. Some open-pollinated.

Henry Field's Seed & Nursery Co.
Shenandoah, IA 51602
(605) 665-9391
  Conventional vegetables and fruits.

Fowler Nurseries, Inc.
525 Fowler Rd.
Newcastle, CA 95658
(916) 645-8191
  $2 for catalog. Selection of fruits, especially for West coast climate.

Fox Hill Farm
444 W. Michigan Ave, Box 9
Parma, MI 49269-0009
(517) 531-3179
  Good selection of herbs.

Garden City Seeds
1324 Red Crow Road
Victor, MT 59875-9713
(406) 961-4837
  Good selection of northern vegetable varieties. Open-pollinated seeds. Some are certified organic.

Grimo Nut Nursery
R.R. 3, Lakeshore Rd.
Niagara-on-the-Lake,
Ontario L0S 1J0
(416) 935-9773
  $1 for catalog. One of the best nut nurseries around for high quality seedlings.

Gurney's Seed &
Nursery Co.
Yankton, SD 57079
(605) 665-1930
  Good selection of vegetables.

Harris Seeds
60 Saginaw Drive
P.O. Box 22960
Rochester, NY 14692-2260
Orders: (800) 544-7938
Other: (716) 442-0410
  Good vegetable selection.

Hartmann's Plantation, Inc.
Box E, 310 60th Street
Grand Junction, MI 49056
(616) 253-4281
Fax: 616-253-4457
  The largest blueberry nursery in the nation. Huge selection.

High Altitude Gardens
P.O. Box 4619
Ketchum, ID 83340
(800) 874-7333
  A nice selection of seeds for short season vegetables, wildflowers, grasses, and herbs -- which all grow at 6,000 feet! Many open-pollinated varieties.

Hilltop Orchards & Nurseries, Inc.
Box 578, C.R. 681
Hartford, MI 49057
(800) 253-2911
Michigan: (800) 632-2951
  Retail and wholesale. Good selection of fruits. High quality. Minimum order of 10 fruit trees.

Horticultural Products
Box 810082
Dallas, TX 75381-0082
  Huge selection of peppers.

Indian Walnut Products, Inc.
1000 North 500 West
West Lafayette, IN 47906
(800) 999-0727
The only source of the patented "Purdue Number 1" seedling.

Johnny's Selected Seeds
Foss Hill Road
Albion, ME 04910
(207) 437-9294
Fax: (207) 437-2165
Good selection of vegetables, especially carrots and greenhouse varieties. Most are untreated seeds.

J.W. Jung Seed Co.
Randolph, WI 53956
(414) 326-4100
Selection of vegetables, flowers, herbs, berries and fruit trees.

Kelly Bros. Nurseries, Inc.
P.O. Box 800
Dansville, NY 14437-0800
(800) 325-4180
Selection of fruits, berries, and ornamentals.

Krohne Plant Farms
Rt.6, Box 586
Dowagiac, Michigan 49047
(616) 424-5423
Large selection of strawberries, and some asparagus.

Henry Leuthardt Nurseries
Montauk Highway, Box 666
East Moriches,
Long Island, NY 11940
(516) 878-1387
Nice selection of fruits. Noted for its selection of espalier trees.

Miller Nurseries, Inc.
West Lake Road
Canandaigua, NY 14424
(800) 462-9601
Fruit and nut tree and berry selection.

Native Seeds/SEARCH
2509 N.Campbell Ave, #325
Tuscon, Arizona 85719
Public Ed. Office Phone (No Orders) 602-327-9123
A non-profit seed conservation organization. They are working to preserve the traditional crops and their wild relatives of the U.S. Southwest and Northwest Mexico. Grains, vegetables, herbs, fruit, cotton, tobacco, books, food, baskets and dye for wool.

NYFT -- N.Y. Fruit Testing Cooperative Association, Inc.
Box 462
Geneva, NY 14456
(315) 787-2205
$5 for catalog and membership. Selection of fruit trees and berries, with a number of experimental new crosses for trial gardeners.

Nichols Garden Nursery & Rare Seeds
1190 North Pacific Highway
Albany, OR 97321
(503) 928-9280
Fax: (503) 967-8406
Good selection of vegetables and herbs, often rare and unusual.

Nolin River Nut Tree Nursery
797 Port Wooden Road
Upton, KY 42784
(502) 369-8551
One of the few nut tree nurseries. Offers specific varieties.

Northwoods Nursery
28696 S. Cramer Road
Molalla, OR 97038
(503) 651-3737
Fruits and fruit trees.

Nourse Farms, Inc.
Box 485, RFD
South Deerfield, MA 01373
(413) 665-2658
Fax: (413) 665-7888
Good selections of strawberries, raspberries and asparagus. Most everything propagated by tissue culture.

Park Seed Co.
Cokesbury Road
Greenwood, SC 29647-0001
(803) 223-7333
Vegetables, especially hybrids, flowers, shrubs and ornamentals.

Plants of the Southwest
930 Baca Street
Santa Fe, NM 87501
(505) 983-1548
Good selection of plants native to the Southwest, and for Western mountains and high plains.

Raintree Nursery
391 Butts Rd.
Morton, WA 98356
(206) 496-6400
Good selection of fruit trees and berries for the Northwest. An informative catalog.

Rayner Bros., Inc.
Box 1617
Salisbury, MD 21801
(301) 742-1594
Huge selection of strawberries.

Redwood City Seed
P.O. Box 361
Redwood City, CA 94064
(415) 325-7333
$1 for catalog. Large selection of unusual varieties, especially from the Orient, Mexico and Europe.

Richters Herb Catalogue
Goodwood, Ontario
Canada L0C 1A0
(416) 640-6677 Fax: (416) 640-6641
Cadillac catalog of herbs for all purposes.

Rocky Meadow Orchard & Nursery
Rt.2 Box 2104
New Salisbury, IN 47161
(812) 347-2213
Nice selection of fruit trees on various rootstocks.

Saginaw Valley Nut Nursery
8285 Dixie Highway, Rte #3
Birch Run, MI 48415
One of the few nut tree nurseries. Offers specific varieties.

Sandy Mush Herb Nursery
Rt.2 Surret Cove Road
Leicester, NC 28748
(704) 683-2014
$4 for catalog. Large selection of culinary, ornamental, medicinal and other purpose herbs.

Seeds Blum
Idaho City Stage
Boise, ID 83706
$2 for catalog. Good selection of heirloom and open-pollinated seeds. A fun and informative catalog.

Shepherd's Garden Seeds
Shipping Office
30 Irene St.
Torrington, CT 06790
(203) 482-3638
  $2 for catalog. Gourmet vegetables, with some flowers and herbs.

Sonoma Antique Apple Nursery
4395 Westside Rd.
Healdsburg, CA 95448
(707) 433-6420
  $1 for catalog. Organically grown antique apple and other fruit trees. Espaliered trees.

South Carolina Foundation Seeds
Clemson University
Clemson, SC 29634
(803) 656-2520
  Sweet potato varieties.

Southern Exposure Seed Exchange
Box 158
North Garden, VA 22959
  $3 for catalog. Open-pollinated and heirloom vegetable varieties. Special varieties for solar greenhouses. Untreated seeds. Very informative catalog.

Southmeadow Fruit Gardens
Lakeside, MI 49116
(616) 469-2865
  $6 for catalog, 112 pp. illustrated, with a free listing update. Huge selection of antique and some newer fruit trees.

St. Lawrence Nurseries
R.D. 2
Potsdam, NY 13676
(315) 265-6739
  $1 for catalog. Very hardy berries and fruit trees for the North.

Stark Bro's Nurseries
Louisiana, MO 63353-0010
(800) 325-0611
Fax: (314) 754-5290
  Fruit trees, berries and nuts. Many common and some unusual varieties. Some varieties listed in this book are offered in their catalog for professional growers.

Stokes Seeds, Inc.
P.O. Box 548
Buffalo, NY 14240-0548
(416) 688-4300
  Good selection of vegetables and flowers. Good greenhouse varieties. Some open-pollinated and untreated seeds.

Territorial Seed Company
P.O. Box 27
Lorane, OR 97451
  Nice selection of vegetable seeds for the Northwest. Many open-pollinated varieties.

Thompson & Morgan Seedsmen
Box 1308
Jackson, NJ 08527
(201) 363-2225
Fax: (201) 363-9356
  Cadillac catalog of flowers and also some vegetables. Many unusual and interesting varieties.

Tomato Growers Supply Co.
Box 2237
Fort Meyers, FL 33902
(813) 768-1119
  Huge selection of tomatoes, most hybrids.

Van Well Nursery
Box 1339
Wenatchee, WA 98801
(509) 663-8189
Washington: (800) 572-1553
  Retail and wholesale selection of conventional fruit trees and berries.

William Dam Seeds Ltd.
Box 8400
Dundas, Ontario
Canada L9H 6M1
(416) 628-6641
  Good selection of vegetables, especially cold-tolerant varieties, and some cover crops and herbs. Untreated seeds.

Windmill Point Farm & Nursery
2103 Perrot Blvd.
N.D. Ile Perrot
Quebec, J7V5V6 Canada
(514) 453-9757
  $2.50 for catalog. Good selection of fruits on a variety of rootstocks and some specific nut varieties.

OTHER SUPPLIERS

Ag Life
1032 Hoffmaster Road
Knoxville, MD 21758
(301) 432-2836
  Botanical and mineral controls, fungicides, soaps, oils, fencing, pet products, more.

Ag Biochem Inc.
3 Fleetwood Ct.
Orinda, CA 94563
  Beneficial insects and other biocontrol agents.

A.M.Leonard, Inc.
6665 Spiker Road
Piqua, OH 45356
(800) 543-8955
  Extensive offering of garden tools, light and heavy.

Arbico Inc.
P.O. Box 42470-CRB
Tuscon, AZ 85738
(800) 767-2847
  Beneficial insects and organisms, traps, soil test kits, compost, fertilizers, more.

Biofac, Inc.
P.O. Box 87
Mathis, TX 78368
  Beneficial insects.

Clyde Robin Seed Co.
3670 Enterprise Avenue
Hayward, CA 94545
(415) 785-0425
  Pest control supplies, beneficial insects, and seed mixes to attract beneficials.

Diggers
P.O. Box 1551
Soquel, CA 95073
  20-gauge galvanized root guard, 3/4-inch mesh in 1 to 5 foot widths, and 15 gallon containers, both useful against gophers.

Evans Biocontrol, Inc.
895 Interlocken Pkwy
Unit A
Broomfield, CO 80020
  Environmentally safe controls for grasshoppers, including "Nolo Bait" which contains *Nosema locustae* to stop them feeding.

Gage Industries
Lake Oswego, OR 97035
Write for your nearest distributor of Dura pots, which are made from recycled plastic.

Gardens Alive!
Natural Gardening Research Center
Hwy 48, P.O. Box 149
Sunman, IN 47041
(812) 623-3800
Row covers, sprayers, beneficial insects, different Bt's, beneficial nematodes, botanical and mineral products, traps, composting and irrigation supplies, pet products, more.

Gardener's Supply
128 Intervale Road
Burlington, VT 05401
(802) 863-1700
Tools, seed starting kits, row covers, organic fertilizers, greenhouses, drip irrigation, composting supplies, sprayers, bird houses, botanical and mineral products, soaps.

Growing Naturally
P.O. Box 54, 149 Pine Lane
Pineville, PA 18946
(215) 598-7025
Traps, composters, beneficial insects, biological controls, fences, soil conditioners & fertilizers, watering devices, row covers, chipper/shredders, more.

IFM (Integrated- Fertility-Management)
333 Ohme Gardens Road
Wenatchec, WA 98801
(800) 332-3179
(509) 662-3179
Promotes ecologically sound orchard, farm & garden practices. Garden equipment, nutrient analysis, soil amendments, foliar sprays, green manures, pest controls, botanical and biological controls, beneficial predators and parasites.

Mellinger's
2310 W. South Range Rd
North Lima, OH 44452
(800) 321-7444
Besides a wide range of plants, offers lots of drip irrigation equipment, greenhouses, pots, planters, sprayers, organic fertilizers, fungicides, insecticides, rooting hormones, traps, tools, beneficial insects. More. Often wholesale prices.

Necessary Trading Co.
P.O. Box 305
New Castle, VA 24127
(703) 864-5103
Fax: (703) 864-5186
Traps, beneficial insects, biological controls, oils, soaps, pheromone traps (mating disruption), fungicides, disease controls, organic fertilizers, green manure crops, soil testing kits, composting supplies, sprayers, more.

Nematode Farm, Inc.
2617 San Pable Avenue
Berkeley, CA 94702
Sells beneficial nematodes.

NPI Nutri-link
417 Wakara Way
Salt Lake City, UT 84108
Mycorrhizal fungi inoculum for blueberries and greenhouse plants.

Peaceful Valley Farm Supply
P.O. Box 2209
Grass Valley, CA 95945
(916) 272-GROW
Catalog $2.00. Tools, composting supplies, row covers, many cover crops and mixes, sprayers, soil amendments, greenhouse covering, seed thresher, and also bulbs.

Ringer
9959 Valley View Road
Eden Prairie, MN 55344
(800) 654-1047
Pest control supplies, garden tools, sprayers, compost supplies.

Reuter Laboratories
P.O. Box 346
Haymarket, VA 22069
Various pest and disease biocontrols.

Safer's Inc.
189 Wells Avenue
Newton, MA 02159
(617) 964-2990
Pest control supplies, beneficial insects, predators and parasites.

Vertical Veggies
728 Fourth Avenue
Salt Lake City, UT 84103
Collapsible 4-sided tomato square cages, 6 feet high, 18 inches on a side. Unlike most cages, these store flat.

STATE GARDENING ASSOCIATIONS
Biodynamic, Biological, Ecological, and Organic
May, 1990

We urge you to contact your local growers association for a list of locally recommended insect and disease controls. It is also a way to get involved in local gardening and farming issues, if you choose.

Issues of disease and insect control vary widely from region to region. Pests in the Northeast may never be seen on the West Coast, Southwest, or Florida, and vice-versa. Most of the following state associations have compiled lists of substances that, for growers to be certified "organic," are permitted, regulated, or prohibited by the organization. Significant debate continues over both the purpose and content of certification lists. None of these lists are final or cast in stone. You may want to obtain a copy -- if only to become aware of which substances used in your area are considered, potentially, most harmful.

For further information at the national level, contact The Organic Foods Production Association of North America (OFPANA) (see page 170). Questions may be directed to the OFPANA Office, P.O. Box 1078, Greenfield, MA, 01301 and (413) 774-7511. The following list of organizations was kindly provided by them.

Ozark Organic Growers Assn
HCR 72, Box 34
Parthenon, AR 72666
(501)446-5604
Contact: Peggy Bonds

Ozark Organic Growers Assn,
South Central Chapter
Route 4, Box 158
Huntsville, AR 72740
(501) 545-3658
Contact: Mark Cain

Ozark Organic Growers Assn,
South West Chapter
Route 2, Box 76
West Fork, AR 72774
(501) 545-3658
Contact: Tim Snell

Demeter Assn for Biodynamic Ag.
4214 National Avenue
Burbank, CA 91505
(818) 843-5521
Contact: Deborah Hawkins

CCOF - Central Office
P.O.Box 8136
Santa Cruz, CA 95061
(408) 423-2263
Contact: Mark Lipson

CCOF - Big Valley
11383 Comstock Road
Stockton, CA 95205
Contact: Mark Jory

CCOF- Central Coast Chapter
747 Shore Road
Hollister, CA 95023
Contact: Grant Brians

CCOF - Desert Valley Chapter
90-571 Avenue 81
Oasis, CA 92274
(619) 397-4379
Contact: Bill Jessup

CCOF - Fresno-Tulare Chapter
42126 Road 168
Orosi, CA 93647
Contact: Nornam Freestone

CCOF - Kern Chapter
P.O.Box 358
Bakerfield, CA 93302
Contact: Joyce Johnston

CCOF- Mendocino Chapter
1021 Greenwood Road
Elk, CA 95432   895-2333
Contact: Al Weaver

CCOF - North Coast Chapter
4395 Westside Road
Healdsburg, CA 95448
Contact: Terry Harrisonn

CCOF - North Valley Chapter &
OCIA - California (CCOF)
P.O. Box 369
Richvale, CA 95974
(916) 882-4551
Contact: Bryce Lundberg

CCOF - OFAC Contact
P.O. Box 146
Weott, CA 95571
(707) 946-2223
Contact: Patti Laboyteaux

CCOF - Pacific SW Chapter
9018 Artesian Road

San Diego, CA 92127
Contact: Bill Brammer

CCOF- San Luis Obispo Chapter
685 Grade Mountain Road
Nipomo, CA 93444
Contact: Glenn Johnson

CCOF - Sierra Gold Chapter
17148 Old Gambetta Road
Mokelumne Hill, CA 95245
Contact: Jim Du Hamel

CCOF-Siskyou-Humboldt Chapter
14431 Old Westside Road
Grenada, CA 96038
Contact: Kirsten Olson

CCOF - South Coast Chapter
541 Janet Wood Drive
Oxnard, CA 93030
Contact: Paul Carpenter

CCOF - Yolo Chapter
5072 Pacific Avenue
Pleasant Grove, CA 95668
Contact: Ed Sills

OCIA - California
1713 Tulare, Suite 117
Fresno, CA 93721
(209) 237-4588
Stan Schletewitz

Colorado Organic Prod Assn
Route 1, Box 659
La Jara, CO 81140
(719) 274-5230
Contact: Tom Hamilton

NOFA - Connecticut
58 River Street
Guilford, CT 06437
(203) 453-3040
Contact: Richard Fisher

Georgia Organic Grow Assn
General Delivery
Madras, GA 30254
(404) 253-0347
Contact: Larry Conklin

Florida Organic Growers
P.O. Box 365
High Springs, FL 32643
(904) 454-3487
Contact: Marc Ketchel

OCIA Florida
1007 Poinsettia Drive
Ft. Pierce, FL 34950
(407) 461-1222
Contact: Steve Rosslow

Idaho Organic Producers Assn
1741 Bullock Lane
Middleton, ID 83644
(208) 585-6140
Contact: Tim Sommer

Land of Lincoln Organic Growers
Assn
2400 Spring Creek Road
Barrington Hills, IL 60010
(312) 658-7400
Contact: Barbara Macarthur

Indiana Organic Grow. Assn.
P.O.Box 208
Patricksburg, IN 47455
(812) 859-4195
Contact: Sophia Hauserman

OCIA - Indiana
RR 25, Box 21B
Terre Haute, IN 47802
(812) 894-3143
Contact: Vaughn Edwards

OCIA - Iowa
Rt 1, Box 176
Harlan, IA 51537
(712) 627-4217
Contact: Ken Rosmann

Iowa Organic Growers & Buyers
Association
22 East Court Street
Iowa City, IA 52240
(319) 351-7888
Contact: Hilary Strayer

Northeast Kansas Organic Food
Producers
Rural Route

Beattie, KS 66406
(913) 353-2414
Contact: Judy Nickelson

OCIA - East Kansas
Rural Route
Goff, KS 66428
(913) 939-2032
Contact: Ed Reznicek

OCIA - Kansas
RR 1
Home, KS 66438
(913) 799-3304
Contact: Joe Vogelsburg

Kansas Organic Producers
RR 1, Box 132
Dodge City, KS 67801
(316) 225-0440
Contact: Allen Moody

Kentucky New Farm Coalition
104 Hanson Street
Berea, KY 40403
(606) 986-8640
Contact: Bill Riley

Maine Organic Farmers & Gardeners
P.O. Box 2176
283 Water Street
Augusta, ME 04330
(603) 648-2521
Contact: Nancy Ross

NOFA - Massachusetts
124 Essex Street
Beverly, MA 01915
(508) 922-4869
Contact: Keith Olcott

Organic Growers of Michigan, Thumb
Chapter
3928 South Sheridan
Lennon, MI 48449
(313) 621-4977
Contact: Lee Purdy

Organic Growers of Michigan,
SW Chapter
26041 County Road 681
Bangor, MI 49013
(616) 427-8986
Contact: Maynard Kaufman

Organic Growers of Michigan,
3rd Coast Chapter
6677 Twelve Mile Road
Rockford, MI 49341
(616) 866-1679
Contact: Fred Reusch

OCIA - Michigan
3915 Dearing Road
Parma, MI 49269

(517) 788-7728
Contact: Tom Summers

Org Grow & Buyers Assn
1405 Silver Lake Road
New Brighton, MN 55112
(612) 636-7933
Contact: Yvonne Buckley

Mississippi Organic Growers Assn
Route 1, Box 442
Lumberton, MS 39455
(601) 796-4406
Contact: Tom Dana

Ozark Organic Growers Assn,
NE Chapter
Route 5, Box 1026
Ava, MO 65608
(417) 683-5109
Contact: Gregg Thorsen

Ozark Organic Growers Assn,
Springfield Chapter
1510 South Jameston Road
Springfield, MO 65809
(417) 865-0593
Contact: Gary Jensen

Organic Certification Assn of Montana
Baker Ranch, Box 94
Shawmont, MT 59078
(406) 632-4528
Contact: Terry Lechner

OCIA - Montana (Northeast)
Box 5035
Wolf Point, MT 59210
(406) 653-2492
Contact: Dewey Forsness

OCIA - Montana (N. Central)
Round River Ranch
Loma, MT 59460
(406) 378-3154
Contact: Bud Berner

Nebraska Sustainable Agriculture
Society
P.O.Box 736
Hartington, NE 68739
(402) 254-2289
Contact: Sam Welch

OCIA - Nebraska
Rt 1, Box 163
Marquette, NE 68854
(402) 854-3195
Contact: David Vetter

NOFA-NH/NHDA Cert Com
RFD 1, Box 516
Andover, NH 03216
(603) 648-2521
Contact: Richard Estes

Organic Growers Assn of New Mexico
1312 Lobo Place, NE
Albuquerque, NM 87106
(505) 268-5504
Contact: Sarah McDonald

OCIA - New Mexico
131 Peak Place #56
Santa Fe, NM 87501
(505) 983-9688
Contact: Mark Rehder

NOFA - New Jersey
RD #2, Box 263A
Pennington, NJ 08534
(609) 737-3735
Contact: Jennifer Morgan

NOFA - New York
RD #1, Box 134A
Port Crane, NY 13633
(607) 648-5557
Contact: Pat Kane

Carolina Farm Stewardship Assn
Route 3, Box 494
Silver City, NC 27344
(919) 663-2429
Contact: Kate Havel

OCIA - North Carolina
109 Landon Drive
Washington, NC 27889
(919) 946-7402
Contact: Brownie Van Dorp

Northern Plains Sustainable
Agrictlure Society
Box 274
Kulm, ND 58456
(701) 647-2693
Contact: Tom Stadler

OCIA - North Dakota
RR 2, Box 79
Mott, ND 58646
(701) 563-4455
Contact: Charles E. Wallace, Jr.

OCIA - Ohio
428 N. Warren
Columbus, OH 43204
(614) 279-3833
Contact: David Baldock

OCIA - Federation
3185 Township Road 179
Bellefontaine, OH 43311
(513) 592-4983
Contact: Betty Kananen

Ohio Ecological Food & Farm Assn
65 Plymouth Street
Plymouth, OH 44865
(419) 687-7665

Contact: David Balbock

Oregon Tilth Provender
P.O.Box 218
Tualatin, OR 97062
(503) 692-4877
Contact: Yvonne Frost

Biodynamic Farming & Garden Assn
P.O.Box 550
Kimberton, PA 19442
(215) 935-7797
Contact: Rod Shouldice

NOFA - Pennsylvania
RR#2, Box 116A
Volant, PA 16156
(412) 530-7220
Contact: Ron Gargasz

NOFA - Rhode Island
89 Country Drive
Charlestown, RI 02813
(401) 364-9930
Contact: Mike Merner

SC Organic Assn
129 Organic Lane
W. Columbia, SC 29169
(803) 791-5733
Contact: Margaret Locklear

OCIA - South Dakota
RD 2, Box 764
Lake City, SD 57247
(605) 448-5465
Contact: Herb Allen, Sr

Tennessee Alternative Growers Assn
Route 2, Box 46A1
Indian Mound, TN 37079
(615) 232-7777
Contact: Martha Yanchyshyn

Mid-South Organic Network
7750 Macon Road
Cordova, TN 38018
(901) 756-8586
Contact: Jeff Restuccio

Texas Organic Growers Resource
Committee
Route 2, Box 840
Lorena, TX 76655
(817) 881-2053
Contact: Dossie Raines

Texas Organic Growers Assn
Route 1, Box 94A
Carrizo Springs, TX 78834
(512) 876-2103
Contact: Bay Laxson

Deep Root Organic Co-op
RFD #1
Bellows Falls, VT 05101
(802) 722-3546
Contact: Paul Harlow

NOFA & Vermont Organic Farmers
RR #1, Box 177
Richmond, VT 05477
(802) 434-4433
Contact: Enid Wonnacott

Vermont Northern Growers
Box 125
Lou Pulver
East Hardwick, VT 05836
(802) 533-7175
Contact: Lou Pulver

Virginia Biological Farmers Assn
Route 2, Box 124B
Strasburg, VA 22657
(804) 971-4832
Contact: Ellen Polishuk
(703) 636-1817
Contact: Patti Nesbit-Habib

Tilth Producers Cooperative
1219 Sauk Road
Concrete, WA 98237
(206) 853-8449
Contact: Anne Schwartz

Mountain State OGBA
Route 10, Box 30
Morgantown, WV 26505
(304) 296-3978
Contact: Keith Dix

CROPP
Route 1, Box 77A
Chaseburg, WI 54621
(608) 483-2604
Contact: Spark Burmaster

OCIA - Wisconsin
RR 1, 1198
Soldiers Grove, WI 54655
(608) 734-3711
Contact: David Engel

Wisconsin Organic Growers
Route 1, Box 160
Spring Valley, WI 54767
(715) 772-3104
Contact: Faye Jones

USDA PLANT HARDINESS ZONE MAP

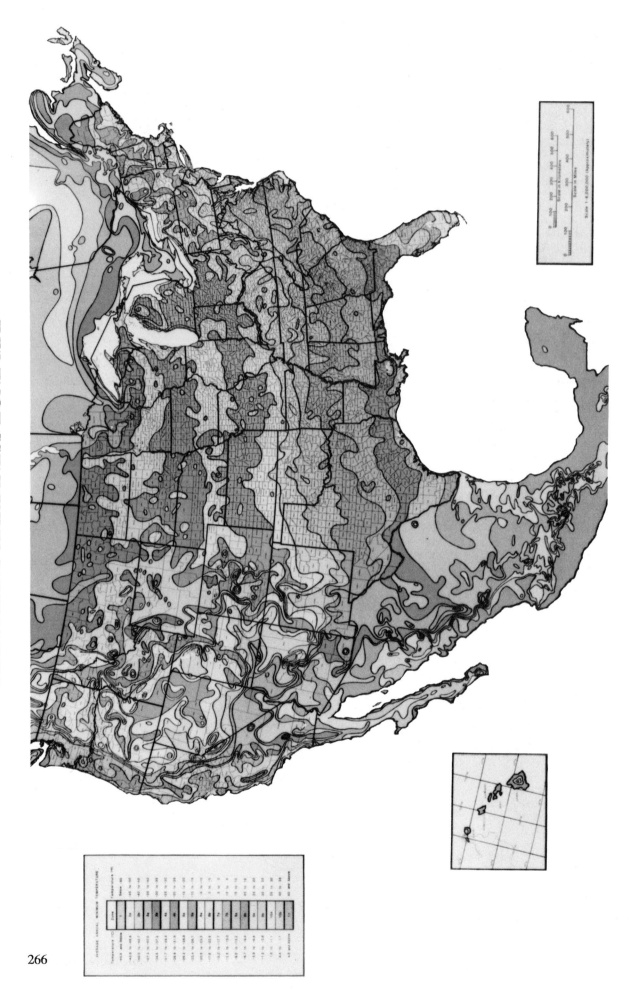

USDA PLANT HARDINESS ZONE MAP

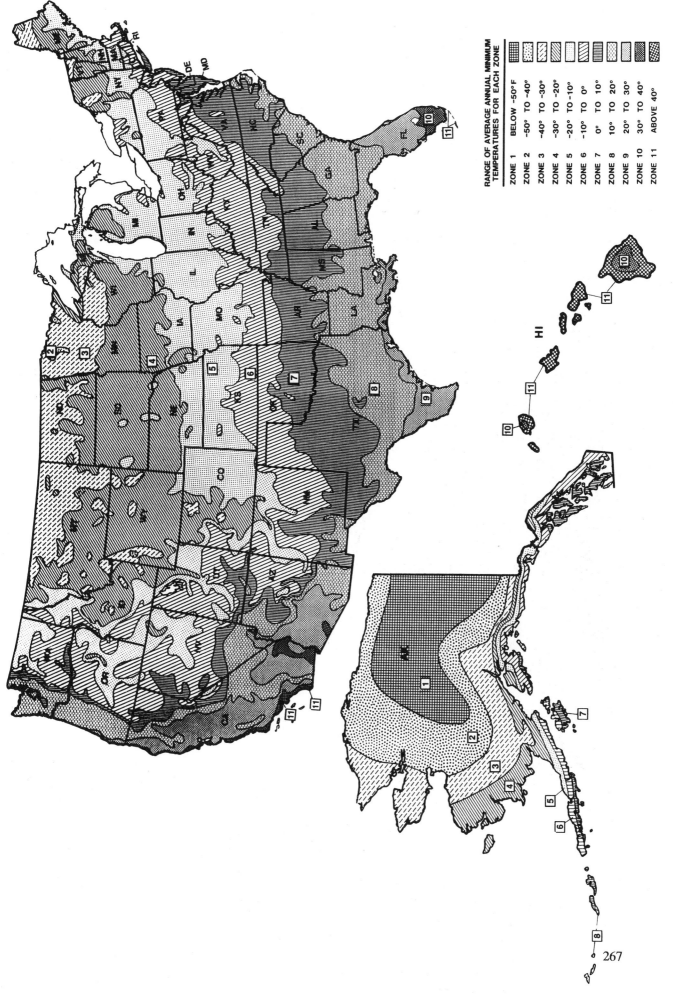

RANGE OF AVERAGE MINIMUM
TEMPERATURES FOR EACH ZONE

ZONE 1   BELOW -50°F
ZONE 2   -50° TO -40°
ZONE 3   -40° TO -30°
ZONE 4   -30° TO -20°
ZONE 5   -20° TO -10°
ZONE 6   -10° TO 0°
ZONE 7   0° TO 10°
ZONE 8   10° TO 20°
ZONE 9   20° TO 30°
ZONE 10   30° TO 40°
ZONE 11   ABOVE 40°

267

INDEX

ORDER INFORMATION

Call Or Write To:

Author's Cooperative Publishing Services
121 East Front Street, Suite 203-A
Traverse City, MI 49684

Toll Free: 1-800-345-0096
24 Hour Service, 7 Days A Week
Visa and Mastercard Accepted

Send a check for $22.95, plus $3.00 for shipping and handling. Please include your name, address, phone and, if different, the name and address of the person to whom you wish the book to be shipped. For information on orders of more than one, call or write Authors' Cooperative.

Please See The Registration Form On The Reverse Page

REGISTRATION

To receive special pre-publication discounts on future editions and other offerings, please fill out the information below and send to the address noted below. *Please print.*

Name: _____

Address: _____

City: _____ State: _____ Zip Code: _____

WE WOULD VERY MUCH APPRECIATE YOUR THOUGHTS

Would you like to see more vegetable, fruit, nut, or herb charts? _____

If so, which ones? _____

Would you be interested in charts on grains? _____

If so, which grains? _____

We would very much appreciate any other comments you may have about this book, as well as growing tips not included in this book. For successful disease and insect controls not listed in the charts, please describe your microclimate and how many times or years the remedy has worked. You will be acknowledged if we decide to use your suggestion in future editions. We hope you'll understand that we can't promise a personal response.

_____

_____

_____

_____

_____

_____

_____

Where did you first hear about this book? _____

THANK YOU VERY MUCH FOR FILLING THIS OUT!   PLEASE SEND TO:

WOODEN ANGEL PUBLISHING
Wooden Angel Farm, Building 1A
P.O. Box 869
Franklin, WV 26807